Fire at Eden's Gate

FIRE
at
EDEN'S GATE

TOM McCALL
&
THE OREGON STORY

Brent Walth

OREGON HISTORICAL SOCIETY
PRESS

Frontis: Governor Tom Lawson McCall of Oregon. (OrHi 90703)

Library of Congress Cataloging-in-Publication Data
Portland, Oregon

The paper used in this publication meets the minimum requirements
of American National Standards for Information Sciences—
Permanence of Paper for Printed Library Materials,
ANSI Z39.48-1984

Printed in the United States of America.

Library of Congress Cataloging-in-Publication Data

Walth, Brent, 1961–
Fire at Eden's gate: Tom McCall & the Oregon story / Brent Walth.
p.   cm.
Includes bibliographical references and index.
ISBN 0-87595-247-X: $29.95
1. McCall, Tom, 1913–83. 2. Governors—Oregon—Biography.
3. Oregon—Politics and government—1951–   . I. Title.
F881.35.M33W35   1994
979.5′04′092—dc20
[B]   94-24277
CIP

For
Shannon,
my best friend and love,
whose faith saw me through;

&

for
my father, mother and brother,
who taught me to believe
anything is possible.

Contents

*. . . and at the East of Eden he placed the cherubim,
and a flaming sword which turned every way,
to guard the way to the tree of life.*

Genesis 3:24

Prologue:

The Sign

T HE SIGN EXISTED ONLY IN MYTH, yet the story of the sign said much about the land and people who claimed it for their own. For as with all myths, the tale of the sign grew to explain to the generations that followed what was otherwise not easily explained.

The land for centuries had been home to native tribes: the Coquille, Yaquina and Tillamook along the coast; the Tualatin, Clackamas and Wasco along the rivers; the Umatilla, Tenino and Nez Perce in the high desert. The powers of Europe—Spain, Russia and Great Britain—at first came to the land out of curiosity, sending ships to probe the shores for an elusive throat of water, a northwest passage, that might connect the Pacific with the Atlantic. The pious soon followed, erecting their missions to bring the Lord to the godless native souls.

None of these motives was responsible for the great western migration. The white settlers who traveled across North America in the nineteenth century did so because of an unspoken desire. They were driven from the eastern cities by grime and despair, or from failures in the midwestern plains and the Missouri region, to seek a new freedom. Farmers and hunters, businessmen and prospectors, preachers and thieves—all had the same desire: to find a land that could feed and shelter them far from encroaching civilization. "In their own time," wrote one historian, "they were called not pioneers, but movers."

People had moved west across the continent before, but these—the Movers—had heard accounts of a land biblical in scale; this was not just the next unclaimed territory, but a Promised Land, or even an Eden.

The Movers believed this new land was not for everyone, but should be reserved only for the righteous. This division of immigrants into people deemed worthy and those deemed unworthy inspired the tale of the sign.

As the story goes, the sign stood at a fork in the deep-rutted wagon road west. One route went south. Along this route sat a pile of pyrite—fool's gold. The route north was marked by the sign, the land's name carved into the weathered wood.

The illiterate and greedy saw the fool's gold and plunged south, into California. The travelers seeking Eden ignored the worldly temptations and understood that a greater reward awaited.

These people, so the myth goes, went north, into Oregon.

ONE HUNDRED AND THIRTY YEARS LATER, another sign marked the boundary between California and Oregon. This sign—quite real—stood alongside a steep stretch of Interstate 5 as the freeway wound through the treacherous Siskiyou Mountains. The sign's tall letters held a simple message for northbound travelers: "Welcome to Oregon. We Hope You Enjoy Your Visit." The sign stood amid brittle scrub plants, the only foliage that could survive the choking fumes unleashed by cars and trucks. In the winter, soot-blackened snow drifted against its posts; in the summer, its words faded, bleached by the sun and scratched by the dusty breeze.

It was no place for a dying man. But Tom McCall was determined to come to this spot anyway, and the misery of the trip was testament to his stubbornness. He was sixty-nine years old during that summer of 1982, and would not live to see seventy. Cancer gnawed its way through his body and climbed his spine like ivy to his brain. The airplane ride south from Portland had been hell. At nearly six-and-a-half-feet tall, he had never fit well into airplane seats, and after logging hundreds of trips, he still dreaded flying. During his years as Oregon's governor, McCall had kept a bottle of gin within reach on airplane rides so he could wash away his fears. There had been no bottle that morning, though, and the cancer only added to his discomfort. He winced at every bump during the flight and the long car ride to the border.

McCall stepped gingerly from the car onto the gravel roadside of the freeway. He squinted under blue July skies and ignored the television cameras that drew near. He was long accustomed to the media's presence. McCall, a Republican, had served eight years as Oregon's governor, from 1967 to 1975. His time in office was seven years in the past, but McCall still made news in Oregon no matter what he said or did.

For four decades, Oregonians had listened to this man—first as a broadcast journalist, then as their governor. He could dominate any situation by his presence alone. His massive frame dwarfed everyone around him, and the sweeping cornice of his jaw was always poised to talk. His voice was as remarkable as his image; words curled from his mouth in a strange barnyard-Harvard accent forged by his desert upbringing and his Massachusetts heritage.

McCall dominated everything around him, however, because of all that he represented to his state. As the Movers had centuries earlier, Oregonians believed theirs was still a land largely unsullied; McCall was the one person who had told them how to keep it that way.

More than other American political leaders of his time, Tom McCall personified the sweeping environmental movement of the 1960s and 1970s. While other politicians had talked of the need to clean and protect the nation's land, air and water, McCall had acted.

McCall entered office when Oregon's heartland river, the Willamette, ran poisoned by the industries and the population growth of its valley. When he left office, the Willamette ran clean. His administration tamed mills that for years had stained the air and water with impunity. He left behind the nation's toughest land-use laws. Through opportunism and force of personality, McCall ended forever the threat of private development of the state's public beaches. He won the first mandatory bottle-deposit law in America, which freed Oregon's streets and beaches of bottle and can litter. When the nation found itself in an energy crisis, McCall was the first political leader to demand—and receive—action on energy conservation.

To McCall, conservation of Oregon's beauty and resources meant more than aesthetics. Protecting the environment meant protecting the state's livability and prosperity. McCall was never a preservationist in the strictest sense. He was a conservationist, one who preferred to protect Oregon's natural resources while allowing for development in a judicious way. He called his doctrine the "Oregon Story," a tale of environmental awareness years ahead of fashion, of reason above politics, and of caution before consumption.

McCall's was an idea-rich leadership, one that made Oregon, as *Newsweek* put it at the time, "Where the future works." But McCall had, most of all, what Americans seek from their leaders: vision and humanity. He was brutally candid and forthright, incorruptible in a profession that breeds deception. He never lost the touch of his first career—journalism—in his determination to speak honestly, no matter who might be hurt. He appealed to a nation dismayed by its leaders during the tumultuous years of Vietnam and the shame of Watergate. McCall warned of increasing American consumption a decade before the excesses of the 1980s, and he foresaw the need to break away from the two-party system and invite a "third force" into politics long before Ross Perot.

By 1982, the national fame McCall had earned for himself and for his state had largely passed, however. Three years before, the nation had slid into a shadowy economic recession, and Oregon had led the way downward. The timber industry—the industry that kept Oregon solvent—had collapsed. Soaring interest rates in the early 1980s meant fewer people wanted to build homes. As a result, fewer people demanded Oregon's lumber. The cost of producing what little lumber could be sold had grown prohibitive; the industry had gutted Oregon's forests, and the price of buying scarce logs meant many lumber companies could no longer operate. In lumber towns throughout the Willamette Valley and the Cascade Range, the mills, once whining day and night, fell silent. Families, who for generations knew only the woods and the mills, found that the jobs had gone for good. Oregon had known no economic collapse such as this since the Great Depression; in many parts of Oregon, the situation was even worse than it had been then.

The recession offered no easy solutions to a new generation of political leaders. But, as unemployment lines grew long and angry, Oregonians demanded answers, and their leaders sought a scapegoat.

They found one in Tom McCall.

It mattered little that McCall had been out of office for seven years, and that the timber industry's collapse was due to economic forces beyond the control of Oregon's leadership. Oregon's current leaders, many envious of McCall's eclipsing fame, blamed him—and the blame stuck. Despite all the success of the Oregon Story that McCall had spun for America, a single quote haunted him, a quote McCall could neither forget nor escape.

During the heady days of his administration, McCall had sought a way to dramatize his commitment to controlling growth in Oregon and protecting his state's livability. In a 1971 interview with the CBS Evening News, McCall issued his message to the rest of the country: "Come visit us again and again," McCall proudly told millions of Americans. "This is a state of excitement. But for heaven's sake, don't come here to live."

After decades of seeing politicians practice unbridled boosterism, the sight of a governor actually shutting the doors to his state stunned Americans. To McCall, however, his declaration made perfect sense.

When McCall took office in 1967, Oregon's reputation was still one of a pristine landscape of mountains, desert, lush green valleys and ocean shores, a place where, as the Movers had a century before, people still lived off the land. Timber and agriculture provided the base for the state's healthy economy.

Oregon, however, faced a tide of post-World War II growth that no one had considered controlling, and that growth threatened the base of the state's economy. As a journalist, McCall had seen first hand that the root of almost every environmental problem—polluted rivers and dwindling natural resources—could be traced back to unplanned, uncontrolled growth. Although his comment on CBS made him sound like an isolationist, McCall only wanted to conserve Oregon and to make sure the inevitable use of its land and resources was carried out wisely.

Oregonians quickly embraced McCall's "visit, but don't stay" declaration. The quip stood for years as the state's unofficial motto, an inside joke that Oregonians relished repeating. One Oregon artist sold "Oregon Un-Greeting" cards. One typical card read: "Tom Lawson McCall, governor, on behalf of the citizens of the great state of Oregon, cordially invites you to visit . . . Washington or California or Idaho or Nevada or Afghanistan." The cards sold like crazy.

McCall's remark gave Oregon a national prominence it had not known since the territory had been heralded in the nineteenth century as a new Eden. His quote inspired so many people to find out what made Oregon worth protecting that McCall inadvertently helped ignite a new migration. Oregon continued to grow during the 1970s at rates above the national average.

Cheery economic times in the 1960s and 1970s had allowed McCall to experiment with Oregon's future. But in 1982, with Oregon in dire economic straits, McCall faced history's fickle judgment. Once eager to praise McCall, the press now turned on him. Oregonians who had considered McCall a modern folk hero only a few years before now eyed him warily. The whispering started: Wasn't he the one who made new industry unwelcome in Oregon with nitpicking environmental laws? Wasn't he the one who said, "Visit, but don't stay"? Wasn't he the one who had ruined this state?

The state that had once embraced McCall's ideas now prepared to extinguish his legacy. With a single vote in the coming November referendum, Oregonians—frightened by their splintered economic fortunes—could repeal McCall's most important work: laws that controlled growth and development in its most valuable lands. The same pollsters who had once proclaimed McCall's stature in his state now said Oregonians were prepared to cast that vote against him and his work.

Embittered and ill, McCall saw the end—not just for himself, but for everything that he had hoped would live on. That is what had brought him to the sign, planted in the roadside along a busy interstate at the California border, with everyone in Oregon wondering if he might recant.

IT WAS AS CYNICAL A MEDIA EVENT as Oregon had seen that year, and even for some time before that. The current Oregon governor, Republican Victor Atiyeh, faced re-election that fall and wanted to appear active in trying to rescue the state's faltering economy. Atiyeh had also learned that Tom McCall's long shadow was difficult to escape; since taking office, he had worked to reverse what he thought was a poor image for the state. McCall's "visit, but don't stay" comment irked Atiyeh most of all. He wanted a media event that would erase the memory of the Mc-Call quote, and he thought of the freeway sign. The "We Hope You Enjoy Your Visit" phrase, Atiyeh said, implied that Oregon still did not want people to stay. For the benefit of television cameras, Atiyeh wanted to blow up the sign with dynamite. His aides talked him out of the stunt, noting the potential damage to the adjacent freeway. So instead Atiyeh called the Oregon press to the border to watch him paste over the offending words. He was surprised when McCall accepted the obligatory invitation to attend the ceremony.

McCall surprised almost everyone by showing up. His enmity for Atiyeh was famous, and he had never blown with the political winds. Yet these were frightening times for McCall, and the press assumed McCall's appearance would be an act of contrition.

On the warm July morning, a clear sky overhead, McCall stepped from the car, moved past the television cameras and walked over to the sign. Someone handed him a hard hat as a prop, and he placed it high on his large head. He watched as Atiyeh climbed a ladder and pasted up a new sign that read simply: "Welcome to Oregon." Atiyeh descended, gave a short speech, and then introduced McCall. "Governor McCall," he said, "will now be the speaker at the funeral of his own prose."

McCall told the crowd he would soften his famous statement for the purposes of Atiyeh's show. But he did so on his own terms.
"I want the terms of this understood," McCall began as the TV cameras panned toward him. "I want the media especially to understand that in accepting this does not represent unconditional surrender."

Everyone laughed, but McCall kept going, his expression grim. Behind him, trucks roared past on the freeway. His words sawed through the noise.

"This sign," McCall said, "is relatively complete. We might have a few embellishments, if they start rolling over the border too rapidly, you might wish you had back again."

People again laughed. McCall still was not smiling. He was vexed, he said, by reporters who had suggested he had changed. Well, he declared, he had not. As he spoke it dawned on those present that this was not a day of contrition after all.

"There's been a lot of bad mouthing about 'visit, but don't stay'."
McCall rumbled on. "It served its purpose. We were saying 'Visit, but
don't stay' because Oregon, queen bee though she is, is not yet ready for
the swarm.

"I am simply saying," McCall continued, his voice lowering to a
growl, "that Oregon is demure and lovely, and it ought to play a little
hard to get."

Then, barely pausing, he shot a quick, impatient look at Atiyeh. "And
I think you'll all be just as sick as I am if you find it is nothing but a
hungry hussy, throwing herself at every stinking smokestack that's
offered."

Through television and newspapers, McCall's message was carried
across his state. The on-lookers at the sign had expected submission.
But his defiance had turned surrender into victory and reminded Oregonians why he stood so tall. The Movers many generations ago had
come to Oregon hoping for an Eden. Even in the darkest of times, Tom
McCall, the sentry at the gate, had dared to rekindle that hope.

TOM MCCALL SOUGHT TO PROTECT OREGON because he loved the land.
But he also did so because he knew what it meant to possess Eden—and
then lose it.

His life had begun in idyllic circumstances. He was born to one of the
nation's wealthiest families, bestowed with an honored political name,
and brought to live on one of America's grandest estates. His family
had been graced in one generation. By the end of the next generation,
however, the glory had vanished. Understanding the life and character
of Tom McCall begins with understanding the forces that drove his family to greatness and, finally, to madness.

The first was a force of pride and ambition—McCall pride and ambition. His paternal grandfather, Samuel Walker McCall, had served for
twenty years as a Massachusetts congressman, and then for three one-
year terms as that state's governor. The McCall name had come to symbolize independence, courage and compassion. When asked why he ran
for office, Tom McCall always spoke of his father's father: "A great
historian, a public speaker, a man of sagacity and brilliance. . . . This influence became stronger, through my will to want to emulate him."

Tom McCall always aspired to the same independence and courage. Yet he could never be all that the austere and prim Samuel Walker McCall had been. Sam McCall had prided himself on his reserve and humility; Tom McCall could not control his explosions of emotion or his hunger for fame. The grandfather had been deliberate, contemplative, cerebral; the grandson, impetuous, reckless, verbose.

Another drive within him—overwhelming and consuming—denied him his full measure as a McCall. It was the force of his mother's father, Thomas Lawson, a ruthless Wall Street raider who made and lost several fortunes, destroying thousands of lives as he went. His was the terrifying gene within the family that was the root of its flamboyance, melodrama—and madness.

The story of Tom McCall begins with the story of his two grandfathers—the colliding forces in his life   and the dilemma of his character: He aspired to be a McCall, but in his soul, he was a Lawson.

PART ONE

*Nature is often hidden;
sometimes overcome;
seldom extinguished.*

Francis Bacon

1

Old Roman and the Copper King

T O BE A LAWSON, for a glimmering moment at the awakening of the twentieth century, meant living the life of royalty. For Thomas William Lawson, that meant the thousand-acre dominion he called Dreamwold. Construction of Dreamwold had taken four years and $3 million. Finished in 1905, Dreamwold, along with stables, racetrack and farm, boasted its own fire department and train station—even its own bank for the estate's two hundred employees.

As a symbol for the estate Lawson had erected a tower of kings. The tower stood 153-feet tall, its conical peak visible from the nearby Atlantic and the Massachusetts shore. Each hour the tower bells chimed across the surrounding farms of Scituate and Egypt, the towns thirty miles south of Boston near where Lawson had placed his estate.

The tower had not been part of the original Dreamwold plan. The city of Scituate had built a water tower on the edge of the estate, and Lawson offered to build a new facade to hide the ugly municipal standpipe. With a typically grandiose gesture, Lawson dispatched architects to Europe to study designs favored for medieval castles. The resulting tower was an audacious sight, not unlike Lawson himself, brooding over the landscape.

When each of his grandchildren were later born in the Dreamwold mansion, he ordered that the tower bells ring. Their song carried over the fields and out to sea, signaling that another Lawson had been delivered. The chimes signaled Tom McCall's birth on the Saturday before Easter 1913. For half of the next nine years, Dreamwold was his home. Nannies and butlers rushed to serve him, chauffeurs whisked him off to school in sleek limousines, and Lawson filled his bedroom with fine toys from F.A.O. Schwartz. He romped through the mansion's dark halls and grand rooms cluttered with bronze statues paid for with Wall Street booty. He raced his pony cart across the estate's grounds. He especially loved the stables, nine hundred feet long, where Lawson kept some of the nation's finest thoroughbreds.

The horses provided another Dreamwold symbol. Lawson had made Pegasus part of the Dreamwold insignia, and he had the winged horse imprinted on the estate's china, linens and iron gate. Once a symbol of Dreamwold's strength, the horses, years later, also represented the Lawson darkness. With his estate in foreclosure, and his brain gripped by demons, Lawson ordered that his horses be shot rather than auctioned to pay his creditors. The horses had been Dreamwold thoroughbreds after all. What other estate could be grand enough to be worthy of them?

LAWSON HAD WRAPPED HIMSELF in glorious eccentricity from the moment he rose from bitter poverty. With thousands of other immigrant families who populated the Boston area in the mid-nineteenth century, the Lawsons lived amid slums, their tenement located along the mud streets of Charleston. Lawson was born in 1855, not long after his father, Thomas Sr., a carpenter, emigrated from Scotland through Nova Scotia. His father died when Tom Jr. was still a boy, and the young Lawson stole food from local markets to help his mother, Anna, feed the family. His efforts were inadequate; he watched as one sister died of consumption brought on by malnutrition.

One afternoon in 1867, Lawson, age twelve and desperate to support his family, skipped school and crossed over the Charles River into Boston to find a job. He found a bank whose window advertised for help. He applied to the manager, who led Lawson to the vault. Beyond the massive door, Lawson watched as workers shoveled mounds of gold coins into canvas bags. "Can you shovel gold?" the bank manager asked the boy. Astonished at the sight of such riches, Lawson nodded and went to work. When Lawson, one of the nation's richest men, told the tale years later, he added, "I have been shoveling gold ever since."

At the turn of the twentieth century, when fewer than two hundred Americans claimed a worth of more than $10 million, Thomas Lawson claimed five times that wealth. Lawson earned his millions not by creating capital for industry, but by perfecting the art of stock price manipulation. He moved from gold-shoveler to teller to clerk in the bank, all the while learning the larceny of finance as he watched Boston stock speculators on State Street. Using what he had learned, he made his first fortune at age sixteen by pooling money of investors, including John F. "Honey Fitz" Fitzgerald, the future Boston mayor and grandfather of President John F. Kennedy. He sank the money into railroad stocks and earned $50,000 in five days, only to see the profits vanish on his next investment. With a flair that became characteristic, Lawson blew his last $157 at a posh restaurant, tipping the waiters with the last of his change.

Lawson never again relied on luck. Fortune, he had learned, was only for fools. He became a promoter of his own investments. Publicity, he later declared, was "the most powerful weapon in the world." Unlike any Wall Street operator before him, Lawson exploited the New York and Boston press for his own ends. With bold speeches to reporters and brash newspaper advertisements, Lawson would drive up stock prices by issuing glowing predictions about a stock's value. The price would soar and Lawson—holding a substantial share of the stocks he manipulated—would cash out. He developed a loyal following because many investors also made money as they rode the crests of Lawson's manipulations.

Lawson did not settle for bombast alone. He gilded many deals with outrageous gimmicks, always hoping to top himself. One Lawson innovation: trading cards, which one of his companies printed and sold with great success. Other enterprises, however, were not above suspicion. In 1891, he claimed he had discovered a rich coal vein in land he had recently bought in Grand Rivers, Kentucky. Local residents believed so deeply in Lawson that they elected him mayor—and then ran him out of town when they decided he was a fraud. In time, however, Lawson amassed the power to sway fortunes for himself and others.

Alongside the robber barons of his era, he rigged Wall Street for his own profit.

Unlike these others, however, Lawson sought one thing more than money: fame. For all his millions, Lawson never forgot how short a trip it was from the pile of gold coins to the slums. He hungered for adulation and praise, forever afraid the public might dismiss him as just another robber baron. He relished all the attention showered on him by the press, and there was a lot of it, because he was always a great story. Tall and lean, with a dark, brooding brow, full mustache and searing blue eyes, Lawson made a mesmerizing figure. He wore garish suits and carried precious gems in his pockets like change. When most ocean schooners had five masts, Lawson built one with seven and named it for himself. The New York and Boston newspapers devoured his antics. "[Wall] Street did not like him," wrote historian Louis Filler, "for he smacked too much of the people." Flaunting his social exile, he demanded entrance into the 1901 America's Cup. When the New York Yacht Club refused him entry, he launched a bold publicity campaign aimed at shaming the club. It worked. His boat was allowed to race, but it lost. Lawson ordered the vessel destroyed and sent pieces of its bronze hull to friends.

Lawson made money so fast that he refused to worship it. He once spent $30,000 to have a hybrid carnation named for his wife, Jeannie, and then spread the exaggerated story that he had paid that sum for a single flower stem as a gift to her. He threw away tens of thousands of dollars at a time at the racetrack. Once, after winning $50,000 on a horse race, Lawson gave the winnings away, dividing it between orphanages for black and white children.

Lawson became best known as the architect of the biggest swindle Wall Street had known, a scheme that Lawson said had been "responsible for more hell than any other trust or financial thing since the world began." It was also a business deal that changed Lawson's life and the destiny of his family.

IN 1897, LAWSON TEAMED UP with William Rockefeller and Henry Rogers, two men who controlled Standard Oil, one of the era's most powerful and despised corporations. Rogers and Rockefeller knew Law-

Thomas W. Lawson, Tom McCall's maternal grandfather, was once one of America's richest men. (OrHi 90709)

son as a fierce competitor who had frequently outsmarted them, so they listened eagerly to his scheme. Lawson proposed that together they try to corner the American copper market. Following Lawson's plan, Rockefeller and Rogers in 1899 bought out copper magnate Marcus Daly and his Montana-based company, Anaconda Copper. The price: $37 million. Yet Rockefeller and Rogers gave Daly only an IOU. They then formed Amalgamated Copper Co., a sham holding company without assets.

Though Amalgamated was an empty shell, it would be promoted as a company loaded with assets and safe for investors. That is when Lawson stepped in. With newspaper advertisements across America and Europe, Lawson promoted Amalgamated's initial stock issue, declaring the company the safest investment he had ever seen—even though he knew the company, without real assets, was worthless. His promotion touched off a frenzy. Investors flocked to New York to buy Amalgamated stock, and Lawson strolled through the jammed hotel lobbies observing the panic he had created. When people recognized him and asked about Amalgamated, he told them flatly, "Go your limit."

Amalgamated stock sold out in hours, hit $175 a share and earned Rockefeller and Rogers a $75 million profit. The pair paid off Daly, assumed control of Anaconda, and unloaded their Amalgamated stock. The stock sales sent the price crashing to $33 a share, wiping out the investments of tens of thousands of people who had trusted Lawson. Several investors committed suicide at the news they had lost their fortunes. Meanwhile, Rockefeller and Rogers, flush with cash, bought back Amalgamated stock at bargain prices as the public unloaded their holdings.

Lawson collected a $5 million fee, plus unknown profits from his own insider trading. He launched himself into the copper trade and fueled his fortune to its $50 million zenith. With his Amalgamated profits, Lawson began construction of Dreamwold.

As he watched Dreamwold rise from the rocky meadow, however, Lawson moped. The Amalgamated affair had created his vast fortune, but it had ruined his reputation with the public. So in 1904, Lawson decided to do what no other robber baron had ever done. He confessed. Lawson wrote a detailed account of the swindle, dubbed his epic "The Crime of Amalgamated" and gave away the story to *Everybody's*, a national general-interest magazine. He freely admitted his own role, then fingered Standard Oil as the real villain. He went on to expose more Wall Street shenanigans, including misuse of insurance company trust funds. To describe the crooked financial world, Lawson coined the phrase "the System."

"The people had dreamed of such a man: a man who knew the heart of corruption, and had turned against it; one experienced in intrigue, who had repudiated his past," wrote one historian. Added another, "[T]here was a strange streak of altruism in the man, a sort of messianic eagerness to deliver the common people from what he considered their bondage." Even in the era of Ida Tarbell and Lincoln Steffens, the American public had never seen such muckraking. The series ran nearly two years. *Everybody's* routinely sold out each month. The revelations often rocked Wall Street, causing one stock crash the press called the "Lawson panic."

His motives in writing the series were mixed. He hoped to embarrass Rockefeller and Rogers, who, following the deal, had again become his enemies, as much as to clear his name. But the articles also allowed Lawson to reclaim his stature with the public. In fact, Lawson recommended stock market reforms that inspired the Securities and Exchange Commission thirty years later.

In the end, the Amalgamated affair made Lawson an outcast on Wall Street, but he did not care. He realized there was little in life—not even a vast fortune—that was more important than being a hero. It was a lesson his grandson, Tom McCall, learned well.

LAWSON'S FLAMBOYANCE had always hinted at a certain mental instability. But his sanity took an irrevocable turn for the worse in the summer of 1904, when his wife, the former Jeannie Goodwille, died. She had been a somber-eyed, sickly girl when he first met her in the Charleston slums, and he loved her deeply. But her heart was weakened by illness, and she died at Dreamwold during a relentless heat wave; in testament to Lawson's fame, her obituary became front-page news in the *New York Times* and *Boston Globe*.

Lawson went wild with grief. He ordered his wife's unembalmed body stretched out on a pool table, where it grew gamy in the heat. He believed her death was God's revenge for the people he had ruined by his Amalgamated scheme. He stalked around the mansion, pistol in hand, threatening suicide.

When he finally buried Jeannie at Dreamwold, Lawson ordered her room sealed. Her clothing and jewelry collected dust for years where they lay exactly as she left them. He ordered his servants to set her a place at dinner each night; once, when a guest mistakenly sat in her empty chair, Lawson screamed in horror and then collapsed in sobs. And every night, his chauffeur drove Lawson to the Dreamwold train station where he waited for his dead wife. When she did not arrive, the limousine then carried Lawson, alone and weeping, back to his mansion.

TWO MONTHS BEFORE DREAMWOLD'S CHIMES heralded Tom McCall's birth in March 1913, Samuel Walker McCall arrived at the Massachusetts State Capitol in Boston wearing his finest clothes. After serving twenty years in Congress, Sam McCall believed he alone deserved the

Tom McCall lived much of his early life at Thomas Lawson's Massachusetts estate, Dreamwold. (From: *Ranch Under the Rimrock*; OrHi 90712)

state's newly vacated seat in the United States Senate, and he had come to Beacon Hill to claim his prize.

McCall was the epitome of propriety and sobriety. Tall and bony, the grim-faced McCall looked more like a schoolmaster than a congressman. Politics to Sam McCall was not a battle between factions but an exercise of reason. A historian and author of wide acclaim, McCall could recite Homer and Virgil in the original Greek, and often laced his floor speeches with quotes from the classics. The Capitol press, inclined toward nicknames, dubbed him "Old Roman."

His years in Congress had established Sam McCall as one of the state's most popular and enduring politicians. His courage won him admiration across the state, though he represented only the Eighth Congressional District comprising Middlesex County and the suburban Boston towns of Cambridge, Somerville and Winchester. Samuel Walker

McCall made it clear that no one—not his party's leaders, nor even his party's president—could control him. He was like a renegade racehorse, as Washington correspondent J.B. Morrow once wrote, "an intellectual thoroughbred with the pernicious vices, from a party point of view of jumping fences, biting and striking at his trainers and running away with those who try to drive him."

So strong was his independence that his own Republican party had targeted him for defeat because he would not follow its doctrine. McCall fought back with a granite will; years later, Boston mayor John Fitzgerald remembered "Sam McCall's voice ringing through the chamber denouncing members of his own party for their unfairness."

He knew his power lay not with party bosses, but with his voters. "If you want a man with the backbone of an angleworm," Sam McCall told his constituents defiantly, "then don't send me back to Congress." The

Eighth District voters, by record margins, sent him back every time.

In seeking election to the Senate, though, Sam McCall would not face voters. In 1913, the assembly picked the United States senators, and the Republican party bosses ran the assembly. Steeped in his own pride, though, Sam McCall believed the public's will that he be elected would overcome the bosses' opposition.

Among the five contenders for the Senate seat, McCall led in the voting but he could not reach the ninety-seven votes necessary for nomination. The balloting went on for three days, and each day Samuel McCall arrived in his finest clothes and top hat, waiting for word of his victory. On the third day, a Friday, the GOP machine rallied behind John W. Weeks, a pliable congressman willing to carry out the party's wishes. During a weekend break, party bosses cajoled and allegedly bribed assembly members. On Monday, after thirty-one ballots, Weeks emerged the winner.

The Republicans had exacted their revenge. Bitterly, Sam McCall went home, still dressed in his finest clothes, his top hat gripped in his hands. "To exaggerate the depths of Mr. McCall's disappointment would be well-nigh impossible," wrote a friend. "The result was a feeling of resentment that was as unfortunate as it was intense." McCall's anger, wrote another contemporary, "became obsessive, a root of bitterness, from which sprang an antagonism that he could not overcome." Such stubbornness and pride characterized the McCalls.

ALTHOUGH THE PATH OF THE FAMILY ANCESTRY is not clear, the first McCall probably emigrated from Scotland in the mid-1700s. The first clear traces of the family lineage appear during the Revolutionary War, when Samuel McCall's great-grandfather died during the Americans' disastrous showing at the battle of Brandywine in 1777.

The McCalls farmed in Bedford County, Pennsylvania, until Sam's father moved to the open prairie in western Illinois. His rural upbringing framed Sam's view of government. He believed that the smaller the role government played in Americans' lives, the better. Too many laws, he thought, infringed on basic freedoms. (In fact, when he left Congress, Sam McCall said he wished he had voted against more bills during his ten terms.) McCall earned a law degree at Dartmouth College; while practicing law in Boston, he bought a newspaper, the *Daily Advertiser*. As its editor, he wrote continuously, eventually publishing five books including biographies of Daniel Webster and Thomas Brackett Reed.

His conservative views attracted attention from the local Republican party leaders, who invited him to run for the state assembly. Once elected in 1888, however, McCall immediately made it clear he was a populist at his core: in three one-year terms in the state house, McCall successfully championed sweeping social reforms, including the abolishment of Massachusetts' debtor's prison and the nation's first corrupt practices act.

He also proved ambitious, winning election to Congress for the Eighth Congressional District in 1892. McCall moved to Washington with his wife, Ella Thompson McCall, who traced her ancestry to the *Mayflower* and the Pennsylvania Dutch. One congressional wife described her as "severe and clean cut," stoic in her "Puritan charm."

Sam, a compelling storyteller, became a favorite of the press, which chronicled McCall's fights with his party's leader, Henry Cabot Lodge, the Massachusetts congressman who controlled Bay State patronage. From his seat on the House Ways and Means Committee, he fought President William McKinley's tariff policies. After the sinking of the battleship *Maine*, McKinley sought a resolution of war against Spain in 1898. McCall was one of only six congressmen to vote against it. He walked home from the Capitol sullen. That night he told his wife his vote would cost him his career. It did not.

Among the Massachusetts Republican machine, however, "his characteristic independence of thought and action made him a marked man," recalled one contemporary. Indeed, McCall's loss in 1913 looked like his end, but it was not. In 1915, McCall ran for governor as a Republican, although he embraced the Progressive party platform of workers' reforms, such as an eight-hour work day. He lost the election, but won many Progressives votes. The next year he ran again and won.

Sam McCall, as he had in Congress, fought for the underdog and the forgotten, not for Republican dogma. McCall became a national figure as he battled the assembly to enact Progressive-style reforms, including a plan to protect all Massachusetts residents under a public health care system. His reputation meant that, in 1916, McCall was proposed as a

Samuel Walker McCall of Massachusetts, Tom McCall's paternal grandfather, was a maverick Republican congressman and governor. (OrHi 9113)

compromise candidate for president when the Republican party headed for deadlock over whether Theodore Roosevelt or Charles Evans Hughes would be the nominee to challenge the Democratic incumbent, Woodrow Wilson. McCall declined. Proud as he was of the offer, he wanted something more. He wanted the United States Senate seat denied him.

Five years later, he had his chance. He would not have to face the Republican machine again; Massachusetts law had changed, allowing voters to choose their senator.

Illness and age had slowed McCall in his third term as governor, and he had handed many of his duties over to his lieutenant governor, Calvin Coolidge. Still, the hardened McCall pride drove him to challenge John W. Weeks, who had beaten him earlier. Kicking off his Senate race, he delivered a blistering attack on his own party and promised a vigorous campaign.

Then, suddenly, Samuel McCall quit.

The reason he gave for bowing out was odd. He said he did not want to disrupt party unity by challenging Weeks. To anyone who knew Sam McCall, the excuse was absurd. In reality, McCall had expected Weeks to step aside out of deference to him. Weeks did not step aside, however, and McCall faced an arduous campaign that his health could not support. Besides, he said later, to campaign for a Senate seat that was rightly his was "repugnant to my inclination."

He lived five more years, until 22 November 1923, writing books and lecturing on government. Although he had retired from the field, Old Roman did not lose his final battle against the Republican party. He was simply too proud to fight.

FOR THEIR CHILDREN, Thomas Lawson and Samuel McCall created comfortable, secure worlds. Their families wanted for little and thrived amid fame.

Dorothy Lawson, for one, wanted no more than to cling to the comfort afforded by her father's wealth. The fourth of six children, Dorothy learned best of all her siblings the lessons of being a Lawson. She was born 12 October 1888 in the midst of Lawson's rise to power. Dorothy found her invalid mother too distant; she made her father the central figure in her life. If she recognized his darkness that often veered into madness, she never admitted it.

Lawson had provided a landscape of privilege for Dorothy and his other children that only increased in scale as they grew up. Dorothy's diary of 1904, when she was nearly sixteen, records days filled with horseback riding and dinner parties—that year she traveled to Boston and New York to see twenty-four plays and operas. In the summer, there was croquet, tennis and late night cruises on the family yacht, the *Dreamer*. Some days she lounged in bed all day, reading the classics, rising only for meals or to allow a servant to wash her hair and manicure her nails. Dorothy spent days at a time designing her dresses; the Boston newspapers' social pages reported her comings and goings.

Suitors lined up by the dozen, not only because of her family's wealth, but because of her beauty. Her neck was long and smooth, her face soft like her mother's, but lacking her mother's sadness. She had a sweet, wily grin and eyes that, like her father's, bored through a person with the penetrating Lawson stare. Dorothy thrived on her suitors' attention, one moment playful and coquettish, the next surly and cold. "The Lawsons had more charm than most people, but were five times more difficult," one of Dorothy's daughters said years later.

Few suitors could compete with her father for her attention, and even fewer could deliver the devotion she demanded. However, when Dorothy was sixteen years old she met a suitor who fulfilled her demands.

She had known Henry McCall—everyone called him Hal—since they were children in Winchester, before the course of their fathers' lives pulled them apart. Hal had attended a prep school, St. Mark's Academy, and, after that, Harvard. He was offered patronage government jobs and diplomatic assignments, but he wanted none of the public glare that came with being a congressman's son. Hal McCall had only two real interests when he met Dorothy, interests that changed little during his somber life. The first was baseball; the second was the dream of living in the West.

Hal had hoped to play major league baseball and he had the talent to do so. He loved the game so much he repeated his senior year at St. Mark's so he could replay the school's rival, Groton, to whom Hal's team had lost the previous year. At Harvard—which he finished in three years to make up for his fifth year in prep—Hal was a star, batting .325 his senior year despite a bum ankle. On the diamond he was, said a student sportswriter, "sensational."

Hal's only real plans beyond college were to try out with the Boston Red Sox, and to save money with the hope of someday becoming a rancher in the distant, romantic West. Since childhood, Hal had been surrounded by his father's colleagues in Congress, and he enjoyed most of all talking to the western congressmen who regaled Hal with tales of the mountains and wildernesses of their home states.

He saw no reason to change his plans even after he began courting Dorothy Lawson. Their friendship had rekindled when Dorothy had attended a St. Mark's baseball game and had seen Hal play. Hal found her brooding Lawson looks alluring; Dorothy found Hal's charm and pride refreshing. As they courted, she listened with detached interest to his talk of playing baseball and moving west; she assumed Hal would abandon these dreams once they were married and accept a diplomatic

Dorothy Lawson, Tom Mc-
Call's mother, about 1905.
(From: *The Copper King's
Daughter*, OrHi 90715)

post or enter politics. Hal, however, quietly assumed that Dorothy
would dutifully follow the pursuit of his dreams, not hers.

Youth and love compounded the errors in their miscalculations.
Dorothy returned to Dreamwold one day in 1909—the year Hal graduated from Harvard—to make a wrenching confession to her father: she
was pregnant.

Tom Lawson exploded in fury at the news. Dorothy, terrified by her
father's reaction, fled to the ocean shore, where, with Lawsonesque
drama, she pretended to try to drown herself. Her brother fished her out
of the waves before she could get more than wet.

Lawson soon mellowed, remembering he had rushed to the altar with
his own wife because she, too, had become pregnant during their
courtship. To avoid scandal, however, Lawson hired a discreet Boston
doctor to perform an abortion. Soon afterward, Dorothy and Hal announced their engagement. In exchange for his blessing, Tom Lawson
issued a firm edict: Hal had to stay clear of Dorothy until the wedding.

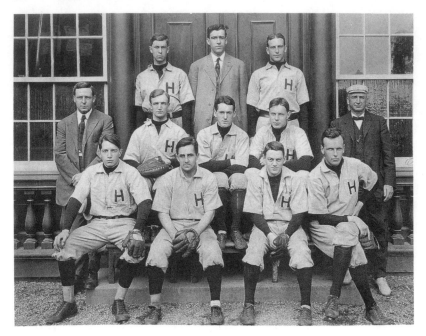

Hal McCall, who would bring the McCall family to Oregon, pictured in about 1908 (front row, right) as a Harvard baseball player. (Courtesy of Jean McCall Babson)

Lawson made sure he was obeyed by sending Dorothy to Paris and enrolling her in the Sorbonne.

Hal faced a year with little to do. A tryout with the Boston Red Sox led nowhere, so he decided it was time to travel west. He accepted an invitation from a Harvard classmate, Hamilton Corbett. "I know a fellow," Hal wrote his father about his travel plans, "in Portland, Oregon, whose father practically owns the town & he might fix me up."

Then—perhaps thinking about the enraged Lawson—he added, "I think the best thing to do is to get away from here, don't you?"

HAL MCCALL ARRIVED IN OREGON fifty years after statehood and when the state already worried about its growth. In the years during which he came west, the state beckoned newcomers, but with increasing caution and reserve. "Oregon welcomes the man who will make the land produce," said the 1915 *Oregon Almanac,* published by the state Immigration Commission. "Oregon has room for all who come with purpose to succeed." However, the state already felt the pain of too-rapid growth and newcomers unable to support themselves. "City bred people of limited means," the *Almanac* warned, "will be confronted by many difficulties if they come to Oregon to earn a livelihood."

To Hal McCall, preparing to marry the daughter of one of America's richest men, money did not matter. He arrived in 1909 in Portland, Oregon's biggest city, which was still little more than a mud-splattered town surrounded by tree stumps. The influence of New Englanders like himself dominated Portland; they had bankrolled the town and kept its Willamette River port busy. They even had a hand in naming it: the city would have been called Boston, except for the outcome of a coin flip. Its founders took pride in Portland's propriety, rarely acknowledging its grimy underside. Portland was, however, a shipping and logging town, with a violent waterfront and well-attended brothels and bars, often located in buildings owned by the city's elite.

Hamilton Corbett's family was a metaphor for the city. The late patriarch, Hamilton's grandfather, Henry Corbett, had come from New England around the time of statehood, and had turned a hardware store and his banking interests into a fortune. The Corbett family took an immediate liking to Hal and sponsored him on a ranch in the Palouse in eastern Washington where he learned the rudiments of farming and animal husbandry. His Harvard-soft hands cracked from his labor, but Hal made no complaint. He was living in the West he had imagined.

After his sojourn on the ranch Hal secured a job at a Corbett-run bank in Portland and returned to Massachusetts to marry Dorothy. He intended to live in Portland and, someday, run his own ranch. He had a significant problem, however: Dorothy cared nothing for his dream.

Before their elaborate winter wedding at Dreamwold in December 1910, Dorothy finally agreed to move to Portland for a year. She promptly regretted her decision. The winters she knew at Dreamwold were snowy and frosted, with servants on call to ferry her wherever she wanted to go in a sleigh. Winter in Oregon was nothing like winter in Massachusetts. When the McCalls arrived in Portland in January 1911, the damp city drowned Dorothy's spirits. "The rain came quietly down

Westernwold, the "ranch under the rimrock," the central Oregon home where Hal and Dorothy McCall raised their family. (From *Ranch Under the Rimrock*; OrHi 90716)

and down," she recalled, "the wind never blew, the sun never shone." As the days went by, she said, "the clouds seemed blacker and the rain wetter." Homesick for Dreamwold, Dorothy each morning walked the ten blocks from their apartment to Union Station. There, she watched the train depart for the East, wishing desperately she were on it.

The climate soon wreaked havoc on Hal's health. Within weeks after they had arrived, a crippling sinus attack felled him. A local surgeon operated on his head to relieve the pressure. The crude operation left an arching, oozing scar on his forehead but did little to relieve the pain. On doctors' advice, Hal and Dorothy took a vacation to the state's desert country to the east where the Corbetts owned land.

At news of Hal's operation, Thomas Lawson rushed to Oregon and joined the McCalls on their trip to the desert. Their train took them east

along the Columbia to The Dalles, then south into the dry lands where the rimrock waited.

THE RIMROCK IS NAMELESS. From the valley floor, the cliff's ragged face rises two hundred feet, a basalt curtain drawn before the desert's auditorium of brush and rock and dust. Its cracked precipice divides the horizon into earth and sky; its scarp tapers to the floor, a slope of chipped rock, fallen against the rimrock's base like shavings from an ancient lathe. In the summer, when the sun floods the land with bleaching light, heat washes upward against the rimrock's grand face. The rising air fills the wings of hawks, which hang effortlessly above the valley, watching for prey.

As it is throughout central Oregon, the land is dry, a hard dry. The

Cascade Mountains to the west—frosted white-blue with snow, frayed with evergreens—rob the rain that moves onshore from the Pacific. The only water is the river—the Crooked, appropriately named—running along the valley's south side, trapping a swath of land north to the cliffs, a land that is flat and lovely and cruel.

In the late 1800s, the first white explorer to record his travels along the Crooked River stopped to marvel at the river's beauty. He learned quickly of the land's power to deceive as a winter storm crushed his camp. "Without forage the horses became gaunt," wrote one narrator, "and sharp ice and rimrock crippled their feet so badly that sometimes the hoof was worn away, leaving nothing but a sickening stump." Meanwhile, the river's thick ice suddenly clenched the travelers' beaver traps, and the white men nearly froze to death. One moment the land had seduced; then, quickly, it betrayed.

Hal saw the rimrock for the first time from a distant bluff after he had stepped off the train in Redmond, a small mill town a few miles to the west. Transfixed by the desert, Hal within days asked Lawson to build him a ranch in the valley. Lawson gave him $50,000 to buy 640 acres from the Corbetts and build a ranch house in the rimrock's shadow. Lawson dubbed the enterprise "Westernwold," and he considered it his wedding gift to his favorite daughter and her husband. With typical Lawson flair, the ranch house was grandiose: five bedrooms, a formal living room, and—unheard of in the region—five indoor toilets. Other ranchers had succeeded in bringing water up from the river for irrigation, but only in small amounts. Westernwold, using electric pumps, pumped water out of the Crooked River—not just a few gallons at a time, but by the thousands of gallons.

Hal knew nothing about running a ranch in the wilds, but he learned his first task was not to tame the desert. His first task was to convince his wife to stay.

During the frantic construction of Westernwold, Dorothy had glowered as she saw her plans to stay in Oregon only one year disappear. She thought herself a misfit in this land, as if she were a strand of fine pearls tossed into the desert shale. The nearest town, Prineville, named for the area's first merchant, was the largest in Crook County. However, Prineville's dirt streets had no charm and certainly none of the culture her soul required. She tried to brighten the yard at Westernwold with flowers and plants—shrubs that belonged in a cool, damp climate; they perished quickly. The young woman who had once beckoned maids to wash her hair now cooked meals, scrubbed the house, and battled the maddening desert dust that coated every surface. In despair, Dorothy fled the ranch and returned to Dreamwold whenever she could.

Each time she left, the breach between her and her husband widened. She left nonetheless, for she had found the perfect, unassailable reason for leaving. "The family used to say," one of Dorothy Lawson McCall's daughters recalled decades later, "that mother got pregnant just so she could go home, because Granddaddy insisted she be at his side for the birth of his grandchildren."

So Dorothy McCall returned to Dreamwold to deliver her children, conceived in the Oregon desert, into Lawson luxury. Into this breach between his parents, a divide as broad as the continent, Tom McCall was born.

2

The World

H E SHOWED HIS CHARACTER AT BIRTH, a howling, nine-pound
baby who exited his mother's womb feet first. Years later his
family would joke—perhaps with much truth—that his mother
scorned him all of his life, as if to repay him for his painful arrival.

With the Dreamwold bells chiming, Dorothy bestowed on the baby
the Copper King's full name: Thomas William Lawson McCall. He was
born 22 March 1913, when Woodrow Wilson was president, radio and
airplanes were still rare and when a world war brewed in Europe. He
was his parents' second child, born two years after Henry McCall, Jr.,
whom everyone called Harry. Tom spent his first nine years shuttling by
train between his homes in Oregon and Massachusetts, oblivious to the
battle waged by his parents over the family's future.

At Westernwold, Tom had an expansive landscape to explore, although at first Dorothy balked at allowing her children to venture outside
the ranch house. Lawson children, she said, should not play where they
might get dirty. In time, Dorothy relaxed her rules, and Tom explored the
rimrock, ran through the alfalfa fields and chased his father's cattle.

The stays in Oregon never lasted long, however, before Dorothy escaped with her children back to Dreamwold. By age six, Tom had made
at least four extended trips to the Lawson estate; by age nine, he had
spent almost half his life there. For Tom, the trips back to Dreamwold
offered only more adventure. "They had the run of the place," Alma

34

Tom McCall, about six months of age. (Courtesy of Audrey McCall)

Litchfield, one of Lawson's secretaries on the estate, said of the Mc-
Call children. "The entire estate was their playground." In later years,
McCall remembered Dreamwold's "sweeping terraces, acres of hand-
some buildings, and the fleet of limousines."

Each trip back to Dreamwold lasted longer than the last, with Dorothy
loathe to return to Oregon. By 1918, she had three children: Harry, Tom,
and a daughter, also named Dorothy, whom the family called Bebs.
When she became pregnant again in 1919, she returned to Dreamwold,
gave birth to twins, and vowed she would never go back to Oregon.

Before Hal could protest, Dorothy enrolled Tom, Harry and Bebs in
the private Derby Academy in Hingham near the estate. When Hal came
to visit his newest babies, he found he could not budge Dorothy from
Dreamwold. "I found myself," Dorothy later said, "torn between my father and my husband." She chose her father, and Hal, after each visit, returned to Oregon, alone.

For Tom, now six years old, Dreamwold had always been a place to visit, but as months passed, memory of the Oregon ranch faded. In all, his final stay at the Lawson estate lasted more than two years—years Tom spent without a father. Soon, Thomas Lawson, not Hal, became the center of Tom McCall's young life. "Granddaddy was king of it all," said Thomas Lawson II, Tom McCall's cousin, who also lived at Dreamwold at the time. "He was king of the family and everyone kowtowed to him. He was a wonderful guy, but of course, he had to be the center of attention. Everything was centered around him."

Lawson lavished special attention on Dorothy's children, dressing them in the finest clothes and spoiling them with gifts. In the mornings, Lawson ushered Tom, Harry and Bebs into his Pierce-Arrow limousine and rode with them to Derby Academy. When school let out, Lawson was there with his footman to pick them up, entertaining them during the trip home with magic tricks or tall tales about his own achievements. "Everyone more or less held him in awe," said cousin Tom Lawson. "We children adored the sight of him."

Tom McCall agreed. He absorbed his grandfather's flamboyance, his theatrics, and his brooding manner. Granddaddy Lawson, as Tom McCall said years later, had him "under his magic spell."

Hal visited occasionally, and when he did, Lawson tried to persuade him to sell Westernwold and return to Massachusetts. Hal refused, instead asking Dorothy to return with him to Oregon. When she declined, he would leave for Oregon without his family. So it went until 1921, when Hal, emboldened by McCall stubbornness and pride, returned to Dreamwold threatening divorce if Dorothy did not return with the children.

THE LIFE TO WHICH DOROTHY CLUNG had been built by the power her father had held. That power, however, had started to fade.

As he grayed, Lawson remained a celebrity, writing books and creating commotion with his pronouncements about corruption on Wall Street. But his power to make money had vanished and his business deals had turned sour. In one deal, he sank the Guggenheims into a failed gold scheme that suspiciously resembled the Amalgamated swindle.

He could have retired comfortably, but he heeded the advice of his

Tom McCall, dressed as a doughboy, in 1918. (Courtesy of Audrey McCall)

late wife. "If the ship ever has to go down," she had told him, "sail her down with all the sails drawing." He ran Dreamwold at full tilt, despite the $200,000-a-year operating costs that he eventually could not meet.

He still valued fame most of all. When Samuel McCall dropped out of the 1918 United States Senate race, Lawson declared himself an independent and jumped in. He toured Massachusetts, giving fiery, populist speeches and drawing enthusiastic crowds. One of his speeches became so incendiary it nearly caused a riot; fighting among members of the audience ended only when Boston mayor John Fitzgerald climbed onto the platform and sang "Sweet Adeline."

Fearing that Lawson would split the vote, GOP leaders begged Sam McCall to intervene. "No one," replied a bemused McCall, "could influence, much less control, Mr. Lawson's course." Lawson did sap the Republican vote by taking five percent, enough to hand victory to the Democratic candidate.

During one campaign trip, Lawson's limousine overturned and he

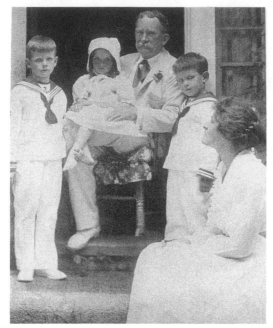

Bracketed by his mother, Dorothy (right), and his grandfather, Thomas W. Lawson, Tom McCall poses with his brother Harry (left) and sister Bebs. (Courtesy Charles Gould)

suffered a broken collar bone. However, the injuries ran deeper than physical pain; brushed by death, Lawson became increasingly morose. His grandson Tom McCall witnessed Lawson's fitful midnight wanderings through Dreamwold. The old man, obsessed by the haunting memory of his dead wife, stumbled about, wailing. Tom also witnessed his grandfather's public humiliation. In April 1920, while the McCall children still lived at Dreamwold, the state of Massachusetts convicted Lawson for illegally advertising stocks. He avoided jail by paying a $1,000 fine.

Lawson saw the end rushing at him, and when Hal returned threatening divorce, Lawson ordered his daughter to return to Oregon. The McCalls fled just ahead of Lawson's final crash. In October 1922, creditors crushed Lawson's empire, once worth $50 million, under debts of $180,000. Auctioneers sold off Dreamwold's riches, speculators carved up the estate into subdivisions, and Lawson moved to a tiny apartment in Boston's Fenway district. Dreamwold's trustees, sympathetic to the old man, gave Lawson $550 in cash workmen found hidden in the mansion's walls. As the family legend goes, Lawson parlayed the cash into a final, profitable binge in the stock market, sent the money to his children, and died.

At his death on 8 February 1925, a few days short of his sixty-eighth birthday, Lawson was a curiosity, a relic of a bolder time. Reporters flocked to Dreamwold for the funeral where the old man was to be buried alongside his wife in a small plot not lost to creditors. The journalists took note of the hundreds of mourners, the pall of fog, the tower bell's mournful chimes and the absence of only one of Lawson's six children. Dorothy Lawson McCall, the one who perhaps adored him most, could not return in time from Oregon for the funeral. Instead, she remained trapped at the distant place she was now forced to call home—Westernwold, the lone surviving piece of the Copper King's empire.

THE MCCALLS' RETURN TO OREGON, when Tom was nearly nine, was traumatic to his siblings, Harry and Bebs. After being chauffeured to a private academy, they now walked through the sagebrush to a one-room schoolhouse—and they brooded over their fate. "It was such a change from living in such luxury," Dorothy "Bebs" McCall Chamberlain said. "We were taken to the wilds. It was a terrible shock."

But not to Tom. Certainly he missed the fun of Dreamwold, but as he would the rest of his life, Tom cared little about money or where he lived. However, just as his grandfathers stamped out the shape of his character, this land left an indelible imprint on him. Years later, McCall traced his own love for Oregon and its land to his childhood days in the Crooked River country. He explored the rimrock crags, waded through the Crooked when the summers thinned the river. The isolation did not bother him, and he reveled in the open spaces, the seemingly limitless bounds of rock and sage and sky.

Hal McCall had gotten what he wanted. He had his ranch and his family at home. But Hal's dream was fragile. Instead of building slowly, Westernwold had risen overnight, and it was never solvent. The collapse of Lawson's fortune, which had propped up the ranch financially all those years, soon exposed Hal's folly. "My father," Tom McCall said years later, "was a hell of a good guy but one who was constantly knocked off balance by destiny."

Running the biggest operation in the valley, Hal McCall did not know the first thing about farming. He raised hay and alfalfa, and his inexperience was compounded by the nationwide collapse of farm prices during the 1920s. While his neighbors raised beef cattle, Hal insisted that Westernwold be run as a dairy. Few dairy operations existed that far out, and for good reason. Most area residents had their own cows, and it was difficult to ship milk and butterfat to larger towns. "That was no place for a dairy, way out there in the boondocks," said Charles Mc-Cormack, whose father ran sheep on the McCall land. "It was a hell of a way to starve to death."

Hal kept Westernwold afloat with a $10,000 line of credit, but the money was not enough. He could not afford decent feed for his cows, which in turn stopped producing milk, nor later could he pay for the dairy's basic needs, such as bottles and capping machines.

The family's other finances suffered as well. Hal signed for a new Buick sedan, and never made a payment. The local utility, the Deschutes Power Co., routinely shut off the ranch's electricity for unpaid bills. Men and women toiled for months at a time in Hal's fields, only to leave the McCall ranch without paychecks. The state demanded its taxes. Neighbor Maude Butler Knorr remembered Hal McCall borrowing pocket change from employees while twenty-dollar gold pieces lay around the house. "The gold coins were gifts to the children from Tom Lawson," Knorr said, "and they never thought of spending them."

As debts piled up, so did lawsuits. Between 1920 and 1931, seventeen plaintiffs sued the McCalls. Most of them won expensive judgments, typically awarded by default because Hal was too proud to show up in court to defend himself.

Whatever his failings as a rancher and businessman, Hal was always a gentleman. Despite their isolation, Hal insisted the children remain well-mannered, even to the point of obsession. Without fail, Hal berated the boys for wearing their hats in the house. Wearing a hat—even in a ranch house—was to Hal the highest violation of etiquette.

Hal clung to his pride, refusing to take menial jobs to pay his debts.

Although Hal's pride did not break, eventually his will did. "He finally gave up," said his youngest son, Sam McCall II, years later. "He sat in his chair all day long while the ranch blew away."

The sadness in Hal McCall's eyes was not lost on his children. "Father never struck me as an unhappy man," Jean McCall Babson, the youngest McCall daughter, said. "Father struck me as a very worried man. We knew how worried he was because of the hat."

Covered with desert dust and overcome by worries and defeat, Hal would sit at his desk, the ranch account books lying open in front of him. Hal would stare at his dirty boots, his Boston manners forgotten amid the ruins of his dream, his battered work hat still sitting firmly on his head.

AS HIS FATHER'S DREAM FAILED, Tom McCall watched the Lawson power rise again in his family. Dorothy Lawson McCall had hated Oregon. Now, however, she fought to protect her own small piece of the desert and the last remnant of the Lawson fortune.

"My husband," Dorothy McCall declared years later, "was ashamed of only one thing—being in debt." Then she added sharply: "I wasn't shamed."

For years, the dominant figure in Tom McCall's young life had been Thomas Lawson. Now the other Lawson, Dorothy, dominated his life, and from her he took a lasting lesson. He learned how to fight.

She relished the fight to protect the ranch as Lawson had his Wall Street battles. She cooked for workers, split wood, and hacked through the river ice to gather water when the pipes froze in the winter. When the Deschutes Power Co. cut the ranch's electricity, shutting down the irrigation pumps, Dorothy stalked down the sidewalks of Redmond until she found the utility's superintendent and tore at the startled man with her razor tongue. Two years later, when the unpaid power bill reached $1,837, Dorothy again harangued the same official until he apologized to her. "I'm sorry you are holding me responsible for the fact you were without lights for 23 days," the superintendent wrote. The utility promptly agreed to restore Westernwold's power in exchange for a fraction of the unpaid balance. "When she started a fight, the other person was usually the loser," recalled Knorr. "When she lost her temper, I tell you, she would swear as much as any man. She'd just rant and rave until she got her way."

When creditors came to repossess the dairy herd, Dorothy first employed her charms to turn them away empty-handed. Other times, at her direction, Tom and his siblings would hide the entire dairy herd in a secluded glen on the ranch. If a process server arrived with a court summons for Hal, Tom remembered, "I used to see dad go roaring past the bunkhouse and by the barn, roaring right by the milk house, just pale-faced, and go right up the cliff." When all else failed, Dorothy met creditors at the gate with a shotgun.

The Lawson Curse at times crept into her senses and Dorothy would perform the role of heiress, as if the Lawson millions waited patiently in a Boston vault. She clung to the ranch house's splendid trappings: crystal from Tiffany's, delicately patterned silver, tall bronze statues. Guests regularly sat down for dinner at a dining room table opulent with crystal, fine silver and delicate china, then received puny servings of food that barely covered the fancy plates. When she could take no more, Dorothy played out a melodrama, wielding pearl-handled revolvers given to her by Lawson, pressing the engraved barrels against her temple and cocking the hammers. Her suicide threats became so commonplace that her children stopped noticing.

While fearsome, Dorothy still fascinated and entertained her children. Each night, she gathered Tom and the other children in Westernwold's living room for a reading session. She took down a volume from the vast library Lawson had provided and read in her lush Boston accent the tales of Tolstoy and Shakespeare, Thackeray and Poe. "We whistled through [the books]," McCall remembered. "We all got tremendous vocabularies, and we were literate people from that exposure to those great books."

During other evenings she spun tales of her glorious childhood. She never missed a chance to burn into her children's minds what the Lawson and McCall names represented. In a house haunted by ghosts of lost power and wealth, Tom Lawson and Sam McCall became mythic figures who fought systems and machines, men who stood alone, always alone.

The lesson in these men's lives, which Tom McCall heard time and again from his mother, was that the pursuit of power was worthy, but, once gained, power came with debts to pay. That was her moral: Use your power to fight for life's underdogs. "She taught us what it meant to be a Lawson and a McCall," said Jean. "She instilled in us a sense we stood for something."

Tom watched his mother's transformation into the family leader and marvelled at the way her power of words and dramatics allowed her to control the entire ranch. Tom wished to emulate her, and often succeeded.

Unlike any other two people in the McCall family, Knorr said, Tom and Dorothy shared "that energy and the ability to go ahead with anything they wanted to get done. They seemed to have an unlimited amount of energy. Everything he wanted to do he did." Often what Tom wanted to do was to compete with Dorothy for the limelight of the family stage. He usually won that attention through mischief. "He was a curious child," Bebs recalled, "always getting into everything." Tom pestered workmen around the ranch, rooting through their tools or chanting, "My granddaddy was the governor of Massachusetts! My granddaddy was the governor of Massachusetts!" When the workmen teased Tom about his Boston accent, he in turn mimicked their drawls. Once, when the workers grew bored with him, he filled their tool boxes with motor oil. After his visits with the crew, he marched into the house spouting the profanity he had learned from eavesdropping on the workers. His brothers and sisters giggled at his boldness even as Dorothy grabbed Tom and scrubbed his mouth with pepper.

His mischief sometimes turned reckless. Once, when he was about ten years old, Tom took the pearl-handled revolvers out of their wall mounting, loaded them and marched outside. He saw two neighbor boys playing nearby and proposed a game of "cops and robbers." Tom fired toward his laughing playmates hidden behind nearby boulders. Suddenly, one of the boys jumped into view as Tom fired, and the bullet nicked the boy. "It was reckless play," said Knorr, who heard Tom's confession to his father about the incident. "[Tom] was very much ashamed of it. But it was the type of mischief Tom liked, and he had their attention for awhile."

Dorothy saw Tom's mischief as a challenge to her authority. "To my mother, life was this stage on which she was always performing," Jean said. "Tom was always trying to horn in on the spotlight. We thought it all terribly funny, but mother could not stand it." While her temper toward the other children was explosive, Dorothy unleashed the most fury toward Tom. "She seemed to be punishing him more," Bebs said. "She punished him terribly." She often whipped him with a riding quirt filled with shot. If he remained unrepentant, she locked him for hours in a broom closet—the one punishment she knew he dreaded. Still, he saw the punishment as the attention he yearned for; he taunted Dorothy knowing the discipline he faced, and often suffered the punishment with a satisfied smile.

Despite the discipline, Tom remained abundantly cheerful and free of the pressures his mother applied to Harry, the oldest son. She insisted that Harry be the one to recapture the family fortune and uphold the family's legacy. The demands weighed Harry down with resentment, as Tom, dismissed by his mother as a ne'er-do-well, spent his days romping through the wilds and daydreaming.

Tom turned his talent for storytelling into entertainment for the twins, Sam and Jean, and he put his tales on paper, often pecking out stories, plays and poems on the family's typewriter. One of the lasting works of his childhood was a newspaper he produced with Harry and Bebs during February and March 1927, when he was thirteen. Cut off from school by the flooding Crooked River, they spent their idle time chronicling the daily events at Westernwold. Appropriately, they named the newspaper "The World."

RIVER IS RISING

The river of this city commonly known as Crooked is rising rapidly. Many refugees have come floating down on rafts and have been taken in by the kindly but simple, Mrs. Henry McCall.

HENS ARE MURDERED

Two hens, known in this city, were found brutally murdered on an old wood pile. . . . Henry McCall, who was caught nearby, was grilled and confessed but it is suspected that he is only a tool of some power.

WOMAN PESTERED

Mrs. Henry McCall of First St. was "pestered" by the World's reporters for news. After several hours of such pestering Mrs. McCall threw a large spoon at the offending reporter.

The children could also make light of the family's deep financial problems.

As there is a conspicuous absence of a certain commodity around these parts, [Hal and Dorothy] plan to bum a ride down and while there, rob a bank. In the murky morning stillness, they will undertake to run the gauntlet of hungry creditors.

Tom's writing showed an uncommon skill and talent for language and wit that marked his career as a politician years later. Tom worked at expanding his word power; each week he picked a new word out of the dictionary, memorized its meaning and worked it into his daily speech. "Each of the children had a marvelous vocabulary," said Knorr. "That came from the nightly readings by Dorothy. But Tom was the one putting it to work."

Nowhere did Tom's love of attention and his control of the language stand out more than in school. The McCall children attended Montgomery School, a one-room schoolhouse near Westernwold, where Knorr taught seventeen children in grades one though eight. Tom McCall enrolled as a fifth grader in 1923 and dominated Knorr's attention with his mischief. When her back was turned, Tom entertained the other children with jokes and tricks. She wanted to scold him, but he would disarm her. "He was the picture of innocence," she said. "He would look at you as if to say, 'You don't want to scold me, do you?' And that little grin would pop out. And there you'd be."

He also showed a remarkable ability to persuade. On the playground, a small, dusty clearing among the brush and rocks, Tom usually wanted to play baseball. With seventeen students and Knorr, Tom had just enough for two full teams, if he could convince everyone to play. "He'd

just argue that was the best game to play, and it would be the most exercise," his teacher remembered. "He had a dozen arguments why they
should do it his way. He always got his way." He also dominated the
game, selecting the teams and the positions everyone played. If he did
not like the players on his team, Knorr recalled, "He'd keep trading
players until he got the ones he wanted. He was a great maneuverer."

When Tom did not get his way—which was not often—he demonstrated a trait that surfaced years later: the ability to follow, but make it
appear as if he was leading. "If he could see all the others were going
against him, he'd change," she said. "The other children would have
their way, but Tom would have made it seem that he had been leading
them all the time."

The charm, the power of language, and the stubbornness all showed
at an early age. "He had the determination to do whatever he wanted to
get done," Knorr said. "You could not but admire the little fellow for it."

The one wish Tom had during these years, though, could not be
reached through determination. He wished to be as graceful an athlete as
his father had been, and his brother Harry had become. By age fifteen,
though, he had shot up, as Tom recalled, into "an uncoordinated,
clumsy, fast-growing mess, possessing the ruggedness of a Stradivarius
in my 6-ft 4 inch 130-pound round-shouldered frame." He could not
run the bases without tripping over his flapping legs, nor swing a bat
without the momentum knocking him off balance. "I couldn't go into a
room where there were two people without being violently embarrassed," he said of his awkwardness. "No one ever saw such an inferi-
ority complex."

His years at Prineville's Crook County High were uneventful, spent
in the long shadow of his athletic brother while he was a "drab nobody."
In his senior year he transferred to Redmond and returned to his gregarious self. He found his towering height and odd accent were novel-
ties to his new classmates, and he soon won election as student body
president. "He always could figure ways to get things done," said Mabel
Teater Goodrich, a Redmond classmate. "I believe he had an eye on
politics even then."

But his years of awkwardness sharpened his dream of the time: to
become a writer. "I was much better writing about [sports] than playing,

and so part of my earliest ambition was to become a sports writer," he recalled. After graduation, he enrolled in the journalism school at the University of Oregon, located in Eugene, a hundred miles west across the Cascades. Samuel Walker McCall's estate had set aside some money for the children's college costs, but not enough, so Dorothy marched down to a local pawn shop and hocked the pearl-handled revolvers. Even with these efforts, Tom sat out long stretches of college when the family could not pay tuition. The delays forced him to spend five years pursuing a four-year degree.

The University of Oregon was the state's oldest public college and in 1931 was also the biggest, though the Depression had cut enrollment. At Oregon, Tom again fell under Harry's shadow. He joined his brother's fraternity, Phi Delta Theta, and Tom stood out among the freshmen having reached his full, towering height of six feet and five inches. His long, sloping face swept out to a jutting chin that dragged out his lower teeth when he spoke or smiled.

At the University of Oregon, though, his mischievousness often ran counter to the Phi Delt's code of conduct. In one instance, the fraternity forbid freshmen to drink in the house. Yet Tom and a classmate built a still in the house's basement. Their moonshine made them both violently ill, but after they recovered, McCall insisted they try again—they ended with the same results.

Such antics made Tom a target for fraternity-style discipline—swats with a paddle or dunks under icy showers. His mischief, plus Harry's determination to punish his younger brother, perhaps spurred on by sibling rivalry, meant that Tom was punished more than anyone else.

Tom's pride swelled whenever he faced punishment. Under the paddle wielded by Harry, Tom never flinched. "At Harry's direction we'd swat him or stick him under the shower until he was numb," recalled Phi Delt member Lagrande Houghton. "Tom had the guts of a burglar. He just took the punishment."

Tom emerged a popular figure on campus who preferred carousing and drinking to everything else. As McCall said of his college years, "I was a gregarious soul. . . . I was a great fun guy and always liked to be with the boys." He became reckless about money. He had a part-time job and a small allowance check from home, but he was always broke.

He routinely hit up fraternity brothers for loans—fifty cents here, a dollar there. His friends learned that Tom was prompt about paying them back—and as prompt in asking for another loan.

The drain on his funds had a prominent cause. Like Thomas Lawson before him, McCall had a taste for gambling. He spent most of his money on pinball or slot machines used in some bars illegally for gambling. The spinning wheels, the feel of the lever, the rush as coins clinked into the tray—it all fascinated him. His affection for the slots was so pronounced that, decades later, another Phi Delt vividly remembered an incident that took place in a tavern close to campus. Charles Heltzel had taken a date into the Three Trees and found McCall hunched over the slot machine. When he ran out of nickels, McCall looked around the bar and spotted Heltzel. "Chas, ol' pal," McCall said, "can I borrow a nickel?" Heltzel's date forbid him to give McCall any money, so McCall shrugged and walked over to the tavern's owner.

"How much would you give me to sweep out this entire bar?" McCall asked the owner.

"A nickel," the owner replied.

McCall grabbed a broom and furiously swept the establishment. When he was finished, the owner laughed and handed him a nickel. McCall rushed back to the slot machine, sunk the nickel and pulled down hard on the handle. His reward: a losing combination of two lemons.

Tom's recklessness with money increased. Harry and Bebs struggled to make sure they received the monthly forty-dollar allowance checks from home that were supposed to serve all three McCall kids. When Tom got the checks first, he cashed them and spent the money.

One night four of McCall's fraternity brothers found a drunken McCall sitting in the large stone fireplace of the Three Trees. Covered with soot, McCall explained that he had blown the entire allowance check on beer and slot machines. When one of his friends asked why he was sitting in the fireplace, McCall sheepishly explained it was his penance, his act of contrition—as in sackcloth and ashes—for having such a hell of a good time.

Meanwhile, McCall ignored his studies. In five years he received only one A, earning it in a freshman music course. He finished college with an even C average, the lowest grade level he could have and still

A University of Oregon senior, McCall as he appeared in his school's annual, the 1935 *Oregana*. (OrHi 90803)

graduate. "He had the smarts but didn't apply himself," said fraternity brother Malcolm Bauer. "He didn't spend the time." McCall had learned that he did not have to spend the time. His talent for writing always saved him. McCall turned out papers and reports quickly, and with a minimum of studying or research.

To graduate from the journalism school, McCall had to write a senior thesis, supposedly a year-long effort. As the deadline approached, though, McCall had not started work. "He wasn't the least bit worried about it," recalled his roommate, Richard Devers. Two days before the paper was due, McCall locked himself in his room and began typing. For the next thirty-six hours McCall consumed nothing but coffee and caffeine pills. He emerged with a finished thesis, and Devers remembered marvelling at its prose, which included passages about the Crooked River valley and the rimrock country. "It was," said Devers, "a beautiful tribute, absolute literature, a verbal photograph." He earned only a C in the class, however.

While his academic studies suffered, McCall devoted his attention to campus activities, especially the newspaper, the *Oregon Daily Emerald*. His work as a sports writer—and later sports editor—showed a writing flair. He became widely known at the University of Oregon as a voice for the school's "establishment." In his daily column, "Sports Quacks," he routinely defended the athletic department against criticism from other student journalists who criticized the use of student fees to support sports.

His classmates sensed a desire for politics that he never fully pursued. Students certainly thought him a leader, electing him president of the Phi Delt house, the fraternity governance council and virtually every club he joined. He also showed a knack for wielding the small doses of power he had. As president of the Inter-Fraternity Council, he investigated hazing violations, uncommon for the oversight board. The inquiry found widespread violations and McCall fined nine fraternities.

Only once did he wade into campus politics as a candidate. In the spring of 1935, he ran an impromptu write-in campaign for senior class president when only one candidate appeared on the ballot. McCall won by twenty votes, but the school stripped him of the election when the University of Oregon Law School dean, Wayne Morse (later a United States senator) ruled the write-in election invalid.

McCall did not take himself seriously, however. With a friend, student newspaper editor Robert Lucas, McCall, in his senior year, launched a mock campaign, running for student body office as the "forgotten man" candidate. He and Lucas stumped the campus giving satirical speeches. "We weren't protesting anything," Lucas said. "We were a couple of terrible hams." The mock campaign, however, underscored McCall's grasp of language. "He'd make me these flowery speeches about almost nothing, no serious issue," Lucas said. "He could make anything sound interesting, simply by his diction and his grand manner. Here was the tall slack-jawed figure making all these gestures. He was funny as hell. He had people laughing. It was all just a big joke."

The joke had some greater meaning for McCall, however. McCall's college years had taught him that not everyone had his colorful background. He began to pay more attention to his family's history and took special notice of Samuel McCall. He read and re-read a biography of his grandfather that detailed Sam's political career. He studied his grandfather's speeches and practiced delivering them. Most of all, he remembered Dorothy's tales of Sam McCall's devotion to the downtrodden.

Around the fraternity, McCall told his classmates he intended to follow Sam's course into politics. When his fraternity brothers chuckled, unable to take him seriously, Tom took exception. "You know," he once declared, unusually earnest, "I intend to be President of the United States someday." The others in the room collapsed from laughter. For once, McCall did not laugh along.

"That 'forgotten man' campaign was only a joke to us," Robert Lucas said. "Tom wasn't serious enough to run for anything. Yet you could see it. He could see it. He had the knack."

3

The Knight of the Underwood

MCCALL SLID THROUGH GRADUATION in June 1936, and at age twenty-three with nowhere else to go, he headed home to Westernwold.

His father's financial problems had eased. One of Dorothy's sisters had paid off the creditors, and Hal had put the ranch into a trust to protect it from foreclosure. But for McCall, prospects for work as a reporter were dim. The Depression still gripped the country, and sparse central Oregon had little to offer a young reporter seeking his break into newspapers. He worked part-time for the *Bulletin* in Bend, a small mill town fifteen miles south of the Crooked River, but he blew what little he earned in card games.

Then, early in 1937, he heard from a University of Oregon classmate who had landed a job selling advertisements for a newspaper in Moscow, Idaho. The paper needed help. McCall left Westernwold for Idaho in February, on his own for the first time.

With just five dollars in his pocket, McCall arrived in Moscow, a farming town sitting high in a nook of the Palouse, just across the Washington-Idaho border from where Hal McCall had first learned about ranching twenty-eight years earlier. Moscow was the biggest town for miles except for Pullman, Washington, a few miles west across the border. The town had a population of four thousand, which doubled each fall when students flocked back to the University of Idaho, located at the edge of town.

Despite the town's size and depressed economy, Moscow supported two daily newspapers: the *Star-Mirror*, and McCall's new employer, the *News-Review,* which had launched a circulation battle a few months earlier against its competitor. The two newspapers fought for readers' attention with bold headlines announcing the latest events at city hall, or the distant rumblings of a new war in Europe.

The *News-Review* typically ran eight pages a day and McCall's job was to fill them. Each morning he scurried around Moscow in search of news stories at city hall, the college, the Latah County courthouse, or coffee shops. By noon he had rushed back to his office and had dashed off his stories on his Underwood typewriter. As that afternoon's paper headed for the press, McCall became the paper's sports reporter. On an average night, he might cover a high school game, rush over to the college and cover another event, and then write late into the night.

McCall's editor was Louis Boaz, a dyspeptic, bulb-nosed man, a lifelong Moscow resident who considered the town his personal journalistic domain. Boaz's temper was legendary. "Louis would pound his desk and throw papers around and then put on his hat and storm out of the office over the slightest thing," said pressman Dick Westwood. "That happened all the time."

Boaz most often unleashed his anger at McCall. In the local newspapers' circulation battle, Boaz pushed McCall to scrape up dirt on local officials. McCall found the assignments unseemly, especially since he had become pals with so many of the town's leaders. "Louis was never happy with [McCall]," Bill Anderson, a Moscow clothing store owner, said. "He was too good. He was too trustworthy. Louis loved nasty stories. And Tom wouldn't write them. Besides, Tom was a hell of a writer and Louis was jealous of his talent."

McCall stood out in Moscow, not only as a newcomer, but because of his size and his strange accent. He relished the attention and remade himself to fit the role. Mimicking Hollywood's portrayal of reporters, McCall affected what he called the "movie scoop" look: "Hat tipped forward over a protruding cigarette and exuding a faint essence of Old Crow." He also copied the lifestyle. He moved into the Day Mansion, a

In 1939, McCall, then a young sports reporter, posed on a Moscow, Idaho, street with his friend William Brown. (Courtesy William and Ruth Brown)

rambling Victorian boarding house on A Street that catered to bachelors. With his twenty-dollar-a-week salary, McCall and his roommates hung around the University of Idaho sororities, where girls were fond of young men with paychecks to spend on them.

Nonetheless, recalled his roommate, William Brown, "Girls to Tom weren't the most important thing at that time." He instead preferred to drink and gamble. McCall roamed Moscow's bars—the Ad Club in the Idaho Hotel, the Elks Club, or the Knobby Inn closer to campus.

He became a hit among the locals. Recalled Morey O'Donnell, a Moscow attorney, "He was a witty, very clever young man. He was not a joke-teller. His conversation was simply funny. We local yokels would just stand around and wait for Tom to make us laugh." He drank beer, as did most of his friends, but he loved gin most of all. "He was amazing," said E.J. "Mike" Sullivan, a University of Idaho basketball player who became one of McCall's closest friends. "Tom could really put it away. He never seemed to slur or lose command. He got better. He got funnier."

McCall's life became a cycle of work and carousing. On an average day, he worked until late, then drank until the taverns closed. Often, he never made it home. In the morning, the newspaper's press operators would find McCall in their shop, passed out on the large rolls of newsprint. McCall would wake up, so hung over that, Westwood recalled, "He could hardly see his hand in front of his face." Dusting himself off, he would start another day and another night of drinking, unaffected by the last. Remembered Art Crossler, owner of the Idaho Hotel, where McCall often drank: "He was not a lady's man. He was a man's man. He liked playing poker and the slot machines and all the things that took money he didn't have."

Gambling followed the drinking, and he gambled whatever money he had. Years later McCall acknowledged his gambling addiction while in Moscow, saying, "I had a little gambling trouble in those days."

"What he meant to say," said Sullivan, "was that he had a *lot* of gambling trouble."

He gambled at cards in Moscow's sleepy beer joints. He gambled on the illegal one-armed bandits at the Idaho Hotel and the Elks Club. He gambled with abandon, as if he intended to lose. "He was lousy at cards but loved it anyway," said William Brown. "He never seemed to win." He played the slots in the dark Elks Club lounge—he "fell in love with the slot machines," as he put it—and would stand before them as if hypnotized by the whirling wheels. "Every week he got his paycheck," said friend Ruth Brown, "in his paycheck would go, all of it, into the slots." Added Sullivan, who gambled alongside McCall, "I can remember going to the Elks Club with him on Sundays, and we would never get out of the place—spent a whole week's pay on the slot machines, both of us." Even if McCall hit a few jackpots, he never left with a dime. "He never won. We saw to that," Sullivan said. "We just couldn't walk away winners."

McCall joked that he had inherited Thomas Lawson's gambling blood, as if to rationalize why he gambled as he did. But that did not justify his habits to his friends. "He was playing the slots too much for what he was making," William Brown said. "He owed everybody." His friends loaned him small amounts of cash, and he lived on his tabs at restaurants and taverns and on credit from local stores.

McCall often paid his debts with advances from his salary. He only paid enough of the debts, however, to get merchants to extend his credit even further. When payday came, McCall pressed his boss for even larger advances, which he often gambled away. Even as his debts grew out of control, he rarely fretted about the money. He plunged into each evening ready to drink and gamble again. It was in his blood, McCall would say, and he could not stop.

His editor, Boaz, frowned on McCall's heavy drinking, scowling when, as McCall remembered, "On some occasions, the air in our tiny joint cubicle reflected my partiality the night before toward a pint of gin." Boaz used McCall's drinking and gambling as excuses to fire him. Each time Boaz tried to fire McCall, however, the newspaper's publisher, Bill Marineau, rescued him. Marineau had taken a paternal liking to McCall. He valued McCall's talents and hoped his reporter would soon grow out of his bad habits.

When the two rival newspapers in Moscow merged under Bill Marineau, McCall's role changed. By 1939, two years after his arrival, the newspaper, now called the *Idahoian*, had given him a daily sports column called "On the Spot." The column gave McCall greater celebrity, carrying as it did a photo of McCall wearing his fedora. He took to calling himself "The Spotter" and wrote as he spoke—loquacious, witty, irreverent. "Everybody read that column," said Westwood. "People were always talking about what Tom was saying."

"His column was especially popular for one reason," Ruth Brown said. "He was always sticking up for the underdog." McCall wrote dutifully about the football and basketball teams, but he sought out the athletes in the obscure sports, such as archery and cross-country, who he portrayed in romantic prose. He followed the fortunes of a local boxer who, while championship material, could not afford to pay his way across country for a title fight.

His columns sought justice for local athletes. One year the University of Idaho's president abruptly fired the school's football and basketball coaches, neither of whom had turned in winning seasons. Still, they were both McCall's close friends and he raged in print against their firings, using one column to skillfully mock the university president. The resulting controversy gave Boaz one more reason to fire his columnist, but McCall had become too popular to let go.

McCall was constantly reaching, stretching for a clever line or turn of phrase, often mimicking the style of the renowned sports columnist Grantland Rice. Most of all, his writing showed his imaginative use of language. A fullback did not carry the ball, he "lugged it"; a coach did not have watchful eyes, he had "vigilant peepers"; football score predictions were "clairvoyant pennings." When he wrote about the university's athletic budget, he rejected dry spending reports. He wrote: "Unsung as a multiplier and believed scarcely able to add the simplest figures, the Spotter is liable to startle the bulk of his buddies today by blossoming forth with a clutch of dollar signs, digits and doo-dads." Once he delivered his weekly football predictions in verse: "A spot of rhyme here and there/Keeps Mr. Fan from tearing his hair/By taking his mind off the errors/Of The Idahoian's prognosticating terrors."

He loved his job so much that even an emergency trip to the hospital did not slow his pace. McCall had suffered a hernia in childhood, and when he reinjured himself, he underwent surgery at Moscow's Gritman Hospital. While recuperating, McCall wrote his column from his hospital bed for more than a week. There, from his "horizontal Hades," he described the sensation of slipping under the anesthesia.

> [A] couple of the west's best cutter-uppers inveigled a henchman into slipping the ether mask over my beak.
>
> That made up my mind—ether is the shortest distance between two points of consciousness and oblivion. It's a tough trip at first: you think your lungs are going to burn up or explode before you can slip into the blessed blackness. Now that the journey's over it would seem that the bellows survived the tribulation. There is, however, a dark brown taste in the chamber reserved for my gnashers, and somewhere south of the border I can detect one hell of a pain.

Nothing stopped him from doing his job, not surgery, not his drinking, not his gambling. McCall lived the reporter's life of movies and books, a raspy, smoky, boozy life. He championed the athletes who did what he was too clumsy and awkward to do himself, and he thought his profession a grand one. To him, sports writers were artists—"scriveners," as he once put it in a column—pounding out history on their chattering typewriters. They were, he wrote, "Knights of the Underwood." And he loved being one of the knights.

MCCALL'S ROMANTIC LIFESTYLE took its toll, his drinking and debts driving him to ruin. He lacked the discipline required to pull himself up, but soon he found someone who possessed it.

One day in February 1939, Bill Marineau assigned McCall to cover a cooking demonstration sponsored by the Washington Water Power Co., the area's utility and one of the newspaper's biggest advertisers. McCall loped next door to the grange hall expecting a routine story. "When I walked in, there was this darling blonde girl seating old ladies and cooking roasts, steaks and cakes all over the place." As the young woman later recalled, "He was a very hungry reporter. He hardly spoke to me. He just ate everything that I had baked." And for good reason, McCall said later: "I hadn't had anything to eat except a pint of gin the night before."

McCall did take careful note of Audrey Owen. "Suddenly," as McCall said years later, "this hungry, hard-writing, burn-the-candle-at-both-ends sports writer reached an incisive conclusion: 'I'm never going to let that sweetheart out of my sight'."

Audrey Owen had grown up self-reliant and strong-willed. Abandoned by her father at age three, Audrey was raised by her mother in Spokane, Washington, with an ambition to survive on her own. In college at Washington State in Pullman she studied home economics. Later, while she was working as a hostess of a local coffee shop, the president of Washington Water Power spotted her and hired her to push electric appliances in hopes of increasing the utility's business. She toured most of Idaho with her cooking demonstrations, showing rural housewives how easily electrical appliances performed exhausting kitchen chores.

With his stomach filled, McCall promptly asked Audrey out. At first she declined, telling him she was already engaged to her high school sweetheart back in Spokane. Besides, she thought, Moscow had plenty of single men already eager to entertain her. None, however, persisted as McCall did, and she finally gave in.

McCall used every trick he knew to entertain Audrey on their dates. Years later, McCall recalled that to make her laugh he had once grabbed an ashtray and dumped the cigarette butts onto his head. "Tom, you made an ass of yourself," Audrey said when McCall told the story. "Yeah," McCall replied, "but I got your attention, didn't I?"

Audrey responded with lavish dinners of steaming roast beef she would fix for him at her apartment. After only a few dates, McCall proposed marriage. Audrey at first laughed him off. Undaunted, he asked again and again. "I can't remember how many times he proposed to me," Audrey said. "It was quite a few times. That's why he got so hard to resist."

During a Friday night date Audrey finally said yes. The next day, 20 May 1939, McCall bought a ring on credit and the two of them slipped into a local church for the ceremony. With only two close friends as witnesses, Tom and Audrey were married. He was twenty-six, and she was twenty-four.

They hoped to keep the wedding a secret. With jobs in short supply, Audrey's employer followed a common Depression-era rule: Married women could not keep their jobs if their husbands also worked. In gossipy Moscow, word of the marriage leaked out and Audrey was fired. Bill Marineau sympathetically raised McCall's pay by $2.50 a week.

The raise hardly covered their costs, not to mention the gambling debts McCall had brought to the marriage. Audrey put McCall on a strict allowance, doling out single dollar bills only when McCall needed the money. "He didn't see any of [the money] then. She took over," William Brown said. "And it's a good thing she did."

McCall's habits died hard, however. Their apartment, in the Idaho Hotel, was in the same building as the Ad Club and next door to the Elks Club—McCall's favorite havens for drinking and gambling. Cut off from his paycheck, he quietly borrowed even more money to finance his nights at the bars and slot machines. Occasionally McCall got to the paycheck before Audrey did and spent it all before she could stash the money away.

Audrey learned that McCall's big heart also took its financial toll. He frequently invited to dinner a stranger with whom he had become fast friends while working or drinking in a tavern. "Every down-on-his-luck guy Tom would meet he'd bring home and Audrey would feed him," Ruth Brown recalled.

Audrey tried to make do with her homemaking skills and encouraged McCall to tone down his social life. But as it had been since childhood, McCall loved to be the center of attention. Audrey found her apartment host for parties every weekend, for which she cooked lavish meals. For entertainment, there was always McCall. He would try anything—stuffing a half dozen lighted cigarettes in his mouth, eating soap—to make people laugh. If a piano was nearby, McCall, while someone else played, would improvise a song about each person in the room. His odd voice mangled the melody, yet he sang with cheer and abandon. As a testament to his control of language, the song usually rhymed the first time through.

To most people in Moscow, McCall was an insatiable reveler and reporter. His friends, however, knew he had hidden passions of which he rarely spoke. And the first was a love for the land.

On many of their evenings out, McCall would sit for hours and describe for Mike Sullivan the wonders of the Oregon desert. There was a longing in his stories, a longing for the Oregon landscape he had left behind. "This love of the land and nature was always part of him, even though he didn't always show it," Sullivan recalled. "You had to really know him to see it." His passion moved McCall to take up conservationist issues in his sports column. He wrote publicity pieces for the Latah County Conservation Federation, a group—which McCall helped run—comprised of hunters and naturalists concerned about farmers' efforts to kill off the region's wild animals.

Even Sullivan was surprised by how deep McCall's concern ran. One night, as they meandered from bar to bar, McCall announced a change of plans. He and Sullivan walked over to the grange hall, where farmers had gathered to hear a University of Idaho agriculture professor lecture on land conservation. The thrust of the professor's talk was simple: Don't overuse your land. "Those farmers were not too receptive about this," Sullivan recalled. "What this guy was talking about was a long-term view of the land. They knew it would cost them a few bucks."

Suddenly the professor introduced McCall as the evening's guest speaker. Sullivan looked on with astonishment as McCall delivered the same message to the farmers, albeit with far more eloquence and caring. "Tom could speak so well," Sullivan said. "And he told the farmers what they didn't think they wanted to hear. What he said was that if you didn't take care of the land, your children were not going to have the benefits of it. Tom was very sincere about it."

Sullivan sat stunned as he listened. Later, he and McCall walked from the grange hall into a nearby bar. Still surprised at McCall's speech, Sullivan kidded him about it. "So, Tom, what the hell did all of that have to do with sports writing?" he asked, laughing.

McCall, however, did not laugh, and his sudden, rare earnestness startled Sullivan. "Mike," McCall said, "I'm interested in what happens to the land." McCall fell silent and Sullivan never teased him about the topic again.

While McCall's first passion was private, his second passion was much more public.

During 1940, McCall, then twenty-seven years old, started talking about running for public office. Moscow's mayor was retiring and McCall decided to jump into the city hall race. The news was no surprise to Audrey, to whom he had confided his ambitions. "It was always understood between the two of us that Tom would someday run for office," Audrey said. "It was his grandfather, you know, the governor of Massachusetts, he looked up to."

According to McCall, the inspiration to run came from the incumbent mayor: "[I]n 1940, Mayor Bill Anderson . . . got me in a room with several other dignitaries and urged me to run for mayor. Bill was a reliable mayor. He was just getting tired of the job—and of chewing those putrid cigars through those long night meetings. I was both honored and excited." McCall talked up the idea to his friends and others around town. Soon, Sullivan recalled, "The word was out that Tom McCall may run for mayor." McCall said his campaign hopes crumbled when his editor, Louis Boaz, told McCall that he could not simultaneously cover city hall and run for it. Faced with losing the sole household paycheck, McCall claimed, he turned down the city leaders' offer.

Anderson, the only surviving member of the group McCall said approached him about the job, remembers things differently. Anderson said that he never offered McCall a chance to take his place at city hall. In fact, records show that in 1940, when he supposedly invited McCall to take his place, Anderson was not yet mayor; he was running that year for the first time. As Anderson put it, "Why would I want him to run when I'm running for the job myself?" Moscow city records show that Anderson served as mayor until 1947, five years after McCall left town. Moreover, Anderson pointed out, why would he and other city leaders choose McCall, of all people? "[McCall] wouldn't have gotten to first base running for mayor," he said. "He was popular, sure, but people knew about his debts and that he played the slot machines too much."

Anderson remembers that, more often, McCall talked on his own about running for mayor someday. "I do remember telling him that he might make a good politician one day, and he really liked to hear that," Anderson said. "It was just a passing remark, if it was anything at all."

McCall's ambition, however, had been laid bare.

HIS TENURE IN MOSCOW ended in March 1942, when Louis Boaz, for reasons unknown, fired McCall. Those in Moscow remember the final fallout. Art Crossler, McCall's landlord at the Idaho Hotel, said McCall told him then he had been fired because of a "tiff with Boaz, which didn't surprise me at all." Anderson recalled a glum McCall entering his clothing store and saying, "Louis just canned me." McCall worried about a hundred dollar debt for a new suit he had bought from Anderson on credit. "I told Tom he could pay me back over time," Anderson said, "and that he would need that suit to look for a new job."

Bill Marineau, who had saved McCall's job many times before, this time did not intervene. Did he want to stay in Moscow forever? he asked his columnist. McCall said no and saw his chance to move on. "Marineau just felt it was time for him to get out and break his bad habits," Audrey McCall said.

His final column was about the local boxer who could not afford to make the trip to his title fight. It ran 20 March 1942, two days before McCall's twenty-ninth birthday. The column contained no farewells to his loyal readers. McCall's departure was necessarily quick and silent, as he did not want to alarm his creditors as he skulked out of town.

McCall had arrived in Moscow five years earlier with dreams of being a reporter; he left a seasoned writer and a happily married man. He had arrived with five dollars in his pocket; he departed as an addicted gambler with $1,200 in debts—almost a year's salary.

Although Audrey had squelched some of his drinking and gambling habits, marriage and debts had sobered him only a little. What sobered McCall the most was his flickering political ambition, which could not be satisfied in a town that knew his vices too well. So he went away to start fresh in a new town. When he left Idaho, said Ruth Brown, "He just grew up. Matured. He stopped being foolish."

THE NEXT FOUR YEARS moved McCall closer to the threshold of that political career, but brought none of the stability that Audrey wanted in their lives. Instead, McCall faced only more change—four jobs in four years—as he tried to start over.

Leaving Audrey behind in Idaho—a "hostage to my creditors," he said—he traveled first to Portland to seek work and found the town bustling. The United States had entered World War II full scale after Japan's attack on Pearl Harbor only three months earlier. Portland was not only a jumping off point for many men enlisting, it was becoming a major shipbuilding center for Henry Kaiser. Finding work proved to be little problem. Most men of McCall's age had enlisted to fight in the war and jobs were plentiful. McCall had been told by the military that his bad knees and a recurring hernia would disqualify him, so he did not try to enlist. Instead he applied at the city's two daily newspapers, the *Oregonian* and the *Oregon Journal,* which were at the height of their circulation battles. With reporting still largely a male profession, the war had depleted the newsrooms. The *Oregonian* promptly offered Mc-Call a job at seventy-five dollars a week, nearly triple his Idaho wage.

He soon discovered the newspaper was a far larger operation than the one he had left in Idaho. The *Oregonian*'s newsroom filled the sixth floor of the newspaper's downtown building. The city room smelled of cigars and newsprint. Dozens of desks sat in sturdy rows, buried under the daily scatter of paper and carbons and battered typewriters. On the floor above, the Linotype machines, setting the hot metal type one line at a time, rattled and crashed as if they were about to break through the aging ceiling.

On McCall's first day, a Sunday, "I saw this tall, Lincolnesque type fellow walk in," recalled Hollis Goodrich, who worked as an editor that day. "So I gave him a desk. He was so damn tall the desk didn't fit him. He just sat there all morning. At noon I told him to go to lunch, and he said, 'Oh. I'm not hungry.' But he sure looked hungry. I said, 'Are you stoney?' That means 'broke.' I gave him a dollar. He went to lunch."

McCall's work immediately impressed his new editors. He worked general assignment and the police beat, often spending all night at the downtown precinct waiting for crime reports to come in. After producing an entire paper everyday in Idaho, McCall knew how to write quickly with flair. "He had a good command of the English language, without letting flowery language get in the way," said J. Richard Nokes, a fellow reporter. As Goodrich remembered, "A lot of us were good. Tom was a hell of a writer."

In that era, few reporters regularly won by-lines, which the newspaper reserved for its "star" reporters, but McCall earned more than his share, writing breaking news, features, business stories and even movie reviews. "By-lines were like winning a gold medal," recalled Audrey, who joined him in Portland after several months.

McCall also displayed his volatility at the paper. "He [was] an emotional person," Nokes said. "He could be terribly depressed, or he could be on the ceiling, exalted over some story he had written successfully. If he wrote a story and someone called him up to compliment him, he'd preen his feathers. All writers do. But this was at a higher level."

"He took great pride in what he wrote," Goodrich said. "Most reporters didn't care. We got our paychecks and that was all that interested most of us. But Tom took pride in it." One editor in particular infuriated McCall by rewriting everything he wrote. McCall would see the rewrite and fume, "I'll kill that son of a bitch." At one point McCall pounded out a resignation letter and stuck it to the typewriter of the managing editor, Jalmar Johnson. Johnson ordered the editor to leave McCall's writing alone. "None of us liked to be edited," Nokes said. "No one but Tom would ever go that far."

Together again, Audrey and McCall felt unburdened. They had a comfortable salary and lived in a big city where they did not meet the people they owed money to on the sidewalk everyday. Portland in 1942 did offer its temptations, however. The city was wide open with gambling operations and night clubs. Audrey nonetheless maintained tight control over money, each day giving McCall no more money than he needed for that day's lunch, a routine she followed all of McCall's life. However, McCall still sunk his lunch money into slot machines at the local press club or into newsroom card games. "He loved to play poker," says Don McLeod, then a sports writer. "But he was lousy at cards. He had no patience at all."

The *Oregonian* provided much needed stability for McCall, but, always restless, he sought a change. The *Oregonian* owned two radio stations, KEX and KGW. One day a station official walked into the newsroom looking for someone to read five lines in a public service announcement, and McCall agreed. His unique voice impressed the station management; they offered McCall a job as KGW's news announcer, and he accepted.

McCall made the shift from print journalism to broadcasting with ease. He proved to be an unusual asset to the radio station. Before McCall, the station had relied on "rip and read"—announcers taking news directly from the wire service teletypes. McCall, however, could rewrite the news as well as add his own reporting.

He had only two problems. One was his nerves. The thought of broadcasting to thousands of people terrified McCall. He stood at the mike, his giant body trembling, and the words tumbling out. During McCall's first few weeks, the station's manager, Arden Pangborn, assigned a backup announcer to stand behind McCall. "He was such a wreck," recalled Pangborn, "I thought he might faint at any time."

The second problem was his name. The stations already had two other announcers named Tom and Pangborn wanted McCall to have a name with more flair. So McCall adopted his middle name. As Portlanders tuned in their radios each day, they began to rely on Lawson McCall for their news.

IN MARCH 1944, nearly five years into their marriage, Audrey gave birth to their first son. They named him Thomas William Lawson McCall, Jr., but always called him Tad. Tom doted on Tad and relished fatherhood. With his young family, he had all that he had lacked a few years earlier: stability, a healthy income and growing celebrity.

McCall, however, soon disrupted the stability. He wanted to go to war, and he was running out of time. By mid-1944, Allied forces had closed in around both Japan and Germany: in June, Allied forces invaded Europe at Normandy and started the long march toward Berlin; in the Pacific during August, American forces wrested the island of Guam from Japanese control, giving the United States a key launching point for its growing offensive. McCall watched as many men his age slowly returned home from the war, and his conscience nagged at him.

In the summer of 1944, Mike Sullivan visited Portland after his three-year stint in the navy. McCall begged Sullivan to tell him all he could about the service. In turn, Sullivan found that all McCall could talk about was politics and his ambition to run for office—any office. They spent a few nights over drinks talking, and one evening, Sullivan said to him, "I think you'd be great in politics, but if you don't have some kind of military record behind you, it's going to be thrown up at you."

McCall leaned back and smiled, and Sullivan realized McCall had already come to this conclusion. "He was going to do this anyway and sign up to go to war," said Sullivan. "He just wanted me as a back up."

Not long afterward McCall marched into the KGW studios and told his boss, Arden Pangborn, that he intended to join the navy. Pangborn was stunned. It made no sense, he told McCall. McCall had a family and a good job where he was needed. Moreover, Pangborn argued, the war would be ending soon.

The more McCall listened, the more frantic he became. Finally, he interrupted Pangborn. "You don't understand," McCall said anxiously. "If I don't have an armed service record, I'll never have any hope to be governor of Oregon."

Pangborn fell silent. He thought McCall was joking but no smile came.

"He was serious," Pangborn recalled. "He wasn't joking. There was no question in his mind. He was quite serious about it when he talked about being governor. I was flabbergasted that a young man had his sights set so far ahead, which he obviously did."

McCall enlisted in the navy in September 1944, leaving behind an angry wife who did not understand his reasoning. "Heavens," Audrey first exclaimed when Tom brought up his idea of enlisting, "how can you consider quitting your job to go now? We're paying income tax for the first time in our lives!"

McCall recognized the sacrifice he was making for his ambitions. "I had a great job . . . a darling little house, a lovely little garden, a new baby," he recalled. "Here I was, scot-free, at an age where it would have been appropriate not to have gone." His desire to serve—and the desire for the service record—outweighed all else, however.

The navy shipped him to Farragut, Idaho, for training. At thirty-one, McCall was the oldest and tallest of the trainees; the others called him "Pops." In one of many letters home, he told Audrey he stuck out like an "elderly idiot." The training proved rigorous for the still-clumsy McCall, who spent much of his time sick or injured. He could not finish the obstacle course without hurting himself. With his long, stringy arms, he could not complete a single chin-up.

After he finished training, McCall spent a frustrating four months in Farragut. He often stood guard duty, and escaped the other menial assignments by ducking out of sight when duty officers showed up. The navy eventually noted his journalism credentials and assigned him to its news service.

Like the army, the navy had started a publicity office dedicated to filling hometown newspapers with accounts of their local sailors in battle. As a battle correspondent, McCall would write the stories while assigned to the front. Given the rank of seaman second class, McCall shipped out to Pearl Harbor in February 1945, where he pulled a soft duty working regular hours in a sunny office that filled with the scent of flowers when the Hawaiian breeze blew through his open window.

As McCall waited in Pearl Harbor, he worried that he would not see his assignment before the war ended. The Allied forces in February captured the Phillipines, and the image of General Douglas McArthur wading ashore signaled the momentum behind the American effort. McCall wanted to "make a name" for himself with battle coverage, he wrote

McCall served as a sailor in the Pacific theater of World War II, where, as a correspondent, he honed his reportorial skills. (OrHi 90695)

Audrey; instead he performed boring rewrites for correspondents in the action.

McCall pressed for sea duty and within a month won his battle assignment on the U.S.S. *St. Louis*, a 608-foot light cruiser headed for the shores of Japan. Its crew had nicknamed the ship the "Lucky Lou" after it had survived kamikaze attacks and a torpedo that blew open its hull.

After McCall had a day-long drunk with other correspondents, he boarded the repaired *St. Louis*, and the ship chugged out to sea. McCall, at nearly six-and-a-half-feet tall, had trouble adjusting to life on the ship. He worked in a small steel room with four other men. Scrunched at a small table, he squeezed next to a typewriter, his bony knees pulled toward his chin. When the *St. Louis*'s giant guns fired, the typewriter would leap into his lap. Ceilings and doorways were too low—"always bumping the noggin," he wrote Audrey—and he was constantly afflicted with heat rash. He spent long hours idly playing cards, waiting for the ship to enter action. When it did, as a combat correspondent,

Seaman Second Class McCall took his battle station on the ship's bridge where he watched the fighting.

By mid-March 1945 the *St. Louis* had caught up with a thirty-ship convoy, Task Force 58, that was ordered to bombard the island of Okinawa in preparation for an Allied invasion which would turn out to be the last major battle of World War II. For two months, the *St. Louis* sat off Okinawa and fired a record 26,265 rounds at Japanese installations on the island. McCall stood at his battle station on the ship's bridge and recorded the airborne fury he witnessed. "Plane after plane dove," he wrote home after one attack, "climbed and rolled until the sky was filled with red-balled wings, some of them in flames, others in the water." The sights quickly satiated McCall's desire for battle. "I don't think I care much for warfare," he wrote Audrey. "It is about 99 parts waiting and one part excitement. And the proportion of excitement is being diluted as time goes on."

He also admitted to fear as he watched Japanese kamikaze flyers try to crash into the *St. Louis*. "[T]he ancient knees were aquiver during the excitement," he wrote. "The way those flaming juggernauts persist in coming and coming and coming is something to turn the scalplock to silver, although mine seems to have gathered only a few more strands of white."

The sight of death, enemy or not, moved him. He described one hapless Japanese flyer who stumbled unprepared upon the *St. Louis*. The plane, McCall wrote, immediately retreated "in a manner that reminded you of the way brakes sound in a movie cartoon." The *St. Louis*'s guns fired and the plane exploded. "No one even bothers to look for the pieces," McCall wrote. "[I]t becomes impersonal after a time. You shoot at mechanisms, not human beings—and we let it go at that."

The *St. Louis* saw no more than six weeks of action while McCall was aboard; it spent the remainder of the war uneventfully steaming around the South China Sea. To kill time, McCall organized stage shows for the crew and helped sailors write letters home to their girlfriends. He honed his radio skills reading the news over the ship's public address system. In his work, though, he was reduced to writing features about the sailors for their local papers back home, and a long history of the *St. Louis* itself.

The idleness brought on waves of melancholy and homesickness. His letters home to Audrey reveal not only his emotions, but his flair for expressing them; they also show he still felt the need to defend his decision to enlist.

> Six months ago tonight we said goodbye [he wrote Audrey in August 1945] and never, at any time since, have I deviated from my contention that it had to be done. I have weakened to the point that I have cursed life for driving such a bitter bargain. . . .
>
> That's why my eyes are ever turned toward the Heights when I do permit myself the exquisite misery of projecting my thoughts past the grey-banked Eastern horizon and over leagues of somber water.

Immersed in loneliness, though, McCall never forgot his purpose, his dreams, and the value of his military service.

> The experience will make me a most competent civilian. When you think about stateside life, and compare it to the sentence war dictates you serve out here, you can see nothing but opportunities—opportunities which can be exploited by expending the strength you used at sea just trying to exist without too much misery. In brief, the leverage you can apply to the problems of civilian life looms as simply terrific.

4

A Most Competent Civilian

WAR IN THE PACIFIC ended with the Japanese surrender on 14 August 1945. Three weeks later McCall transferred off the *St. Louis* with hopes of an early return home. Caught in the crush of servicemen also heading stateside, he languished at Cavite Naval Base in the Philippines, surviving for weeks in a ramshackle tent under torrential rains. He did not see home or family for five more months. He arrived in Portland in January 1946 for a warm reunion with Audrey and Tad, now nearly two years old.

When the navy rejected his application to become an officer, the thirty-two-year-old McCall turned again to his ambition of entering politics. He decided the quickest way to gain a political foothold was by building his own name through broadcasting.

One of the city's biggest radio stations, KEX, offered him his own nightly talk show. Broadcasting again as Lawson McCall, he called his program "Around the Town." The fifteen-minute show aired weekday nights and featured a mix of news and gossip. Still the reporter, McCall worked the entire city each day to fill his show. He often beat the newspapers to big stories—such as the police chief's resignation and the new chief's hiring. With his wry humor and engaging accent, McCall also took up the causes not of the city's VIPs, but of its underdogs.

In segregated Portland of 1946, McCall actively promoted civil rights. He cheered the end of white-only jobs at the shipyards, boosted the Urban League's campaigns against racism, and scolded establishment organizations such as the Daughters of the American Revolution for excluding blacks from its functions. His concern for the disaffected knew no scale. He told the story of a crippled boy whose dog was stolen just as he faced a serious operation. He shared the tale of a single mother harassed by city inspectors as she tried to add rooms to her house.

Portlanders loved the novel show and fan mail piled up in McCall's office. As one woman listener described the show: "It's full of the things I wish my husband would tell me when he comes home every night— but doesn't."

In January 1947, as McCall built his name in Portland, he was stunned by news from Westernwold: his father had died.

After thirty-six years of struggle, Hal McCall had fulfilled the dream that brought him to Oregon. Through the booming war years, Hal had operated Westernwold with a profit. However, at age sixty, he was worn down. In the bitter cold of late January, Hal told Dorothy he had pains in his chest. He drove to Redmond, where his doctor told him he probably suffered only from indigestion. The next morning, he rose to milk the cows and the pain returned. He collapsed, paralyzed and unable to speak. Within hours, he was dead.

Hal McCall had wanted nothing more from life than to be a rancher. His independence meant for him rounded shoulders and roughened hands, while bearing the decades of failure and embattled pride. The independence had drained him, and his once-smooth face had long ago become as cragged as the rimrock. Yet Hal's fight to survive the lean years had created deep respect among others who lived in that hard country. His neighbors, along with the workers whom Hal often could not afford to pay, carried his casket to the grave.

Hal was independent, but he was never free. He could not even call the ranch truly his own. To save the ranch from creditors years earlier, he and Dorothy had transferred it into a trust. In the end, after four decades spent trying to survive, Hal McCall died with just $735 to his name.

AS TOM MCCALL BECAME MORE WELL KNOWN through his radio show, he devoted time to the causes he championed. He volunteered for the Urban League and Easter Seals. He cared most for the Oregon Prisons

Association, a watchdog group founded by Claire Argow, a local activist. The treatment of prisoners—especially juveniles—in city and county jails outraged Argow. McCall joined Argow's battles after interviewing her on his show; he soon became the group's president. He investigated abuses in local jails, wrote reports, and then publicized the problems on his radio show. The group's work led to a legislative investigation of the state penitentiary and the firing of the warden.

McCall pursued other activities for the connections they might offer. George Birnie, a University of Oregon classmate, served on the local symphony board, and McCall sought a way to join the board himself, admitting to Birnie he knew nothing about classical music. "He wanted to be on [the symphony] board so it might lead to something else," Birnie said. "That was the first time I'd seen him set out with a plan."

McCall devoted himself to one purely political group, the Young Republicans. Before the war, Portland's Young Republicans chapter had served chiefly as a starting place for young businessmen hoping to impress the city's corporate elite. Now, the Young Republicans chapter was filled with men more interested in reshaping the party itself. The men, typically more liberal than their predecessors, hoped to move the Oregon Republican party away from its support of racial segregation. "A lot of us didn't have strong ambitions of our own," says Robert Elliott, who was a Young Republicans organizer at the time. "We were interested in trying to make the party more progressive."

Within the Young Republican ranks, however, a handful of members made it clear they intended to enter politics themselves. "Tom always fit the category as one of the future candidates," said Elliott. Added another Young Republican, Clay Myers, "The thought of Granddaddy McCall, that's what drove him. He was always conscious of that legacy."

McCall wrote Young Republican policy papers and delivered speeches to Republican clubs throughout the state. "The group gave him the kind of exposure he needed then," Elliott said. "And he loved getting the exposure." In early 1949, McCall's connections to the Young Republicans made him prominent enough that Oregon's newly elected governor, Douglas McKay, considered him for the job of his top aide. Two of McCall's friends in the Young Republicans, Elliott and Sig Unander, had visited McKay and urged him to hire McCall. After hearing McCall speak at a luncheon, McKay was convinced. In June 1949, the governor offered McCall the job.

The new position meant sacrifice. McCall earned $7,200 a year as a broadcaster, but McKay could offer him only $6,000. McCall had no financial reserves and still carried seven-year-old debts from Idaho. But in the end, McCall could not resist. The state's highest ranking Republican was offering him the top job in his office, and the opportunities it would afford him were enormous.

That McCall aspired to political office himself was no secret, judging by the editorial applause to his appointment. The *Oregonian* said that McCall had "ability, aggressiveness and a consuming curiosity about the processes and possibilities of politics. . . . [I]t will not be surprising if the political seasoning which he will acquire on the governor's staff leads him to apply later for approval of the voters for public office." The *Oregon Statesman* in Salem foreshadowed McCall's future more succinctly: "Clearly McCall is a man for Oregonians to observe."

TOM MCCALL BECAME A REPUBLICAN by family tradition. But tradition or not, being a Republican in Oregon meant everything to an aspiring politician. The party had dominated state politics for decades. Democrats built the first political machine, but the GOP started to run the state soon after the Civil War.

Many of the Movers coming into Oregon had seen their opportunity not for land or business but for political patronage. "Western carpetbaggers, they have been called," wrote historian James Hendrickson, "who went out to take advantage of the unusual opportunities awaiting those who were able to exploit them."

Both parties exploited the state's growing political corruption. "Oregon," Lincoln Steffens wrote, "was in that stage of corruption where the methods were loose, crude and spontaneous." The legislative assembly elected the United States senators, and, as one lawmaker of the era recalled, "There was never a time that the [United States] Senatorship wasn't up for barter or sale." Votes of a single legislator went as high as $10,000. (Democrats could usually be bought for less.) In 1896, railroad giant Southern Pacific paid $225,000 to re-elect Republican senator Jonathan Hipple Mitchell. Mitchell's foes—among them, Henry W. Corbett, whose family ushered Hal McCall west—squashed the effort with their own bribery. Rather than buy votes, Mitchell's opponents, in 1897, paid legislators not to show up. Republican leaders spent the considerable sum of $80,000 to entice lawmakers with cash, prostitutes and liquor to shack up in Salem hotels. The legislature never had a quorum and never chose a senator because the house failed to convene. Predictably, the crooked process produced crooked senators. One was Mitchell, who was later convicted for taking bribes in a sweeping timber land fraud case that also saw an Oregon congressman and thirty-one other state and federal officials convicted.

Practiced openly, the corruption eroded public confidence in state government. After the 1897 "hold-up" legislature, wrote one journalist of the era, "Forty years of corruption in the legislature had reached its logical outcome in anarchy." Oregonians responded with the most populist reforms the nation had yet seen: the initiative and referendum, which gave voters a direct say in writing state laws. Under pressure from voters, lawmakers approved the initiative and referendum system in 1902, the direct primary in 1904, and the recall in 1910.

Oregon's progressive reforms did not shake Republican party control, however. Republican party registration at the start of the twentieth century outnumbered Democratic party membership by two to one. With rare exception, the GOP controlled the the office of governor and secretary of state, as well as the seats in the United States Congress and leadership of the state legislature. In turn, a clique of business leaders—known loosely as the Arlington Club, after the posh Portland club to which many of them belonged—controlled the party and operated the state in the best interests of business.

Meanwhile, the Democrats languished because they offered few appealing candidates. Those who were elected were controversial. For example, Walter Pierce, elected governor in 1922, had links to the local Klu Klux Klan, which was waging an anti-Catholic movement and which all but controlled the 1923 legislature. Charles H. "Iron Pants" Martin, a retired major general, was elected to Congress in 1930, and swept into the governorship four years later by a brief Democratic surge in Oregon that followed President Franklin Roosevelt's New Deal reforms. Martin detested the New Deal, however. Even with thousands of Oregonians suffering during the Depression, he blocked state participation in many federal job programs. Martin also soured the Democrats' image with his callousness. When he learned of the high cost of keeping hundreds of mentally handicapped children at a state institution, Martin suggested the children be put to sleep, like unwanted pets in an animal pound.

Most Oregon governors in the 1900s were like Doug McKay: Republican and conservative. James Douglas McKay was a patriot above all else. The son of a Portland carpenter, he was born in 1893 and worked to support his family after his father died. When World War I came, McKay went as an infantryman to Europe and nearly died during a battle in the Meuse-Argonne. His injuries left him disabled, but he considered his military service his greatest honor. A stubby man, McKay grew several inches as he straightened to attention whenever he saw an American flag.

In Salem, McKay founded one of the country's largest Chevrolet dealerships. He served as Salem mayor and later as a state senator. He also helped found one of the first powerful business lobbies, the Oregon Automotive Dealers Association, and turned the group into a formidable political machine. The association promoted highway construction projects, believing more roads would sell more cars. Later, McKay and his association organized political campaigns, and in 1942 helped elect fellow car dealer Earl Snell as governor.

Tragedy soon sent McKay in pursuit of the governorship himself. In October 1947, Snell, Secretary of State Robert Farrell, Jr., and Senate President Marshall Cornett were killed in a plane crash in southern Oregon, wiping out the line of succession to the governor's chair. The job fell to Oregon House Speaker John Hubert Hall. Hall proved a hapless governor, and McKay defeated him in the 1948 primary election and easily won the governorship.

Within his first months, however, McKay realized he needed help. He was a poor public speaker and lacked a chief of staff. He knew he needed a younger man to handle the work and protect his image. McKay found his man when he found Tom McCall.

BUOYED BY HIS PRESS NOTICES, McCall moved his family to Salem, to Winter Street near the State Capitol, and began work for McKay on 1 July 1949. By this time, his family was larger; two months earlier, Audrey had given birth to their second son, Samuel Walker McCall III. McCall had some regrets about transplanting his family to Salem and doing so on a smaller salary, but the possibilities of the job placing him at the heart of state politics quelled his concerns.

McCall's office was on the second floor of the Oregon State Capitol in the governor's suite. The Capitol building itself was only eleven years old, an edifice of Vermont marble, the interior in the Art Deco style popular in the mid-1930s. The building replaced a Corinthian-style Capitol destroyed by fire in 1935. The new statehouse, with its clean, classical lines, held aloft on its dome a twenty-three-foot, gold-leafed statue of a pioneer man, ax in hand, his head turned west. Inside, the rotunda, with its 106-foot ceiling, was flanked by broad staircases leading to the senate chambers on the left, and the house chambers on the right. One level up, straight ahead, there was a breezeway that opened to the offices of the governor. The office suite opened up into a ceremonial office, paneled in walnut.

McCall was given a small office in the suite's southwest corner, near McKay's private office. McKay proudly showed his new assistant around the building. The short governor and his tall, loping assistant struck the Capitol crowd as an odd pair. After seeing the two standing next to one another, a legislator asked McKay, "Did you hire him as an assistant or a bodyguard?"

McCall was at first leery of his new boss, who was far more conservative than he was. But McKay's style impressed him. "He was a tremendously feisty guy," McCall said of McKay. "He was the dynamic salesman type. He was honest and not afraid to take a position." Nor was McKay subtle. McCall one day heard shouts from McKay's office, where the governor was meeting with the leader of the Oregon Education Association. The group's leader had somehow offended the governor, and McCall watched as McKay grabbed the leader by belt and collar, led him to the door and flung him into the hallway. "I'll be damned," McKay shouted at the crumpled lobbyist, "if you'll impugn my honesty."

McCall was still trying to figure out his new role in the governor's office. His official title was executive secretary, but he was the governor's only assistant; as a result he did almost everything in the office. He served as liaison to the public, met and briefed lawmakers, reporters and bureaucrats, wrote thousands of constituent letters, and greeted groups on McKay's behalf. McCall quickly made himself more useful beyond his regular duties. Like a reporter working the beat, he prowled the Capitol for information. He soon became a valuable source of inside information for the governor.

McCall saw another duty in his job: moving his conservative boss to take more liberal positions on key issues. He found McKay's ideology rigid from the start. Even though he oversaw the governor's daily appointments, McCall could not stop the business lobbyists from sneaking in the back door and bending McKay's sympathetic ear.

McKay respected his aide enough to listen to McCall's appeals that he take more liberal stands, although he sometimes showed impatience. In at least one case, McCall wrote a speech for the governor that McKay found too cerebral. When McKay took to the podium, he held up the draft and said, "This is the speech Tom McCall wants me to give." He then delivered impromptu remarks. "He never really understood me," McCall said of McKay. "Everyday he must have given a sigh of relief that he'd survived this liberal."

McCall did succeed in pursuing some progressive issues with McKay. Civil rights was one. McCall saw few Oregon politicians willing to talk about civil rights in 1950. "[Politicians] had been very bland, with nominal appearances with the token Negro on the campaign trail when necessary," McCall remembered of the era. The Urban League and other organizations had been fighting for years to outlaw discriminatory real estate covenants that kept blacks and other minorities out of certain neighborhoods. McKay assured McCall that his administration would help ban such discrimination.

Not everyone in the administration got the message. McKay's real estate commissioner, Claude Murphy, assumed the opposite—that anyone in a Republican administration wanted to maintain segregation. When liberal legislators introduced a bill to outlaw a discriminatory housing covenant, Murphy slyly confided to McCall, "I think we've got

Oregon Governor Douglas
McKay (1949-52). McCall
served as McKay's top aide.
McKay later served as
President Eisenhower's
secretary of the interior.
(National Park Service photo;
OrHi 7633)

a way to get around these guys." McCall reared up. "I happen to be one
of those guys," he shot back. It was, McCall said, "a jarring awakening
for me: the realization that civil rights hypocrisy dwelt so close to the
governor's office."

McCall and other liberals—including a future rival, then-State Representative Mark Hatfield—helped move some anti-discrimination bills
through the legislature, including fair employment and public accom-
modations acts, measures most states then refused to consider.

McCall also learned more about a governor's power. For example,
lawmakers had refused to outlaw insurance companies' discriminatory
practices. At the time, the companies automatically made blacks pay
the premiums for high-risk drivers, regardless of their driving record. To
Robert Elliott, who was also working on the civil rights issue, McCall
suggested drafting another bill to remedy the problem. "You don't need
legislation," Elliott said. "Just tell McKay to order his insurance commissioner to fix it." McCall agreed and persuaded McKay to do exactly

that. "It was a revelation for Tom about the power he had," Elliott said. "Tom created something of a small civil rights act just like that."

McCall also invested his newfound influence into the first piece of environmental legislation he ever touched. Before 1951, Oregon had no air-quality standards. Several activist groups had been pushing the legislature to create standards for factories. McCall spent months working with two Oregon State College professors to craft a bill that created industrial emission rules and a watchdog commission to enforce them.

None of the rules had teeth to them, however. Years later, McCall acknowledged the bill was only a small step, but an important initiation. "It was really a preamble," McCall said of the bill, "a statement of policy that air quality and the health of the people and Oregon's climate would be maintained."

The enterprise taught McCall an important lesson: When faced with opposition to environmental proposals, take the idea to the public—or at least threaten to.

While it was under consideration in the legislature, the bill was pounded by industry lobbyists at its first hearing, and the committee promptly tabled the measure. McCall watched in disbelief as his months of work vanished with the drop of a gavel. However, groups fighting for the bill did not give up, including the Oregon State Grange, a liberal, grass-roots force in the state's politics. Politicians feared the grange for its ability to rally public support and quickly launch initiative drives. McCall gathered industry lobbyists in a room to negotiate the tabled bill, and the lobbyists would not budge. McCall then ushered in the grange's veteran lobbyist, Elmer McClure. "Boys," McClure drawled, "if you think this is a tough bill, wait till you see the one the grange is going to initiate and put on the ballot."

The sight of a conservative governor's aide standing united with the liberal, activist grange leader stunned the lobbyists, who reversed course. As McCall put it later, "The bill came off the table and we passed it."

McCall's concern for the environment, while strong, remained only one of many reformist issues on which he concentrated. His work as McKay's top aide gave him the chance to pay more attention to prison reform. The prison reform crusade taught McCall more lessons about the use of executive power and its ability to sway public opinion.

The Oregon prison system then came under authority of the Board of Control, a three-person panel made up of the governor, the secretary of state and the state treasurer. The Board of Control set policy for all Oregon institutions, from the mental hospitals to the home for retarded children. However, the Oregon State Penitentiary, with its 1,300 inmates, consumed most of the board's attention.

The board members knew McCall from his days as president of the Oregon Prisons Association. The group's work had led to the hiring of penitentiary warden, George Alexander, regarded as a prison reformer himself. Other members of the board, Secretary of State Earl T. Newbry and State Treasurer Walter J. Pearson, disliked the reform ideas because they appeared to make the state look soft on felons. McKay was at first uncomfortable with the ideas, too, but he trusted McCall and gave his aide freedom to pursue reforms. By August 1951, a few of the reform ideas were in place. New policies put tighter controls on the use of severe punishment of prisoners. Inmates also received more opportunity for education and job training and could form a governing council to take grievances to the warden.

McCall's efforts, however, were soon imperiled. On 14 August 1951, two prison guards decided to discipline a black prisoner for a minor rule infraction. One guard held the prisoner down while another beat him severely with a club. Outraged, the prison council demanded that Alexander fire the guards. Alexander refused and instead publicly defended the guards' actions. The prisoners' council then called for a work strike until the guards were disciplined. Prisoners also listed their grievances, which included such simple requests as the right to take regular showers. Refusing to concede, Alexander abolished the prisoners' council, locking all 1,300 inmates in their cells and denying food to any striking prisoner—an apparently popular move. "Warden Alexander is right," grumbled the *Capital Journal* in Salem. "Let the convicts work or starve."

The swift punitive action against the prisoners distressed McCall. But with the tough-looking warden playing well in the press, McKay and the other Board of Control members refused to step in. McCall thought the guards' actions reprehensible but could find no one in power willing to stand up against public sentiment.

After years of working around the penitentiary, McCall had dozens of prisoners who confided in him, and they told him tensions within the prison over the work strike and the beating could lead to riot. Summertime temperatures burned into the high nineties while the prisoners remained locked down in cramped, sweltering cells.

Meanwhile, some hungry prisoners were giving up the strike and returning to work. McCall knew that if the strike broke, the reforms would die as well. So after seven days of the strike, McCall went into the prison, alone, to settle the strike with an unofficial council of prison leaders. "They had eight murderers on this committee," McCall said of the group. "I walked right in by myself with no gun over me." McCall offered a deal: Give up the demands that the guards be disciplined and end the strike now. Prison leaders scoffed at the plan. What would they gain? McCall gave his word that McKay would reinstate the reforms and stop future beatings by guards. He also suggested that the guards involved in the beating might still face disciplinary action.

In making such a promise, McCall spoke for the entire Board of Control. It was a risky stance, for only McKay had any idea of what McCall was offering. It remains unclear if the other two Board of Control members knew McCall was even negotiating. Nevertheless, McCall pressed his offer, read it over the prison's public address system, and the prisoners agreed to the deal. As McCall described the scene years later, "A great, coarse shout of joy just rang out over this huge compound," McCall recalled, "and then it was over."

Despite his value in ending the prison crisis, McCall found his style had caused him trouble. The other Board of Control members were furious at the deal he had cut with the inmates. Even though McCall's deal simply restored conditions prior to the strike, the board members thought his work made them look weak. McKay took the heat for his aide, but McCall gave the governor reason to lose patience.

McCall, despite his loyalty to the governor, never forgot that his job promised him political exposure. He capitalized on this opportunity in large part because Douglas McKay hated to give speeches.

It was part of McCall's duties to sift through the scores of speaking requests that came in each month for McKay. The governor, who had a dull voice and physical stature that left him barely able to see over most lecterns, accepted very few. The only speeches he enjoyed were rousing, patriotic orations saved for Veterans Day or the Fourth of July. The routine luncheon and dinner talks remained undelivered.

McKay encouraged McCall to appear in his place, so McCall worked the circuit of Rotary Clubs and chambers of commerce. Before these groups, McCall honed his speaking skills and tested favorite turns of phrase. His reputation as a public speaker spread, and before long the invitations coming into the governor's office were not for McKay, but for McCall.

McKay at first did not mind the extra attention his aide was receiving, but that was before McCall went too far toward self-promotion. "Tom always had a strong sense of public relations," Robert Elliott said. "Tom used to write press releases that began, 'Governor Douglas McKay announced today. . . .' and Tom eventually changed that to 'T. Lawson McCall, executive secretary to Governor Douglas McKay, announced today. . . .'" The press corps, many of whom were McCall's friends, often paid more attention to McCall than McKay. One reason was that McCall was the one making news—often to McKay's dismay. McCall had slowly shifted the focus of his speeches from McKay's positions to his own. Soon, McCall's opinions were being written up as McKay administration policy. In one speech McCall denounced the Republican party for hosting a dinner in honor of Wisconsin senator Joseph McCarthy, who was then at the height of his anti-Communist crusade. In another case, McCall spoke openly for a sales tax. Oregon had never had a sales tax, and voters always opposed it. The speech set off a small storm as politicians wondered if McKay wanted a sales tax, too. McKay did not, and McCall found himself backpeddling.

McCall's boldest step came when he began pushing to have himself called lieutenant governor. The state did not have an office of lieutenant governor. McCall, however, thought his duties equalled such an office and started referring to himself under that title. One of McKay's closest advisers, Harry Dorman, who McKay named to run the state budget office, told McKay to fire McCall. "This is getting out of hand," Dorman confided to another state official. "We have to make sure McCall knows which one of them is governor."

Throughout McCall's tenure, McKay only spoke of McCall with the highest regard. However, both he and McCall realized that McCall's service had its limits. McCall's $6,000-a-year salary had been a financial stretch from the start, and he compounded his financial woes by spending a large amount of money each month to entertain politicians and lobbyists in his home. "We could hardly make ends meet," said Audrey McCall. "We were slowly going broke down there."

Most of all, McCall, at thirty-eight, had grown impatient to start his own political career. His two years with McKay had given him a first-hand look at the way state government worked. It had also given him the credentials he needed to enter politics on his own. McCall confidently told his friends in Salem that he would be back someday as an elected official.

Recognizing McCall's ambitions, reporters tried to prompt McCall into a declaration about his political plans as he left McKay's office for the last time. "If the call to public duty comes again in the future," McCall said coyly, "I suppose I would heed it."

5

On a String

MCCALL HAD NEVER BEEN SHY about his ambitions, but he had been without focus. "I never had what you might call desirous eyes fixed on any ambitious goal," McCall said later. "You ride to beat hell and then you look up and see where you are."

By 1953 he had looked up and found a goal. He had looked back into his family's history and been inspired to follow Samuel Walker Mc-Call's course: the United States House of Representatives, the governorship and—the height Sam McCall never could reach—the United States Senate.

There was a significant roadblock in Tom McCall's path to the first step, however. He lived in Oregon's Third Congressional District, which covered the city of Portland and the remainder of Multnomah County. And that congressional seat already had a Republican holding it—and holding it firmly.

That Republican was Homer Angell, seventy-nine years old and serving his ninth term in Congress. Every election year, Angell suggested he might retire, but every election year he ran for re-election and won handsomely. Bland and pompous, Angell proved a harmless politician, producing little as a congressman, yet providing little reason for his constituents to vote him out.

Certainly Angell was old, yet McCall knew it might be years before the congressman retired or died. Waiting was no longer in McCall's plans, however. He needed a reason to challenge Angell. Suddenly, the reason was slapped into his hands.

That reason was power—not political power, but the electricity generated on the Columbia River.

Surging rivers defined the Pacific Northwest, creating its boundaries and carving out the valleys in which the Native Americans and first white settlers lived. The Columbia was unmatched in its force, plowing 1,200 miles to the Pacific as it gained momentum from dozens of wild rivers. Engineers in the 1930s began to harness the Columbia's power, and the great dams that followed—such as Grand Coulee and Bonneville—corralled the river and sent it shooting through titanic turbines. The hydroelectricity made the region attractive to new industries that required plenty of power to operate. The power was cheap, too, because the costs of the dams had been borne by federal taxpayers, as part of Franklin Roosevelt's New Deal programs. The federal government kept control of the dams and brokered the electricity they produced to utilities. The system of federal control worked, and no politician from the West, regardless of party, seemed willing to change it.

No one, that is, until the Democrats lost the White House.

In 1952, Americans elected the first Republican president in sixteen years: Dwight Eisenhower, the five-star general and war hero. Eisenhower moved quickly to reverse any government policy he believed bad for free enterprise. The Northwest's dams, like the Tennessee Valley Authority projects, provided a example of New Deal enterprise—and Eisenhower did not like them. Eisenhower could do little about the federal dams already built. He could, however, change the outcome of dams still on the drawing board.

To do that, he needed someone as secretary of the interior who understood the West's politics, someone who, in military fashion, would carry out his orders. So he gave another military man the job: Oregon governor Douglas McKay.

McKay was a predictable choice for the Eisenhower cabinet; he had helped Eisenhower secure the Republican nomination during critical hours at the GOP's convention. But he was an unlikely choice to overturn federal policies on hydroelectric power—policies he generally supported. McKay arrived in Washington uncertain about how to handle the federal power issue. Eisenhower, though, wanted change, and McKay sought to carry out his duties. When he did, he triggered forces that helped alter Oregon politics forever.

The change centered around the United States Department of the Interior's plans to build a new dam in Hells Canyon across the turbulent Snake River. The river, running through a magnificent gorge, divided Oregon and Idaho at Oregon's northeastern corner. As sketched by engineers, the Hells Canyon Dam promised to be one of the toughest engineering feats ever pulled off by federal builders. At 742 feet high, the dam was to be the world's tallest, and it would sit at the bottom of an inaccessible, 6,000-foot-deep canyon. The Truman administration had already made it clear it wanted the dam to be a federal project, and the Department of the Interior, in 1948, had given its approval. However, the department had failed to finish the project, and the Hells Canyon Dam remained an engineering sketch when Eisenhower took office.

Alongside the federal plan in the Interior Department's files sat another proposal from the privately owned Idaho Power Co. Rather than building one giant dam, the utility proposed building a system of three smaller "pygmy dams." The smaller dams could recycle water as it rushed from one set of turbines to another. The proposal had gathered dust in the Interior Department's files, rejected outright because the utility had proposed private construction and ownership.

McKay did not consider Idaho Power's plan at first, either. As Oregon governor, McKay had supported federal development of the dams and saw no need to change the strategy. Eisenhower and his aides, however, saw that private industry wanted a piece of the hydroelectric business, and the administration determined that the investment would begin in Hells Canyon.

According to an account of the time, McKay at first decided to settle the issue objectively. He asked Interior Department officials to study both plans and recommend the best choice. Analysts picked the single, giant federal dam. As the story goes, McKay sat in his office not long afterward discussing the report with a friend. The phone rang and McKay took the call from Sherman Adams, Eisenhower's chief of staff. McKay listened intently to Adams and then hung up. "You can tear up that report," McKay said, referring to the Hells Canyon study recommending the federal project. "The White House has changed my mind."

Although Eisenhower's ideology drove him toward private control of

Hells Canyon, the site that inspired political divisions in Oregon during 1954. Surveyors examine the site where the federal government wanted to build a hydro-electric dam across the Snake River. (Bureau of Reclamation photo; OrHi 90681)

the Pacific Northwest's waterways, he did not understand the politics of the region. That is where McKay should have warned his president of the pitfalls.

The fight over control of the utilities in Oregon—a fight between private corporations and the public—had been the single most divisive issue in the state for the past four decades. Most often private utilities had won the battle. The companies were part of national utility trusts operated from Chicago or New York. The utilities understood early, however, that state government was the key to their survival. State government regulated rates, assessed utility property values, and controlled their taxes. Most of all, state government created the rules by which citizens could form public utility districts. These public utility districts took away the private corporations' control. The utilities spent millions influencing Oregon politics, both in the legislature and in public utility elections, to maintain private control.

By the 1930s, politicians in Oregon were divided not by party but by their position on power—public or private? On the public power side, grass-roots organizations such as the Oregon State Grange made the utility question its single campaign issue. As a result, populist sentiment often fell to the public power advocates. The only independent governor Oregonians ever elected, Julius Meier, jumped into the 1930 race to protest the pro-private power candidates nominated by both Republican and Democratic parties—and won on the strength of his stand. Within eight years, public power advocates were on the verge of forming their own party, the Oregon Commonwealth Federation. The federation's 1938 candidate for governor, Henry Hess, ran as a Democrat and defeated the incumbent, Governor Charles "Iron Pants" Martin, in the primary. Hess lost to a liberal Republican, Charles Sprague, in the fall, and the Oregon Commonwealth Federation never scored another win.

By the time McKay became secretary of the interior, the public-private power debate had cooled, but the issue had never died. So McKay made news when he marched into Portland in 1953 and, during a luncheon speech, abruptly announced Eisenhower's new policy: The days of federally operated dams were over and private industry was stepping in.

Tom McCall was in the audience that day, and he was as struck by the announcement from his former boss as was everyone else. Afterward, McCall left with Monroe Sweetland, a long-time Democratic party operative who had helped lead the public power Oregon Commonwealth Federation in the 1930s.

"Wasn't it refreshing to see a member of the cabinet throw away his script and tell you without a note what he really thinks about these great issues?" McCall said to Sweetland.

"It's great," Sweetland replied. "But you wait and see. He'll never survive."

McCall missed the significance of McKay's speech—not only for McKay, but for himself. McKay's announcement instantly reignited the old power debates. McKay had talked about one dam project, the one in Hells Canyon. The issue was not just this dam project, however, but the future of the entire Pacific Northwest hydroelectric system.

The old public power alliance rallied again for a new fight. Oregon senator Wayne Morse, who had just abandoned the Republican party and become an independent, had long been a public power advocate. Outraged, Morse denounced the Hells Canyon project as Republican larceny. "When you see a purse being snatched, do you calmly tell the culprit's admirers that he is a sterling fellow?" Morse bellowed in one speech. "No. You shout, 'Stop thief'!"

Hells Canyon emerged as the single biggest political issue in Oregon in 1954. Republicans lined up to back Eisenhower and McKay. Any Republican politician who opposed Eisenhower and Douglas McKay was a man the Oregon Republican party could do without.

That is where Tom McCall first missed the significance of Hells Canyon Dam. Homer Angell was just such a man.

Angell was a survivor. Born in 1875, the son of pioneers who arrived by covered wagon in Oregon during the 1850s, he grew up on a farm near The Dalles. When he was a child, Angell's right hand was blown off by flying buckshot when an old gun misfired. He stuck the bloody stump into a bag of flour and patiently waited for medical help to arrive.

Angell had survived in Oregon politics by following a simple rule: Tell voters what they want to hear. Trained as a lawyer at Columbia University, Angell became a skilled political hand in Oregon's state legislature. In 1938, Angell unseated the Third District's Democratic incumbent, Nan Wood Honeyman, a devout New Deal supporter. Angell, however, proved even more devoted to Roosevelt than Honeyman.

To survive in office, Angell conformed to his district's biggest political forces. The Third Congressional District was a labor union stronghold. Dockworkers and shipbuilders unions especially formed the district's Democratic party machine. Angell thrived by accommodating the unions in every way. He also cultivated a loyal following among the local Townsend Clubs.

The clubs were an outgrowth of the writings of Dr. Francis Everett Townsend, an Illinois physician who, in 1933, two years before Congress passed the Social Security Act, advocated a national pension system for senior citizens. There were more than one million members in an estimated seven thousand Townsend Clubs nationwide, many of which were centers of political activity. Typically, Republicans believed

Congressman Homer Angell. He ignored McCall's primary election challenge, and it cost him his Third Congressional District seat in the House of Representatives. (OrHi 12153)

Townsend was a socialist and vehemently opposed his plan. However, Angell supported the Townsend plan early on, and his constant attention to the members' concerns gave him a loyal following among the district's older voters.

Together, the unions and the Townsend Clubs forged a political girder that kept Angell standing. Angell, however, had one other support to his incumbency: he favored public power.

As a ranking member of the House Interior Committee, he chaired that panel's Subcommittee for Rivers and Harbors. In addition to giving him clout with the job-granting port and docks authorities, the position gave Angell the power to crush a dam project he did not want. And he made it clear in 1953 that a privately run Hells Canyon Dam was a dam Homer Angell did not want.

Until 1953, the Oregon Republican party and the Arlington Club had suffered Angell, for he had been a benign, ineffective congressman. His outright opposition to Hells Canyon Dam changed that, and early in

1953, Republican leaders began looking for a candidate to challenge Angell in the 1954 GOP primary.

The leaders, however, were operating outside the party itself. During his 1952 campaign, Eisenhower had set up a political machine, known as Citizens for Eisenhower, with chapters in major cities. The chapters carried out campaign operations outside—and sometimes in competition with—the Republican party. The Portland branch was especially strong; in fact, in 1952, the organization had delivered Multnomah County to Eisenhower despite its heavy Democratic registration, and Ike remained popular in the county as 1954 approached.

While no record exists of a White House order to defeat Angell, the Portland chapter of Citizens for Eisenhower made Angell a target. Its leaders included the city's most powerful businessmen: Ralph Cake, a top banking official and Oregon's most prominent Republican operator; Joseph W. Smith, a laundry company owner who maintained financial pipelines with the national Eisenhower network; and Gordon Orputt, station manager at KGW radio.

These three men sought a potential challenger to Angell. Orputt did not have to look far. He had a broadcaster at his radio station who talked incessantly about entering politics, a man who had obvious talents and boundless ambition. Cake and Smith agreed to meet the broadcaster, Tom McCall.

As McCall recounted the offer years later, "There was an Eisenhower wing of Republicans, including some businessmen at the Arlington Club, who thought it was time for Angell to step down. They thought I might be a suitable person to run against him."

Certainly McCall knew of the Arlington Club's dissatisfaction with Angell, and probably had promoted himself earlier to Orputt. Still, McCall made sense as a challenger. Young and handsome, McCall could be portrayed as a loyalist to McKay, his former boss. And he was well known. Since leaving McKay's office eighteen months earlier, he had worked to build his fame. He had returned to KGW radio and launched a new show, which aired for fifteen minutes each week night at 5:30 P.M., and which was devoted entirely to politics. McCall also parlayed his reputation as a public speaker onto the statewide banquet circuit. When the Portland Chamber of Commerce booked him for a speech in April

1953, it billed McCall as "a man who has watched Oregon legislation both from the inside and out and who has established himself as a widely recognized commentator on affairs of government." Loving the lime-light, McCall pursued any angle he could to stay in the public eye. He even appeared regularly on television as a guest on a local game show called "Treasure Hunt." McCall each week appeared on the game show's celebrity panel as a "news expert" alongside a gossip colum-nist, a disc jockey and a model.

By 1954, McCall was easily as well known as Homer Angell—prob-ably more so. Still, he would not have challenged another Republican without the support and encouragement from the local Citizens for Eisenhower leaders. Upon accepting their offer, McCall became in-debted to these men, for they offered him credibility, a political ma-chine and money. Smith personally signed for $5,000 in bank loans to create a McCall for Congress Committee.

After years of longing, McCall would finally run for office. He an-nounced his candidacy for Angell's congressional seat on 6 February 1954. He was forty years old.

Oregon Republican party leaders were disturbed by McCall's overly ambitious nature. They also questioned his ability to win the election. Mervin Shoemaker, the *Oregonian*'s long-time political reporter, echoed the Republicans' doubts about McCall in a February article: "Some influential Republicans . . . prefer Angell's demonstrated vote-getting ability in the fall election to the question of McCall's strength against a Democratic candidate."

McCall expected his radio celebrity to give him a hefty advantage in the election until he discovered a problem. He was running for Con-gress as Tom McCall, but for ten years he had been known on radio as Lawson McCall. McCall's campaign presented a greater political dilemma, however: How to strike clear differences between himself and Angell. Angell was a liberal. So was McCall. But he could not win a Re-publican primary by portraying himself as more liberal than Angell. This made his position difficult. For example, he strongly supported labor unions—he had even been president of the local of his union, the American Federation of Television and Radio Artists. As a candidate, however, to make a distinction between himself and Angell, he suggested that he might favor management over unions. And he often echoed Eisenhower's call for overturning many of Roosevelt's policies.

Most of all, though, McCall talked about Hells Canyon. Angell opposed a private dam and wanted to protect the federal control over the Columbia Basin river system. So did McCall. But he could not say he agreed with Angell without risking his campaign and the support of his Arlington Club sponsors.

As a result, on an issue with no compromise, McCall straddled the fence. He proposed that the federal government leave the final decision on private ownership in Hells Canyon up to the wisdom of the Federal Power Commission, a regulatory board overseeing such projects. On its face, McCall's position sounded judicious: Allow a federal panel to weigh the facts and rule on the evidence. It was nothing of the kind and he knew it—it was instead "a cop out," he admitted years later, "because the [Commission] was Republican."

At first, Hells Canyon Dam did not stand out as a decisive issue in the race. Instead, the race centered on style—the flamboyance and charm of Tom McCall, contrasted with the musty incumbency of Homer Angell. The *Oregonian* soon summed up the McCall-Angell contest as "Youth vs. Age." That summary suited McCall just fine and he worked hard to underscore his vitality. He attacked the tasks of campaigning as he had every other job in his life—relentlessly, working long hours and pushing himself to exhaustion. His experience giving speeches had honed his delivery and his message. He loved campaigning, and he had a touch for it. He dominated any room in which he stood by his sheer size and with the tenor of his voice. He was charming and affable and had a flair for impressing voters with his earnestness. Whenever a voter spoke or asked a question, this giant man leaned down, bending to the side and cocking his head, so he could listen intently.

From the start, the Portland press—as it would be for his entire career—was generous to McCall. Each night McCall would type out a press release about his latest speech or endorsement. His friends in the newspapers—especially at his former employer, the *Oregonian*—made certain the releases ran, often word for word. Both Portland newspapers endorsed his election.

So McCall headed into the spring of 1954 with a successful campaign operation. But McCall's campaign succeeded most of all for one reason: Homer Angell refused to fight back. When, in January 1954, Angell told his constituents, "I have decided to stand for re-election," he meant exactly that. He stood for re-election. He did not run.

Angell initially dismissed McCall as a nuisance. He portrayed himself as a congressman on the job who did not waste taxpayers' money by campaigning. As he had in previous elections, Angell campaigned through his congressional newsletter, produced and mailed with public funds. "I have always followed the practice," Angell said in one newsletter during an earlier re-election campaign, "of remaining here on the job and attending to my work here, feeling that I am paid for that and my first duty is to do what I am paid to do and let the chips fall where they will."

His overconfidence meant that Angell did not activate his own campaign machinery—the unions, the Townsend Clubs and the Republicans still loyal to him. His newsletters, however, reflected Eisenhower's popularity in his district; he seemed to forget his New Deal roots and hailed Republican proposals just as McCall started to campaign against him. Angell's endorsement of Eisenhower's policies had one exception: his strong opposition to a private Hells Canyon Dam—a view with which political surveys were finding most Multnomah County voters agreed.

As the primary neared, Angell heard from his friends back home that McCall was gaining ground. Fearing he had lost touch with voters, Angell—again using his franking privileges, the free postage available to congressmen—mailed a questionnaire asking voters how they felt on a range of issues.

This effort by Angell—the most humble of campaign gestures—backfired. McCall cleverly pounced on the questionnaire, telling reporters he "was surprised to learn that our congressman apparently is deluging the precinct . . . with campaign literature, some of which was mailed at the taxpayers' expense under his free franking privilege."

Then he took one of Angell's questionnaires, filled it out and provided his answers to the newspapers. Where, he demanded, were the congressman's answers to his own questionnaire? Back in Washington, Angell at first refused to respond. All the while, McCall worked the sidewalks of Portland. He gave speeches, appeared on radio, granted interviews, made phone calls, wrote letters. He did everything well and did everything right. Angell eventually sent his completed questionnaire to the Portland newspapers, and started attacking McCall in his congressional newsletters. By then, however, the attacks did not matter. A winner in the race had emerged.

ON PRIMARY ELECTION NIGHT, Friday, 21 May, McCall led and never looked back. He collected 40,026 votes to Angell's 26,142. By noon the next day, Angell had conceded defeat.

Despite McCall's successful campaign, few people had expected an upset. The Associated Press touted McCall's victory as one of the biggest congressional races of 1954, and the national press viewed the win as an off-year bellwether for Eisenhower.

To many observers, McCall was certain to become the Third District's next congressman. How could he lose? He had beaten the incumbent, the district had gone heavily for Eisenhower in 1952, and McCall had portrayed himself as a pure Eisenhower man.

To beat Angell, McCall had posed as more conservative than he truly was. Now was the time to move back to the middle and show voters the real Tom McCall: liberal, progressive, independent. However, McCall owed his fortunes to Eisenhower's Oregon machine. He had fallen into the debt of men who did not want him to be liberal or progressive—and certainly not independent. The men who had helped McCall fulfill his dream wanted what they had seen during the primary: a candidate who would follow the Republican party line at every turn. And that is what they got.

He had no choice. He had finished the primary with $288 in cash and the initial $5,000 loan still outstanding. To continue his campaign he needed ongoing GOP support. The National Republican Congressional Committee donated $2,000, and Joseph W. Smith and other businessmen upped their loans to $11,000. So although McCall admired Eisenhower personally, his enthusiasm about linking his campaign to the president's policies was driven by expediency.

Republican publicists designed a campaign theme, "Power, Payrolls and Prosperity for Portland," that tied McCall to Eisenhower's policies. In June 1954, he flew to Washington for a meeting with Eisenhower himself, and stood in line with a score of other Republican candidates to pose with the president for publicity photographs. McCall's campaign managers reprinted the photo on almost every brochure and flyer they produced. If anyone ever questioned where McCall stood, it was clear that he stood with Eisenhower.

McCall accepted his role. Victory was the point. Once he had that, he reasoned, he could again become his own man. He had, after all, managed to win the primary. Now, how could he lose?

THERE WERE THREE WAYS Tom McCall could lose. The first way was in assuming that the Republicans would hold their grip on Oregon politics. For half a century the Democratic party had been in shambles, disorganized and often corrupt. However, starting in 1948, two men, Monroe Sweetland and Howard Morgan, had brought the Democrats a new liberal agenda and the steely resolve to initiate it.

Sweetland was raised in Michigan on the doctrine of Wisconsin progressive Robert LaFollette. The soft-spoken Sweetland aligned himself with Socialist party movements in Oregon; later, he backed Roosevelt and the New Deal when top Oregon Democrats—including Governor Charles Martin—refused to do so. As a result, Sweetland landed a job in the Roosevelt administration and gained power through the federal patronage he controlled. He rewarded people who were also devoted to a liberal political agenda, which often excluded many top Democratic officials, and built a loyal following within the Democratic party.

With Morgan—a political streetfighter raised in Portland's tough Albina district—Sweetland engineered a party coup that broke the hold of the Democratic party's old guard. During the 1948 elections, Sweetland and Morgan stuck with beleaguered President Harry Truman against Republican Thomas Dewey even when many Democrats abandoned the president. Truman rewarded their loyalty with more power to make patronage decisions, which increased their influence in Oregon.

In 1950, however, the Democrats in Oregon were still losing elections. "We've got the best ideas," Richard Neuberger, a Democratic state senator from Portland told Sweetland repeatedly. "We've got all these things going for us, but we don't nominate people who themselves command respect from the voters."

McCall campaigned in 1954 as an Eisenhower Republican (above). (From the McCall Collection, OHS; OrHi 90802) In June 1954, after his defeat of Angell, McCall visited President Dwight D. Eisenhower at the White House (opposite). (Eisenhower Library; OrHi 90688)

So in 1952, the new Democrats pushed aside the old faces and instead chose untested—and untainted—candidates. "We knew in 1952 that we weren't going to win races," Sweetland said. "The idea was to introduce people who would be winners in future elections."

One of the new faces was Edith Starrett Green, a former home economics teacher. Green was precisely the kind of candidate the new Democrats wanted. Dimpled and charming, Green, at first glance, looked like a housewife who had naively wandered into politics. However, Green was a talented legislative lobbyist for the Oregon Education Association. She possessed a bullwhip tongue and a propensity for lashing it at anyone who crossed her. "She always had this façade as the perfect lady," said Jean Young, a Republican organizer who knew Green before she entered politics. "She was nothing of the sort."

Green stepped forward in 1952 to run for secretary of state against incumbent Republican Earl Newbry. She proved to be an engaging candidate but, as did most Democrats that year, she lost. Newbry won state-

wide by 68,322 votes out of 682,110 cast—about ten points. But the returns yielded hope: Green had defeated Newbry in Multnomah County
with nearly fifty-two percent of the vote, despite a strong GOP showing
that gave Eisenhower a three-to-two margin there.

Given those results, Green was an obvious choice to run against Angell in 1954. But now she would face McCall. "We thought Edith would
run well against Angell, with her being younger and more personable,"
said Sweetland. "We hadn't counted on Tom McCall. . . . He was personable, pleasant, sophisticated, and an extremely popular commentator.
He was very fast in debates. And in joint appearances he always looked
good. We didn't know how to cope with someone like Tom McCall."

But as Green watched the Republican primary, she saw that coping
with McCall would not be as difficult as she had first thought. "For Tom
to win," Sweetland said, "he had to prove to the Republicans that he
was safe. Tom had been a liberal and a progressive. A lot of his campaign was to work to show that he was not as liberal and progressive."

That was the second way McCall could lose the election, by ignoring Homer Angell's past supporters, the unions and the Townsend Clubs. Bound by demands of his Republican supporters and feeling secure in his nomination, McCall did not court Angell's labor supporters. But Green did. "There wasn't a union local that we didn't contact within forty-eight hours of the primary election," said Ken Rinke, who became Green's key campaign operative. "The unions were furious at McCall for grinding up Angell. They all made it clear that they were out to get McCall."

Nor did McCall seek out the Townsend Clubs. "It was the same thing here," Rinke recalled. "Within those same forty-eight hours we contacted every Townsend Club in the district. These contacts were not made just on the grounds that [Green] was in favor of the Townsend group, but on an anti-McCall basis, because he had defeated their darling."

McCall might have overcome the growing Democratic strength and the loss of Angell's supporters. But there was one more way that he could lose the election, and that was McCall himself.

He had built a reputation as a clear, progressive thinker and a persuasive speaker. He was, however, at his core, a Lawson, erratic and emotional. "I had seen Tom in social situations in which he did not take to criticism well," Rinke said. "I liked Tom . . . but he always had a thin skin."

Green—already a seasoned campaigner—decided to cut that skin and see how thin it really was. She started by adopting the slogan, "You get straight answers from Edith Green." The slogan was chosen carefully. "We planned to set out to show that you couldn't get straight answers from Tom McCall," Rinke said. "Of course, you could get straight answers from McCall. But it didn't look that way when we finished." Green started to run brief television commercials in which she appeared and declared, "I challenge my opponent to a debate anytime, any place." Rinke recalled: "The beauty of that was that voters thought McCall was ducking a debate with Edith Green. In fact we didn't want a debate. But, see, if you say it often enough, the public gets the impression Tom is the one refusing to debate."

Green left most of the stabbing into McCall's thin skin to surrogates. Launching an attack on him herself would have meant surrendering the

In a pose belying the eventual acrimonious campaign in the general election, Democrat Edith Green and Republican Tom McCall listen to primary election returns that won them their respective nominations in the 1954 congressional campaign. (OrHi 90699)

advantage her gender offered the campaign. In 1954, women rarely ran for office, and when they did, the press treated them with deference; Portland newspapers called Green the "Lady Candidate," and she found the title useful. She was not going to make herself appear less a lady with an open attack on McCall.

Howard Morgan began the attack on her behalf, charging McCall had concealed campaign contributions in his public disclosure reports. In a calculating message to the press, Morgan pointed out that McCall reported spending thousands of dollars more than he had taken in campaign contributions. How could that be? he asked.

The explanation was simple. The thousands of dollars in campaign loans McCall received were reported in a separate financial report. That made the books, on the surface, appear out of balance. The press fell for the ploy, however, and McCall spent the next few days trying to explain the accounting quirk. By then, however, the Green attack had moved on.

Morgan then told the press that McCall wanted to foist a sales tax on the working folks of Portland. McCall denied the charge, forgetting that, three years prior while speaking on behalf of Governor Douglas McKay, he had said he favored a sales tax. Rinke produced a newspaper clipping quoting McCall's speech, and McCall had to backtrack quickly.

Rinke and Morgan toured the district delivering speeches against McCall. They noted that McCall had been the chairman of the local Easter Seals chapter for the past two years and that his name still appeared on the chapter's fund-raising letters. Morgan charged McCall with exploiting the charity for his personal benefit. McCall—speechless that his work for charity could be used against him—had Easter Seals remove his name from the letters. In another attack, Green's operatives held up a newspaper photograph of McCall loading his car for a family vacation. "There was a picture of the boys and the dog, and I was putting golf clubs into an old Ford to go on a week's vacation," McCall said. "Jesus Christ, they tore me to ribbons. Because Eisenhower played golf. Talk about a cheap shot." Morgan even went so far as to attack McCall's name: Who was McCall really? Lawson or Tom?

Rinke came up with other gimmicks that were far more clever, for example, the Friday elevator rides at Meier & Frank. This major department store in downtown Portland held a weekly "Friday Surprise" sale that always brought shoppers flocking to the store. Each Friday, Green's campaign aides rode the department store elevator. When the elevator filled with shoppers, the campaign aides talked loudly about McCall's finances: how the guy never paid his bills, how he had welched on loans, how he could not be trusted. McCall indeed had money troubles, but nothing like the comments suggested. The two aides would continue their conversation to the top floor, until the last shopper filed out of the elevator. As the elevator descended and new people entered the car, the two would start the conversation over. "We may not have changed many votes with this idea," Rinke said, "but we certainly demoralized McCall."

Suddenly, McCall found himself surrounded by charges of all kinds. "It was just a bunch of passionate crap . . . just personal vitriolic attack," McCall said.

Green had dug into McCall's skin and found it was not deep at all. As she had hoped, her tactics drew out the raging Lawson emotions. Mc-

Oregon U.S. Senator Wayne Morse. (OrHi 90702)

Call wanted to strike back. But at whom? The attacks were coming from Rinke and Morgan. Striking back at them distracted him from his real opponent, Edith Green.

The operators behind McCall's campaign—particularly Joseph Smith, the Citizens for Eisenhower chairman—wanted McCall to strike back at Green directly. McCall refused. "Tom had been brought up in a family that respected women," Audrey McCall said. "It was very hard for him to campaign against a woman." He also knew beating up on the Lady Candidate would make him appear ruthless and crass. Still, he found his patience taxed whenever they shared a stage. "They shrewdly exploited our joint appearances—the little woman against the big man," McCall said. Often he was so agitated by her aides' attacks, "When Mrs. Green and I would finally get together, I'd be about ready to explode. Here was the big man being discourteous to the little woman."

Still unsullied by her aides' war against McCall, Green enlisted the meanest campaigner in Oregon: Senator Wayne Morse.

Morse, a Republican-turned-independent, had been ranting about

Douglas McKay's power policies at the Department of the Interior since McKay had proposed private control of the Hells Canyon Dam project. Now Morse blasted McCall's credibility on the dam issue, calling him nothing but "a spokesman for the influences that control the Republican party." In a circuit of powerful stump speeches, Morse attacked the public power "giveaway" and pointed to the two men many people thought were behind the scheme: Paul McKee, president and chairman of Pacific Power & Light, the area's largest private utility, and Secretary of the Interior McKay. In doing so, Morse used memorable alliteration, pounding away at the "giveaway team of McKee, McKay and McCall."

The "McKee, McKay and McCall" attack was withering in its potency, and left McCall stuttering for a response. "Morse was the hardest hater I've ever known," McCall said years later, as if still shaken by the memory.

To fight back, McCall realized he needed to distance himself from Douglas McKay and, ultimately, Eisenhower. He found he could not bring himself to do so. "I was shrouded by these affiliations through a sense of loyalty to the Republican party," McCall remembered. "I really wouldn't have minded the loss of Republicans if I had exercised some independence in enunciating positions that were contrary to party dogma. But I would have really minded hurting Secretary McKay. So, Morse recognized me as a good fellow and drove it home."

That was the issue that kept McCall silent: Douglas McKay had given him his break in politics, and loyalty ran deepest of all McCall's emotions. McCall found too late that he was not simply running for Congress, he was taking a Republican loyalty test. And the most difficult part of the test still lay ahead.

DESPITE THE TONE of Edith Green's campaign, McCall still believed his victory was inevitable. He worked even harder than he had in the primary, and spent a record amount of money for that era, $27,366, to fill the airwaves and newspapers with McCall ads. His confidence brimmed. As the election approached, he considered selling his Portland house in preparation for a move to Washington, D.C. He even told a few friends he considered them possible appointments to his congressional staff.

However, a poll published by the *Oregonian* on 24 October 1954, nine days before the election, rocked his confidence. The front-page poll showed McCall with only a three-percentage-point lead. Green had gained on him. If the trend held, Green could pass him before the election on 2 November.

Panicked, McCall's Arlington Club supporters decided that he had to strike back at Green. Joseph Smith arranged for television air time and commissioned a slashing speech he wanted McCall to deliver. The speech represented more than a campaign tactic, however; Smith wanted revenge for the Democrats' attacks on Eisenhower and McKay.

A few days after the *Oregonian* poll appeared, Smith invited McCall and Audrey up to his suite in the Congress Hotel. They arrived to find Smith surrounded by the businessmen and Republican operators who had financed McCall's campaign. Smith handed McCall the seven-page speech and ordered him to deliver it on television the next night.

McCall read the speech with shock. It was "the raunchiest speech I'd ever read," McCall said later. He jumped up and waved his long arms in anger at Smith and the others in the hotel room.

"I wouldn't touch one word of that shit!" McCall screamed. He went to an open window and tossed out the speech, its pages fluttering as it vanished from sight.

Smith grabbed his chest, as if he were having a heart attack. McCall, knowing Smith had a history of heart trouble, fell silent. "I'm going to ask you one thing," Smith said, gasping with great drama. "It may be my last request. Give that speech."

McCall sobered at the sight of his stricken campaign manager. "Go get it," McCall said sheepishly.

"Suddenly," McCall remembered years later, "Joe sprang to his feet perfectly well."

An aide retrieved the speech and Smith thrust it back into McCall's hands. McCall read the speech again and his revulsion grew. At home, Audrey read the speech as well and insisted he not deliver it. These were not his words, she said. These were the words of the private utilities and the Arlington Club. But as much as the speech disgusted him, McCall felt another emotion running even deeper: the craving to win.

Many years later, McCall said he had thought his campaign was lost even before he agreed to give the speech. But if that were true—if he

still had not held some hope of becoming Congressman McCall—he
would never have delivered it.

On the evening of 25 October, McCall went to the KPTV studios in
Portland to deliver the speech. A few minutes after 7 P.M., Portlanders
saw their regular programming interrupted as McCall's familiar voice
and face filled their television screens.

> Ladies and gentleman [McCall began] among the many
> things which have been kicked around by the extremist
> bosses of the opposition and their candidates in this political
> campaign is one which has taken an especially punishing
> treatment, and I refer to the priceless commodity known as
> truth.

His delivery was precise, his diction crisp. He showed no regrets, no
reservations. He punched at each word, as if this speech were the campaign message he had intended all along.

> The anti-Eisenhower extremist faction, which is running my
> opponent's campaign, has kicked the truth around, slammed
> the truth around, mauled it, twisted it, slugged it, beaten it,
> high-jacked it, black-jacked it, and slapped so much mud on
> it, in an effort to disguise it completely, that I'm sure they
> must now gleefully think the voters of Oregon will never
> recognize the truth under any circumstances!

Without hesitation, McCall did what he had not done for the entire
campaign. He turned on Green herself. He first raised the Hells Canyon
Dam issue, charging that Green's support of public power had made her
a pawn of "bureaucrats" and the "Eastern Big Bosses" of the unions.

> The Lady Candidate has called me a giveaway candidate!
> Or I should say the Eastern Big Bosses who are such clever
> ventriloquists have put the words into the lady's mouth.
> Friends, it's mighty hard to fight a puppet! If I could meet

the Big Boys from the east—the extremist gang which is pulling the strings and writing the words for their puppet to say—I would pull no punches on denouncing them, to their faces, for the band of cut-throat opportunists they are.

It is they who manipulate the policies of the Lady Candidate. . . . Does she think Oregon incapable of developing and managing its own resources? . . . The ventriloquist's puppet doesn't appear to think very much of Oregon, does she?

Then McCall gave vent to his own emotions as he seared Green. All the frustration at the indignities her henchmen had heaped on him boiled out.

I do not belittle the personal career or accomplishments of this very nice lady, but in fairness to myself, and in fairness to the voters who are to choose between us, I must point out that the Lady Candidate offers as her background for political office some years as a teacher of home economics, and a short time as a cooking authority on a local radio station.

No one appreciates the fine art of cooking any more than I do—I happen to be married to an excellent cook, I'm happy to say—but I cannot feel that being an expert in the home economics field qualifies anyone for politics!

I am sure the lady is an expert in the kitchen, but ladies and gentlemen, it takes more than a cookbook to cope with the destinies of the people of Oregon and this great nation.

McCall went on, attacking the labor unions and repeating his support of Eisenhower. But none of that mattered. The damage was already done.

FROM THE MOMENT the television lights blinked out that night, McCall regretted what he had done. "I did go to the gutter," McCall said of the speech. "It was the most shameful thing I ever did."

What McCall did not understand, however, was that the attacks

Green had launched against him were never intended to cost Tom Mc-Call votes. They were intended to ignite his temper. Just as Green hoped, McCall had lost his patience—and his dignity.

Since the start, Green had hidden behind the shield of her gender and allowed others to carry out her attacks. McCall's speech now allowed Green to step forward and portray herself as the victim.

On 28 October, three days after the speech and four days before the election, McCall and Green arrived for a joint appearance at the downtown YMCA. They had shared the stage at events a dozen times, but no joint appearance had been like the one McCall faced that night. He arrived to find Green had set up a record player next to her podium. When he asked why the record player was there, Ken Rinke cheerfully explained that the Lady Candidate had had an audio tape of McCall's speech made into a record and intended to play it for the audience.

McCall exploded. He pleaded with the debate's moderator, Judge Lowell Mundorff, to prohibit use of the recording. Mundorff, a Republican, sided with McCall, but before doing so, he recognized Green's ploy. "I'm going to rule in your favor, if you insist," Mundorff told McCall. "But in all fairness I should tell you, I think that if you do insist, you will regret it."

McCall did insist, and as the debate opened, Green announced she would not be giving an opening statement. Instead, Green—who had counted on McCall protesting the recording—pulled out a transcript of McCall's television speech. She read the most offensive passages, pausing with painful drama to glance over at McCall. When finished, Green put down the transcript. "You wouldn't believe that he said that, but he did," Green said with disgust. She then pointed to the silent record player. "I have it right there on a recording. But he won't let you hear it."

McCall had been set up. The audience of 250, stacked with Green's supporters, stomped and howled at him. Each time he tried to respond, hecklers drowned out his words. The debate was so lopsided Mundorff mercifully ended the affair thirty minutes early. If McCall had not already known how disastrous the night had been for him, he soon learned. As he stepped off the stage, a woman from the audience tried to club him with her purse.

The disaster at the YMCA, he recalled, "just did violence to my psyche." But Green was not finished. Until that night, McCall's friends in the newspapers had ignored the speech, but Green's tactics at the YMCA had made it impossible for reporters to ignore it any longer. Newspapers carried accounts of McCall's refusal to let Green play his speech; two days later Green issued a full transcript of the speech to reporters. She then bought television time and went on the air to read the offending passages.

The backfire of the speech deafened voters to anything else McCall had to say. Everywhere McCall went he heard about his speech. If voters had not heard or read parts of the speech, they knew of it or the controversy it had created. Wherever McCall went during the closing days of the campaign, he had to defend himself for attacking the Lady Candidate. McCall could do nothing but wait for the inevitable.

On election day, as returns came in, McCall emerged with a large lead, igniting cheers at his victory party. The *Oregonian* went to press that night declaring he held a two-point edge and ran a photograph of Tom and Audrey grinning and embracing.

McCall relished the moment, knowing that it could not last. The final votes counted that night came from the blue-collar northern precincts, the union vote crucial to Green. At midnight, McCall led Green 33,221 to 31,750—a margin of 1,471 votes. As the vote counting went through the night, about 133,000 more votes came in—and a considerable majority went to Green.

By dawn, as the morning paper declared McCall held the lead and showed him celebrating with his wife, the tally had turned against him.

IN THE END, Green's victory was clear but narrow. Out of the 198,344 votes cast, she had collected 103,976 to McCall's 94,368—a victory margin of five percent.

Her victory was only part of the larger story in 1954 for the Democrats. The action by Douglas McKay to reverse federal power policy gave the Democrats the single issue they had needed so long—the weapon they could turn against the Republicans. The GOP lost a United States Senate seat when Richard Neuberger defeated incumbent Guy Cordon; the congressional seat won by Green; and a record number of legislative races.

Election night, November 1954: Tom and Audrey McCall celebrate his early, and temporary, lead against Edith Green. (The *Oregonian*)

The Democratic flood that swept over McCall, though, did not completely explain his defeat. What had defeated Tom McCall was his own ambition and recklessness. Stroked by the Republican business interests, McCall had believed cautious adherence to GOP doctrine—and reliance on GOP money—was the route to victory. He had abandoned the basics he truly needed to win. McCall had forgotten that his strength came from his own progressive ideas, and his ambition had overwhelmed his common sense. In attacking Green, McCall had become little more than that which he had accused Green of being: a puppet on a string, controlled by hidden interests.

Losing in itself was not the tragedy. It was the way in which he lost. In his hungry pursuit of victory, he had forgotten the lessons of independence taught by Samuel Walker McCall's life. He did not truly learn those lessons until that night of defeat in November 1954. But the learning had come too late.

Sleepless and hung over, McCall concedes to Green the day after the election. (OrHi 37444)

WEDNESDAY MORNING, the day after the election, McCall agreed to meet Green in the *Oregonian* newsroom, where he would concede the race. McCall appeared disheveled and boozy; he had not slept at all. When his campaign party at the Congress Hotel had shut down, he and Audrey had retreated to a friend's house where he got drunk. Green, who had slept only an hour, arrived in the newsroom to find reporters consoling McCall. Towering over her, he greeted her warmly. The usual news-room clatter halted as reporters and editors looked on. Respectful of the moment, everyone in the room allowed McCall and Green to speak alone.

As they talked, McCall and Green paced the length of the newsroom, and overcome by emotion, he apologized for the speech. "I didn't want to give it," McCall said. "They made me do it."

As he apologized, McCall wept. Green graciously accepted McCall's apology, posed with him for photographers and, with an aide, walked out of the newsroom. Once out of earshot, Green stopped. She turned to her aide, her eyes narrowing.

"If there was anything that convinces me Tom McCall should not be in Congress," Green said, "it's his admission that other people can make him do something."

Back in the newsroom, McCall sat down at a desk and typed out a concession statement. He handed the statement to a reporter, gathered his coat and left.

Outside, cars scurried along sw Broadway and passers-by filled the sidewalk. He watched the people, their lives unchanged by the election that had crumbled his dreams. The November sky was gray and threatened rain. McCall hunched his shoulders and began walking, a weary and defeated man with nowhere in particular to go.

PART TWO

6

Redemption

UNTIL NOVEMBER 1954, Tom McCall's life had been a grand crescendo. He had escaped his mother's grip, outrun a besotted legacy in Idaho, served in state government at its highest level, and thrived as a journalist and a broadcaster. In politics he had hoped to move swiftly, as if his long stride could take him to the United States Congress in a single step. When he stumbled, he might have appeared noble, even in defeat. But not after the campaign he had run. All that he had gained—his credibility, his financial strength, his good name—was gone.

So in 1955, at the age of forty-one, Tom McCall began again.

He began submerged in debt. His savings were wiped out and he was personally liable for $2,500 in unpaid campaign loans—an amount equal roughly to half a year's take-home pay. But now he had no job. With his hangdog face, McCall went to every radio station in Portland, asking for a chance to return to the air. No one wanted him without a sponsor, and no sponsor wanted to associate his name with McCall's. Always a hearty drinker, McCall began drinking even more, and his ambition vanished.

For the next few months, McCall scraped by. Sympathetic Republicans provided him with piecemeal press release work. For awhile, McCall put out a syndicated column called "The Second Look." Even though filled with McCall's snappy writing, the column dwelt almost entirely on Republican gossip, as if Republicans were the only sources available to him. As a result, the column was a dud financially, at its peak appearing in only three small newspapers around Oregon.

Things improved a bit for McCall when two former *Oregonian* reporters, Ed Snyder and Hollis Goodrich, made McCall a partner in the public relations and advertising firm they had started. It was the only time McCall went into business for himself. He decorated his office as if it were the congressional one in Washington, D.C. he had failed to win. With its wallpaper and curtains emblazoned with flags and eagles, "It was as presidential as you can get," Goodrich said. "You could almost hear the drapes singing 'The Star-Spangled Banner'."

McCall was lousy at the public relations game, however. He wrote press releases for the bricklayers' union and a truckers' group—"just hacking and whacking the stuff out," he said of his work. "I didn't even have enough to starve on properly." Recalled Snyder, "His heart was not in it. He wanted to be elsewhere."

After six months, McCall's prospects brightened. Gordon Orputt, his former boss at KGW and one of the chief financial backers of McCall's congressional campaign, smoothed over the concerns of the station's advertisers, and he hired McCall in June 1955 as a commentator. McCall was excited about the work, though it was only part time. However, he soon turned to a new medium—television.

Portland was the last major city in the United States to get a television station. The first station, KPTV, went on the air in 1952. In the summer of 1955, the station expanded its news operation with what was then a radical notion: a fifteen-minute newscast, with sports and weather, and camera crews to film stories around the city. The news director, Ivan Smith, hired McCall as a reporter and news analyst. Most other television announcers at the time first had been disc jockeys or radio announcers. "Many of us came from different careers, but almost no one had been a reporter," said Smith. "McCall had journalistic ink in his blood." Rather than simply reacting to news events, McCall again prowled the city for stories and gossip he could turn into news reports.

Viewers liked his on-air style. Unlike the bookish, bland announcers of the time, McCall on TV had a special charm, with his tall face sloping out to the end of his jutting jaw, his large ears flaring like wings. His mouth, with its unusual curve, wended across his face like a river, rising gently on the left, sweeping down and climbing again on the right.

His unique voice was as intriguing as ever. But viewers at first had trouble with his strange eastern accent. "People were turned off initially because of his accent," said Dick Althoff, a KPTV cameraman. "The station got a lot of complaints about this guy who people thought was faking the accent. In time they accepted it and it became his trademark."

Just as radio had lifted his profile in Portland, McCall believed television could repair and restore his image. But the switch to television was not without its own ordeals. The nervous attacks that had rattled him during his early radio days returned as he went before the cameras. He had to dictate his commentaries before going on the air because he was too nervous to sit and type them out.

He was also easily confused by the bustle and confusion of the studio. One night, as McCall read a particularly long commentary, he mistook a director's signal and started reading the cue cards meant for the commercial announcer. McCall stopped his commentary in mid-sentence, read six lines extolling the sponsor's chocolates, and returned to his script without noticing what he had done.

The television job provided McCall a steady income and the exposure he always enjoyed. But he longed to return to politics. In March 1956, McCall traveled to Salem with cameraman Althoff to cover deadline day for candidates filing for state office. McCall was edgy and anxious all day as he watched the tote board fill with names of candidates. Altoff thought McCall might run up at any moment and add his name to the list. "The urge would come, and he fought it," Althoff said. "You saw it in his eyes." When the 5 P.M. deadline came, McCall finally relaxed.

Later that evening in Portland, McCall saw his former business partner, Ed Snyder.

"I only wish I'd had twenty-five dollars with me today," McCall told Snyder.

"What would you have done with that?" Snyder asked.

"Why, I would have filed as a candidate," McCall replied. "That's what it costs to file."

"But for which office?" Snyder asked.

"Hell," McCall replied, "any of them."

McCall stayed on at KPTV through the 1956 election season and became a hit with viewers. But in December 1956, his boss, Ivan Smith, abruptly quit when KPTV management ordered him to deliver the newscast with a jug of a new sponsor's anti-freeze product at his elbow. When Smith refused and walked out, the station manager turned to McCall. "You're going on in place of Smith," the manager told him. McCall instead reached for his hat and coat. "I'm no Quisling!" he shouted, and followed Smith out the door.

Along with Smith, McCall went back to KGW. Its owners had won approval for a new television station. For the next seven years, McCall would be a fixture on KGW-TV's news team. His work for the station not only established his celebrity in Oregon, it propelled him into the governorship.

The station's parent company, Crown Stations of Seattle, appealed to McCall. Crown's owner, Dorothy Stimson Bullitt, an heiress to a Seattle real-estate fortune, had built her radio and TV stations into the Pacific Northwest's biggest broadcasting company. Bullitt insisted her stations put concern for profits behind local coverage, and she dedicated the news departments to a tradition of in-depth public affairs reporting.

To launch the Portland station, Bullitt sent Tom Dargan. A former Marine and a producer at KING-TV in Seattle, Dargan had realized early on television's power to inspire social change. "Television was like a pulpit to Tom Dargan," said Althoff, who also left KPTV to join KGW's new station. "He was years ahead of everybody else in how television should operate and what news should be." McCall called Dargan a "very imaginative fellow—a crusading kind of fellow."

Dargan and McCall were a perfect match. McCall wanted to be controversial, and Dargan encouraged him. "Dargan gave McCall a long leash," recalled Ken Yandle, a KGW-TV producer. "Longer than he gave anyone else." At Dargan's direction, McCall and others on the KGW-TV news team injected aggressiveness and enterprise into the Portland television market.

In its first year on the air, KGW-TV proved itself with its coverage of one of the major news stories of 1957. The *Oregonian* had uncovered an organized crime network behind the Teamsters local. In the fallout, a grand jury indicted the former county sheriff, Terry Shrunk, for bribery soon after Schrunk became Portland's mayor.

Unlike other stations, KGW-TV kept pace with the newspapers. Dargan sent camera crews to Schrunk's trial. KGW-TV cameras in the courthouse captured the scene—through the courtroom windows—as the verdict of not guilty was read. They also filmed Schrunk's testimony before the mob-busting Senate committee, chaired by Senator John L. McClellan of Arkansas and staffed by a young Robert F. Kennedy, that later went after Teamster boss Jimmy Hoffa.

These were heady times for a news television station, and McCall thrived. Aside from working his government and politics beat, he produced nightly commentaries and news analysis. He also launched "Viewpoint," a weekly discussion show format he pioneered in the region.

With "Viewpoint" McCall covered diverse subjects. He hosted candidate debates; devoted time to civil rights issues, in particular the race riots in Little Rock, Arkansas; and even invited experts to discuss the appropriate bedtime for children. McCall consciously chose guests he knew would clash openly. But he remained the centerpiece. "He punched up the show," said Yandle. "If you had to tread on somebody's toes, he could do it."

McCall quickly became KGW-TV's star. Despite his growing fame, however, McCall never lost the sense that he was there to serve the average Portlander. "People would call him from all over to talk about their problems, whether it was a lost dog or a problem with their insurance company," said Richard Ross, KGW-TV's anchorman. "He would start answering questions and complaints and sad tales of woe from any and everybody who called him."

While his colleagues admired his work and his spirit, they wondered how he ever succeeded, given his chronic disorganization. Out on a story, McCall took exhaustive notes until he filled his reporter's notebooks. With nothing else to write on, McCall scribbled on cigarette wrappers, envelopes or any other paper scrap he mined from his busy pockets. He once scrawled his notes on an envelope only to discover later he had accidentally mailed his story. Back at KGW-TV's newsroom, McCall would dump his tattered notes onto his desk, already lost under

McCall's name recognition came through his radio and television presence. He sharpened his image with his show "Viewpoint," a program that focused on political issues. In January 1961, McCall (center) leads a discussion among (left to right) Representative Robert Duncan of Medford, State Senator Harry Boivin of Klamath Falls (both Democrats), and their Republican counterparts, State Representative F. F. "Monte" Montgomery of Eugene, and State Senator Anthony Yturri of Ontario. (*Oregonian* photo; OrHi 12491)

a tide of paper that became a KGW-TV legend. A co-worker once measured the paper heaps and found them nearly a foot deep.

Amid this chaos McCall pecked out his commentary on a typewriter, cursing with farmhand's language each time his large fingers punched the wrong key. As the 6:30 P.M. air time approached, McCall rushed up a flight of stairs to the news set. KGW-TV's studios were located in a converted German Society health club on SW Thirteenth Avenue. The news set was in a former gymnasium on the fourth floor. When the heavy cameras moved during a broadcast, viewers could hear the studio's rickety wooden floor squeak. After appearing on the set for the show's opening spot, McCall would dash back downstairs, frantically finish his script, and hurry upstairs again in time for his cue. Once, McCall had written so much of his commentary along the margins that he had to rotate his script to follow along.

He read into the camera, hunched slightly to make up for his height, the skill and confidence of years as a broadcaster shining through. After each broadcast, McCall's mood wavered. If he had performed flawlessly, he gushed. If his performance had been rocky, he skulked away. If a technical problem had marred his segment, he could be ferocious. After one broadcast, when one of his film stories had accidentally run without its soundtrack, McCall roared and punched his foot through the control room wall.

Dargan understood McCall's emotional nature and learned how to harness it. He encouraged his analyst to tackle the larger issues facing Oregon—and that is how McCall learned of television's power. He used that power to make his first statement about how protecting Oregon's environment protected the state's economy.

The issue he tackled involved the Klamath Indians of southern Oregon. McCall had studied the Klamath while earning extra money in 1957 as the lone staff member for the legislature's Interim Committee on Indian Affairs. (Today, newsroom ethics discourage reporters from working for committees they also cover. However, the rules were looser then, and Dargan, knowing the debt-laden McCall needed the extra income, looked the other way.) McCall's job was to write a lengthy report on the conditions of Native Americans in Oregon, including the quality of their jobs, health care and education.

McCall discovered that in southern Oregon, the Klamath Indian tribe held control over the largest Native American reservation in the state, covering 1,107,846 acres and including some of Oregon's most valuable timberland. The giant forest itself enveloped precious wetlands that served millions of migrating birds and a delicate watershed that furnished much of southern Oregon and northern California with its water supply.

The virgin Ponderosa pine forest had been carefully managed by the Klamath tribe under the practice of "sustained yield," which limited timber harvests based on how quickly the trees would grow back. In 1957, most of the forest remained in old-growth stands. It was threatened, however, by a new federal law, passed by Congress in 1954, that allowed any member of a certified tribe to demand his share of the tribal assets.

The law presented the tribe with huge economic problems. Many Klamaths wanted cash payments for the value of the tribal lands. Yet if too many wanted to cash out, the tribe would face bankruptcy. As with any collapsed business, the tribe would have to sell off its holdings, including its forests. The trees probably would go to private timber companies. In fact, many tribal members were being urged to demand their payments by timber interests who anticipated buying up the forest. In effect, McCall noted later, "'Boom or bust' land speculators and lumber interests plotted to control the Klamath basin."

McCall saw that liquidation of the Klamath's assets—and the forest—promised calamity for the region. In 1957 the Klamaths had valued their timber holdings at $100 million. That meant a private buyer would have no choice but to clearcut virtually all the forest to cover the purchase price. In a matter of years, the entire Klamath forest could be wiped out. That would spell ruin for the region's economy. The timber market would be flooded with pine, depressing prices and wasting a long-term source of jobs. More than that, however, McCall foresaw the obliteration of the Klamath wilderness and what he called its "priceless scenic values."

McCall was not the only conservationist alarmed by the prospect of the Klamath forest being clearcut. His greatest ally was Senator Richard Neuberger of Oregon.

If Tom McCall had a role model in Oregon politics, Neuberger was that person. If not for his untimely death in 1960, Neuberger probably would have commanded the state's political stage for the next generation, perhaps overshadowing McCall. Like McCall, Neuberger had risen into politics out of journalism. A year older than McCall, Neuberger, already had seen great political success. He had been born in Portland in 1912 to a well-to-do family. Neuberger had a flair for language, and also aspired to become a sports writer. The *Oregonian* hired him while he was still in college, and he entered the University of Oregon for its journalism school in 1931, the very same year McCall arrived at the University of Oregon from Prineville.

There the parallels end. While McCall partied amid fraternity life, Neuberger spent his days as a campus activist. Out of college, Neuberger established himself as a nationally recognized writer. By the age of twenty-six, he had published three books and was a regular contributor to *Life* magazine. He later entered Democratic party politics and won election to the Oregon Senate in 1948. His wife, Maurine, won a seat in the Oregon House two years later. In 1954, Neuberger won election to the Senate and led the Democratic party sweep that ended the Republicans' historic hold on Oregon politics.

McCall and Neuberger shared basic values: a desire to protect Oregon, and a determination to lift up the underdog. These concerns drew them both to the Klamaths' plight. Neuberger had opposed giving the Klamath the power to dissolve their tribal control of the forest, fearing the action would trigger a land grab. A year before McCall wrote his report on Oregon's tribes, Neuberger had introduced a bill that called for a federal buy-out of the forest, which would ease the economic pressure on the tribe to clearcut its timber. "The federal government was the only one who could afford to take it and save it, and cut it according to sustained yield," McCall said later.

Neuberger's plan, with its $120 million cost, ran into opposition from private timber companies, salivating over the prospect of controlling the Klamath land. In addition, the senator's efforts, while publicized in Oregon, had failed to ignite any real emotion in the state. McCall convinced Dargan that the story needed the force only a documentary could provide. Using his research from the committee, he pieced together a sixty-minute film, "Crisis in the Klamath Basin," that reflected McCall's evolving conservationist ideology: the need for a clear balance of environment with jobs, with government— not the free market—in control of natural resources.

In 1958, a long news documentary was an unusual enterprise for a local station. What made this documentary even more unusual was McCall's presentation. As a news commentator, McCall offered insight into and analysis of the day's news. However, with the documentary McCall became an advocate. He crafted the film so that it first explained

U.S. Senator Richard Neu-
berger. In Oregon politics,
Neuberger was a pioneer
conservationist. His untimely
death in 1960 created a
political vacuum that fellow
journalist Tom McCall filled.
(OrHi 54008)

the problem, then marched to an inevitable, convincing conclusion: Keep the Klamath forest out of private hands and let the federal government protect it.

"Crisis in the Klamath Basin" won McCall the first of many environmental awards—the Golden Beaver from the Isaac Walton League of Oregon—but the show had greater rewards. The documentary aired just as Neuberger's fight with the Eisenhower administration began over the federal purchase of the land. Neuberger played McCall's documentary for congressional staff; McCall thought the film helped win support for Neuberger's buy-out plan. By September 1958, Neuberger had pushed the timber purchase through Congress and President Eisenhower had signed the bill.

McCall marvelled at Neuberger's accomplishment. "The age of Sputnik had just dawned and public opinion and Congress were bent on catching up with the Soviets," McCall said. "It was into education that we were putting all of our dollars. And here was a tribe of Indians, way out in southern Oregon, that Neuberger managed to get $120 million for."

The experience taught McCall the power of a dedicated, focused leader such as Neuberger. Over the years, McCall envied other politicians whose mercurial ascents might threaten his own success, but he never expressed envy for Neuberger. He was shaken when Neuberger died of cancer in 1960. In praise he never granted any other Oregon politician, McCall said of Neuberger, "Oregon will never have a better senator."

LATE IN 1957, a newspaper reporter asked McCall if he had considered quitting television to run for office again. "I'm in politics up to my neck," McCall replied, "as anyone is who comments on the news or explores controversial subjects before the public."

As his friends and KGW-TV colleagues knew, McCall's ambition still burned. In 1958, Marko Haggard, a political science professor at Portland State College and a regular guest on "Viewpoint," was traveling the state campaigning for the re-election of Democratic governor Robert Holmes. Everywhere Haggard went, people asked about Tom McCall. "What's he like?" they would ask. "Don't you think he would make a good candidate?" Or, frequently, "Why doesn't he run for governor?"

When he returned to Portland, Haggard told McCall, "I'm convinced that you could get elected governor yourself, with all the popularity you have out there." Haggard thought McCall might be flattered or surprised. But McCall just leaned his head back and gave Haggard a knowing smile. "I thought I was telling him something that he didn't know," Haggard recalled. "This was something that he knew well and was clearly on his mind."

In 1958, however, the governorship was snatched away from Holmes by another bright Republican star: Mark O. Hatfield. Young and handsome, bright and progressive, Hatfield had a potential matched only by his ambition to rise from one office to the next. In the years that followed, no other Oregon politician gained power as fast or kept it as long.

In time, McCall and Hatfield would ascend in Oregon politics and become the state's two most prominent leaders. They might have been the closest of friends, for they were both outspoken liberals willing to chal-

Mark O. Hatfield (here pictured about 1958) preceded McCall as Oregon's governor. He later won election as U.S. senator. (OrHi 83427)

lenge their own party's doctrine. Instead, their relationship was steeped in jealousy, one always envious of the other's success.

Hatfield saw success first. He grew up in rural Marion County, in the Willamette Valley town of Dallas. His father was a railroad blacksmith, but it was his mother—a pious Baptist—who spurred him into politics; at age ten, he displayed "Hoover for President" banners on his toy wagon. After his graduation from Willamette University in Salem—located across the street from the State Capitol—Hatfield went on to Stanford University, where he literally diagramed the course of his political career: state legislature, governor, United States Senate—then he left a blank.

While teaching political science at Willamette University, Hatfield in 1948 won an eleven-way Republican primary race for the Oregon House. Four years later, he ran for and won a seat in the Oregon Senate. His legislative career was distinguished only by his ambition. To other legislators he was aloof. He avoided the social scene around the legislature and instead used his off hours to travel the state, delivering speeches to civic groups and quietly building a following. In 1956, Hatfield won election as secretary of state and promptly plotted a run for governor.

The incumbent, Governor Robert Holmes, was a radio station manager and former state senator from coastal Clatsop County. Holmes lacked Hatfield's vigor, and he had made a few damaging decisions. His opposition to the death penalty allowed one convict on death row to get a reprieve. Hatfield, also a foe of the death penalty, nonetheless exploited the capital punishment issue skillfully against Holmes. Hatfield's cleverness as a campaigner alarmed Democratic leaders who cast about for a way to tear him down. The result was one of the more scurrilous attacks in recent Oregon history.

The attack was leveled by Senator Wayne Morse, who had since joined the Democratic Party. Morse had dug into old laws books and unearthed an eighteen-year-old lawsuit involving Hatfield. In 1940, when Hatfield was in high school, he had struck and killed a seven-year-old girl with his car while driving on a country road south of Salem. Hatfield faced no criminal charges, but the girl's parents won a civil case against his parents. The tragedy had never been aired publicly. But late in the campaign, Morse used speeches in the southern Oregon towns of Klamath Falls and Medford to detail the tragic case. Morse pointed to what he said were major discrepancies between the young Hatfield's sworn testimony and the evidence. Hatfield, he charged, had testified that the girl had suddenly stepped into the road from behind a clump of roadside grass. Morse then waved the testimony of other witnesses who said the girl had stood in plain view before Hatfield's car struck her. Hatfield, he said, could not be trusted. Once a liar, Morse alleged, always a liar.

Morse's charges were splattered across the state's newspapers, yet voters were sympathetic toward Hatfield. Aware that the incident might someday come to light, Hatfield pulled from his files a prepared statement: "Those who conspire to profit thereby have my compassion." Holmes—who denied being behind Morse's attacks—was drowned in the tide of spite the senator had unleashed, and Hatfield won the governor's seat with fifty-five percent of the vote.

As a reporter covering the race, Tom McCall admired Hatfield's stamina in withstanding Morse's attacks—stamina he had lacked in his congressional campaign. But he envied Hatfield's success. The two had met in the late 1940s at Young Republicans meetings. When McCall worked for McKay, Hatfield, then a legislative freshman, often had dinner at the McCalls' home.

Their differences ensured that they never grew close. McCall could be convivial, boisterous, cheery and boozy; Hatfield could be aloof, chilly, sober and brooding. Where McCall was impetuous, Hatfield was calculating. Hatfield prided himself for his reasoned, academic approach to politics. McCall acted from his gut and his heart. "They were as different as you'd expect a born-again teetotaler and a party boy to be," said James Welch, an editor of the *Capital Journal* who knew both men well. "Mark considered Tom a noisy clown, and Tom thought Mark was a candy-ass."

The bitterness began in 1958, when Governor-elect Hatfield acted as if he wanted to offer McCall a plum job: Hatfield's position as secretary of state, which he would soon be vacating. After his election victory, Hatfield invited McCall to Salem to talk about the job. McCall eagerly accepted the invitation, and for good reason. The duties of secretary of state were often ceremonial, but the office had a high profile. The secretary of state had a seat on the state Board of Control, which oversaw state institutions, including the state penitentiary, one of McCall's key interests. Most of all, the office had a reputation as a reliable jumping off spot for the governorship, a job that offered political prominence with little risk.

During their meeting, which lasted most of an afternoon, Hatfield made it clear that he was considering McCall for the post—at least that was the way it sounded to McCall. McCall said later that he emerged from the meeting convinced Hatfield would give him the post. Hatfield, in recollecting the meeting, however, was vague about what he might have said to McCall.

In any event, there was no job offer. Travis Cross, a Hatfield aide and McCall friend, recalled that Hatfield thought the meeting was a courtesy, nothing more. "Hatfield never seriously considered McCall for the job," Cross said. In fact, McCall's personality made him precisely the kind of person Hatfield did not want in the job. "Hatfield considered McCall unreliable," Cross said. "Part of it was the drinking. And part of it was Hatfield wanted to have a secretary of state who wouldn't cross him as Tom might."

Indeed, McCall was independent to his core, and Hatfield did not want to endure what he would consider disloyalty. But he never told McCall that. Instead, Hatfield remained silent.

Rather than take Hatfield's silence as rejection, McCall allowed his hopes to soar. Soon, hope overcame common sense, and McCall convinced himself that Hatfield could not possibly appoint anyone else. McCall began telling friends and his family he had the job. At KGW-TV, McCall even told Dargan that he planned to resign as soon as Hatfield offered him the position.

On the day of Hatfield's inauguration, McCall traveled to Salem wearing his finest suit. Ostensibly there as a reporter, McCall expected Hatfield to call a press conference and invite him up to the podium to accept the appointment. McCall was still running his acceptance speech through his head when Hatfield announced that he was naming someone else to the post: Howell Appling. A complete unknown, the Texas-born Appling ran a farm equipment store in Portland and had volunteered for Hatfield's campaign. By the end of the campaign, Appling was running the Multnomah County operation and had impressed Hatfield with his administrative skills. Appling was everything that McCall was not—and exactly what Hatfield wanted—a colorless bureaucrat who would not overshadow him.

McCall watched, crestfallen. "You could just see him collapse inside," said Dick Althoff, who was with him that day. "McCall was dreadfully disappointed—total disappointment and personal defeat."

The years that followed—years during which Hatfield and McCall should have worked together for Oregon—barely eased the betrayal McCall felt. During the drive back to Portland, McCall sat silently for long stretches, and then exploded with confused rage. "He couldn't understand why," Althoff said. "He was more hurt than disappointed. Tom felt Hatfield purposely led him on."

MCCALL'S REJECTION as secretary of state was a hidden blessing. He would spend the next six years working for KGW-TV, the most stable job he would ever have aside from his two terms as governor. These years were also remembered by his family as the happiest.

The McCalls lived in a nice home in a wooded neighborhood up Canyon Road, just minutes from the KGW-TV studios. Audrey, his wife of twenty years, was the pillar of the house. She had given up her career as a home economist and devoted her life to the family. "I took complete responsibility for the house: cooking, laundry, bookkeeping. Tom never had time for any of it, he was always so busy," she said. "I enjoyed it. It was my contribution to Tom's career, to keep things good for him at home."

Tom's schedule was, as always, a panic. Appearing on the evening and nightly news, he worked until nearly midnight. What spare time he had he stuffed with civic activities. To help pay off his debts, he took on extra work, as he had when he served as staff for the legislative committee on Indian issues. His older son, Tad, had a lasting memory of his overworked father: Tom writing at home during the evenings, pounding away on his manual typewriter, the sound of the tapping keys drifting through the house as Tad fell asleep.

For once, the McCalls' finances were stable, although they still had debts to pay from the congressional race, and worries about money haunted McCall. Once, a KGW-TV colleague found a photograph of the *Thomas W. Lawson,* the seven-masted schooner built by the Copper King. McCall looked at the picture and sighed. "If I had just one-tenth of the money my grandfather piddled away, I'd be a rich man," he said.

McCall remained impetuous about spending money. His sons delighted in his passion for foreign cars. He loved shopping for cars and made it something of a hobby. "We never had an abundance of money," Audrey said. "But Tom was one of those people who believe that when the tires needed replacing, you go out and buy a new car." He finally settled on a Morris Minor. The tiny convertible looked like a toy car with McCall at the wheel, his giant head and large shoulders sticking up out of it as he zipped down the road.

Despite his rigorous work schedule, he carved out generous amounts of time for his sons, Tad and Sam. As his mother often had been to her children, McCall was a grand source of entertainment for his own boys. He was a great storyteller, emulating Dorothy at times by reading aloud or spinning tales from his childhood or the life of his grandfathers. Tad and Sam both remembered, as Tad put it, that he "was a kid at heart. We all knew Mom really had three boys to raise." Indeed, he was as gregarious and mischievous as ever. Audrey was the family's rudder, the symbol of discipline and authority. When the boys did something wrong, Audrey often asked Tom to carry out the scolding. "Mom would say, 'Tom, I want you to take care of this'," recalled Sam of the times he was to be punished as a young child. "So he would pull me away and act quite angry, until Mom was out of earshot. Then we'd laugh and he'd say, 'If your mother asks, tell her I scolded you'."

The family enjoyed tennis and golf, but McCall's favorite pastime was fishing. He loved the sport, although he was as uncoordinated at it as anything athletic he had ever tried. His fishing buddies from KGW-TV called him "C.B." McCall, the C.B. standing for "closed bail." When casting, he usually forgot to open the bail to allow the line to unfurl. As a result, the line would yank short as the lure came to an abrupt stop mid-cast, and his reel in minutes would become a snarl. It did not matter to him. McCall was childlike in his love of fishing and the outdoors. Family vacations usually consisted of trips to central Oregon lakes, where they might stay in a cabin or camp out. Before dawn, McCall would jump out of bed, spend a few hours fishing, rush back to his still-sleeping family, rouse his boys, and return for more fishing. "These were the best years for the family," Audrey recalled. "It was a really wonderful, very pleasant time."

Only one event interrupted the McCalls' comfortable life—a car accident that could easily have killed him and Audrey.

In April 1960, they were speeding home along Canyon Road in the Morris Minor when a Chevrolet sedan roared up from behind. "I looked in my rear-view mirror and it suddenly seemed as if a stranger were in the back seat," McCall remembered of the on-rushing car and its driver. The Chevrolet slammed into McCall's small car, sending it left, across the oncoming lane, soaring off the far shoulder and plunging down a three-hundred-foot embankment. The car landed upright in a shallow marsh. The crash shattered Audrey's right knee, and Tom suffered a

During the family's happiest times, McCall, Audrey, Sam and Tad gather for their 1959 Christmas greetings photograph. (Courtesy William and Ruth Brown)

broken back and cuts on his chest, legs and his head. He spent the next six weeks in a hospital and the following months in a cast that stretched from his waist to his neck. The accident left McCall with a slight stoop and back pains that nagged him for the rest of his life. Despite the severity of his injuries, McCall reported back for work sooner than he should have. Before he went on the air each night, McCall simply pulled up his shirt collar and fixed his tie high enough so that viewers could not see his cast.

NOT EVEN A NEAR-FATAL ACCIDENT kept McCall from looking ahead to re-entering politics. As the 1960s opened, McCall had spent twenty-five years as a journalist. As he approached his fiftieth birthday, his hopes for another shot at politics remained high. Yet McCall lacked two key ingredients that a major campaign—such as one for the governorship—required. One was the courage to stand for election again. The loss to Edith Green still gnawed at him, as did the thought of sinking back into debt. The other ingredient was his sense of purpose. He wanted to be governor—but what would be the ends of his pursuit?

Soon McCall satisfied those needs, and he did so with a single documentary. It was a story that forever changed the way Oregonians thought about their state's environment. To find this story, the one that changed the course of his life, McCall looked no further than the heart of the state and the filthy banks of a polluted tragedy named the Willamette River.

7

Who Are These Foul Strangers?

THE NATIVES had called the river "Wal-lumt." One historian thought it translated to "spill water," a reference to the waterfalls at Oregon City twenty-six river miles above the Willamette's confluence with the Columbia. For the natives, the Willamette was a vein of life. It carried the harvest of salmon, the silver muscle of fish that once swarmed through the water. Over time, the river carved out a lush, green valley that white settlers chose over the brittle, dry land to the east. Eventually, three-fourths of the residents in Oregon lived along or near the Willamette; the valley hosted the state's biggest cities: Eugene, Albany, Salem, Oregon City, and, finally, Portland with its busy waterfront.

From its initial bubblings in the Cascade Range to the east and the Coast Range to the west, the Willamette's two forks join near Eugene and the river meanders north for about 190 miles before reaching the Columbia. The river provided the first key transportation route through the heart of the state; sternwheelers in the late nineteenth century plied the river from town to town, and loggers floated rafts of freshly cut trees to mills built along the river's banks.

Over time, the river was not used only as a resource, however, but as a trough for raw municipal sewage and industrial wastes. Slaughterhouses emptied their bloody bins of flesh and entrails into the water, and manufacturing companies dumped in used chemicals. The worst offenders of all were the pulp mills. The mills boiled wood chips in giant vats of chemicals to create pulp, then flushed the vats' hot liquors into the Willamette.

The wastes robbed the river of life. The chemicals mixed with the raw sewage to feed algae, which covered the river like a tepid green sheet. The algae consumed the Willamette's oxygen, the source of a river's viability.

In the natural course of things, the river would clean itself. In the fall and winter, heavy rains kept the water level high and the river fresh. In the spring, runoff from the snowy Cascades also washed the Willamette. Every time the river splashed or churned, it replenished itself with oxygen.

Eventually, though, the pollution became too great for the river to fully recover. During the summers, when water levels fell and pulp mills ran at a high pitch, the pollution was at its worst. Salmon, trout and other fish returning to the Willamette to spawn swam blindly into a smothering cloud of waste, and were forced to retreat or suffocate.

The Willamette quickly became a public scandal that everyone recognized, but that no one in power seemed willing to halt. State and local health officials began closing the river to swimming in the 1920s; in 1926, the state board of health created an Anti-Pollution League to draw attention to the river, but without much effect.

The next year, the city of Portland started the first careful study of the river's pollution. The tests found that, in the city harbor, oxygen levels fell below the five parts per million that scientists considered the minimum for sustaining aquatic life. That same year, the Portland City Club declared the river "intolerable" and "ugly and filthy." The City Club's report found that, within the city limits, the city itself, with its sewage outfalls, was the worst polluter.

The report and study alarmed the public; anti-pollution groups demanded the state and local government leaders take action. Politicians in the legislature and on the Portland City Council listened politely, and then did nothing.

So more studies followed. In 1933, Governor Julius Meier ordered the state to study how much pollution was caused by the five pulp mills operating in the Willamette watershed. The report was conclusive: The

For years, the Willamette River proved a playground for the public. Here at an Oak Grove beach, across the river from Lake Oswego, Oregonians enjoy the clean Willamette. Eventually the growth of mills along the stream led to a pollution so severe that the river grew dangerous to public health. (Gifford & Prentis photograph; OrHi 89602)

mills were not just contributors to the pollution but the major culprits. The state report, however, was not made public for three years. Another report on the river at Portland, this one issued by the private Charlton Laboratory in 1934, described "sludge banks forming at the outfalls of some of the sewers because there are continual bubbles rising to the surface and large pieces of decaying matter churned to the surface." The scientific findings of all the reports echoed earlier studies: the oxygen levels in the Willamette near Portland were falling.

Politicians soon learned they could win votes by denouncing the Willamette's condition. In 1937, State Treasurer Rufus Holman dramatized the river's sorry state when he led a delegation to the Portland water-

Along the Willamette's banks, pulp mills, such as this one in West Linn pictured in 1905, dumped wastes into the river. Devouring the river's oxygen, the wastes would suffocate fish. (S. P. Davis photograph; OrHi 9725)

front. There, he lowered a cage of salmon into the river and, several minutes later, removed the cage to find the fish dead or gagging. "The fish," said one delegation member, "would live longer in a frying pan."

Soon, the public outrage over the river compelled politicians to act as if they might make good on their rhetoric. In 1936, the pollution study on the pulp mills ordered by Governor Julius Meier was finally made public. In response, the 1937 legislature proposed a bill strictly controlling the dumping of industrial wastes into the river. It was a bold stroke, but it could not withstand lobbying pressure from the paper companies. The industry used what became a time-honored tactic—they threatened to shut down and throw hundreds of people out of work if the state imposed pollution regulations. Legislators backed away from their proposal and, in the end, passed a stripped-down measure that actually exempted industrial wastes from state regulations. However, even the weakened bill went too far for Governor Charles Martin's tastes. He vetoed it on sight.

Voters, too, balked at cleaning up the Willamette. In 1933, the city of Portland proposed building sewage treatment plants, and voters approved a $6 million bond measure. Delays caused the bonding authority to lapse, and voters twice refused to renew the bonds. Only threats of a health crisis made a difference. In 1938, the *Oregonian* reported that scientists had found the Willamette's filth carried E. coli, the harbinger of typhoid. Faced with that news, Portland voters approved the construction bonds for the treatment plants.

So went the long, sorry history of the Willamette River: polluted during years of indifference, ignored by windy politicians, abandoned by voters, everyone hoping someone else would pay for cleaning up the river.

During those years, scientists kept a careful vigil; study after study chronicled the river's decline. In 1944, scientists at Oregon State College (OSC) added one more report.

Starting from the Willamette's highest reaches, the OSC study charted the falling oxygen levels as the river flowed north, becoming more burdened with septic and industrial discharge with each city it passed. By the time the river reached the falls at Oregon City, life in the Willamette only flickered. From there it flowed into the Portland harbor, where large sewer pipes poured in more wastes.

Earlier studies had shown the Willamette in the Portland harbor to have low levels of oxygen. The OSC study changed that conclusion. Where the Willamette reached Portland, oxygen in the river was not simply lacking, or depleted, or inadequate.

There was no oxygen at all. The Willamette was dead.

WEARY OF DELAY, Oregonians finally demanded action. In 1938, voters approved, by three-to-one, an initiative to create a state board empowered to clean up Oregon's rivers. The Oregon State Sanitary Authority made the Willamette its special case. Because the Willamette flowed

Public outrage over the polluted Willamette led to protests about its condition, and created opportunities for politicians. Here, Portland mayor Joseph Carson (center with drum) leads a "Clean River" rally in 1938. (Photo-Art Studio photograph; OrHi 001253)

within a single state, the Sanitary Authority had sole control over it. But the authority had few pollution laws to enforce; those that did exist were weak. Four years passed before the Sanitary Authority proposed its first answer to the Willamette's pollution: dilution. Rather than control what went into the river, the authority decided to regulate the river flow. The United States Army Corps of Engineers planned to build a series of dams on the Willamette's tributaries. With careful timing, discharges from the dams could wash the river clean of mill wastes. The authority, however, had to wait for the dams to be built. With delays caused by World War II, more than a decade passed before the authority's strategy could even begin.

Meanwhile, the mills and cities kept dumping. In 1943, a joint Wash-

Cities along the Willamette dumped raw sewage into the stream, further choking the
river. In this 1938 aerial photograph, the arrow points to effluent billowing from a
sewer outlet under the Burnside Bridge in downtown Portland. (OrHi 014541)

ington-Oregon commission studying pollution in the Columbia River
found that mills and sewer lines were causing problems in that river,
too, but the biggest source of pollution in the Columbia was the Willamette River.

In September 1950, low water levels made the Willamette's pollution
especially potent. Thousands of dead fish—even carp, which survive
in the worst of conditions—littered the river's stinking edge. When a reporter asked a Sanitary Authority engineer about the fish kill, he replied
that he was indeed surprised. No, he was not surprised fish were dying.
He was surprised that so many fish survived in the Willamette in the
first place.

Without strict laws to enforce, the authority could only pursue a policy of voluntary compliance with industry. "The only real tool we had in

those years was a company's fear of publicity," said B.A. "Barney" McPhillips, who joined the Sanitary Authority in 1943. "We could threaten to expose them as a polluter at a hearing, or they could clean up their act. It wasn't much of a tool."

Waste treatment was still experimental and prohibitively expensive, and companies threatened closure—and job losses—if the state forced them to install pollution controls. In 1952, the authority called the mills' bluff and ordered them to stop dumping their wastes directly into the Willamette. The mills followed the letter, not the spirit, of the rule. Three pulp mills poured the wastes into pits, then drained the pits into the river; another, Crown Zellerbach in Oregon City, hauled its wastes on barges to the Columbia and dumped them there.

By the 1960s, the authority had had a few victories. The agency had encouraged every city along the river to treat its sewage at least once before discharging it into the Willamette. When the state ordered secondary treatment, the city of Portland balked, and the authority sued, forcing the city to comply.

But the Willamette Valley's growing population put greater demands on the river, and the authority could not keep up. By 1962—nearly a quarter of a century after voters had approved the Sanitary Authority—on-going studies showed the river was as polluted as ever.

During those years, many of the eight governors to hold office spoke of their concern about the Willamette, but none made it a true priority. A few journalists questioned the state's efforts, but overall the Sanitary Authority did a good job of convincing Oregonians that the Willamette was in fact growing cleaner all the time.

Tom McCall was one of the few journalists who did not buy the authority's story. Since joining KGW-TV, McCall had paid close attention to the Sanitary Authority's work. In late 1961, his focus sharpened on Oregon's pollution problems in general and the Willamette in particular. "I had sort of been hinting, in some of my commentaries, that perhaps Oregon had symptoms of malaise—environmental malaise that had attacked the Potomac, the Cuyahoga and a lot of other streams and areas that man had laid waste to," McCall remembered of this time. After one of these commentaries, his boss, Tom Dargan, suggested that McCall hit the pollution issue hard, that he, as McCall put it, "get on the back of the state Sanitary Authority because of the deterioration of the Willamette."

Dargan proposed they produce a documentary and McCall agreed. As they planned the piece, Dargan blamed the pulp mills and other industries for the pollution, but he especially blamed state officials for failing, after so many years, to keep the Willamette clean. McCall, however, having served in state government, was reluctant to blindly blame a state agency without investigating.

When he did investigate, he was stunned by what he found. He had believed that Oregon, with the exception of the Willamette, had been spared environmental damage. He found he had been wrong. "We were beginning," McCall said of his findings, "to develop the symptoms that in other places had proved to be the basis of the disease that was destroying the environment." Much of the fault, he found, could be placed at the door of state government.

McCall soon produced a one-hour documentary script that laid blame and named names. "[The polluters] had to be portrayed as culprits for something to happen," KGW-TV cameraman Dick Althoff said. "Good guys and bad guys. Tom felt there had to be an adversary relationship between us and those that were polluting." By the spring of 1962, McCall was ready to set off with his camera crew to film the pollution sources. "He had already been to many of these places," Althoff recalled. "He knew exactly where he wanted us to put the camera and what he wanted us to film."

The crews returned with lurid footage of waste dumping. At the Crown Zellerbach mill in Oregon City, Althoff set up a camera on a retaining wall above the mill's outfall pipes. As the camera began rolling, the mill—as if on cue—suddenly released thousands of gallons of pulp wastes. The film caught the swirling waste bubbling below. Later, Althoff rented a boat and, with cameras rolling, followed the Crown Zellerbach barge laden with pulp wastes on its regular dumping trip to the Columbia.

The documentary began to take a toll at KGW-TV. The station had never spent as much money on a single show as it was spending on McCall's documentary—$18,000, McCall remembered, an enormous budget for the time. In addition, many of the companies cited in the film threatened to sue or pull their advertisements unless McCall killed the project. Dargan ignored the threats and told McCall to keep at it.

For the next six months, McCall worked to fit his script to the footage; the exhausted McCall eventually brought in another writer to help him finish the film. Editors added a ponderous musical soundtrack to the film that at times made the production melodramatic. But McCall wanted the drama.

He named the documentary "Pollution in Paradise." Although he never appeared on screen, he narrated the piece in the distinctive voice now familiar to Oregonians. KGW-TV anchorman Richard Ross opened the film by reading a brief passage that—pure McCall in style—set the documentary's tone.

> America is wild and clean and beautiful. But there is also a dying dream of America where the waters are poisoned by the wastes of man and the breeze is strangled by the fires and fumes of civilization.
>
> No part of America still retains more of Nature's original works than the state of Oregon, a paradise for those who treasure the unspoiled in sight, in smell, in sound.
>
> But who are these foul strangers in Oregon's paradise?

McCall then picked up the narration. Detailing case studies from all over the state, he carefully made the case that Oregon's livability was in peril. He first talked about the threat to Oregon's land. As footage of crop lands rolled, he spoke of the deterioration—an echo from his speech to Idaho farmers twenty-five years earlier.

> Insecticides that sometimes upset nature's balance and the less well-known threat of chemical pesticides are poisoning man's environment. Many man-made chemicals, acting in the same way as radiation, live in the soil and enter into living organisms, or travel in subterranean waters and emerge to plague vegetation and livestock and trigger strange human maladies. Insecticides, indiscriminately applied, are massacring birds, mammals, fishes and indeed every form of wildlife.

McCall also talked about the quality of the air. He noted that cities, such as Los Angeles, were already facing air pollution alerts—and that Oregonians were mistaken to think their cities would escape the same fate.

> On some mornings, when the city should sparkle in the sun, guarded by the clean silver cone of Mt. Hood, Portland is shrouded as if by the murk of some filthy twilight in a shadow world.

He pointed to the plumes of industrial smoke coming from plants around Portland, describing them as the "culprits' trail stretching in a great canopy from the mill stacks." He noted that federal officials at the United States Department of Public Health had declared that Portland and Eugene suffered from acute air pollution problems.

McCall even used sarcasm to help make his point. As an example, for years Oregonians who drove the state's primary north-south highway near Albany had passed through a nauseating, rotten-egg cloud from a nearby pulp mill. "Motorists on Highway 99 often are assailed by billows of offensive smoke from the pulp plant of Western Kraft Company," McCall said as viewers saw the plant's chimneys issuing smelly steam. "The process here is another that puts unrecovered waste either in the water or in the air. This plant is doing a little of one and obviously a whole lot of the other."

He then looked at industries along the Columbia River, where sunny hillsides produced a rich fruit crop. "In lush orchards," McCall said, "a sort of tragedy strikes." He showed nearby aluminum plants, located along the Columbia for easy access to inexpensive electricity, and pointed out the classic dilemma: The orchardist needed the climate, the aluminum makers needed the cheap power, yet the industries could not coexist. The aluminum plants' air emissions had caused a rain of metallic dust that was killing the orchards. One company, Harvey Aluminum, had already agreed to pay damages for the destruction of fruit crops.

McCall then jumped to the town of Newport, along the Oregon coast. Aside from fishing, Newport's economy drew its strength from tourism. "A resort and motel town that depends on tourism," McCall said, "Newport found itself shunned by travelers. Property values began to sag and the slide continued as word got out that Newport was the stink center of the Oregon coast."

The problem was a Georgia-Pacific pulp mill in the nearby town of Toledo, eight miles east. The pulp waste aromas had filled Newport with the rotten-egg smell for years. Finally, Georgia-Pacific had agreed to pump the wastes away from the plant into the Pacific Ocean. "At long last," McCall said, "did the Sanitary Authority cautiously agree that Georgia-Pacific had largely cleaned the Newport sea breeze of its stinking cargo."

That had solved the problem for Newport, but not for the Pacific or nearby Toledo. Toledo residents blamed their increasing respiratory problems on Georgia-Pacific. "[T]he bad air in this long suffering little town," McCall said, had been labeled by health officials as "a veritable time bomb."

McCall showed the most concern for the Willamette River. Many Oregonians believed the Willamette was actually cleaner in 1962 than when the Sanitary Authority first went to work. McCall showed that the river was, in fact, no better than before. He pointed to the raw human sewage that still poured into the river from municipal waste systems, houseboats, barges and cargo ships. The ships, McCall said, carry crews that, when put all together, are "enough to populate a medium-sized American city and all of whom are using the river as an open sewer."

McCall saved his most colorful descriptions for the worst polluters. He showed viewers the footage of the Crown Zellerbach mill dumping thousand of gallons of waste into the river. Against that image, McCall spoke indignantly.

> The pulp and paper industry [is] the largest contributor of organic wastes to the water of Oregon. Where these wastes are not treated in a safe manner, the effluent becomes an oxygen-gulping, slime-making scourge. It destroys fish life, fouls fishing gear and fishing boats. Sometimes it churns at river's bottom, forming into rafts that rise to the surface in sluggish, foul-smelling masses of filth.

The river, McCall reported, carried twenty to three hundred times the allowable level of disease-causing bacteria. He also noted that health officials linked the Willamette's pollution to Oregon's hepatitis rate— the nation's highest. With the same drama McCall described the sum of a putrid Willamette.

> Test nettings in the Willamette show that only carp and other warm-water trash fish can survive. And at times even these scavengers perish for a lack of oxygen. There is scarcely a season when fishermen's nets do not become weighted with the thick foul slime created by bacterial action in wasted, bloated waters.

He had shown Oregonians the problem. With growing indignation, McCall asked the single question:

> Do we have the right to ask why more hasn't been done by more people?

McCall placed accountability for Oregon's pollution problems squarely on the Sanitary Authority. He cited examples of the authority's success, noting that the number of cities with sewage treatment plants had grown from thirty-eight to two hundred since the authority had been established. But, he said, the authority was not acting fast enough to keep up with the state's growth. "Oregon," he said, "finds itself running ever faster just to keep up."

McCall then faulted lawmakers for failing to give the Sanitary Authority the power it needed to enforce the state's anti-pollution laws. He cited the 1951 air pollution bill that he had helped write as an important start. Although the agency needed a large statewide staff, he noted that the authority had nine employees—only nine—to police hundreds of industrial sites.

At one point, McCall interviewed an industry lobbyist who said that pollution was a "small inconvenience" for a healthy industrial economy. In case after case, however, McCall showed that the state did not have to choose between jobs and a clean environment. A lax environmental policy protected jobs, he said, but only in the short run. Oregon's livability and its long-term ability to provide jobs was in peril. This was the moral that McCall wanted to leave with his viewers.

> There can be no compromise with this invader. And it could be only the beginning. For how far pollution marches in Oregon is a matter in the final analysis of citizen responsibility, should the citizens face up to it.

McCall intended the documentary to be both a protest and a call to arms. He produced exactly that. "Pollution in Paradise" aired for the first time the evening of 21 November 1962. For all its limitations of style, the documentary was a breakthrough. McCall had produced a smashing report void of the timidity and equivocation rampant in local television reports of that era. He had placed unpalatable images in front of Oregonians that no one in the state had been willing to broadcast. "When Tom blew the whistle," said KGW-TV producer Ken Yandle, "it really made a difference for a long time to come."

The Oregon press quickly acknowledged the power of the documentary. "[I]t will be something of a shocker for those people oblivious to the scope of the problem," said an *Oregon Journal* editorial. "It has some bite. It steps on some toes. It can be rightly called controversial."

Dargan sent copies of the documentary to schools and community meetings around the state. Then, with careful timing, he scheduled and heavily promoted a second broadcast of the show in January 1963, a few days before a new legislative session convened. When the session opened, lawmakers found themselves inundated with letters and phone calls from angry viewers. The legislature responded with a bill, sponsored by Portland state senator Ted Hallock that, for the first time, gave the state the power to shut down a polluting company. The bill itself was a landmark, the single biggest legislative move to clean up the Willamette to that time.

Passage of the measure signaled a change in Oregon politics. For the next twenty years, politicians gave environmental concerns high priority in their rhetoric. Oregonians, they knew, wanted—and demanded—results.

McCall raised the question of the quality of Oregon's environment on the rising tide of growing national concern about pollution. Authors such as Barry Commoner and Stewart Udall, then United States Secretary of the Interior, described the decline of quality in America's land, air and water. But no one did more to raise concerns about the environment than biologist Rachel Carson with her 1962 book, *Silent Spring*. Carson tracked the deadly trail of manmade chemicals and pesticides through the environment, and her writings led to the banning of several chemicals, including DDT.

In Oregon, McCall's challenge to his state had been clear. The effect it had on him personally was profound. Oregon itself needed a champion—but had none. The tenets of his concern for the land were rooted in him as firmly as the sun-hardened juniper of Westernwold. Yet "Pollution in Paradise" was an awakening. What did he offer Oregon that no one else could? He could suddenly answer that now. He could fight for the state itself, its water and air and land.

And if he could generate such passion with a single television show, what could he do as a candidate?

Or as governor?

8

The Two Deals

FOUR YEARS LATER, Tom McCall took the oath as Oregon's thirteth governor. He ascended showing he had learned from his mistakes in his congressional race by waging a sincere, gentlemanly
campaign, one of the last Oregon witnessed. He stood apart from his
political party and won on the strength of his personality and his message of protecting Oregon.

Temptation to sell out, however, surrounded him. Before the election, McCall was offered two political deals in exchange for help delivering him the governorship. One deal—a raw political proposal from
fellow Republicans—he rejected. The second, however, was so subtle
and alluring that he saw it as accommodation, not as an outright deal. He
did not foresee its implications, and he accepted it. Both could have undermined his political career. One nearly did.

In early 1963, with the momentum of "Pollution in Paradise," McCall
talked openly of running for office. In May 1963, Doug Baker, the gossip columnist for the *Oregon Journal*, noted that he often relied on "inside" sources and what he called "inside inside" sources. "My 'inside inside' sources (a pretty good bet)," Baker wrote, "now say definitely that
Tom Lawson McCall, the TV commentator, will make a bid for governor on the GOP ticket." Considering his friendship with Baker, who also
worked at KGW-TV, McCall was probably the "inside inside" source.

His path to the governorship cleared in late 1963 when Oregon Secretary of State Howell Appling announced he was retiring from politics at the end of his term. McCall had reported the possibility of Appling's retirement on KGW-TV on 13 December. In a later broadcast McCall commented that if Appling were to step aside, "the line will form on the right" to replace him. When Appling made his formal announcement, McCall told other reporters he thought the opportunity was great, but added, "Despite the temptation and the encouragement, the odds are about 80 to 20 against my taking that action."

Even as McCall gave long odds, he was working on his campaign. The secretary of state's term lasted four years, but McCall had no intention of serving that long. "We saw this as a means to my end," McCall said later. And that end was the governorship.

The day after Appling's announcement, McCall and Audrey sat down with Clay Myers, one of McCall's Young Republican friends, to plan the campaign. Audrey resisted the idea, recalling the debt and pain that had followed the 1954 congressional race. McCall could not afford to run for the secretary of state's office without a steady paycheck; he also knew KGW-TV would take him off the air as soon as he announced his candidacy.

One day at work, McCall cornered his boss, Tom Dargan, at the company soda machine.

"Damn it," McCall exclaimed to Dargan, "I could be governor if you let me."

Dargan, accustomed to McCall's outbursts, replied calmly, "I think it would be great. How do I stand in your way?" McCall explained, and Dargan agreed to reassign McCall to an off-camera job while he ran for office.

With this financial security, in January 1964 McCall booked a statewide speaking tour as a warm-up for the campaign. In February, at one of the stops on that tour, McCall spoke before the Oregon Junior Chamber of Commerce state convention. There he attacked the Oregon Republican party for its inflexible views on taxes and civil rights. He took the party to task for its devotion to Arizona senator Barry Goldwater, the conservative Republican seeking the presidency, whom McCall disliked. He also articulated his vision of a stronger state government, one that took control of Oregon's destiny rather than simply reacted to noisy interest groups.

The speech was classic McCall—and it won him the devotion of two people in the audience who helped him launch his campaign.

One was Edward Westerdahl, a twenty-eight-year-old lobbyist for Portland General Electric (PGE). A former Army intelligence officer and cryptographer, Westerdahl, in only three years with PGE, had forged a reputation as an effective, bull-headed lobbyist who prided himself on his steely, emotionless style.

Elsewhere in the Jaycees audience sat Ronald Schmidt, also twenty-eight, a public relations man for Portland's Lloyd Center, the nation's first major shopping center. A California native, Schmidt had a remarkable talent for promotion and a taste for populism.

Both Schmidt and Westerdahl walked out of the hall after McCall's speech believing they had found a man they could follow into politics; Westerdahl quit his job the next day and offered his services to McCall.

Schmidt arranged for a series of lunch time meetings at the Lloyd Center, where the three talked about McCall's political future. McCall was impressed with them despite their youth, and during one lunch he confided his fears about sinking into debt again. Westerdahl and Schmidt promised the campaign would remain solvent. "OK, I'm running," McCall said, and he turned to Schmidt. "I now appoint you my campaign finance chairman." He stuck Schmidt with the bill for lunch.

Schmidt and Westerdahl became McCall's most valuable aides. Westerdahl was charged with keeping McCall focused and calm. Schmidt handled the press and managed McCall's flamboyance for the best coverage.

Schmidt leaked news of McCall's impending candidacy so that the story appeared in Sunday newspapers on 16 February. McCall—as if he needed it—won more publicity a week later when the National Conference of Christian and Jews gave him its 1964 Brotherhood Award; his portrait from the ceremony landed on page one of the *Oregonian*. Two days later, riding this crest of attention, McCall formally announced his candidacy, telling reporters, "I am running as an extension of a life devoted to public concern. I feel compelled to go out on a limb."

That night, KGW-TV's news broadcast led with McCall's announcement. On the news script, someone had typed the headline: "McCall announces for Secretary of State," and then added, not for broadcast, "Oh Fateful Day!"

Ron Schmidt (left) and Ed Westerdahl (right) were critical to Tom McCall's successful campaigns and his administration. (Gerry Lewin *Statesman Journal* photo and
Photo-Art Studio photo; OrHi 90678)

AFTER TEN YEARS, Tom McCall was again a candidate. His work as a
journalist had produced in him a growing awareness of the threat to the
state's livability, and he wanted to make that concern the centerpiece of
his career. But first he had to prove he could win.

His own party was most skeptical. McCall's liberal views and attacks on polluting industries, Schmidt said, guaranteed "we were not
the choice of the Republican party by any stretch of the imagination."
Still, Schmidt tried his business contacts to raise money. Friends told
him that any Republican hopeful could expect a sizable donation from
John Higgins, a Portland lawyer who traditionally gave large contributions to GOP candidates. So Schmidt put on his best suit and rehearsed
the speech he would give Higgins. Once inside the lawyer's office, however, he found Higgins matter-of-fact. "Here," Higgins said, pointing to

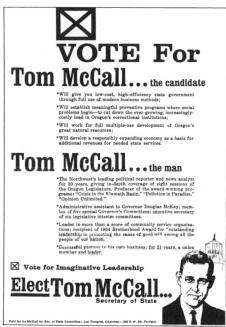

The cover of a McCall for Secretary of State flier (above left) and a page from one of the campaign's mailers (above right). (OrHi 90808 and 90805)

an envelope on his desk, "You give this to Tom McCall." Schmidt raced back with the campaign's first Republican contribution. McCall tore open the envelope and pulled out its contents: a one-dollar bill.

Despite the reluctance among GOP leaders to support him, McCall breezed through the primary. His only opponent was Dan Mosee, a Portland appliance dealer. McCall obliterated Mosee, winning seventy-nine percent of the vote. He lost only one of Oregon's thirty-six counties— Malheur, the least populated and farthest from Portland—and by just thirteen votes.

The general election proved more difficult as McCall had no advantage from party registration numbers: in 1964, out of 932,461 registered voters, there were 110,637 more Democrats than Republicans. His opponent, Alfred H. Corbett, was a state senator from Portland and a descendant of the family that had welcomed Hal McCall to Oregon fifty-five years earlier. Corbett was a Harvard and Yale-educated lawyer with liberal credentials, but he lacked McCall's fame. "[McCall] should be happy," one Corbett backer groused. "Television has given him millions of dollars worth of free advertising—and paid him for it."

Schmidt played on McCall's familiarity with slogans such as "An Old Friend for a New Task," and "You Know Tom McCall." Schmidt added flair to the already flamboyant McCall style. The campaign rented an eighteen-foot motor home when such vehicles were still rare, and the candidate traveled the state in his "McCall Bandwagon." In the streets of small and big towns alike, he was the perfect candidate—charming, articulate, and funny, a true celebrity.

Westerdahl and Schmidt discovered McCall could be the worst kind of candidate, too—thin skinned, nervous, shaky. "His loss in 1954 never let him forget the pain of losing," Westerdahl said. "He was antsy, nervous, always afraid something was going to come up and lose the election for him." Schmidt found that even strong poll numbers did little to calm McCall. If the poll numbers showed even an insignificant shift of voters toward Corbett, McCall would slip into a funk. "He never looked at a poll and said 'Fifty-eight percent of the voters like me'," Schmidt said. "He'd say, 'Why do thirty-eight percent hate me'?"

McCall's thin skin had become legendary after the 1954 race, and that also worried Schmidt and Westerdahl. "My whole weakness as a politician was in wanting to retaliate," McCall admitted later. Tom Dargan suggested McCall apply the "big dog, little dog" technique. "Let the little dog yip and snap," Dargan said. "Don't react, except after a considerable period of time, when you're tired of it, just lift your leg and piss all over them."

McCall tried to follow Dargan's advice, but his rattled nerves often sidetracked his campaign. During one of McCall's statewide tours, a labor newspaper mistakenly reported McCall's position on a workers' compensation issue. Corbett used the erroneous report to charge McCall had flip-flopped. Any other candidate would have recognized the small scale of the issue and dispatched an aide to handle the response. Not McCall. He heard of Corbett's accusations while campaigning in rural Polk County. He flew into a rage, pacing and cursing to himself.

Then he cancelled his tour, rushed to Portland, and held an angry press conference, drawing more attention to Corbett's minor charge. "This attack was a big nothing," said Floyd McKay, a reporter for the *Oregon Statesman* who was traveling with McCall. "It was Mickey Mouse stuff. But Tom felt like he had to respond. And he derailed his own campaign efforts in doing so."

Even at the times he should have been sharp, he often collapsed into a nervous wreck. During a taped television debate with Corbett at KGW-TV's studios, McCall stammered and muttered through several painful, tense minutes. It was so bad so that, as Westerdahl remembered, "Tom was making even dull Alf Corbett look good."

As Westerdahl and Schmidt watched helplessly in the studio's shadows, Tom Dargan walked up from behind.

"Tom isn't doing very well, is he?" Dargan whispered to Westerdahl.

"He sure as hell isn't," Westerdahl replied.

"What if," Dargan said, "we had a technical malfunction and had to start all over?"

Westerdahl grinned. "Yes," he replied. "Why don't you have a technical malfunction?"

Dargan nodded and headed for the control room. A minute later, the director's voice boomed through the studio, announcing that a problem with the studio equipment required them to start over. Westerdahl pulled McCall aside and calmed him down. He delivered a far stronger performance the second time.

Recognizing how rattled the campaign made him, McCall handed over his campaign strategy and planning to the cool, logical Westerdahl. "He generally knew that the strain of campaigning was almost too much for me," McCall later said of Westerdahl. "He was brilliant. He was the antithesis of Tom McCall [and] the most infuriating son of a bitch I've ever known."

Westerdahl was careful about the topics McCall broached. McCall wanted to talk about all kinds of issues—especially the environment—and he desperately wanted to attack his party's own presidential nominee, Barry Goldwater, who McCall thought had exploited racial issues to win over conservatives. Corbett was trying to link McCall with Goldwater, and McCall, apoplectic, wanted to respond. Westerdahl would not let him. Privately, McCall wrote an "Affidavit of Conscience," a statement denouncing Goldwater. He never issued it, and the stress of remaining silent increased the tension between him and Westerdahl.

Westerdahl was also charged with keeping McCall's behavior above reproach and McCall sometimes resented it. During a campaign swing in Eugene, Audrey, Tom and Westerdahl stopped to visit Tad McCall, then a freshman at the University of Oregon. Recalling his own college days, McCall agreed to buy beer for his underage son and friends. Westerdahl did not see it as a fatherly gesture; he saw it as recklessness. As he drove Tom and Audrey to their next stop, Westerdahl lectured McCall that if the boys were caught with the alcohol and it was traced back to him, it could cost him the election. McCall exploded. "You rotten son of a bitch!" he screamed at Westerdahl, pounding his fists against the back of the car seat. "I've taken the last criticism I'm going to take! Get out! Fight!" But Westerdahl calmly kept driving until McCall cooled off.

Voters saw little of McCall's twisted nerves, but Schmidt and Westerdahl worried he might crack in the campaign's final days. So they took no chances. They sent McCall into hiding.

On 21 October, thirteen days before the election, McCall took one last campaign swing through the southern Oregon town of Klamath Falls. McCall felt ill and friends called a local doctor, Raymond Engelcke, who diagnosed the flu. He put McCall in a local hospital, recommending he stay in bed four days. But McCall was in the hospital for no more than two days. After that, Engelcke said, "He was fine and walked out under his own power."

However, his campaign continued to report that the candidate was in the hospital for observation. Actually, McCall rested under wraps in Portland while Audrey campaigned in his place. The ruse, which never became public, put everyone at ease. Years later, McCall still tried to keep the ploy secret. "I had campaigned so hard that I had to spend the final week of the campaign in the hospital in Klamath Falls," he noted in his memoirs. But at the time, Westerdahl said, "A lot of the reporters knew where Tom was. They were his friends and weren't about to report that he wasn't in the hospital."

McCall waited out the final result in nervous seclusion, but the general election vote on 3 November was no surprise. McCall beat Corbett handsomely, collecting 432,150 votes to 338,487 for the Democrat.

McCall's electoral strength was, in short, remarkable. He had pulled in the Democratic and independent vote across the state, and he had won twenty-nine of the state's thirty-six counties, losing only where Democratic registration was heavy. McCall had also run contrary to a powerful trend: Republican Barry Goldwater had performed disastrously in Oregon, becoming the first Republican presidential candidate in twenty years to lose the state. McCall's ability to withstand this anti-GOP current made his thrashing of Corbett all the more impressive.

At fifty-two, McCall was, for the first time, an elected official. "I am tremendously stirred by it," he delightedly told a reporter the day after his victory, "and I will burst a gasket to do a good job."

MCCALL RESIGNED FROM KGW-TV and, with Audrey and their younger son, Sam, moved into a large state-owned house just three blocks from the Capitol. He took the oath of office for his $16,500-a-year job on 4 January 1965. Each day, McCall walked down Summer Street to the secretary of state's office suite in the Capitol. The suite, which filled one corner of the building, was down the stairs and around the corner from the governor's office in which McCall had worked thirteen years earlier.

His duties put him in charge of the state's elections, accounting, auditing and buildings. He also had a seat on both the Board of Control, which oversaw state institutions, and the Land Board, which managed state forests. His office's more menial tasks ranged from handling legislative payroll to fielding complaints about the Capitol's heating system.

In all, he now had authority over dozens of employees and an annual budget of about $500,000. McCall had never run a business or an office or even a tidy desk. Although professional managers ran most of the operations, McCall had no idea how to oversee the office.

"He was terribly disorganized," said Wanda Merrill, McCall's chief secretary and a holdover from Appling's administration. Merrill had grown accustomed to Appling's crisp management style. Each day, Appling promptly read and answered his mail, then went down a formal list of daily tasks. But Merrill would enter McCall's office to find the mail unopened and realize McCall had slipped out a back door. "He was always distracted, always up out of his office doing something else," she said. "He was usually somewhere in the building, talking to people, gathering information, talking issues. It came from his background as a newsman."

Although bored by detail, McCall devoted his attention to broader issues, especially the Board of Control. Twenty years after he first worked for corrections reform, McCall now had a direct role in overseeing the penitentiary's rehabilitation programs.

Even in that pursuit, McCall struggled, for one reason: Governor Mark Hatfield, with whom McCall would have to work for two years. (Hatfield was not seeking re-election in 1966, instead eyeing a seat in the United States Senate.)

Like many other politicians in Salem, Hatfield viewed McCall as a lightweight who had won office only through television fame. McCall hoped to prove himself, but Hatfield did little to help. He demanded loyalty out of McCall; McCall often refused to give him that loyalty. Hatfield, for example, had grown accustomed to meeting with Board of Control members in secret, then convening public sessions as a formality. McCall, however, insisted on public meetings only. Unlike Hatfield, he wanted public debate, especially on issues that affected the welfare of people in state institutions.

Hatfield also had grown accustomed to having the other Board of Control members follow his will; McCall often refused. The board's third member, State Treasurer Robert Straub, would watch as Hatfield lashed out not at him, the board's only Democrat, but at fellow Republican McCall. Recalled *Oregon Statesman* reporter Floyd McKay, "Hatfield would go after Tom and put him in a corner and make it appear as if Tom didn't really know what was going on. Mark could do that very skillfully." Added Straub aide Ken Johnson, "Mark was just cutting up Tom something awful. But Tom would just sit there and take it." McCall soon found himself aligned with Straub, and together they repeatedly outvoted Hatfield on key issues.

The alliance Tom McCall and Bob Straub forged survived throughout their careers despite their own rivalry for the governorship. There was more in Straub to respect than resent. Like McCall, Straub, then

Democratic State Treasurer Robert Straub and Republican Secretary of State Tom McCall confer on the March 1966 filing day, when they registered to run against each other for the governorship. While political foes, they were allies on many issues, including environmental protection. (OrHi 74881)

forty-five, was a political oddity whom few people took seriously. He was born in San Francisco in 1920, graduated from Dartmouth College and went to work for Weyerhaeuser in Springfield after World War II. He became comfortably rich from timber and a contracting business, won a seat on the Lane County Board of Commissioners and later a seat in the Oregon Senate. Straub, however, showed little promise as a politician and struck many people as ambitious beyond his abilities. Straub always had high hopes for himself, though. In 1962, after one term in the state senate, he abandoned his seat to run for Congress; he finished a distant third in a three-way Democratic primary. Undeterred, in 1964 he challenged Republican State Treasurer Howard Belton, a Hatfield appointee. Straub was dismissed as a longshot, running, in essence, against the popular Hatfield administration. Yet Belton was no match for Straub, who proved to be a dogged campaigner; Straub defeated him.

McCall and Straub were most often aligned over the state's failure to clean up the Willamette River. After twenty-seven years, the Sanitary

Authority had seen only humble results of its work. Sewage treatment plants served half the state's population. In 1964, the agency finally ordered the Willamette Valley's seven pulp mills to solve their waste disposal problems; the result was a marked increase in the quality of water in the Willamette. Although these results created hope for the Willamette, that hope soon faded in the summer of 1965.

It turned out that the Sanitary Authority had simply been covering up pollution problems with the Willamette's augmented water flow. When the dams upriver were open, the mills could pump their waste into the river and the extra water would flush the Willamette clean. However, when the year's rainfall was less than normal, the dams held less water and the river could not purge itself. The year of 1965 was exceedingly dry. As the summer approached, the river shrank, the pulp mills fired up, and dumped their loads in the river. Without adequate reservoirs to flush itself clean, the Willamette clogged with waste. The conditions grew so bad that the pulp mills actually shut down—a case of pollution finally taking an economic toll on the industry that created it.

The Oregon press treated the summer of 1965 as a dramatic setback for the Willamette. A series of news reports, all in the aggressive tone of McCall's "Pollution in Paradise," detailed the Sanitary Authority's failures. Although the state had won a lawsuit against the city of Portland, thirty-six city sewage pipes still spit raw waste into the river. The agency had never exercised its full power, granted in 1963, to close down a polluting mill. As long as industry showed "good faith," the authority declined to crack down on pollution. As one reporter put it, the Sanitary Authority files were "jammed with dreary records of orders and excuses, requests and arguments, demands and feet-dragging."

Hatfield had talked a good game about the Willamette, said B.A. "Barney" McPhillips, a long-time Sanitary Authority member, "But he never showed all that much interest in what we were doing." Hatfield's budgets denied the authority adequate funding, providing its ten scientists with less than $2,000 a year to fight its legal battles against polluters. Hatfield's priority had been Oregon's economy; he wanted to diversify the job base, and his record suggests that he saw strict pollution controls in conflict with that goal. "Hatfield," McCall later said, "was a grabber of payrolls at almost any cost."

With the Willamette a canal of swill in the summer of 1965, the 1966 race for the governorship became a referendum on the river and the state's environmental future. A special legislative panel studied pollution issues during the fall of 1965 and provided McCall and Straub with a forum. Testifying before the panel, Straub called Hatfield "grossly derelict" for failing to do more about the Willamette. Hatfield, he charged, "must carry personal responsibility for the disgraceful, stinking mess of the Willamette River."

Although McCall was also disappointed with Hatfield, before the legislative panel he avoided attacking the governor and concentrated on defining a new Oregon policy toward the state's environment. Under Oregon's current policies, McCall said, the state had tried to clean up the mess that existed. He called for foresight and wise planning that prevented pollution and the loss of valuable land resources from uncontrolled urban growth.

"Oregon is at a crossroads," McCall told the committee. "There is still a chance to choose between the polluted chaos of Southern California and cleanliness." As a reporter on hand recorded the rest of the comment, "McCall said a 'line must be drawn' in fighting pollution, even if it means saying to a major industry you cannot locate here if you are going to pollute our rivers or air."

ONLY FIVE MONTHS after becoming secretary of state, McCall turned to his campaign for governor and found his way blocked. "McCall is fighting for his political life," said a Bend *Bulletin* editorial in June 1965, "And the opposition comes not from Democrats but from his fellow Republicans. What started as mild disaffection with McCall during the early days of his term in office has turned into a full-fledged 'stop McCall' movement. He still has nothing to fear from Democrats. But some Republicans are after him in full cry."

Indeed, conservatives had not forgiven his refusal to back Goldwater, and he had made matters worse once in office by launching an investigation into the local John Birch Society's finances. Business leaders saw him as a threat, and his frosty relationship with Hatfield did not help.

Republican leaders hoped to knock McCall out in the primary by recruiting State Senator Tony Yturri of Ontario, who first said he would run and then dropped out. They then encouraged House Speaker F.F. "Monte" Montgomery to join the race. Montgomery, an insurance agent from Eugene, had held little ambition for higher office before 1965. His mind changed as his GOP house colleagues implored him to prevent McCall's rise to the governorship. "Our people," Montgomery said, "were as much anti-Tom as they were pro-Monte."

Montgomery, trailing McCall two-to-one in surveys, sent a signal to the thin-skinned McCall that the race would be rough by bringing into his campaign a name out of McCall's past: Ken Rinke, the brains behind Edith Green's assault on McCall in 1954. The news of Rinke's hiring chilled McCall. "Rinke," McCall said privately at the time, "will put me in [the Oregon State Hospital] whether I win or not."

McCall, however, did not flinch in his determination to run, and Montgomery decided his heart was not in a campaign he did not think he could win. To salvage something for Montgomery, the speaker's top lieutenant, House Majority Leader Robert F. Smith, tried to cut a deal with McCall.

On the last day of 1965, Smith visited McCall at the small beach house he and Audrey had purchased a year earlier in the Roads End area north of Lincoln City. At first McCall did not know why Smith had asked for the meeting, but Smith was direct. Montgomery would not run for the governorship, Smith said, in exchange for a promise from McCall that he would appoint Montgomery secretary of state when McCall assumed the governorship.

McCall stiffened. He told Smith that no such deal could ever be kept secret. Smith said Montgomery had already worked out a cover plan to bow out of the primary campaign—he would announce that polls showed him too far behind, giving that as a reason not to run.

Then, Smith aimed a clear threat at McCall: without the deal, he warned, Montgomery would unleash a bitter campaign intended to destroy McCall's chances for winning in the general election.

McCall got the message: Make Montgomery happy and there would be no contested primary, no Rinke-run assault on his character. But McCall smelled a trap. He knew Smith was offering a deal that was patently illegal—Oregon's Corrupt Practices Act prohibited a candidate from

Oregon House Majority Leader Robert F. Smith (left) proposed that Tom McCall cut a deal by pledging to appoint House Speaker F. F. "Monte" Montgomery as secretary of state in exchange for Montgomery's withdrawal from the 1966 governor's race. McCall believed Smith's plan was illegal and refused. (Al Monner photo; OrHi 018053 and Wayne Easternburn Eugene *Register-Guard* photo)

offering someone a job to keep him out of a race. The secretary of state himself was responsible for enforcing that law. If McCall went along, Montgomery could make the deal public and shame McCall right out of politics. McCall refused Smith's offer.

After Smith left, McCall typed out a confidential memo that served as the record of the meeting. "I oppose such manipulating, in principle, even if it were not outlawed," McCall wrote. "Say, for sake of argument, I made such a deal, it could never be kept undercover; it would be politically dangerous, as well as immoral and illegal."

His bluff called, Montgomery announced in January 1966 that he would not be running for governor. McCall had shown a new political maturity by risking greater GOP anger by shirking Montgomery and by inviting a vitriolic campaign against him.

A second deal, however, had a different ending.

McCall had cleared a path to the nomination even though his own party's leaders considered him a third-rate choice: unpredictable, untested, unsteady and too ambitious for his own good. His popularity with Oregonians made him immune to the concerns of GOP insiders, and he understood why the corporate leaders opposed him. He could not be bought.

Later in his career, McCall relished his role as a maverick. But in 1966 he did not want to win the governorship without respect from Oregon's business leaders, for he wanted the legitimacy they could offer his campaign. So in early 1966 McCall paid a visit to the one man in Oregon—a man of singular power—who could provide him with that respect.

HIS NAME WAS GLENN JACKSON, and for three decades his name in Oregon was synonymous with power. His adulators sought fawning titles to bestow on this mousy man. The title that followed him the most was "Mr. Oregon," a tribute to his considerable civic work. Tom McCall gave him a more fitting title, "The General."

Jackson was a self-made millionaire whose business interests spanned the state. He controlled the state's largest utility and sat on the boards of the state's biggest bank, its biggest retailer and its biggest insurance company. He also held controlling interests in newspapers, timber, real estate, mining, airlines, railroads, cattle ranching, farming, tourist resorts and a country club. At his death in 1980, Jackson was worth $20 million, an underestimate of his real financial worth at his career's peak.

His business career alone does not account for the influence he held. Unlike other business leaders who aided politicians based on their allegiance to the Republican party, Jackson held no fixed ideology. He took no sides in politics. He simply made himself valuable—indeed, he made himself necessary—to any politician who hoped to hold high office.

For twenty years, Jackson ran the powerful Oregon Highway Commission, overseeing construction of the state's interstate freeway network. The position gave Jackson an intimate knowledge of the needs of every major business interest in Oregon. For three decades, governors and senators turned to him for help, and hopeful candidates sought his blessing.

Despite the power he held, Jackson remained a phantom to most Oregonians. As a prominent business leader, Jackson enjoyed publicity, yet many of the fertile tales of his power remain secret, protected by his loyalists, even now.

Jackson was born in Albany in 1902, a descendant of a pioneer family and the son of a successful businessman and publisher of the town's newspaper, the Albany *Democrat*. An uninspired student, the scrawny Jackson showed an unusual determination in business. "I've always been a little squirt, and one thing I couldn't stand was for someone to say something couldn't be done," Jackson said in later years. "So then I'd go out and do it, just to prove the bastards were wrong."

Jackson went to work for the California-Oregon Power Co. (COPCO), in 1928. He started as a COPCO appliance salesman and ended as chief stockholder. He built his empire from Medford in southern Oregon through innovation and aggressive investments. Soon after World War II, Jackson bought an old army base and built one of the nation's first industrial parks—although no one at first knew what to call White City, with its lumber mills, manufacturing plants, fire department, railroad, small shopping center and housing developments for workers. His influence expanded when he engineered a corporate coup, going behind the back of COPCO's president (Jackson was then the utility's vice president) to merge it with Pacific Power & Light (PP&L), the state's biggest private utility. The deal, in which Jackson cast aside his enemies, foreshadowed his ascendance to the chairmanship of PP&L a few years later.

The merger signaled that Jackson got whatever he wanted in business; his political friendships guaranteed he got whatever he wanted from government. "Jackson was a doer who frequently didn't bother with committees," Hatfield aide Travis Cross recalled. "He created such a commanding fear, especially behind the [PP&L] desk with that low voice. You had a regard for him and knew you should respond to whatever he might be asking to be done. After all, one man's high regard is another man's fear."

Jackson's role as a political dealmaker started with his long alliance with Senator Wayne Morse. Morse had been ostracized by business leaders for abandoning the Republican party in 1952; his often mean, vindictive actions did nothing to broaden his appeal. Jackson, however, knew how to charm Morse. In turn, Jackson held the kind of power no other business leader could—access to Oregon's bombastic but powerful senior senator.

Mark Hatfield had also benefited from Jackson's help. Jackson had been the first major business leader to anoint Hatfield's campaign for governor in 1958. Jackson's influence reached its peak when Governor Hatfield rewarded him with the chairmanship of the powerful Highway Commission, which set policy for the Highway Department.

The appointment concerned Travis Cross. The Highway Commission would be siting the new interstate freeways in Oregon; Cross wondered if Jackson might use his new power to help his various businesses.

"Doesn't he have a conflict of interest?" Cross asked Hatfield at one point.

"He has so many conflicts they cancel each other out," Hatfield replied.

Jackson's accomplishments as Highway Commission chairman were dramatic. During his tenure the Highway Department spent more than a billion dollars to build seven hundred miles of interstate freeways and more than eight hundred bridges, including three major spans in Portland and Astoria. While many states struggled to finish their freeway systems, Jackson delivered to Hatfield a finished Interstate 5 before the end of the governor's second term. The ceremony celebrating the freeway's completion, in fact, conveniently took place in the midst of Hatfield's campaign for the United States Senate in 1966.

Jackson never escaped questions of conflicts of interest. Many people close to Jackson saw the conflicts, but understood that his political influence guaranteed he would never be held accountable for them.

A Jackson case history: As an economic development ambassador for Hatfield, Jackson courted the Minnesota Mining & Manufacturing Co., better known as 3M, which sought a new west coast manufacturing site. Although the opening of the 3M facility would provide jobs for Oregonians, Jackson had a secondary business interest in bringing the manufacturer to Oregon: Jackson wanted his utility to sell electricity to

Glenn Jackson, for years *the* most powerful man in Oregon. (OrHi 90687)

3M. When 3M decided to move to Oregon, in March 1964, it surprised few people that the company announced it would locate in White City.

Nine months after the 3M announcement, which probably increased the value of the industrial park, Jackson sold White City for $4 million. The buyer: Commonwealth Inc., a real estate holding company. As part of the deal not made public, Commonwealth also gave Jackson a seventeen percent ownership in the company, a seat on the board of directors, and oversight of new projects.

A few weeks later, Commonwealth purchased options for 184 acres in Tualatin, a small community south of Portland along Interstate 5. Not long after that, the Oregon Highway Commission, with Jackson at the gavel, announced that a new freeway, Interstate 205, would have its junction with Interstate 5 in Tualatin—close to the land Commonwealth now controlled.

Jackson escaped scrutiny until Congresswoman Edith Green, in November 1965, directed the General Accounting Office (GAO), the investigating arm of Congress, to look into the freeway siting decision. The GAO found no evidence that Jackson had provided Commonwealth inside information on Interstate 205's proposed location, however. The GAO investigators also noted that federal law prohibited highway officials from speculating on land over which freeways would run—but did not prevent them from speculating on land that happened to be well-positioned near new freeways.

The extent of Jackson's influence was not measured by his ability to bring about this kind of business deal, but by the fact that most Oregon leaders—and the state's press—looked the other way when it came to the deal's questionable aspects.

MCCALL KNEW THAT JACKSON was the one person whose endorsement could give his campaign legitimacy with wary business leaders. In his pursuit of Jackson's endorsement, McCall had a key ally: Ron Schmidt.

Jackson admired Schmidt and had bankrolled his first business venture. Schmidt set up a meeting and went with the anxious McCall to Jackson's top-floor suite in PP&L's offices. Jackson was candid. He considered McCall too liberal, too unfamiliar with business concerns, and most of all, a "loose cannon." But Jackson was pragmatic. He saw McCall's overwhelming advantage over Straub and knew he would probably be dealing with McCall as governor soon. So Jackson, in what appeared as a passing remark, offered McCall what ultimately became the second deal he faced in his pursuit of the governorship.

Jackson first granted McCall his blessing. He would spread the word with his business friends that they should support the McCall campaign. McCall was so thrilled by Jackson's endorsement that he did not pay much attention to what Jackson said next. He told McCall he was having trouble locating a highway along the Oregon coast. If elected governor, would McCall support the Highway Commission's efforts to get the job done? Before asking what the highway project entailed, McCall gave his promise to help any way he could.

DESCENDING FROM THE COAST RANGE, the Nestucca River has carved a wide basin as it meanders toward the Pacific. As if reluctant to meet the sea, the Nestucca turns abruptly south within a few hundred yards of the ocean, then runs parallel to the shoreline for two miles before emptying into Nestucca Bay. Caught between the river and the bay is a long sandy finger of land, three miles long and half a mile wide.

The Nestucca Spit remained one of the last wild stretches of land on the well-traveled Oregon coast in 1965. The main coastal highway, U.S. Highway 101, cut inland as it reached the turnoff to Pacific City, the small town near the Nestucca's mouth. Even farther off the main road, the spit was accessible only by crossing a small bridge over the river and hiking across grassy dunes. Hikers could walk for two miles along the beach without seeing a house or motel or gift shop.

It was across this undisturbed land that Glenn Jackson wanted to build a new highway. The Oregon Highway Department had undertaken a realignment of U.S. 101 to remove the road's dangerous curves. The department had other motives as well, namely, to bring the road closer to the ocean to improve the view for motorists, and to boost business in coastal towns otherwise isolated from the main road. As Jackson's engineers had designed it, the new U.S. 101 would cut west to the beach just south of Nestucca Bay, bridge the bay, slice the Nestucca Spit up the middle and continue north to catch up with the old route.

The Nestucca Highway was the first realignment of U.S. 101 to cut so close to the beach; Jackson needed the project to justify and continue U.S. 101's realignment up the coast. He knew that the proposed route might cause a public outcry. He was right. The Highway Commission held a hearing in Pacific City in August 1965 and approved the plan with little debate. Soon afterward, angry residents and owners of vacation homes in the road's path demonstrated their opposition during the Dory Days parade, Pacific City's summer festival, by hanging effigies of Jackson and Governor Mark Hatfield from telephone poles.

The protests caught the attention of Robert Straub. Straub traveled to Pacific City, walked the spit and decided he could not stomach a four-lane highway along the beach. Certain that Oregonians would not accept the highway either, Straub, on 8 May, Mother's Day, brought two busloads of protestors to Pacific City and led a "Mother's March" to save Nestucca Spit. The event earned Straub some publicity and angered local highway supporters, who, not to be outdone by opponents, responded by hanging Straub in effigy.

Nestucca Spit, with the river-fed bay on the right and the Pacific buffeting the sands on the left. The state proposed running a highway along the beach. The plan was a center of controversy for McCall, Glenn Jackson and Robert Straub. (Alfred Monner *Oregon Journal* photo; OrHi 90707)

Jackson had never seen such opposition to a highway before, and he wanted the debate quieted. Normally, he had all the authority he needed to build a highway. But he needed the cover of the governor's office— and the governor—to help him in this case, for the publicity endangered a secret Jackson did not want exposed: the state of Oregon had no legal authority to build the Nestucca Highway.

The spit had a patchwork of ownership, divided between private owners and the United States Bureau of Land Management (BLM). The Highway Department had bought or condemned private property in the route. But the state could not condemn the federal land, and the highway would run over two BLM parcels, one of forty acres stretching across the spit, and another of less than an acre at the spit's south tip. The BLM refused to sell the property but instead offered a patent, which would convey the parcels' ownership to the state, but only under strict conditions. The BLM wanted to protect the area and keep it wild, so when the Highway Department agreed to take over the land, the state promised to use the land "For State Park Purposes for Public recreation in connection with the general public use and enjoyment of the beach as an addition to Nestucca Sand Spit State Park." The agreement of the Highway Department made the patent legally binding.

No sooner did the state take control of the BLM land, however, than the Highway Department laid plans to break the agreement. In fact, maps showing the four-lane highway running over the park land had been finished even before the agreement was signed. Jackson apparently hoped that work on the highway would progress so far that the BLM would give in to pressure and allow the state to break its agreements to protect the spit.

Jackson kept these details secret from McCall on the day they talked about the governorship. Of all the decisions McCall made regarding the environment, few were made as recklessly. But McCall's agreement to support the highway was made in a vacuum, without understanding what it meant. "Supporting that highway ran contrary to every bone in his body," Schmidt said. "This was not a project Tom McCall would have wanted. The only reason he went for [the highway] was because Glenn Jackson wanted it." Added Straub years later, "Tom's heart was in the right place on these issues. But on this one, Glenn Jackson trapped him. He got snookered."

In July, McCall visited Pacific City and publicly endorsed the highway route. The news of McCall's position on the Nestucca Highway issue stunned Straub. "I had expected McCall to oppose the highway, and I just wanted to be the first to do so," Straub said. "I was shocked when he did not oppose it. After that, I tried to beat McCall over the ahead with it. It was about the only thing I had."

Straub believed—correctly—that Oregon's environment would dominate the 1966 governor's race, and he campaigned using the Nestucca Spit as an example that he—not McCall—was the only candidate willing to protect the environment at all costs.

Although Straub's instincts were right, his timing and the issue

Tom McCall kicks off his
1966 campaign for Oregon
governor. (Courtesy the
Oregonian)

proved wrong. When he talked about the spit, Oregonians wondered why they should care about a distant strip of sand and a highway not in their backyards. Meanwhile, reporters, reluctant to investigate McCall, dismissed Straub's attacks as those of a publicity hound. Editorial writers blasted Straub for exploiting such a small issue against his opponent.

Within days, the Nestucca Highway faded from the 1966 governor's race and from public debate. That would change—painfully so for Tom McCall—but not soon enough to hurt him or to help the fading campaign of Robert Straub.

THE OUTCOME OF THE ELECTION WAS NEVER IN DOUBT, and the 1966 race for governor remained polite. McCall's popularity kept him well ahead of Straub in the polls, and the press remained friendly; every major newspaper, except for the *Oregon Journal*, endorsed him. McCall made his election a referendum on the future of Oregon's environment

Cover of a Tom McCall
campaign booklet. (McCall
Collection, OHS; OrHi 90804)

and made "livability" his campaign theme, promising to protect Oregon's air, water and land as a condition of economic growth. "Progress to me is measured in terms of progress for the people of Oregon," he said in a typical speech, "in terms of the land young people will inherit. It is closely allied to maintaining the livability of our state, a livability we must preserve and enhance. It is our duty to keep the scenery unblighted, the air fresh and unsullied, the water pure and sparkling."

Straub followed the same theme, and the press gave up looking for differences between them. "He and I had the 'Tom and Bob Show'," McCall said. "That's what [the press] called our campaign, because we agreed on so much."

Blurred distinctions only hurt Straub's campaign. Struggling to distinguish himself from McCall, Straub posed for pictures at the Willamette's coughing sewer outfalls and pulled fish carcasses out of the river for television cameras. He even hired chemists to take water samples of the seven main tributaries of the Willamette to dramatize the pollution. No surprise in the results: the waters were still polluted far beyond state standards.

Whenever Straub did try to distinguish himself, McCall diluted the effort by agreeing with him. "McCall and Straub, despite their competition, were often two men with the same mind," Straub aide Ken Johnson said. "That never worked to Straub's advantage, because Tom was always much better known and often more charismatic. . . . It was very difficult for us to try to carve out any niche in which Bob could disagree with [McCall]. Over and over again, Bob would come up with things and Tom would say, 'Yeah, I agree with that'."

McCall agreed most effectively in July, when Straub proposed a novel idea for the Willamette: a state-owned greenway running entirely along the Willamette's banks. When the press picked up on the idea, McCall endorsed it. "It totally diffused the issue," Straub recalled. "He had the ability to use the glittery words. And after he endorsed [the greenway], it became his idea after awhile."

As always, McCall's campaign staff knew that the greatest threat to victory was McCall's own nerves. Ed Westerdahl, who had kept McCall disciplined during the 1964 secretary of state race, had stayed out of the governor's race. His presence was missed. McCall was unfocused, rattled and nervous. Straub often outperformed him in joint appearances. During a key debate with Straub at the Portland City Club, the usually eloquent McCall stumbled and flubbed. When Straub glowed over his strong showing, McCall feared Straub would challenge him to another debate. In a panic, McCall grabbed a phone and called KGW-TV to announce he was making the challenge and wanted the station to carry the debate.

Given McCall's shaky nerves, a televised debate as the campaign closed promised disaster. When Ron Schmidt heard of McCall's rash action, he resurrected a 1964 campaign trick: he sent Tom McCall into hiding.

Schmidt convinced Westerdahl to return to the campaign for one last service. They reserved a room in Portland's Imperial Hotel, and there McCall waited out the campaign, with Westerdahl standing guard. "It was just the two of us," Westerdahl said. "No one came in and no one

Governor-elect Tom McCall
celebrates his 1966 victory
over Robert Straub. (David
Kennerly *Oregonian* photo;
OrHi 90692)

left." As McCall remembered it, "They had me chained to a bed for the rest of the campaign." Westerdahl and McCall peacefully ate meals from room service, played gin rummy and watched movies on television.

Meanwhile, Straub and KGW-TV officials searched for McCall in vain. "We were ready to air the debate, but we couldn't find McCall after that," said Forest Amsden, who had taken over as KGW-TV news analyst and was the person McCall had contacted about the debate. "They had hustled Tom clear out of sight."

ON 9 NOVEMBER 1966, a Wednesday, Bill Anderson, the former mayor and clothing store owner in Moscow, Idaho, read in the local newspaper that Oregonians had elected Tom McCall their governor with fifty-five percent of the vote. Anderson recalled McCall's raw political ambition from twenty-four years earlier, but he could hardly believe that the lanky, debt-ridden sports reporter he had known in Idaho was now Oregon's top elected official.

About a week later, Anderson received a letter from McCall. "I still remember the note," Anderson said. "Tom had bought a $100 suit from me when he left town all those years earlier. He had been paying it off in little bits, but I hadn't heard from him for years and had long ago written off the bill as a bad debt. So inside the letter from Tom was a check for the exact amount he still owed on the suit. And there was also note from Tom that said, 'Well, I'm finally in a position to pay off that bill'."

PART THREE

Heroes are not giant statues framed against a red sky.
They are people who say:
This is my community,
and it's my responsibility
to make it better.

Tom McCall

9

The Politics of Sand

THE OREGON THAT TOM MCCALL INIIERITED in January 1967, at
first glance looked vastly different than the one his parents had
discovered sixty years earlier, or that the Movers had yearned
for fifty years before that. The state now had freeways, airports, television—all the features of modern life. Yet Oregon was fundamentally
the same as it had been a century before: a state that survived off the
riches of its land, a land that continued to lure seekers of Eden.

Gushing rivers, harnessed by dams, still produced cheap hydroelectric power, giving manufacturing businesses low-priced electricity and
an economic advantage over the rest of the country. The state's beauty
drew thousands of tourists each year who poured millions of dollars
into the state economy. Farming and ranching combined, though,
ranked as the state's second biggest industry. In 1967, one-third of Oregon was still in farms producing wheat, potatoes, pears, filberts, cherries
and grass seed.

The titan of the Oregon economy remained timber. The year McCall
won the governorship, Oregon produced 8.2 billion board feet of lumber—a board foot being equal to a piece of lumber one foot square and
one inch thick—only slightly below the 9 billion-plus board foot record
cut during the 1950s. Oregon remained the nation's top producer of
lumber—one of every ten jobs in Oregon was linked directly to the timber industry. Timber gave stability to towns such as Roseburg, Molalla,

179

Willamina and Sweet Home, and to loggers, truck drivers, mill workers and longshoremen, who loaded the lumber onto ships.

However, the industry was routinely rocked by every quiver in interest rates. Rising interest rates meant fewer new homes, and a drop in lumber demand. Like the end of a whip, Oregon felt the magnified snap whenever the economy moved up or down. Oregon politicians could do little to control the gyrations; the industry learned to live with boom and bust times, confident that the next boom always waited, like the fresh Cascade rains building over a distant ridge.

Oregon's stable economy, supported by the timber industry, created an air of comfortable insulation for the whole state. All but two percent of Oregonians were white, and their incomes kept pace with the nation's while the cost of living stayed low. Its cities, still relatively new compared to those in the East, lacked blight and urban decay, and the strife that often followed. Cities elsewhere—Los Angeles, Newark, Detroit— were torn by riots and violence; Oregon remained serenely immune to such trouble. Historian Arthur Schlesinger, Jr., summed up the Oregon of that era: "A pleasant, homogeneous self-contained state filled with pleasant, homogeneous self-contained people, overwhelmingly white Protestant and middle class. Even the working class was middle class, with boats on the lakes and weekend cabins in the mountains." Oregon remained what it had been a century earlier: a land to desire. People moved to the state in droves.

McCall saw the droves as the greatest threat to his state's livability. When he took office, Oregon had two million residents—twice what the population had been when he worked as an aide to Governor Douglas McKay only fifteen years earlier. The growth was due to the World War II boom that had brought tens of thousands of people to the Portland shipyards, and the post-war economic boom in the lumber industry. The population growth strained state and local governments' ability to keep up. McCall saw that Oregon was unprepared for the onslaught, and that rapid growth threatened the very qualities that had brought so many people to Oregon in the first place.

McCall took the oath of office on 9 January 1967, at the age of fifty-three, "in the proudest hour of my life." In his inaugural speech, McCall expressed his gratitude to the Oregonians who had elected him, and then

Tom McCall takes the oath as Oregon's thirtieth governor, 9 January 1967. (Verne Lewis photo; OrHi 90708)

laid out a legislative blueprint for education, jobs, tax reform and, most of all, the environment. McCall emphasized that everything else important to Oregon depended on protecting the state.

> Health, economic strength, recreation—in fact, the entire outlook and image of the state—are tied inseparably to environment. Water, air, land and scenic pollution threaten these and other values in Oregon. . . .
> The overriding challenge—the umbrella issue—of the campaign and the decade is quality—quality of life in Oregon.

As McCall left the podium a band struck up one of his favorite songs, "Battle Hymn of the Republic." He headed for the office vacated by outgoing governor Mark Hatfield, who had been elected to the United States Senate. Hatfield had ensured McCall did not have an easy transition. When McCall arrived in his new office, he discovered that Hatfield's staff had stripped all the files clean, and had even gone so far as to rip the labels off the files.

McCall hired as his top aides the two men he had learned to trust most: Ed Westerdahl, named the new chief of staff; and Ron Schmidt, the press spokesman. The three of them promptly turned their attention to the beleaguered Oregon State Sanitary Authority.

After years of operation without much attention from the governor, authority board members suddenly found McCall looming over every action they took. "No governor before Tom ever cared much what we did," said Barney McPhillips, who had served on the authority under six previous governors. "Tom was the only one to take an interest in what we were doing and push us. The only thing Tom didn't understand was that these things took time. He wanted action immediately."

The authority had already ordered the Willamette Valley's seven pulp mills to cut back on waste dumping by 1968. McCall wanted faster action, especially when, in February 1967, the United States Water Control and Pollution Authority released the first comprehensive study of the Willamette in decades. The results proved harsh. While noting modest progress in improving the quality of the river, the report explicitly charged the pulp mills with polluting the river and cited the authority for its failure to act sooner.

To underscore his commitment to the environment, McCall used his skills as a newsman to make news. Oregon governors had rarely appeared before legislative committees in public. McCall changed that tradition when, in March, he testified before a packed hearing of the State Senate Air and Water Quality Committee. McCall's appearance before the committee—and the emphasis he placed on anti-pollution bills before the panel—ensured that lawmakers would not ignore the legislation, which included money for new sewer systems, tax credits for businesses that installed anti-pollution equipment, and new powers for the Sanitary Authority. McCall insisted the legislature help him "draw a line" against pollution. From now on, he said, "Oregon has propounded—and enforces to the hilt—an 11th commandment: Thou shall not pollute."

His testimony increased the pressure on lawmakers to act, but he wanted more pressure on the Sanitary Authority itself. Privately, he thought it might be time for the authority's long-time chairman to go. For twenty-eight years, the authority had been chaired by Harold Wendel, seventy-four-year-old president of Lipman Wolfe & Co., one of Portland's largest department stores. Wendel had been one of the earliest civic leaders to demand the river be cleaned up, and as chairman, the colorless Wendel had gently nudged the authority forward. While he admired Wendel's dedication, McCall wanted to give the authority a more dynamic leader. Westerdahl encouraged McCall to fire Wendel, or at least ask for his resignation. McCall agreed with Westerdahl, but could not bring himself to fire someone so devoted to state service.

Then, on 17 April, a few days after McCall and Westerdahl's conversation, Harold Wendel died of a heart attack. McCall swallowed hard over the decision he had nearly made. If he had fired Wendel, he said, "[Wendel] would have dropped dead anyway, and we would have been blamed for being insensitive, inconsiderate and ungrateful to the point that we had caused his death." McCall quickly issued a heartfelt statement: "[Wendel's] departure leaves a void in my administration it would be impossible to fill."

McCall, however, soon found a person to fill that void, a person willing to demand action from the Sanitary Authority and attract plenty of attention: he named himself.

On 25 April, McCall called the members of the authority into his office, announced he was appointing himself to the board and said he expected to be elected chairman. The authority's board members did what was expected of them and handed McCall the gavel.

No Oregon governor had ever appointed himself to a regulatory board, let alone taken control of one. The event underscored McCall's boldness; Oregonians now saw him leading and running the clean-up of the Willamette.

Before he could prove himself with the Sanitary Authority, though, McCall had the chance to protect Oregon's livability in an even more dramatic way. For along the Oregon coast, in the small oceanfront town of Cannon Beach, a motel owner had quietly altered the political agenda of Oregon. He did so by putting up a fence on the beach.

IN THEIR STATE OF EXPANSIVE NATURAL BEAUTY in its mountains, rivers and deserts, Oregonians considered their beaches sacred, and for good reason. Unlike states such as California, where private ownership had carved up beaches, and New Jersey, where ramshackle boardwalks had scarred the shores, the Oregon Coast had remained public and unfettered.

The tradition of publicly owned beaches had existed almost from the start of statehood. It had become scripture in 1913, when Democratic governor Oswald West, fearing exploitation of Oregon's dramatic 320-mile-long coastline, came up with an idea to protect it.

Born in Canada, West moved to Oregon at age four. As a Salem bank teller, West watched legislators deposit into their accounts mounds of cash they had collected as bribes. West became a state land agent in 1902 and was part of investigations into land schemes and timber thefts that returned to public ownership nine hundred thousand acres fraudulently acquired by private interests. Years later, in 1910, West stood on a Portland sidewalk and watched Republicans—many of whom had deposited bribes in his bank—march in a political parade. The next day, the disgusted West filed as a candidate for governor.

West had dim political prospects at first. "He found himself," wrote one historian, "at 37 without money or influential friends, with no political machine and a Democrat in an overwhelmingly Republican state." Undaunted, West began a lonely campaign across Oregon. He worked the small communities typically ignored by politicians, shaking hands and giving brief, informal speeches from the bumper of his car. He slowly built an organization from the county land agents he knew, and wrote fifteen thousand personal letters to Democrats asking for their help. West campaigned on a prohibitionist platform and promised four years of clean government beyond the influence of greedy corporations. Still burning with the populist fever, Oregonians embraced West and elected him over the incumbent, Republican Jay Bowerman.

To save the state money, Governor West rode horseback, sometimes for hundreds of miles, to attend meetings. He ordered tighter regulations on banks and railroads, and improvements in workers' compensation laws. When the Republican-controlled legislature tried to halt his reforms, West vetoed a record sixty-three bills. Meanwhile, he ap-

Governor Oswald West (1911-15). Pictured on a 1910 campaign flier, West was the first governor to protect public access to Oregon beaches. (OrHi 6425)

OSWALD WEST
"THE MAN WHO DELIVERS THE GOODS"

pointed a special commission to investigate Portland's rampant gambling, bootlegging and prostitution. To West's delight, the commission found that Portland's most respected Republican families owned the buildings that hosted the vice operations.

His experience as a land-fraud investigator told him that the state's base of natural resources remained vulnerable; he worried most about land speculation along the Oregon coast. From the Columbia River south to the California border, rugged cliffs and mountains loomed over long sandy stretches of beach. Unlike Washington state's coast, dominated by impassable bluffs and rocky shores, Oregon's coast was accessible. And unlike the coast in California, no one had fenced off the Oregon beach for private development—yet.

West wanted the state to take control of the beaches to protect them, but he realized that doing so openly would alarm the legislature; he also worried the public might start a buying spree of coastal land before the state locked it up.

So West moved with stealth and deception. As he recounted his scheme later:

> I came up with a bright idea. And this was very much a sur-
> prise for I have enjoyed but few of such in a lifetime. I
> drafted a simple short bill declaring the seashore from the
> Washington line to the California line a public highway. I
> pointed out that thus we would come into miles and miles of
> highway without cost to the taxpayer.

West's sixty-six-word bill was a masterstroke. He knew the High-way Commission—even then a power in Oregon—yearned to control more land and would support the plan. He also knew that, once control-ling the coastline, the commission would never surrender an inch. Said West, "The legislature and the public took the bait—hook, line and sinker."

The beaches fell into public hands—and would stay there. Over time, the pretense that the coastline should actually be a highway was forgot-ten, and the concept of public ownership and protection flourished. In 1947, the legislature changed the designation of the sands from "high-way" to "recreation area."

West had not simply prevented development of the shoreline, he had made the Oregon coast sacrosanct—or so almost everyone thought for the next fifty-four years. West's bill, however, contained an undetected flaw: it declared that public ownership extended over the shore from low tide to high tide. In other words, the public owned the so-called "wet sands." Few people thought the distinction noteworthy. Legally, however, the dry sands were up for grabs.

The coast became a crazy quilt of ownership. In some areas, the state or counties bought entire beaches—wet sands, dry sands and the grass-lands that rimmed the coast—for parks; in other areas, private owners assumed control of beach-front land adjacent to their property. By 1967, 112 miles of dry sands on the coast had been taken over by private own-ers, but the state and the public considered the beach—all of it—as be-longing to everyone.

In 1966, however, one man thought differently.

William Hay was a Portland real estate broker who counted among his investments the Surfsand Motel at Cannon Beach, a sleepy village on the northern Oregon coast that offered one of the closest beach accesses to Portlanders. The Surfsand was a low-slung building perched on a seawall adjacent to a busy beach access. Hay decided he wanted his motel to have a special attraction no other motel in Oregon offered: he wanted a private beach. So he put up a fence in the sands.

When Cannon Beach visitors walked down the public access road and turned right onto the beach, they met Hay's fence and a blunt sign: "Surfsand Guests Only." The fence ran from the seawall out to the high-tide line. Then it ran for about two hundred feet north and south, parallelling the seawall under Hay's motel and the shoreline. At high tide, Hay's fence—reaching with technical precision to the end of the dry sands—blocked the path of people wanting to walk north and south. In August 1966, a Highway Department investigator examined Hay's fence and found that Hay had erected tables and cabanas for his guests. When he went to examine the area more closely, a motel employee ordered him out of Hay's "private beach."

Highway Department attorneys scoured the law and discovered the loophole in Oswald West's bill. The state could not order Hay's fence down, because, simply, the state did not own the dry sands as everyone had assumed it did. So the state Highway Department proposed fixing the problem in the 1967 legislature with a bill that gave the state ownership of all the beach, from the wet sands to the vegetation line above the dry sands.

The measure, House Bill 1601, looked like a dull technical change in the law and arrived in the legislature without fanfare. However, opponents to the measure soon came running to house Republicans. Majority Leader Robert Smith, a member of the House Highway Committee, where the bill got its first hearings, saw the bill as an infringement on private property, giving the state the right to take away property from its legal owners without compensation. In a more personal sense, the bill threatened lawmakers' friends; for example, the former chairman of the Oregon Republican party, Peter Gunnar, who already had plans to build a 120-unit condominium project, the Inn at Spanish Head, at Lincoln City. As designed, the condominium would sit against a cliffside with its foundation sunk into the dry sands. If HB 1601 passed, the project was in peril.

Nonetheless, the Highway Committee chairman, Republican Sidney Bazzett of Grants Pass, wanted the bill and tried to send it to the house floor. But when Bazzett tried to make technical changes in the bill, Smith used his influence to help pass an amendment that actually took away the right of public access in some cases. Bazzett found the amended bill lacked enough votes to either move it to the house floor or kill it outright, so the measure hung in limbo.

Few Oregonians followed the action on the bill until one reporter in the Capitol press corps, the Associated Press's Matt Kramer, began highlighting it, referring to it as the "Beach Bill." Kramer crafted each story so that readers understood what was at stake. When the committee stalled again on releasing the bill, Kramer opened his story, "Beach goers joined the battle for the Oregon beaches Tuesday—and lost."

As Kramer wrote about the bill, McCall, already watching the Highway Committee deadlock with dismay, grew more agitated. Fifty-four years after Oswald West, the Oregon coast again stood open for private development, victim of a Republican blockade.

So McCall tore down the blockade.

After Bazzett tried again unsuccessfully, on 2 May, to free the Beach Bill from his committee, McCall dashed off a letter ostensibly to Bazzett but aimed at house leadership. "We cannot afford," McCall wrote, "to ignore our responsibilities to the public of this state for protecting the dry sands from the encroachment of crass commercialism."

Both men knew the letter was really intended for the public, and McCall promptly leaked it to reporters. The next day, the front pages of daily newspapers across Oregon boomed McCall's rage: "McCall Backs Continued Public Use for the Beach," declared the *Oregon Statesman* in Salem. Added the *Oregonian*, albeit inaccurately: "McCall Slaps GOP's Tabling of Beach Bill."

The page one blasts marked the first time many Oregonians had heard of the Beach Bill or the threat to public ownership of the coastline. And McCall got the result he wanted. "When Tom did that, holy cow, the lid blew off," House Speaker F.F. "Monte" Montgomery recalled.

Overnight, Capitol telephone lines jammed and offices filled with angry letters. House Republicans, once defiant over the Beach Bill, ran for cover. Montgomery stormed up to McCall's office, outraged that McCall had gone to the press before asking him about the bill.

"Do you really want this bill?" Montgomery asked McCall.

"Of course I do," McCall replied. "If you don't give me this bill I will go straight to the press and the people."

Montgomery shivered. "I thought I understood McCall's popularity when I declined to run for governor," Montgomery said later. "I learned then that his power over the press and the public ran deeper than I thought."

McCall's blast brought the Beach Bill to the attention of the rest of the Oregon press. Within days, reporters turned the measure into a crusade. On 9 May, McCall's former employer, KGW-TV, broadcast an emotional editorial calling for Oregonians to contact their lawmakers about the Beach Bill. Public response to that single editorial deluged legislators with tens of thousands of letters and phone calls. Bazzett said his committee counted forty thousand responses in all.

At first house Republicans ignored McCall's threats, but as the public pressure instigated by McCall grew more intense, proposals and protests about the Beach Bill gushed from almost every legislative office. "Every politician rode off wildly in every direction," McCall said later, "each determined that he would be the 'new Os West'."

Smith and the other Republicans blocking the Beach Bill panicked and immediately called for a new hearing on the measure to save face. The original bill proposed that the line of vegetation along the dry sands serve as a legal boundary, but everyone recognized that was an inaccurate and unreliable line. So house Republicans proposed that the state establish a survey line of seven feet above sea level as the boundary line of public ownership. McCall spotted the proposal as bogus; the Republicans' bill actually surrendered much of the state's claim, placing the boundary line closer to the ocean than the current law did.

Smith and his allies tried to force Bazzett into a hearing to vote on the plan, but the chairman ignored them. Bazzett wanted a rejuvenated measure that truly protected the coastline. And he could now wait and let Smith and the other Republicans squirm, because he knew Tom McCall had a plan.

THE MORNING OF 13 MAY broke bright and clear on the Oregon coast. Beachcombers near Seaside walked along the shore, accompanied only by the sounds of gulls and waves.

Suddenly, the air snapped as two helicopters rose over the mountains with the sun. The helicopters set down on the beach, the wind from their blades whipping the dry sands into a storm.

Tom McCall jumped out of the first, followed by scientists, surveyors and reporters. He marched up the beach, giving orders. Within minutes, the surveyors pounded stakes between the dry sands and the water.

"The politicians and the lawyers have got this beach situation all fouled up," McCall told the reporters. "Now the scientists are here to straighten it out." He explained that his aide for environmental issues, Kessler Cannon, had learned from oceanographers at Oregon State University that a sixteen-foot elevation line—not the seven-foot line proposed by Republicans—best defined the entire beach. Surveyors went to work marking lines and pounding stakes into the sand.

McCall stood by, wearing sunglasses, a dark suit jacket and a dark shirt buttoned to the neck. When the stakes were in, McCall walked to the stake highest on the beach. This stake, he said, marks where the public ownership should start. Then he marched to the second stake at the edge of the dry sand. "This is where the state's ownership now ends," he said. Then he took several long strides toward the ocean to a spot near the waves. This, he said, is where the Republicans want the line.

The scene captured all of McCall's flamboyance and anger. With McCall's inspiration, Ron Schmidt had staged the event carefully— adding the helicopters for the drama—to extract the biggest possible play in the press. The cameras missed none of it.

The group flew on and repeated the surveying down the coast. In Cannon Beach, McCall ordered the helicopters to land next to William Hay's motel. McCall stomped toward the "private beach" now blocked off with a log barrier. The motel guests sitting inside the closed-off area looked up to see the governor of Oregon peering down at them, muttering in anger. "He wasn't talking to anyone in particular, he was just mad as hell," said Don Jepsen, a United Press International reporter at the scene. "He was just talking to himself, swearing like hell at Hay and the people inside this area."

The next day, Sunday, Oregonians awoke to newspaper photographs of McCall standing on the beach and literally drawing the line of public ownership in the sand. As McCall suspected, it was a powerful image that lawmakers could not withstand. He arrived back in Salem on Monday with his plan for the sixteen-foot elevation boundary. Although scientists surveying the beach Saturday had determined the correct elevation was 13.7 feet, he insisted on the higher boundary.

McCall, however, had not solved a key problem: Did the state have the right to take land away from private owners?

Many beach-front land owners had never planned to develop their land, yet they had held the title and had paid property taxes on it for years. A land grab by the state could cost millions of dollars in compensation to the owners. House Republicans declared they would not allow a bill that took the land away.

Two lawmakers saw a solution: Lee Johnson, a Republican from Portland, and James Redden, a Medford Democrat and house minority leader, both lawyers and astute legislative tacticians. Johnson and Redden realized that the state did not need to own the beach; it just had to control it. The very day that McCall was staking off the sands, Redden and Johnson rewrote the Beach Bill to give the state the power to zone any beach it did not own, and to outlaw any development or construction not allowed by the state Highway Commission.

Faced with the Redden-Johnson proposal and McCall's attention-grabbing stunt, Republicans caved in. Bazzett sent the strengthened Beach Bill to the full house, which approved it fifty-seven to three. The no votes came from coastal lawmakers, who opposed the bill at all costs. After learning from the house Republicans' painful lessons, the state senate sped the bill to McCall, who signed it into law on 6 July 1967.

The Beach Bill has stood for decades as a landmark of conservation and typified the McCall doctrine: Preservation over development, aesthetics over commercialism.

The bill was also McCall's first political victory, one that revealed the style that would characterize his career. He understood the deep desire Oregonians had to protect their state, especially its coast. When faced with opposition, McCall had appealed directly to Oregonians, using his keen publicity sense. In a single stroke, he had moved the

Beach Bill from nowhere to page one, and in doing so snatched credit for the results.

McCall relished the success and, at the bill's signing, quoted Oswald West on the protection of Oregon's beaches: "No local selfish interest should be permitted, through politics or otherwise, to destroy or even impair this great birthright of our people."

His victory may well have remained unsullied, but for a forgotten political deal. For on 7 July 1967, the day after McCall signed the Beach Bill into law, Glenn Jackson began to carry out his plans to pave the Nestucca Spit.

TRUE TO HIS NATURE, Glenn Jackson never surfaced publicly during the Beach Bill debate, but lawmakers felt his presence and his pressure for passage of the bill. When Bill Holstrum, a coastal Republican on the House Highway Committee, balked at voting for the measure, Jackson called him, subtly mentioning all the proposed highway projects Holstrum wanted for his district. Holstrum changed his mind and voted for

McCall knocked down barriers to the passage of the Beach Bill in 1967 by increasing public pressure on lawmakers. Arriving by helicopter on 14 May, he performed his own surveys of the beach at Rockaway to demonstrate how public access was at stake (above and right). (*Oregonian* photos; OrHi 52629 and 66579) McCall (opposite) also glared at the Surfsand Motel at Cannon Beach. The motel owner had blocked off the beach in front of his property —and in turn sparked the new "Beach Bill" debate. The log barrier shown here had temporarily replaced a fence. (*Oregonian* photo; OrHi 52610)

the measure. When another lawmaker asked him why he had switched, Holstrum grumbled, "Glenn explained it to me." Jackson also worked another lever: after McCall signed the Beach Bill, the Highway Commission, with Jackson at the gavel, approved construction of the Inn at Spanish Head, the first development allowed on the newly protected beach.

Jackson wanted the Beach Bill for all the right reasons: to protect the coastline from development. But he also planned to use that bill as a tool to pave the beaches, or at least pave right up to their sandy edges.

In 1966, opponents to the Nestucca Highway had argued that Jackson wanted to put the highway on the beach, a claim most damaging to the proposed road. Now, however, Jackson and the state could argue that the highway would not be on the beach—not technically, according to the new Beach Bill. The highway project, in fact, would sit just above the sixteen-foot survey boundary and run alongside the beach. This would do nothing to protect the spit or to maintain wildness of the area.

On 7 July, Jackson called the Highway Commission together at Pacific City to reaffirm the routing of the proposed Nestucca road. The action surprised McCall. State Treasurer Robert Straub went wild at the news and pleaded privately with Jackson to stop the road. Jackson told Straub that if he could show that the public opposed the highway, he would stop it.

Jackson may have doubted that Straub could generate any public outcry. After all, Straub had already tried to exploit the issue during the gubernatorial campaign and failed. But one year earlier, Oregonians had had no frame of reference within which to consider the proposed road. The Beach Bill debate had not yet filled the front pages of newspapers across Oregon. The governor had not yet drawn lines in the sand.

Straub launched a loud barrage against the highway in July 1967. Coming so soon after the Beach Bill fight, the press and the public took notice. Reporters turned the highway issue into another crusade, while a few enterprising journalists dug through Highway Department files and found that Jackson's agency planned to build similar beachfront highways on other undeveloped stretches of Oregon's coast. The editorial pages that had once mocked Straub for exploiting the Nestucca debate suddenly praised his courage.

Straub demanded Jackson hold another hearing on Nestucca. When Jackson refused, Straub called his own meeting, the audience packed with highway opponents. McCall sent Kessler Cannon, his aide for environmental issues, to speak for the highway, but Cannon could hardly be heard through the jeers.

McCall watched the debate with discomfort and dismay. He called opponents of the highway "Oregon's noisiest minority," and said they had "made a mountain out of a sand dune." But by now he realized he was on the wrong side of the Nestucca issue. He had impetuously agreed to back the project to win Jackson's support in the campaign; now he knew that Jackson had not divulged to him the entire scope of the project. Publicly, he stood steadfast, out of pride. But privately he confessed his error, as he did when Medford *Mail-Tribune* editor Eric Allen, a Jackson ally, wrote an editorial blasting Straub. McCall wrote Allen a letter agreeing that Straub needed a scolding for his tactics. Nonetheless, he wrote, "In the main [Straub] is pretty much on course."

McCall's staff implored the governor to change course or face political disaster. "Tom was the environmentalists' golden boy," Ron Schmidt recalled. "And they were saying, 'He's advocating paving the beaches.' All of a sudden, we woke up." Ed Westerdahl remembered it more bluntly: "We were getting creamed on this issue." Schmidt and Westerdahl appealed to Jackson for compromise, but the Highway Comission chairman would not budge, leaving full retreat as McCall's only route.

Straub did not give McCall the chance to retreat. He had discovered the fatal flaw in the Nestucca Highway plan, the secret that Jackson had kept from McCall and the public, that the Highway Department wanted to pave land it had promised would remain natural and wild.

When state officials had taken control of the Nestucca Spit from the Bureau of Land Management (BLM), they had agreed in signed land patents that the land would be used for park uses only. Now, the Highway Department was working feverishly to break those land patents and force the highway through. Highway Department officials had already appealed to the BLM and the United States secretary of the interior, who oversaw the agency, to allow construction.

Straub not only had support at home in Oregon but, in 1967, with a Democratic administration in the White House, Straub had partisan sympathies on his side. Secretary of the Interior Stewart Udall was a respected conservationist; he agreed to meet with Straub in Washington, D.C., to discuss the issue. During their 15 August meeting, Udall told Straub that he did not know why such a small issue required cabinet-level attention. Straub handed Udall color photographs Straub had taken the previous year of his wife and daughter walking along the spit's wild, grassy dunes. "Mr. Secretary," Straub said, jabbing his finger at the photographs, "this is where they want to put their highway. And you have the power to stop them."

Impressed by Straub's passion, Udall personally intervened and rejected the highway plan. In doing so, Udall scolded McCall in a letter that the Department of the Interior rushed to make public.

"Quite frankly, it is my opinion your aides have given you bum advice on this question," Udall wrote. "The old argument by highway engineers that it is 'cheaper' to route a road through a beach or a public park was always outrageous from a conservation standpoint. . . . If the new route costs a little more, so what? In our time a wise resource use demands that we always search for the best solution for the long run—and never settle simply for the cheapest solution."

Oregon newspapers reprinted the letter, and McCall winced at the public lashing. What made the letter more painful was its irony. The tone and message of the letter could just have well come from McCall himself; but he now looked like one of the developers he had been so fond of denouncing.

However, Udall's rejection of the project gave McCall an escape from the issue, and he took it. "As far as I'm concerned," he said, "this closes the Nestucca Sandspit issue." Later, in an aside to a reporter, he added, "If I ever catch a highway engineer looking even cross-eyed at a sandspit, there will be the devil to pay." McCall replied defensively in a letter to Udall: "We in Oregon are not beauty wreckers. In sum, though, the state of Oregon will bow to your will."

Glenn Jackson, however, bowed to no one. While McCall declared the Nestucca Highway a dead issue, Jackson's engineers drew up a new plan: a rerouting that would dodge the forbidden BLM land by only a few feet. The highway would no longer line the beach, but instead would eviscerate the spit's grasslands.

Jackson leaked the plans to the press on 20 September without warning McCall about his new strategy. The next day, Straub held a press conference in the Portland Hilton to protest the new plan. Unaware that Straub was in the hotel, McCall, by coincidence, showed up there for another meeting. The two nearly collided in the hallway as they were leaving the building. With reporters looking on, Straub opened a fierce debate in the hotel lobby over the highway plan. McCall and Straub— six-foot-five and six-foot-two respectively—squared off. As they shouted face to face, their aides watched stunned.

"You said there would be no highway on the Nestucca—the issue is dead," Straub said to McCall.

"I said," McCall replied, "if any highway engineer ever looks cross-eyed at another sandspit. . . ." His voice sputtered to a halt. He caught his breath and declared, "I oppose highways on the beaches," he declared.

"Then why did the commission [propose] the sandspit route?" Straub asked.

"Because the route was not eliminated in a democratic way," McCall blurted out, referring to the fact that Udall, not Oregon voters, had vetoed the plan.

"You eliminated it, according to the papers," Straub said.

Straub insisted there be another hearing. McCall suggested they hold a hearing halfway between the coast and Portland. Straub stopped for a moment, realizing the halfway point was in the center of mountains and forest, miles from any sizable town.

"For Christ's sake," Straub said, laughing, "That's in the middle of nowhere."

"Yeah," McCall said as he quickly walked away. "Exactly."

The state of Oregon never built the Nestucca Highway. After his confrontation with Straub, McCall ordered Jackson to cancel the idea entirely. As Westerdahl put it, "We had to remind Glenn Jackson who was in the governor's office."

McCall learned to be more wary of Jackson, and never again made a decision regarding environmental issues as capriciously. But the Nestucca debate unraveled much of the goodwill McCall had built in his first nine months. In July, the Beach Bill made him a hero. By September, Nestucca had made him appear a hypocrite, even though over time

the lasting influence of the Beach Bill itself overshadowed the soon-
forgotten highway project.

Twenty years later, the state established a wildlands park on the spit
and named it for Bob Straub. McCall's only consolation over the Nestucca Spit was that the state never built a highway that might well have
been named for him.

OBSCURED AMID THE UPROAR of the beaches debate, the state's Sanitary
Authority quietly moved forward with the environmental policies Mc-
Call had promised. The immediate outcome of these fit his ideals, but as
with the Nestucca issue, the public image of his work took a beating.

After naming himself to the authority, McCall oversaw approval of
tougher air and water regulations on industry. He had originally intended to keep his post until November 1967. He had found the authority's work too tedious and detail-driven for his tastes, however. He resigned after ten weeks, naming his budget director, lawyer and former
Republican legislator John Mosser, as his replacement. His resignation
allowed him to sidestep a looming fight over construction of yet another pulp mill on the Willamette.

McCall had shown he was willing to say "no" to industry that worsened Oregon's environment, but he was also willing to say "yes" to
companies able to live up to the new anti-pollution standards.

In April, the American Can Co., a New York-based maker of paper
containers, had announced plans for the pulp mill, promising four hundred new jobs and a $4-million payroll for the small town of Halsey, on
the Willamette eighty miles south of Portland. Although pulp mills had
for years been the Willamette's worst polluters, American Can proposed
an efficient waste system that would dramatically cut the effluent going
into the Willamette. The new pollution regulations approved by Mc-
Call would start the following year; the American Can plant would be
the only pulp mill capable of meeting the standards. "There will be a
pinch of stink, that's true," McCall admitted, then added, "I'm hopeful
this will be a showpiece kind of plant, one which will inspire others in
the state by its efficiency."

As Mosser recalled, McCall had assured him that the Sanitary Authority faced no looming problems when he appointed Mosser chair-

man. Mosser soon realized, however, that McCall had left him with an enormous dilemma. "As soon as I became chairman," Mosser said, "there was American Can." Given McCall's loud commitment to a cleaner Willamette, the specter of a new polluting giant sparked widespread public opposition. With the existing seven pulp mills' sorry environmental history, the burden of proof was on American Can.

Few opponents believed the company's promises about the proposed plant's anti-pollution devices, and the opposition grew more emotional as time wore on. Mosser found he could hardly hold a hearing without opponents shouting down the plant's supporters. During a hearing in Eugene, eighteen miles from the plant site, one opponent broke open a vial of percaptin, the chemical that produced the pulp mills' rotten-egg odor, filling the room with the familiar pulp mill stench.

The more the press wrote about the American Can mill, the more public opinion turned against it. In September, Mosser polled the Sanitary Authority's members: two members opposed the mill, and two favored it.

Mosser did not know how he would vote—nor did he know how McCall wanted him to vote. So he telephoned the governor and asked him what he should do.

"Why do you need to know how I think you should vote?" McCall asked.

"I thought you would want to make the decision on this matter," Mosser said.

"Goddamn it," McCall replied, "that's why I put you in there."

Mosser voted for the plant. The authority's three-to-two vote created a new firestorm for McCall. Other state leaders, including long-time McCall allies, roundly attacked the decision, saying it fell short of the governor's promises for environmental standards. However, as McCall said in his memoirs, "Mosser's vote, for approval [of American Can], marked a new era of industrial development with pollution controls."

Over time the plant lived up to McCall's promises. Approval of the plant showed he was not one-sided in his environmental beliefs, as his critics later claimed. McCall's problem was that he did not make that case strongly at the time. Had he stood up publicly to explain his decision—or had he stayed on as authority chairman—he could have stared down the critics. Instead, his timidity in defending his policies made him look weak. That was not the case. On the same day the authority approved American Can, the panel ordered that two other pulp mills—one owned by Crown Zellerbach in West Linn and the other owned by Publishers Paper in Oregon City—shut down temporarily because of their poor pollution records. The press paid little attention to the shutdown orders, and McCall missed his chance to play them up.

McCall's reaction to the events in his first year in office illustrated his strengths and weaknesses. His sense of drama had saved the Beach Bill and made him a hero on the issue, but the Nestucca's marshy problems had soured much of the goodwill he had earned. His decision on the American Can issue and the Sanitary Authority's action against polluting mills, while strong on principle, were short on the flair McCall needed to dramatize his policies. Overall, his first year had been uneven and erratic. The frustrations he felt faded only when new troubles arose.

10

In a Wringer

OR ALL HIS STRUGGLES, McCall in his first year as governor remained popular with Oregonians. The state had had a succession
of stuffy and dull governors, and McCall could not help but be
different. He was articulate and forthright, impetuous and insecure,
childlike and profane. He never tried to reconcile his complexities. Most
of all, he never hid his humanity. "Understanding why McCall was as
loved as he was is not difficult," said Darrel Buttice, one of McCall's
aides. "He was a common man, and yet he was so uncommon."

For starters, McCall ended the imperial nature of the governor's office that Mark Hatfield had established. He ate regularly in the Capitol
coffee shop, and wandered the building like a tourist. Legislators who
could hardly remember seeing Hatfield in the Capitol halls soon discovered McCall was everywhere. He held a weekly open house and
spent hours talking with whomever walked into his office. When people
reverently called him Governor, he insisted they call him Tom. "It was
like someone opened the windows to the Capitol when McCall came
in," said Harold Hughes, a veteran political reporter for the *Oregonian*.
"It was like a fresh breeze blowing through the halls."

The open houses served a purpose other than portraying McCall as
accessible: they kept him in touch with people. McCall had feared the
governorship would insulate him from Oregonians. So he worked the
gatherings as if he were still a reporter, collecting as much information

as he could about the public mood. "That's the trouble with politicians," McCall said years later. "Politicians hardly ever get the truth. . . . The politician doesn't hear enough of it so he resents it. It's a strange sound to him."

He loved people and loved the attention. His staff found it difficult to manage his appearances, if only because McCall rarely turned down invitations. He lunged at any opportunity to mix with Oregonians. "Nobody was a stranger to him," said Doris Penwell. "They'd ask him to do something and he'd say, 'Oh sure, I'll definitely do it.' Then we would be inundated by those people. Even though we would decline invitations, he would read about the event and say, 'I ought to do this,' and just show up."

McCall was more than a political figure, he was a celebrity. He could not go anywhere in public without being swarmed by people. In restaurants, his food grew cold while he chatted with other patrons. When he shopped for gifts for Audrey, an aide often had to do the buying because McCall would be surrounded by customers. Observed Ron Schmidt, "He loved people and people loved him. He thrived on times like those."

Aside from a small state police escort, the McCalls had no domestic staff. Audrey did all the cooking and entertaining on the governor's $23,000-a-year salary. He could not understand politicians who surrounded themselves with pomp, especially his neighbor to the south, California governor Ronald Reagan. They both had entered office in January 1967, but Reagan was already eyeing the presidency; the national media was touting him as the contender to control the GOP's Goldwater wing. McCall had little respect for the former actor. He disliked Reagan's strident rhetoric, and bristled at any suggestion that the two shared a history because they had gained fame in the same way—through television. "In all my years as a broadcaster, I never smiled at anyone," McCall snorted. "You can't say I beguiled them."

A month after they took their respective offices, McCall invited Reagan north for a visit, and the California governor arrived with a fleet of aides and bodyguards. McCall knew that one of his secretaries, Wanda Merrill, admired Reagan. After introducing Reagan to her, McCall ushered the California governor into his private office. McCall soon reappeared, a mischievous grin on his face. "Tom snuck out to my desk and said, 'I just want you to know that as we speak, Governor Reagan is going to the bathroom.' Tom found it hilarious that Reagan would do anything human."

McCall tried to avoid being swept up in others' pomp and felt ill at ease when he could not avoid it. During a trip to Boston, his host, Massachusetts governor John Volpe, insisted on giving McCall a last-minute car tour of Boston. Meanwhile, McCall's flight—he had a coach seat on a commercial plane—was preparing to leave from Logan International Airport. When Volpe learned McCall was worried about making the flight, he had an aide call the airport and order the plane grounded until McCall arrived. McCall's car arrived on the tarmac, surrounded by an escort of howling police cars. "He just cringed and sank into his seat," said Schmidt, who was with McCall. "He hated that sort of thing."

McCall boarded the Oregon-bound plane, painfully embarrassed. Once airborne, he got up, walked down the plane's aisle and apologized to every passenger. Said Schmidt, "Tom couldn't relax until everyone on that plane knew he hadn't used his influence as governor to hold everyone else up."

He remained as fun-loving as he had always been, and he still loved to drink. He never drank during business hours, however, and rarely showed signs of drunkenness or hangover, no matter how much he had had the night before. Yet McCall religiously observed cocktail hour; his staff joked about how nervous McCall grew after five o'clock, his mind on the icy martinis waiting at home. When he frequented legislative parties, he preferred drinking with Democrats rather than with fellow Republicans.

He even planned official functions with good times in mind. The governor's house was a modest Tudor-style house on Winter Street, a few blocks from the Capitol. However, the place was so small that the McCalls had to hold large parties in shifts. So McCall planned the parties accordingly: the dull guests were invited for the early shift, the partygoers in the last shift. "When the last group came in," remembered one aide, "away went the cake and coffee and out came the bar cart."

Even with his fame and position, McCall longed for camaraderie, and his drinking was his vehicle of conviviality. Then-State Represen-

 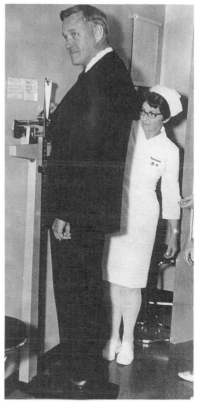

McCall relished his contact with Oregonians as the "people's governor," becoming one of the most visible state leaders in decades. McCall loved the public spotlight whether he was breaking ground for Portland's World Forestry Center (above left), being weighed at Mountain View Hospital in Madras (above right), serving ice cream to eager Keizer elementary schoolchildren (above opposite), or showing off his riding skills in a parade (lower opposite). (Bob Bacon *Oregon Journal* photo; OrHi 90689. OrHi 77955. *Statesman-Journal* photo; OrHi 90706. Gerry Lewin *Statesman-Journal* photo)

tative Jason Boe recalled sitting in a Salem lounge with his wife one evening when the bartender handed him the phone.

"You're in the legislature, aren't you?" the bartender asked. Boe said yes. "Well," the bartender replied, "This is for you."

Boe took the phone and heard McCall's unmistakable voice on the other end.

"Who's this?" McCall asked.

Boe identified himself, and McCall said, "Jason, old chum, mind if I join you?"

McCall arrived a few minutes later and spent the evening enthralling the Boes with his tales and humor. Only later did Boe wonder why the governor would call on him, a lawmaker he did not know that well. Boe realized that McCall had probably called several bars around Salem until he found someone—anyone—he could join for a drink. "He was just lonely," Boe concluded. "Most people in his job would just want to hide away. Tom needed constant companionship."

ALMOST EVERYONE IN SALEM found a reason to like McCall—except members of his own party.

Although Republicans ran the house, the GOP leadership had largely ignored McCall's wishes. McCall had made tax reform a top priority, for example, but Republicans had tossed his proposals directly into the trash can. Later, lawmakers had dragged themselves through a pointless three-week special session to discuss tax reform in the summer of 1967, and all McCall could do was look on as a helpless spectator, disregarded by GOP leaders.

Republicans disliked him in large part because he cared little for partisan politics. McCall had pledged to ignore party labels in filling government posts, and he did. However, that did not please everyone. Montgomery in particular resented that McCall had passed over him for promotion. Even though McCall had made no deal with him, House Speaker F.F. "Monte" Montgomery thought he should have been named as the replacement for secretary of state. Instead McCall named another liberal, his assistant, Clay Myers, to the job.

In the governor's office McCall surrounded himself with aides who could compensate for his faults. Ed Westerdahl, his chief of staff, kept

McCall on track, while press spokesman Ron Schmidt handled McCall's human side, serving as much as psychologist as public relations man.

However, even McCall's closest aides could not protect him from his own weaknesses, one of the greatest of which was indecision. Mc-Call found decision-making torturous, especially when his choices might hurt someone. Rather than looking at the big picture—as a sleek, efficient executive might—McCall agonized over the details, the family whose welfare check had been cut, or the prisoner who could not enter a rehabilitation program.

During his first term, for example, his aides discovered $19-million miscalculation in the state's welfare budget that could only be corrected by ordering cuts in services to recipients of state assistance. McCall ground his teeth and signed the order.

A few days later, McCall rushed into a staff meeting and demanded his budget order be rescinded. He had just received a telephone call from an elderly Salem woman, a widow troubled with a bad heart who was unable to leave her home. Her telephone was her only lifeline, and her financial assistance from the state paid for the phone. That assistance had been part of the cuts ordered by McCall. He wanted to give her telephone back.

Robert Davis, McCall's budget director, recalled how wounded Mc-Call looked because his order had hurt this one woman. As Davis described the meeting,

> Tom immediately ordered and demanded a revocation of the [budget] order. I explained to him—and continued to argue with him— that you could not terminate an order that was part of a budget process. . . . When we finally prevailed and made him understand he could not change that order, he said, "Well," and reached into his pocket—he never carried much money—and said, "Let's take up a collection." And so we did. And every month thereafter, until the budget crunch was over, she had her telephone. That was Tom's approach to things. He couldn't believe that the government could let people go like that.

"I get scolded that I would live longer if I weren't so conscientious," McCall once said. "I'm not boasting about it, because it is something of a handicap." McCall perhaps best described his trait, years later, in a letter to his friend Nelson Rockefeller: "I wear my heart on my sleeve and my brain on my shoulder."

Not only his indecisiveness but his thin skin made him vulnerable. He suffered from every critic's stab, no matter how small. When Democratic legislators delivered floor speeches criticizing his policies—typical partisan drama—McCall, cussing, stormed out of his office in search of the lawmakers. Even letters to the editor in the state's newspapers stung him, and he would rush into Schmidt's office waving the torn clippings from the letters page. Although Schmidt would try to calm McCall, reminding him that the attack was not personal, that would not satisfy McCall. A few minutes later, the letter-writer, enjoying a quiet breakfast in his home somewhere in Oregon, would be interrupted by the phone ringing. On the other end of the line he would hear a voice both irritated and sad, and oddly familiar: "This is Tom McCall, and I've been reading your letter. Why don't you like me?"

Oregonians rarely saw McCall's weaknesses. What they saw came filtered through the Oregon press, which routinely described McCall in glowing terms.

As they had during his campaigns, reporters went especially easy on McCall, their old colleague. But their treatment of McCall went beyond simple favoritism. McCall understood what the press needed: access to the governor, a constant flow of news and the color to give stories a flair. McCall delivered them all.

The Salem press corps had just emerged from eight years of Hatfield's aloof closed-door style. When McCall took over, he opened the doors to his office. Staff meetings, once held in secret, were opened to the press. (The gesture had more value for appearance than substance; reporters soon found the meetings boring and stopped showing up, but they never forgot that McCall had extended the invitation.) "The first impression I had of McCall was of genuine, and not calculated, candor," recalled Henny Willis, the political reporter for the Eugene *Register-Guard*. "He truly disliked deceit and the machinations other politicians liked."

For decades Oregonians had listened to his commentaries and reports. McCall saw no reason to stop delivering them now that he was governor. "People were naturally curious," McCall wrote years later, "about the transformation from reporter to news analyst to newsmaker. They soon discovered that once a commentator, one is always a commentator."

As a result, not only did the press have a cooperative governor, it had a governor coming directly to them with news. While many politicians fretted over who around them leaked news to reporters, McCall became his office's biggest leak. In his wanderings about the Capitol, McCall often hailed reporters he saw and shared his thoughts and troubles for the record. "He was always a walking press conference," Hughes said. "If you let him out of your sight, he might unload some great quote that you miss but some other reporter gets." McCall's staff learned that when they could not locate the governor, they should look in the press room. McCall usually would be there holding an impromptu chat that became the next day's headlines. "When he showed up," said United Press International's Don Jepsen, "you knew—you just *knew*—you'd get something good." After watching McCall in action for a year, the *Oregonian* put it this way: "Silence, to a radio man (such as McCall), never is golden; it is an embarrassing vacuum that must somehow be filled."

Many times McCall shared tips about problems in state government, even if they might prove embarrassing later. He would repeat for reporters the latest gossip he had heard about his own administration. Often he ended private meetings with state officials and legislators by admonishing them not to tell reporters about their briefing. Then McCall himself emerged, located the nearest reporter and tugged on his sleeve. "We just had the most interesting meeting," McCall would say. "You should ask me about it."

"The fastest way to get information around the Capitol was to tell it to Tom and then tell him it was a secret," said then-Secretary of State Clay Myers. Added Lee Johnson, one of the few house Republicans who supported McCall, "He couldn't keep his mouth shut in front of reporters. He just talked their ears off." Once, in response to a reporter's question that begged only a "yes" or "no," McCall initiated a lengthy answer by saying, "I'll just open my mouth and see if the brain is running on it." One reporter summarized the governor's style best by defining a McCallism: "A reflex action brought about when confronted by an open microphone . . . (that) worries the author, and delights the publisher. From the public it invariably brings the response, 'Oh, that's just old Tom'."

Reporters not only loved what McCall said, but how he said it. "Tom, because he had written enough news in his time, knew that if he said certain things in a certain way, he knew what the lead would be," said Russell Sadler, a free-lance journalist and political commentator. "Tom knew what he wanted to get across, and he just spoke in a way that any reporter from the laziest to the most skillful would pick up on it." Added UPI's Jepsen, "He was a master. He would sit there and think for a second and come up with a great line and—boom—you'd think, there's my lead."

Often McCall's most memorable lines were self-deprecating. When house leaders ignored him during a three-week session on tax reforms, McCall told reporters, "In politics you have to take half a loaf, but I didn't expect to get a dog biscuit." Later, he gave reporters a colorful description of his eroding relationship with GOP leaders. "The press is wont to talk about a honeymoon," McCall said two weeks after the legislative session had opened. "If, in light of this bipartisan torture, the honeymoon is still going, then romance must be dead. . . . The wrangling started before we could get out of the church—let alone reach the motel."

Reporters also found McCall frustrating. Because he talked aloud as he thought, McCall might tell one reporter one thing, and, minutes later, float the opposite idea to another reporter. Later, the reporters would compare notes and shake their heads. McCall also insisted on improving his quotes, just as he had sweated over his television scripts right until air time. Hours after being interviewed McCall would track down a reporter to spice up his comments. "You could tell he'd been running his quotes around in his head all day," the *Oregonian*'s Hughes said. "We thought, 'OK, he gave me a quote.' But here he is dwelling on it hours later." Reporters also labeled McCall quotes as "before five" and "after five"—a reference to the more colorful quotes they got after McCall had had a few drinks. The prudent reporters used little of what McCall said after five without checking with McCall's aides first.

For all its appearances, however, McCall's open conversation with reporters was not haphazard. He could be calculating, knowing how to skillfully manipulate reporters into dropping embarrassing lines of questioning. He maintained a private correspondence with editors across the state, in which the editors helped McCall hone the messages and ideas the governor later tried out on reporters.

McCall understood he could control the news agenda by dominating reporters' attention. "The press always knew they could get a direct answer from me," McCall said years later. "I was embarking on a policy where people talked about my foot being in my mouth. It was an awfully big foot, and you have to be somewhat calculating to get a big foot in your mouth. So it wasn't always rattling off without thought of the consequences." When he did put his foot in his mouth inadvertently, he said, "It is done with sincerity."

Despite the mutual admiration and utility, reporters also suffered from McCall's thin skin. "I'm an incurable old pro as a newsman," he said. "I chafe once in awhile. But it is the chafing of an old hand who would have written it differently." Three months after McCall took office, Hughes wrote a story that quoted unnamed lawmakers who were complaining about McCall's lack of performance on tax issues. The small story ran deep inside the newspaper, and Hughes thought nothing more of it. The next morning at 4 A.M., Hughes' phone jolted him awake.

"Harold, what are you doing?" McCall asked when Hughes picked up the phone.

"Sleeping," Hughes replied groggily.

"Now about this story," McCall asked, without explanation as to the timing of his call. "You're not out to get me, are you?"

As Hughes recalled years later, "Four o'clock in the morning to ask me if with one damn quote I was out to get him. I said 'Well, of course not, Tom.' That satisfied him. He said good-bye and hung up."

And despite McCall's warts, reporters rarely challenged him. "They were brethren," Westerdahl said. "They were blood brothers. And neither side violated that."

McCall's friendly relationship with reporters helped protect him politically. Here McCall meets reporters at the 1967 Republican governors' conference at Jackson Hole, Wyoming. (OrHi 90806)

AFTER APPOINTING HIMSELF commentator-as-governor, McCall was unable to keep his attention focused at home. He found the allure of national politics irresistible. When people in Oregon suggested McCall had grown more interested in politics beyond the state, though, he insisted he had not. Events suggested otherwise—and he paid a price for his distractions.

The first distraction was Vietnam.

When Tom McCall took office in January 1967, the United States had already begun a full-scale escalation of the war in Vietnam. In early 1965, Lyndon Johnson, deciding that South Vietnam could not fend off North Vietnam's Communist-led Viet Minh with American advisers only, had begun flooding Vietnam with American troops. At the start of 1967, the United States had 400,000 troops in South Vietnam; 6,664 had been killed and 37,738 wounded, a fraction of what the final toll would be. Yet Johnson had little to show for that price.

Nevertheless, Americans' attitudes had not yet turned against the war. That would not happen until the January 1968 Tet Offensive, when the North Vietnamese launched a surprise attack against the South. In early 1967, the Vietnam War had only begun to divide American opinion and, in turn, the Congress. Within the Senate, however, a handful of men had already taken an irrevocable stance against Lyndon Johnson's war. Two of the war's loudest and most devoted senatorial opponents came from Oregon: Democrat Wayne Morse and Republican Mark Hatfield.

Hatfield had expressed his opposition to the war in 1965, while still governor, although he had couched his denouncement carefully, hoping to appear at once brave and non-controversial. Not so with Morse, who had been a bitter critic of what he considered the United States' illegal involvement in Vietnam long before the 1964 Gulf of Tonkin incident. The incident had prompted a congressional resolution giving Johnson unlimited power to make war in Vietnam. Morse was one of only two senators to vote against the resolution.

McCall's position on the war had appeared cloudy at first. When he announced his candidacy for governor in January 1966, a reporter had asked him whether he was a hawk or a dove on the Vietnam War. "I'm neither a hawk nor a dove," McCall replied. "I guess I'm a duck."

McCall, though, was a stout hawk. He had watched Morse and Hatfield's opposition to the war with dismay and growing anger, considering their opposition to the war an embarrassment to Oregon. Soon after his election, McCall sent Johnson a private, hand-written note that read, "I have supported your policy every step of the way in southeast Asia."

"Tom was a red-hot patriot," Westerdahl recalled. Added Schmidt, "Tom had staked out his position of absolute, unequivocal support for the president of the United States, period." When, in March 1967, McCall visited the White House, he again underscored to Johnson his war support. Later, on the Pennsylvania Avenue sidewalk, he repeated his support to members of the national press, adding, "Oregon is back on the track on Vietnam."

McCall had promised to speak his mind on any issue put before him. However, the Vietnam War especially ignited his passions. He talked about it foremost out of patriotism, but he also spoke out frequently for the war because his nemesis, Hatfield, opposed it. McCall's aides, who largely opposed the war, begged him to tone down his attack on Hatfield and Morse. McCall refused.

In April he uncorked his feelings before a state Republican convention. He declared Johnson had used "honest manpower against the tide of overt and covert aggression." The growing legions of war protestors, he said, would only "prolong and intensify the bloodshed. It is they—not the Johnson administration—who escalate toward genocide."

Three months later, before an American Legion convention in Eugene, McCall came as close as he ever had to attacking Morse and Hatfield personally. McCall said he felt "contempt for the apologists who divide us and the name callers who would weaken our national purpose."

He had never been an outspoken anti-Communist, nor was he a warmonger. What drove him to such harsh speeches? Was he attacking the war's opponents solely to get at Hatfield? After one of many arguments with his staff over the war, McCall in July 1967 sat down at a typewriter and tapped out a long, rambling, passionate memo that offered insight into his motives. McCall wrote:

> A governor owes his support to the people his nation sends to war overseas. A governor, more than any other kind of elected official is a grassroots figure—a symbol of home and an image of nostalgia. . . . It would be unthinkable for him to cast doubt on his commander in chief's motives or fault the cause that sends out men into history's most brutal and frustrating combat. . . .
>
> The main point involves the men over there. It's unconscionable to argue whether it's a bum, purposeless war and still imprison them if they refuse to go and get killed in it. . . . The words of backing are owed the men and their mission. And this must never get lost in the morass of doubt or the growl of dissent.

His support of the war was no mystery after all. McCall had surveyed war's ugly landscape and come to a true-to-form conclusion. Whatever the issue, McCall sought out—and embraced—the underdog. In this case the underdog was the soldier fighting the war.

His frustration over Oregon's senators' stance on the war prompted McCall to briefly contemplate running against Morse in 1968. Political survey results had shown Morse was vulnerable—Oregonians had simply grown tired of his tirades. However, McCall never really gave any serious thought to running for the Senate—he shivered at the notion of facing the man who had savaged him during the 1954 congressional race. "Oh, I could beat him," McCall said of Morse. He then added, "But what would be left of me? There would be nothing left of me but hamburger."

LYNDON JOHNSON REMEMBERED MCCALL'S SUPPORT when, in July 1967, Johnson announced he would hike American troop strength by 50,000 men, bringing the total to 525,000. He had asked Congress for a ten percent income tax surcharge to help pay for the war, a move that had eroded public confidence in the president; more than half of Americans polled that summer disapproved of the war's course. To increase public support Johnson decided to prove American soldiers truly fought for democracy. He pressured South Vietnamese military leaders running the country to hold open elections in September 1967. Because past elections in Vietnam had been shams, Johnson decided to prove the elections were legitimate by assembling a team of election observers. To that team, Johnson named McCall.

McCall joined twenty-one other observers, including such dignitaries as Maine senator Edmund Muskie, and Henry Cabot Lodge, the United States ambassador to South Vietnam. McCall, however, gravitated away from other politicians toward the journalists on the team: Eugene Patterson, editor of the Atlanta *Constitution*, and John S. Knight, founder of the Knight-Ridder newspaper chain and one of journalism's harshest critics of the war.

The charge from Johnson was straightforward: Make sure the South Vietnamese elections remain free of undue influence. McCall had been told by Johnson that he and the other team members would have free range to examine the elections. Instead, once they arrived in Saigon, South Vietnamese Army officials put the team through a tightly scheduled series of briefings.

Frustrated by the restrictions, McCall and Patterson, on 31 August, took an impromptu flight fifty miles southwest to Caolanh, a village in the Mekong Delta province of Kienphong. He began to doubt the election's legitimacy as he witnessed the arrogance of army officials charged with overseeing the balloting.

The next day McCall and Patterson again split from the official tour and flew north, to Phanrang in the seaside Ninhthuan province. McCall inspected polling places and ballot boxes, and he compared the voting procedures with a checklist of election standards he had brought with him from Salem. Through interpreters, McCall interviewed election workers, peasants, police officers—anyone he could find willing to talk about the election. They told McCall about threats made by the North Vietnamese Communist guerillas against people participating in the election. He learned how frightened the villagers felt about facing democracy. "I don't think the people know who they are going to vote for," McCall told one reporter. "The significant choice is between going and not going to the polls."

The trip into the countryside made McCall feel like a member of the press again. Upon his return to Saigon he borrowed a reporter's typewriter and pecked out a dispatch for the Associated Press (AP). In his account, which ran worldwide, McCall wrote that he refused to dismiss the elections as a "sterile exercise." The Vietnamese he interviewed, McCall said years later, "seemed to have a dogged faith in this democratic exercise. It permeated everything they felt. They said it was the kind of thing to do in order to start building a strong, free country."

On election day, 3 September, McCall flew with Muskie and New Jersey governor Richard Hughes to Hue, 375 miles north of Saigon, to observe the voting. He watched old peasants, some barely able to walk, make the journey to polling places despite guerilla threats. At the sight of the large turnout—officially reported at eighty-three percent—McCall joined the chorus of observers endorsing the election's fairness.

(What McCall and other observers saw—and praised—of the 1967 election has since been seriously questioned. The military did influence the election in the hinterlands where observers did not travel. "Though not flagrantly fraudulent . . . the contest could hardly be labeled fair—the word used by American officials to describe it," wrote Vietnam historian Stanley Karnow, who covered the elections for the *Washing-*

ton Post. After the election, Nguyen Van Thieu, the general elected as South Vietnam's president, promptly jailed the election's second-place finisher.)

Before leaving South Vietnam, McCall insisted he spend time with the soldiers he defended at home. The United States military offered him a walking tour of an outpost twenty miles north of Saigon in the Mekong Delta. Unsatisfied with the tour, McCall spied a group of soldiers across a swamp. He took off through the filthy, waist-deep water to meet them. "If we had as much composure back home as they have out there," he later told an AP reporter of the soldiers he had met, "we could wind this thing up in twenty months."

After talking with the troops, and after experiencing long days with uncertain security while traveling in the country, McCall expressed doubts about the United States' success to date in Vietnam, doubts he never made public. On 6 September he flew from Saigon to Honolulu, and then directly to Washington, D.C., for an hour-long meeting with Johnson and a White House luncheon. McCall found himself surrounded by celebrities, from cabinet members to CBS anchorman Walter Cronkite. When Johnson asked about what he had witnessed in Vietnam, McCall shrugged off any doubts he had and joined in the enthusiasm for the elections.

In the end, McCall had helped Johnson get what he needed to continue waging his war. "Lyndon Johnson," Karnow wrote, "had . . . a Saigon regime that could be displayed to the American public and the world as a legal government."

IT WAS ALL HEADY STUFF: presidential assignments, foreign affairs, White House lunches. McCall returned home less willing than ever to settle back into the mundane affairs of running state government. Although McCall had eagerly asked Johnson for another Vietnam assignment, he never received one. Eager to stay on the national stage, McCall found another outlet: the 1968 presidential race.

The leading choice of Republicans was former vice president Richard M. Nixon. However, despite his support for Johnson and the war, McCall wanted a liberal Republican like himself to take the White House in 1968. The man he wanted was New York governor Nelson

Rockefeller. Rockefeller represented the Republicans' progressive wing, a counterbalance to the harsh 1964 rhetoric of Barry Goldwater.

McCall, during his White House visit in March 1967, had talked to the governors about holding off support for any candidate until Rockefeller had made his plans clear. After an impromptu conversation on the sidewalk outside the White House, McCall recruited a core of twelve liberal GOP state leaders, including Maryland governor Spiro T. Agnew, to a campaign to hold off Nixon's momentum.

McCall thought he could help deliver the GOP nomination to Rockefeller—and for good reason. Despite its small size, Oregon had found that its primary election had become a major political test in presidential races; in the late 1960s, far fewer states held primaries than hold them now. Often, candidates shopped for primaries in which they could perform well. Oregon's ballot system also forced presidential candidates to compete because state law required the secretary of state to place all serious presidential candidates on the ballot. Moreover, Oregon held its election only one week before the landmark California primary. As a result of all these factors, candidates treated Oregon as a crucial battleground, giving it importance well beyond its small population.

However, as 1968 approached, Rockefeller refused to move toward a candidacy. McCall was in a quandary. His Republican choices dwindled to Michigan governor George Romney—whom McCall considered a lifeless bore and whose campaign was "lying dead in the water," according to McCall—and Nixon, whose mean-spirited politics McCall detested.

Rockefeller was coy about his candidacy for nearly a year, showing his appreciation for McCall's support by inviting him to speak at a fundraiser for New York senator Jacob Javits in Manhattan. It was a glitzy affair, held at the Waldorf-Astoria, and covered by the national media. McCall shared the head table with Nixon, who had emerged as the frontrunner for the GOP nomination. When McCall spoke, however, he barely glanced Nixon's way as he heartily proclaimed that he hoped Rockefeller would repeat his 1964 victory in the Oregon primary in 1968.

Nixon, sitting only a few feet away, blanched. "A silence such as when a child has pulled off a tablecloth, with all the china, ensued," wrote Washington *Star* columnist Mary McGrory, who witnessed the speech. The snub was the first chill between Nixon and McCall, but McCall did not care. He believed wholeheartedly that Rockefeller would join the race and swamp Nixon. McCall was betting that, as Rockefeller's star rose, so would his own.

MEANWHILE, TROUBLE BREWED AT HOME. Oregon House Speaker Monte Montgomery had felt jilted by McCall's refusal to appoint him secretary of state, and had decided to run for the office in 1968 against McCall's Republican appointee, Clay Myers. His candidacy meant a showdown between McCall's liberal wing and the GOP old guard, who backed Montgomery. But what started as Republican infighting exploded into a crisis of the first order, a disaster that McCall considered the biggest tragedy of his career.

From the start, Montgomery ran a campaign of attack. One of his primary targets was the Oregon State Penitentiary. The penitentiary warden, Clarence Gladden, had been hired after a 1953 prison strike to discipline and reform the penitentiary. Although he was seen as a reformer, Gladden still hung on to many of the old, rough ways of handling prisoners. For example, as punishment, Gladden used "The Box," a darkened, six-by-eight foot cell furnished only with a hole for a toilet. Guards dumped naked prisoners into the Box, leaving them there for weeks at a time without even bedding to keep them warm.

Despite the resentment he caused among prisoners, Gladden remained popular among state leaders. The legislature had even passed a special bill exempting him from mandatory retirement. However, by 1968, Gladden's authority had weakened. The warden's health was failing, and the lines of command within the penitentiary were blurring.

Montgomery's office engineered a series of damaging leaks to the press about deteriorating conditions at the penitentiary. Montgomery exploited internal problems, planting stories about a contraband smuggling operation, violent escape attempts and a string of suicides during the previous year. With these stories as a backdrop, Montgomery publicly attacked Myers, who, as secretary of state, sat on the Board of Control, charged with overseeing the prison.

Montgomery succeeded only in enraging Tom McCall, who at first did not believe there were problems at the penitentiary. He trusted Gladden and the state's chief of corrections, George Randall, whom McCall had helped hire while serving as secretary of state.

Randall, though, was not forthright with McCall. He first told McCall that Montgomery had exaggerated the problems at the prison. Finally, on 7 March, Randall admitted to McCall that problems did exist. The warden, Gladden, had been bed-ridden for weeks, dying of cancer. Neither Gladden nor Randall had named anyone to run the penitentiary in the meantime. The institution was out of control.

McCall then made a fateful decision. He agreed with Randall that the state should keep Gladden's illness secret. He feared, as Randall later put it, that forcing Gladden out at that time would be "throwing him to the wolves." They would wait until the political storm kicked up by Montgomery died down, and then name a replacement for Gladden.

The plan meant that McCall had to delay taking action on the penitentiary's problems. Although McCall wanted to quiet Montgomery's attacks, he could not trust the house speaker with the confidential news about Gladden's health. On 7 March—the same day McCall learned the seriousness of Gladden's illness—Montgomery wrote McCall a scathing letter that demanded a full investigation of conditions at the penitentiary. Before McCall could read the letter, however, Montgomery's staff leaked it to the newspapers.

The letter created new furor in the press and dread in McCall's heart. From his experience as the chief negotiator quelling the 1951 prison strike, McCall knew the prisoners read the newspapers carefully. That meant that Montgomery—unaware of how out of control the prison really was—risked igniting the combustible mood inside the prison.

The next day, McCall scolded Montgomery in a confidential letter: "I must further warn you that the attack you are making on the prison in an effort to further your personal political ambitions is fraught with danger. . . . Your careless, heedless efforts to build a case will accomplish nothing of a positive nature and, indeed, are sowing the seeds of riot within the walls."

Montgomery scoffed at McCall's warnings about a riot and continued his attacks. Meanwhile, McCall's attention was drawn away from Oregon again: Nelson Rockefeller was calling.

McCall had remained active in his efforts to encourage Rockefeller to run for president in 1968. He had helped start a petition drive to put

Rockefeller on the Oregon primary ballot and, in January, had flown to San Francisco for a secret meeting with George Hinman, Rockefeller's chief political aide, to discuss strategy. However, he had seen nothing but a lack of enthusiasm on the part of the New York governor.

Now Rockefeller said he wanted to prepare a presidential campaign. McCall thought Rockefeller's entry into the race was too late to keep the nomination from Nixon. Rockefeller disagreed. He invited McCall to New York City for a 9 March strategy meeting at Rockefeller's Fifth Avenue home. McCall accepted and—at Rockefeller's request—kept his travel plans secret.

On 8 March, the day he had privately castigated Montgomery about inciting a riot in the penitentiary, McCall invited trouble of his own: he decided to use his relationship with reporters to quiet Montgomery for good. He invited a handful of reporters to tour the penitentiary. The superficial tour showed reporters only a quiet and orderly prison—far different from the one depicted by Montgomery—and produced newspaper headlines McCall thought would defuse Montgomery. "Reporter's Tour of Pen Finds No Sign of Letdown in Morale, Control," said a headline in the *Oregon Statesman*. Declared the *Oregon Journal*, "Prison Troubles, if any, Elusive."

Satisfied with his public relations move, McCall flew off on the morning of 9 March to meet with Rockefeller. To cover the trip and keep his meeting with Rockefeller secret, McCall planned to go on to Washington, D.C., the next day for a meeting with Interior Secretary Stewart Udall to receive a grant for the Willamette Greenway.

McCall arrived at the Rockefeller apartment at 812 Fifth Avenue to find Senator Jacob Javits, New York mayor John Lindsay and six other governors, including Agnew of Maryland and Winthrop Rockefeller, Nelson's brother, of Arkansas. Rockefeller pondered whether he should enter the Oregon primary, his first real opportunity to challenge Nixon, and McCall enthusiastically joined in the debate. Surrounded by Picassos and looking out over glittering Manhattan, McCall again felt the heady rush he enjoyed.

At 11 P.M. eastern time, less than an hour after McCall had arrived, the telephone rang. Someone handed the phone to McCall, and he received grim news: the Oregon State Penitentiary had exploded in riot.

A FEW MINUTES AFTER 4 P.M., PACIFIC TIME, on Saturday, 9 March, penitentiary guards had escorted a handful of prisoners from the prison's recreation area to their cells. One prisoner had suddenly stepped out of line and jumped a guard. Other prisoners followed, overpowering the remaining guards. Within minutes, the inmates had taken possession of the penitentiary's control room area.

The attack, by most accounts, was spontaneous—an impulsive response to the months of difficulty inside the penitentiary and the press reports on the outside. But the Oregon prison riot unfolded in a series of missteps by corrections officials. Within minutes of the prisoners' attack on the guards, corrections chief George Randall arrived at the scene. Although the prison had a specific riot control plan, designed to contain prisoners during a riot's early moments by using tear gas to corral rioters, Randall ignored it; in fact, Randall told guards not to use tear gas. He then refused to release a riot platoon of thirty guards trained for such an outburst. As a result, rioting prisoners spread unstopped throughout the prison. They took control of several buildings and captured dozens of prison guards and officials as hostages. By nightfall, four buildings inside the penitentiary were ablaze.

When McCall was finally notified, the riot was four hours old. McCall bolted from the meeting and raced to La Guardia Airport. When he called the prison at midnight, eastern time, he learned that riot leaders then held only four hostages, all prison guards, and were threatening to kill one captive every twenty minutes unless their demands were met.

McCall scrambled to find a plane home, but fog hung over New York City; he boarded two different flights, only to have them grounded. He dashed across town to Kennedy Airport, and then back to La Guardia, trying unsuccessfully to charter a private plane. Distraught, McCall in the early morning telephoned the command center at the penitentiary to explain he could not get home. "My prison is burning," the governor of Oregon said, his voice wavering, "and here I am, trapped."

None of the members of the Board of Control were in town. At the penitentiary, McCall's chief of staff, Ed Westerdahl, had arrived within two hours of the riot's outbreak to find chaos. With McCall in Washington, D.C., State Senate President E.D. "Debbs" Potts was technically acting governor. Potts quickly handed his power to Westerdahl. A few

The burning of the Oregon State Penitentiary during the March 1968 prison riot. (Gerry Lewin *Statesman-Journal* photo)

minutes after midnight, pacific time, on the morning of 10 March, Westerdahl, Randall and a handful of reporters entered the prison to hear the prisoners' grievances. Six prisoners, speaking for the rioters, issued nine demands, which included the resignation of Warden Gladden and the right to take a shower every day. Randall frustrated Westerdahl's negotiating plan by quickly agreeing to all nine demands.

But in the next five hours, no hostages were released; the hostages and riot leaders remained in the open prison yard in clear view from the top of the prison wall. During the early morning hours, Westerdahl ordered an ambush. He stationed police sharpshooters along the prison wall and organized a squadron to storm the gates. At 6 A.M., as dawn broke, police would give rioters a final warning. After that, sharpshooters would open fire on any prisoner standing near a hostage.

Westerdahl waited as dawn approached with no word from the riot leaders. Then at 5 A.M., the riot's leaders asked for another meeting. Randall began talking with them by bullhorn, but when he began to give away more concessions, Westerdahl rushed over and grabbed the bull-horn away from him. After that, Westerdahl moved the assault team into place. At 5:40, twenty minutes before Westerdahl was to give the order to shoot, the prisoners agreed to end the riot.

It was all over before McCall made it back home late the next day, 11 March. After becoming trapped in New York, McCall had decided to attend the Department of the Interior meeting in Washington, D.C., after all. The decision made for an uncomfortable juxtaposition in the press: a wire service photo of McCall appearing in Washington alongside photos of the charred prison.

Once back in Oregon, McCall rushed to the penitentiary and surveyed the damage. The arson fires had destroyed what McCall considered the soul of the prison. The prison factories and workshops, and the buildings that housed the school, social services center and the library—all things McCall had fought to bring into the prison—were gone. "The Oregon State Penitentiary," wrote one reporter at the scene, "looks like a town devastated by war."

As McCall walked through the ruins, wet soot and ash caked his feet. Steam rose from still warm timbers, and a smoky stench filled the air. It was all he could do to hold back tears. "Why?" McCall asked aloud as he stood in the charred rubble. "Why did they destroy all the things that were of value to them?"

He never received an answer.

ALTHOUGH NO ONE DIED, thirty-one guards and prisoners were injured in the riot, and the penitentiary sustained more than $1.6 million in damage. The riot also ended the careers of several people. As the prison burned, Westerdahl dismissed Gladden, who died two months later. A Marion County grand jury report issued in April savaged Randall and his handling of the riot, ending his career in Oregon.

McCall denounced the grand jury report as a "hatchet job," but it was one of McCall's more insincere declarations. McCall knew by this time that Randall was to blame for much of the riot; confidential investigations conducted by both the Oregon State Police and members of McCall's staff had told him as much. Randall had allowed the riot to grow out of control by failing to order the anti-riot squads into the prison and by quickly caving in to rioters' demands. The reports concluded that the widespread fire damage was due largely to inaction.

Meanwhile, Randall was telling the press and public a far different story, claiming he had followed the riot plan as prescribed. McCall decided that Randall was guilty of both incompetence and deception, and he forced his prison chief to resign in July.

The riot also finished Monte Montgomery. In the riot's aftermath, McCall blamed Montgomery for igniting the riot. He released his confidential 8 March letter to the press in which he had warned Montgomery about his inflammatory rhetoric. The letter, which had proven prophetic, proved embarrassing for Montgomery. He spent the rest of the campaign for secretary of state explaining that he was not responsible for inciting inmates in the penitentiary. However, in the election, voters believed McCall; Myers won the primary and, later, the general election.

And what of McCall?

McCall had sensed a prison riot coming, even though Gladden and Randall had hidden the penitentiary's problems from him. McCall believed he could have averted a riot. "That," said Schmidt years later, "was a major failure in his life."

For all the heartache he felt, McCall had learned the greater lesson of accountability: No matter whose actions sparked a riot, or who ran the prison, the governor took the blame.

McCall had made critical mistakes. In the confidential investigation into the riot's causes, it was found that McCall's failure to promptly dismiss Gladden contributed to the tension in the prison. That had not been McCall's greatest blunder, however. While he had privately castigated Montgomery for milking the penitentiary situation for publicity, McCall had done so himself. His impromptu prison tour for reporters on 8 March helped enrage prisoners; as they rioted, many prisoners had waved copies of the newspaper headlines proclaiming all was well in the prison. As a confidential report by McCall's own staff concluded: "Imprudent comments to the press by both Governor McCall and Speaker Montgomery . . . were inflammatory and possibly a triggering cause."

McCall's greater lesson, however, would follow him throughout his first term.

From Vietnam to the White House to Fifth Avenue, McCall had pursued a public dalliance with national fame for his benefit, not Oregon's. The prison riot had caught him unaware—as if to punctuate his absence from duties. The riot made McCall appear far more inattentive to his job than he truly was. But it underscored that, between the dull machinations of running a state and the lure of national politics, McCall had not found a balance.

If McCall thought for a moment his inattention to his job had been overlooked by Oregonians, one letter arriving in his office four days after the prison riot brought reality crashing back:

> Quote from the street of Redmond to brother: "Well, this time he's got his tits caught in the washer."
>
> Pipe down, Governor, stop running amok and govern the old home state.

Three days later, a second note followed.

> Misprint in quote. Word should be "WRINGER."

The notes were unsigned but, to McCall, not anonymous. They came from his mother.

11

Mother and Son

MCCALL'S UNSIGNED MESSAGE from his mother was a reminder that, not only did he have a public life, he had a sometimes dark and troubling private one. Tom McCall was haunted by what his family euphemistically called the Lawson Curse. The inheritance of eccentricity—some said mental instability—handed down from Thomas Lawson had, by 1968, cast a shadow over McCall's family. His mother Dorothy was the most public and prominent case in point. Dorothy believed that she—not her second son—should be the most famous McCall. "She was at once proud that her son was governor, and bitterly jealous that he received more attention than she did," said Audrey McCall, who never made peace with her mother-in-law. "She wanted everything he was getting in the way of attention for herself."

Widowed more than twenty years, Dorothy lived in the creaky Westernwold mansion only in the summer. Most of the year she lived in a small Portland apartment, only blocks from the suite where she and Hal had first lived nearly sixty years earlier. Within a few months of moving back to Portland, Dorothy strutted about town as if she owned it. She soon became an Oregon celebrity in her own right, the star of newspaper articles and television news.

She volunteered tirelessly to raise money for United Cerebral Palsy and did an occasional dramatic turn in benefit theater productions. (One local theater group appropriately cast her in *Apple of His Eye* as a busybody in a small farming town.) Dorothy also took it upon herself to clean up several local nursing homes suffering from deplorable conditions. She launched her own surprise visits, then turned in the offenders to local health inspectors.

Dorothy feared no one in her righteousness. Her youngest daughter, Jean McCall Babson, recalled having lunch with Dorothy in the Portland Hotel, a downtown landmark. Nearby, a group of Royal Rosarians, a civic group self-appointed as the city's officials hosts, berated a young black waiter serving their lunch. "The head Rosarians were just being awful to him," Jean recalled. Everyone in the room looked on and said nothing—everyone, except Dorothy Lawson McCall. "She went over to the chief Rosarian and just gave him hell," Jean recalled. "She said he had no right to treat this boy like that—and that he should be ashamed of himself." Later, the head waiter, an older black man who had worked at the hotel for years, pulled Dorothy aside. "We can't say anything to defend ourselves," he told Dorothy. "We appreciate eternally what you did." Dorothy smiled, raised her chin and strolled out. "That," said Jean, "was mother at her best."

Although she might be a hero to others, Dorothy, toward her children, remained overbearing and punishing. Dorothy controlled their lives. "She knew how to get to them, and she would exploit it," said Borden Beck, a long-time family friend. "She knew each one of their weaknesses. She would find a weakness in character and bore in on it."

Her demands took heavy tolls. Harry, the oldest, made a comfortable salary, but never became as wealthy as Dorothy insisted he should. Dorothy hounded Sam, her youngest son, most of all. Sam, a professor of history and political science at Bakersfield College in Bakersfield, California, returned each year to take care of Westernwold with Dorothy. He had once hoped to marry, but Dorothy had driven the woman away with vindictive attacks. Sam never married and, like others in his family, fell victim to alcohol.

Of the five children, Tom was the only one to escape Dorothy's grip, and Dorothy tried to horn in on Tom's fame. "She was jealous of his fame," Audrey McCall said. "He was accomplishing the kinds of things she dreamed of doing." In an attempt to upstage her son, Dorothy collected essays she had written throughout the years and merged them into a lively book, *Ranch Under the Rimrock*. The 166-page memoir told of the McCalls' life in the Oregon desert with her—and not her famous son—as the central character. Published by a Portland company, the book went into five printings and gave Dorothy celebrity of her own. In a dig at McCall, she invited his nemesis, Mark Hatfield, to write the book's foreword. She later wrote a second autobiographical account, *The Copper King's Daughter*, that told the story of her father's career and her life at Dreamwold.

Dorothy believed her position as the governor's mother made her a political figure in her own right. She took it upon herself to tongue-whip any public officials she thought stepped out of line. Filled with Manhattans, Dorothy spent nights on the phone, offering her commentary on politics to whomever she felt needed to hear her opinions. After McCall took office, reporters and politicians found that their lives included taking late-night calls from Dorothy. "She would call—talk and talk and talk," recalled Monte Montgomery. "At first it would annoy me. Then I got to the point I would love the old gal. She would talk and talk—and then you would hear an alarm—this alarm clock she had set so she would not talk so long, because the kids had complained about her telephone bills." As McCall aide Ron Schmidt recalled, "If I had a call at three o'clock in the morning, I would pick up the phone and say, 'What is it Dorothy?' and she'd just start talking."

On this new audience, Dorothy employed the tricks she used at Westernwold years earlier. Her favorite attention-getting stunt remained the suicide threat and she frequently sprang it on her son's acquaintances. They would call the governor with the frantic news that his mother was going to kill herself. He would only shrug; he had heard it a hundred times before.

Dorothy delivered tongue lashings to anyone who attacked McCall. For example, during the 1966 gubernatorial campaign, McCall and his opponent, Robert Straub, had one of their debates. Later that night a phone call disturbed Straub's sleep.

"This is Dorothy Lawson McCall," said the ferocious voice.

Before Straub could respond, Dorothy tore into him. "Mr. Straub, I have been listening to news reports about your debate with my son, Tom. Now, Mr. Straub, it is my understanding that you went to Dartmouth."

Dorothy Lawson McCall loved to horn in on her son's limelight. Pictured in Portland in 1970, she took the opportunity to promote her memoir, *Ranch Under the Rimrock*. (Jim Vincent photo courtesy of the *Oregonian*)

Straub paused for a moment, still groggy and confused by the call. "Yes," he said after a moment, "I went to Dartmouth."

"Well, Mr. Straub," Dorothy said, "I have trouble believing that because I thought all Dartmouth men were gentlemen." Then she slammed down the phone.

Straub, who had never been treated to a Dorothy Lawson McCall phone call, worried that during the debate he had indeed said something offensive. The next day, he sought out McCall and spoke with concern about Dorothy's phone call.

"Don't worry about it," McCall replied. "Just feel fortunate she hung up when she did."

"She could get anyone on the phone," said Jean McCall Babson, "and just give them hell." Anyone, that is, except McCall. He refused to give Dorothy his home phone number. If by some trickery she obtained it anyway, he had the number changed. The governor's staff was ordered to screen her calls. Enraged by this practice, Dorothy once so terrorized a receptionist—"I'm the governor's mother and I'll see to it you're fired today!"—that she sent the woman into tears.

Once in 1968 when Dorothy could not reach McCall, she angrily dialed the White House. "This is Dorothy Lawson McCall!" she bellowed at the White House operator until she convinced someone that she was a person who might need to talk to the president, Lyndon Johnson. A little while later, a White House official called McCall's office. When a McCall aide confirmed Dorothy's identity, the White House relayed Dorothy's message to Tom: "Call your mother."

Dorothy later boasted to McCall about her long conversation with the president. McCall scoffed. But a few days after the incident, he was stunned when he received a letter from Johnson that included a handwritten postscript: "I had a nice talk with your mother. Lyndon."

But not even Dorothy's call to the president would prompt McCall to give her his home phone number.

Never one to surrender, Dorothy reached her son with telegrams.

> Will have you impeached as Governor. Am fighting mad, Tom. Stay away from me. My friends and I are dangerous.

> Cannot reach you, Tom. When my reports come out through the Oregonian and Oregon Journal advise that you retire. Am through with you Tom stay off my neck and don't bother me as long as you live.

> Wouldn't it be wise to give me your home phone number and not subject me to so much humiliation. . . . If I pay for another Western Union I will vote for every enemy you have.

Your unjustifiable excoriation last night cannot be forgiven
Governor McCall. I would not vote for you for dog catcher's
job.

Have seven burning issues please call me and help me out or
otherwise boy good night forever. P.S. I have the biggest
Western Union and telephone bill in the state of Oregon and
am a penniless widow with Social Security.
    Step on it, brother.

Dorothy's comic intensity was harmless, but it was a reminder of the
dark cloud hanging over the McCall family. As a boy, Tom McCall had
seen his grandfather's frenzies as ghosts overcame his mind. His
mother's sister, Marion, had died in a Boston mental institution, committed there after she had announced that she was Jesus Christ. Another
of Dorothy's sisters, Gladys, drank herself to death on gin; two other
siblings, Doug and Jean (whom everyone called Bunny) suffered ferocious bouts of depression.
    The tendency toward mental instability and addiction carried on into
a fourth generation of Lawsons as well.
    McCall's younger son, Samuel Walker McCall III, had, in many
ways, turned out like Tom himself. He was cheerful, exceedingly bright,
prone to mischief, and full of the Lawson charm. But by seventeen, Sam
was also a hopeless drug addict. He had been an addict for nearly three
years and would be for the rest of his life. He took every kind of drug he
could find, favoring stolen prescription drugs sold on the street.
    At first Tom McCall could not understand why his son had fallen to
drug use, and why Sam never shook his habits. Over the years, the reason became clear: Sam thought his happy home life had been disrupted
by his father's political career and Sam lashed out as if to extract revenge. Delusional, Sam grew to see himself in grandiose Lawson terms,
as a soul destined for greatness, while acting as if he wanted to destroy
his life and his father's. Looking back through the later years' drug haze,
Sam remembered the years before McCall's entry into politics, when his
father belonged to him, not the state. He also recalled his own happiness
that came with those years. "My parents called me the sunshine boy," he

said. "The roof could fall in—or I could be punished for doing something—and in five minutes I'd be happy again."

When Sam was thirteen, he collapsed at school, complaining of stomach pains. Doctors assumed he had appendicitis and operated, only to find his appendix normal. Sam was diagnosed with a stomach ailment and spent weeks in the hospital, isolated from friends as the pain persisted. "Sometimes I was doubled up and screaming," Sam said. "[The doctors] didn't know what to do. Some of them thought it was all psychological. And some just kept giving me this pain medication." Sam quickly learned that he could get shots of a powerful pain killer on demand. The shots sent him into a happy, hazy lull. By the time the hospital discharged him, doctors had discovered Sam's extensive reliance on the pain killers and stamped his chart with another diagnosis: medically addicted.

McCall and Audrey scarcely understood what medical addiction was or how to treat it. Doctors responded by giving Sam more pain medicine, which he ate like candy. When one doctor closed off Sam's supply, he insisted his parents find him another doctor who would reopen it. Soon the McCalls blamed the doctors for Sam's troubles.

Bewildered by their new problem, McCall and Audrey showered their other son, Tad, with all the praise they could. Certainly he deserved it. Tad McCall had turned out as perfectly as any parent could dream. Tad excelled at everything: he was valedictorian in high school and Phi Beta Kappa at the University of Oregon. Tad was also unceasingly faithful to his father's political goals. Although he enlisted in the ROTC in 1967, he later considered resisting service in Vietnam; he finally decided against resistance, fearing that it might hurt his father's image as a politician. Later, Tad was sent to Vietnam and won honors as a PT boat captain. Tom made no secret that Tad had fulfilled their hopes. "He is," McCall said of Tad to reporters for all the world to hear, "our favorite son."

Sam could not compete with his successful brother. McCall remembered when the family learned Tad would graduate Phi Beta Kappa. The family celebrated together, and then Sam vanished. "He went out the door and, Jesus Christ, he was stoned for a week," McCall said.

Although the McCalls blamed doctors for Sam's addiction, Sam did not want to be cured. "I never liked to admit it," Sam said years later. "I loved drugs, I never wanted to stop taking them."

He became clever in getting them, too. He memorized the *Physician's Desk Reference*, the standard guidebook to pharmaceutical drugs. He became a drug gourmet, understanding the particular effects of each prescription. He then faked symptoms that he knew would win him the drugs he wanted. "It was too easy," Sam said. "It was almost always prescription stuff. I was charming. I liked playing the little games. I liked getting the drugs. The whole thing snowballed." When he could not con his way into a prescription, Sam said, "I went to the street to get what I wanted."

He became a skilled thief and liar who loved the thrill of deception as much as the rush the drugs gave him. In his Salem school Sam flaunted his fame as both the son of the governor and a fast-running hood who knew drugs. He stole money from his parents to buy what he needed, or stole their prescriptions of Valium. He used his parents' credit cards to buy merchandise, and then returned the goods for a cash refund later. He stole trinkets from the house and got quick cash at pawn shops. "I became very manipulative and very good at it," Sam said of his knack for deception. "At home, I'd be the perfect gentleman. I had a job to do. I was the governor's son."

Sam kept his habits a secret, until one night he overdosed in the governor's house while shooting drugs into his veins. "I passed out on the bedroom floor upstairs, and . . . [my parents] came in and saw the syringe," Sam said.

They were shocked, but few others were surprised. His relatives had routinely found Sam rifling their homes, looking for money or prescription drugs. McCall's staff had orders from Westerdahl to deny Sam access to the governor's office: Sam had stolen keys to the office from his father and been caught pawing through desks one night. "We couldn't trust him at all," said one aide who, much to his regret later, had allowed Sam to stay in his home while McCall and Audrey were out of the state on business. "He stole at every opportunity. It was a very difficult week."

Despite Sam's crimes, McCall and Audrey fought to protect him. Audrey especially denied Sam's wrongdoings. "Audrey believed the world was ganging up on her son," Westerdahl said. "With that resistance there was little that could be done."

McCall was also slow to blame his son. Once, during a quiet dinner at the home of friends, one of the McCalls' hosts mentioned some trouble she was having with her own physician. McCall suddenly reared up and slammed his broad, open hand hard against the table. Dishes and glasses jumped, their contents sloshing from the impact. "Damn the doctors!" McCall roared, then dropped back into his chair and fell silent.

However, McCall in time grew more realistic about Sam, and as he did his resentment grew. After a day of worrying about running the state, McCall returned home to face the horrors created by Sam. Sam often left the house for the night, leaving McCall awake until dawn worrying about him. When he was home, Sam would be abusive or would fall ill from drugs. "McCall would show up in the office looking absolutely haggard," said Jason Boe, a Democratic legislator who knew McCall well. "He would look like hell, and we would be told later by one of his aides that he had been up all night on one of Sam's escapades." Added a McCall aide,

> Tom was a tremendously emotional person anyway. He just wore his heart on his sleeve and just cared about things. . . . They were always trying to keep track of [Sam]. It kept the governor up a lot. He lacked a lot of sleep when he needed it the most. He would come in the morning and tell us about how difficult it had been the night before. He'd be so worn out he could barely face the issues of the day.

Oregonians did not see the troubles in the McCall home. Though police often arrested Sam for various petty crimes, he was never booked and reports were never written. "Tom never wanted to believe Sam got special treatment because he was the governor's son," said one person close to McCall. "But there's no doubt that he did." Once, when Sam stole the family silver, state police investigators traced the goods to a well-known Salem "fence," a crook who bought and sold stolen items. Hoping to keep the theft quiet, the police offered to negotiate a deal for the return of the silver. The fence agreed. Following his instructions,

Audrey McCall in 1966 with son Sam, whose drug addiction threatened his father's political career. (David Kennerly *Oregon Journal* photo; OrHi 90782)

state police officers dropped a bag containing $100 in cash into a trash can near the Capitol. They returned an hour later to find the money had been replaced by a sack containing the silver. The police returned the silver and never told McCall how they had retrieved it.

Members of the press, too, knew about Sam's problems, often from McCall's candid admissions. "It was a tragedy and nobody wanted to write about it," said the *Oregonian*'s Harold Hughes. "It was like writing about somebody who was crippled." Added the Eugene *Register-Guard*'s Henny Willis, "It was a very private thing, an agony that Tom had to deal with on his own. He never traded on it. I don't ever recall him asking any reporter not to write about it. It was treated differently in a different era as something private and sad."

McCall's staff recognized Sam's potential for violence and believed him capable of injuring or killing his parents. He was also a scandal waiting to happen. During McCall's first year in office, he and Audrey flew to the east coast on business. While they were gone, police in Lin-

coln City found Sam and dozens of high school kids partying in the Mc-
Calls' beach house. The party included a young fugitive from Hillcrest,
the state school for troubled girls. Police hushed up the incident, preventing news stories about Sam giving minors alcohol and harboring a
fugitive at the governor's vacation home.

When Tom returned home, he confronted Sam about the incident.
As Sam sputtered out his excuse, McCall uncocked his long arm and
smacked Sam across his mouth. "I don't want to hear any of your explanations," McCall boomed. Sam stood there, stunned. His father—
the loving, genial man who had never liked disciplining his sons—had
never hit him before.

McCall finally realized the danger his son now presented. At the urging of Schmidt and Westerdahl, McCall sought a treatment program for
Sam; in 1967, however, such programs were both rare and expensive.
Knowing the McCalls could not afford a treatment program, Schmidt
and Westerdahl turned to the man who could discreetly raise the money:
Glenn Jackson. Jackson promptly agreed to help. Schmidt and Westerdahl pitched in, appealing to many wealthy Oregonians who had supported McCall's campaign. "We would say, 'We have a problem here
and the boss doesn't have any money'," Schmidt said. "It was a campaign unto itself." Added one of the business leaders who chipped in, "It
wasn't big dough. But it was big dough to Tom." How much they raised
is unclear. McCall believed it was no more than $4,000. The actual
amount, however, was probably far higher. Schmidt estimated at least
$10,000 to $15,000 was raised; Westerdahl believed it was even more.

McCall took enormous political risk by approving the fund-raising.
His opponents could have used the information to show that people with
a personal interest in the actions of state government were secretly giving McCall cash. McCall never knew who gave the money, although he
did know Jackson was behind the effort. The tie to Glenn Jackson could
have proven especially damaging, coming as it did soon after McCall's
support for the Nestucca Highway project. Nevertheless, the cash gifts
remained secret until years after McCall had left office.

The money paid to send Sam to the Menninger Clinic in Topeka,
Kansas. Once there, however, Sam began playing on his parents' fears.
"I don't think Audrey could stand the fact Sam was away from them

and that she wasn't aware about how he was being treated," one McCall aide said. "Sam was real artful. He was as good with words—as good as Tom McCall ever was—and was able to make sure his family knew precisely how horribly he was being treated." In short order, the guilt overcame Audrey and she insisted Sam be sent home. He returned no better than before.

Tom McCall saw only one more choice. He asked a Marion County judge to commit Sam to a state mental institution. The judge held the commitment hearing in the McCall's living room to avoid publicity. However, the psychiatric hospital had little affect on him. "All they do is lock you in your cage at night," Sam recalled. "My rehabilitation was mopping long hallways two hours a day."

In passionate letters and wrenching phone calls, Sam pleaded with his parents—especially his mother—to release him. The McCalls would have him released—then they would send him back when he acted up.

Sam often bragged of how he "conned" his parents into springing him from the institutions. "They never would leave him there until the doctors felt he had been cured," one aide recalled. "We all felt that was why he never got over his addiction. . . . And so it went on and on."

McCall knew his son's problems could not remain secret for long, and he was right. During his commitments to Dammasch State Hospital, Sam began a series of escapes. The minimum security hospital in Wilsonville, about fifteen miles south of Portland, lacked fences or bars. Whenever he wished, Sam walked away, only to have state police officers track him down and haul him back. Sam's frequent escapes put Tom on edge; until the police located his son, he would not sleep, and would drag himself into work the next day frayed and exhausted.

In July 1969, Sam ran away, hooked up with two friends, got drunk and drove off, heading north on Interstate 5. As Sam approached a construction site near Tualatin, he swerved and struck a highway flagman. The worker suffered a broken leg and police arrested Sam.

This time, Sam's crimes could not be covered up. Schmidt rushed a statement to reporters that gave full disclosure of the accident. Sam pleaded guilty to drunk driving, received a $200 fine and returned to the psychiatric hospital. After the court appearance, Schmidt issued another statement to the press.

The strategy helped McCall fend off suspicions that Sam was receiving preferential treatment, although Audrey complained bitterly about the publicity the press statements had brought into Sam's troubled life. But Sam brought even more trouble on himself. In March 1970, Sam escaped from Dammasch again and fled to the home of a hospital worker he had befriended. Rather than call the police, the worker allowed Sam to spend the night at his house. Police captured Sam the next day, and Dammasch officials fired the worker for harboring the governor's fugitive son. The firing brought on a flood of news stories that detailed Sam's troubled past. "The publicity did not help anyone, especially Sam," said one McCall aide. "But it did show Oregonians how much Tom had on his mind. I think people finally saw his burdens."

Soon after the second publicized escape, Sam agreed to enter a methadone program. Still experimental at the time, methadone was a synthetic drug that was supposed to help addicts ease off their dependency. In the spring of 1970, NBC newsman Sander Vanocur asked McCall if he and Sam might consider talking about Sam's addiction and the program. Sam agreed, and, over Audrey's protests, McCall and Sam sat for a long interview. Sam recounted his slide into addiction and told of how his parents had discovered him with a needle hanging from a vein in his arm. The interview aired in July 1970 on NBC's "First Tuesday," and won McCall praise for his public courage, and sympathy for Sam as well.

To put aside his troubles, McCall would immerse himself in his work. "His moods changed for the better when he was on the job," Westerdahl said. "His work became his one escape." Added his assistant, Doris Penwell, "He had so much on his mind, and he then went on to do so much. When you think about the hell he had to deal with at home, it's amazing that Tom was able to accomplish all that he did."

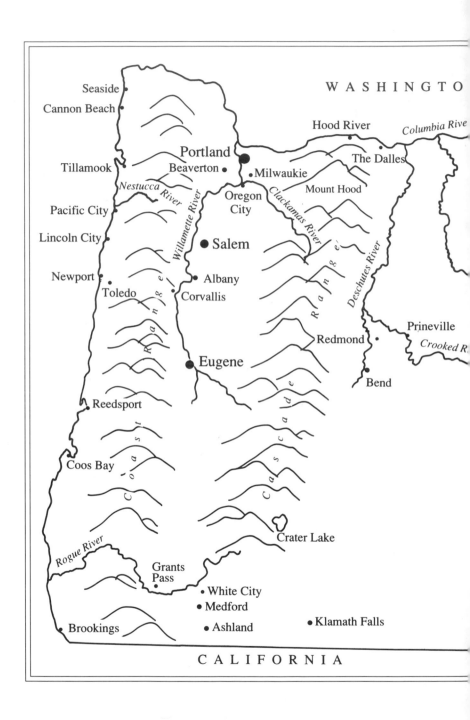

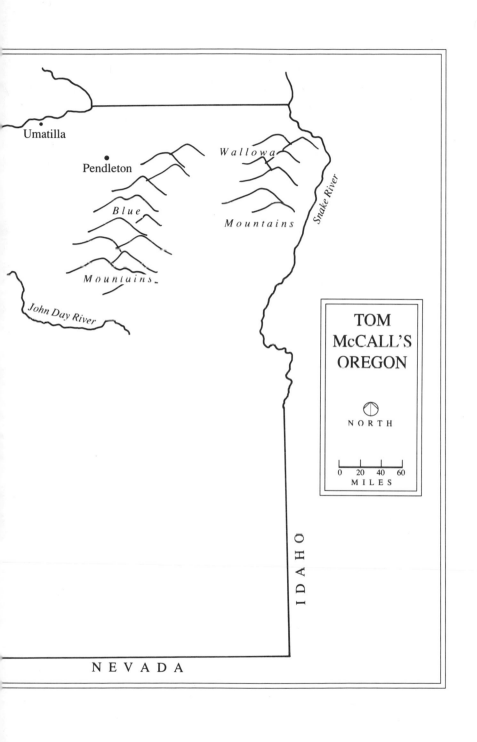

Umatilla

Pendleton

Wallowa

Blue

Mountains

Snake River

Mountains

John Day River

TOM
McCALL'S
OREGON

NORTH

0   20   40   60
MILES

IDAHO

NEVADA

12

The Doctrine

AFTER STRUGGLING THROUGH his first year and a half in office, in 1968 McCall returned to his bedrock theme: protection of Oregon's environment. He had declared in his inaugural address that "the overriding issue of the next decade is quality—quality of life in Oregon." McCall already had championed the Willamette River clean-up and greenway, and protection of public beaches. Those stands were popular and, as a result, quite easy for him to take. Moving to the heart of Oregon's environmental problems promised to be more difficult, however.

His experience as a journalist and governor had taught him that most environmental damage—dirty rivers, industrial pollution, destructive development of pristine areas—had a single root cause: poor planning for growth. McCall wanted Oregon to emerge from the booming 1970s with a new doctrine dedicated to controlling industrial and residential growth. And the only way to control growth was to protect the precious resource most at risk: the land.

As a state that relied on its natural resources to survive, Oregon had a critical stake in protecting its land. McCall understood this better than any politician of his era. He had seen what had happened to areas where development had run its course. Everywhere progress was chewing at the edge of Oregon's natural resource base. Home builders had covered rich Willamette Valley farmland with subdivisions. Timber companies had knocked down forests to build commercial developments, or had not replanted trees after a harvest. McCall realized that no laws or regulations existed to prevent the same fate from befalling the rest of the state.

McCall's decision to move Oregon toward statewide land-use planning evolved into the single most important crusade of his life. He made his doctrine simple: Growth only for growth's sake was foolhardy and irresponsible; development had its place, but under strict control and guidance. He intended to establish a tough test for anyone hoping to cut into Oregon's farm and forest base, and he was willing to usher anyone out of Oregon who did not meet the test.

The kind of planning he envisioned had never occurred in the United States. To succeed, he would have to inspire Oregonians to support his plan by turning land-use planning into an evocative standard for Oregon's protection. Yet it was hardly a tantalizing political subject. In Oregon, as in the rest of the United States, zoning was the most common device for controlling development. However, zoning was often used by local governments not to conserve land, but to protect property values by isolating blight and ghettos. Local control often meant no control, because for city councils and county commissions, development meant fatter tax rolls. Local officials could not resist the lure of short-term jobs that followed new homes and shopping malls. Even well-intentioned local governments in the 1950s and 1960s often felt pressured for development for which they were ill-prepared.

In 1947, Oregon gave its cities and counties the power to create "comprehensive plans," which were intended to guide zoning decisions and were supposed to be more resistant to development pressure. In the few places in which comprehensive plans existed, they wilted in the face of a surging Oregon population: the state's population had doubled between 1940 and 1970, from one million to two million. The surge came from so-called "in migration," with as many as half of Oregon's new residents coming from California.

By the mid-1960s Oregon was growing out of control. One journalist wrote that the state was on a "ticky tacky treadmill" of development. Overloaded sewer systems, patchwork zoning and writhing road schemes were the legacy of development-happy local officials. In

coastal Lincoln County, for example, the county board of commissioners allowed developers and speculators to build countless poorly constructed motels and other tourist attractions along U.S. 101. When, in
the early 1960s, the local chamber of commerce proclaimed Lincoln
County's beach the twenty miracle miles, Governor Mark Hatfield dryly
dubbed it the "twenty miserable miles."

More troubling, however, were the accumulating pollution problems
that were the result of poor planning. By 1968, local health officials in
Lincoln County had located fifty cases of raw sewage flowing into
rivers or onto public beaches, largely from poorly located housing projects with inadequate public services.

In the vast, arid desert of central and eastern Oregon, these kinds of
projects were called "leapfrog" developments, because they landed
miles from the closest water and sewer lines. Often, the developers,
whom McCall ridiculed as "sagebrush saboteurs," lured out-of-state
buyers to these sites through newspaper ads, failing to note the lack of
basic services. The developments were also fire hazards, springing up
on dry, tinderbox lands far from the nearest fire protection.

Not only did the lack of strong land-use planning permit festering
eyesores and contribute to pollution, it threatened the economic strength
of the state. Farming was the state's second biggest industry, falling
only behind timber production, yet farmlands were slowly vanishing
under the bulldozer. Flat farmland was the kind developers found deli-
cious. In the mid-1950s the Willamette Valley had 2.8 million acres of
farmland. In the next fifteen years, developers paved five-hundred thousand acres—nearly twenty percent—for subdivisions and commercial
buildings. That land vanished fastest in the areas around Portland—
namely, rural Washington and Clackamas counties. Clackamas County,
stretching from the city of Portland eastward to Mount Hood, lost one-
third of its farmland during the 1960s alone. "Oregonians," one writer of
the era put it, "have reason to fear that Portland will ultimately merge
with Salem, and Salem with Eugene to make one continuous conurba-
tion, a nightmare of tract houses, clogged highways, factories and commercial strips."

From his own upbringing, McCall understood the financial pressures
on local farmers. Nearby development pushed the speculative value of

Land-use planning was intended to protect productive farm land (such as in this aerial view along the Willamette River north of Albany) from development as the state's population grew. (State Parks photo; OrHi 55547)

farmland so high that the tax burden was immense. Whenever a farmer sold out to a developer, the value of his neighbors' farms shot up. The higher assessments brought higher taxes, often prompting the neighbors to also sell out. The cycle of destruction fed itself. In 1961, the state legislature approved special tax status for agricultural land intended to take financial pressure off farmers and make them less likely to sell their land to speculators and developers. The provisions had little effect.

Not everyone at the local level remained blind to the problematic quilt of unrestricted growth stitched by local governments. Many local officials talked of taking planning decisions out of local hands and giving the decision-making to the state. A few pointed to land-use programs in other states. Hawaii, for example, in 1961 had enacted statewide zoning in response to requests by plantation owners who wanted cane and pineapple fields protected from rampant commercial growth.

McCall was prepared to take on the challenge of statewide land-use planning, although in later years, his detractors tried to use his crusade to show that McCall wanted to lock up Oregon altogether. However, on this issue McCall was not an environmentalist by definition, but a conservationist. He had begun campaigning for his conservation ideas as early as 1965, recognizing that Oregon would some day use up its natural resources such as land. As a conservationist, McCall hoped to guarantee those resources were used wisely—but ultimately used. "[W]e don't have a 'no growth' policy," he reflected later. "We have a wise growth policy."

Wise growth still looked like no growth to business. But McCall cared little for the idea that resources should be used as industry and developers demanded them. "Tom never put much reliance in the idea of supply and demand," said Eldon Hout, then a member of the Washington County Board of Commissioners and an early land-use advocate. "He didn't believe the market system should work when it came to land. He thought land was too valuable for that."

McCall's staff and the Interim Committee on Agriculture worked for a year to write legislation that took the first steps toward state-run growth planning. Of the four bills they produced, none proved more far reaching than Senate Bill 10. The bill contained a strongly worded set of nine land-use "goals." These goals called for protecting open spaces and prime farmland while allowing development "commensurate with the character and physical limitations of the land." That last goal was vital. Designers of the bill believed they could steer commercial and residential development toward more appropriate sites. Under this plan, subdivisions might not go where developers wanted them, but they would go where they fit in with other growth, and where services such as water and sewer could reach and support them.

McCall saw that the threat to Oregon's land was not in what state government did, but in how local governments acted. So SB 10 required all local governments to finish their zoning plans within two years. As a penalty, the state reserved the right to take over local zoning if the cities and counties failed to meet the deadline.

With the bills in hand, McCall needed cooperation from the legislature, but his experience with lawmakers had been rocky. Republicans who controlled the legislature still disliked him. Other legislators remembered the way he had steamrolled them on the Beach Bill. After his troubled year, McCall did not look as politically strong as he had at first, and lawmakers were not eager to help him.

Although House Speaker Monte Montgomery was gone, the new speaker, Robert F. Smith, distrusted McCall as Montgomery had. (Smith had been the one who, three years earlier, had offered McCall the deal that would have promised Montgomery the secretary of state's post in exchange for Montgomery staying out of the governor's race.) McCall wanted to make peace with Smith and the Republicans, but the peace they offered came at a high political price: they wanted a sales tax.

Oregon remained one of the few states without one. The state had only two taxes—income and property taxes. Because the state relied on the two taxes as its only sources of revenue, both were onerous. However, few Oregon issues had proven as unpopular as the sales tax. Voters had always rejected the idea. Still, Republicans hoped the money generated by such a tax would ease the burden of property taxes, although it was charged that the three percent sales tax they had in mind would have shifted that burden onto those who were less able to pay.

McCall had never taken a firm stand on a sales tax. He had supported one while serving as aide to Governor Douglas McKay, but he had backed away from the idea while running for office. Now, he agreed to support the Republicans' plan in exchange for peace.

McCall agreed to give his name to the plan and even campaigned mildly for the tax, playing up its promise of helping schools with funding. However, even as McCall took responsibility for the tax bill, the Republicans who had supported it in the legislature began to oppose the bill that they now called the "McCall sales tax."

McCall had guessed the plan would go down by a two-to-one margin; the final result: a crushing eight-to-one. He told reporters the day after the vote, "I knew in my bones that it was going to be a tough time, especially when I was down in Brookings riding in a parade. I knew it was going to be a tough election when I got some boos and a dog barked at me."

Even after the disaster, McCall continued to take the heat from voters for the Republicans' blunder. "I have heard from my board of directors," he told reporters. "They have told me that I'm all wet." Although he bore voters' ire well, having to take personal responsibility for a plan he disliked, he said later, "was very distasteful."

With the tax debate over, McCall was free to draw attention to land use. He had already tried to do so with a characteristic turn of phrase when he had introduced his land-use plans:

> The steady scatteration of unimaginative, dislocated urban development is introducing little cancerous cells of unmentionable ugliness into our rural landscape whose cumulative effect threatens to turn this state of scenic excitement into a land of ascetic boredom.
>
> . . . Let us never be charged by our inheritors that in 1969 we failed the test, that we buckled and floundered, when everything rode on our grace as leaders who valued our sentimentality but who knew it took much more than loving platitudes to preserve it.

McCall quickly learned that land-use planning would not generate the public support that had greeted the Willamette River clean-up and the 1967 Beach Bill. He was no longer attacking the abstract polluter or talking grandly about the state's aesthetic beauty. He was directing his efforts at every private landowner in the state.

Opposition to the bills came from the largest landowners, many of whom feared that local land-use decisions would be taken away by the state government, which was much more difficult to influence than were local officials. Opponents such as timber companies, including Georgia-Pacific, and industry lobbying groups, led by the powerful Associated Oregon Industries, opposed the bills on the grounds that the legislation invited too much government intrusion. So did the city and county governments, which did not wish to lose their zoning authority. When the bills came up for legislative hearings, several opponents likened the whole idea to the Soviet Union and its centralized planning.

McCall's plan as introduced failed to pass because too many legislators did not understand how land-use planning fit into McCall's larger plan to protect Oregon. McCall had failed to make his case, and the fierce opposition of industry lobbyists only stymied his effort.

In the end, McCall did emerge with one part of the plan: SB 10, which required local governments to finish their zoning plans within two years. Once the deadline passed, the bill would give the governor the authority to impose zoning restrictions in areas where none existed. However, as if to doom even the remnants of McCall's plan, legislators cut the funds intended to help cities and counties finish their zoning plans by the 1971 deadline. McCall feared he had ended up with far too little— a symbolic step toward land-use planning, but little more. Land-use opponents, however, thought he had gone much too far. After McCall signed SB 10, a posse of conservative activists launched a recall drive against him.

The "Recall McCall" effort quickly faded. The group needed 146,000 signatures statewide out of the state's 800,000 eligible voters and only 5,000 voters signed up. Pining for devotion from every Oregonian, however, McCall interpreted the results in his own somber way. "I didn't revel in the knowledge that 795,000 [voters] didn't sign the petitions," he reflected later. "But I fretted with the knowledge that 5,000 people did."

PROTECTING OREGON'S LAND AND ENVIRONMENT was only part of the doctrine that Tom McCall wanted to introduce. The other part was economic prosperity. That meant the need for new jobs.

McCall understood that Oregon needed to broaden its industrial base. The timber business, Oregon's leading employer, was only as strong as the national economy. A recession meant less construction, less demand for lumber, and layoffs across Oregon. McCall had watched his state's economy bob like a cork, from crest to trough, on the nation's economic waves.

Diversification was the key: bring in businesses that did not suffer such sharp cycles. McCall believed that Oregon could walk a thin line, encouraging economic diversity while controlling growth and making industries accountable for their pollution. Yet bringing in new business was difficult. Corporations, when considering interstate moves, first look at the bottom line. When looking at Oregon, companies found several conditions that affected their profitability.

Oregon's tax structure proved to be the first impediment. Without a sales tax to help pay state government's way, property taxes and income taxes were comparatively high. Another problem was Oregon's location. Manufacturing companies saw its isolation from major population centers and soured on the high cost of shipping their goods. And then there were the environmental roadblocks.

McCall had made his priorities in the dilemma clear: new industry was welcome only if it agreed to follow the state's tough environmental rules. The trade-off for McCall was simple. Oregon's environment was its greatest resource, and he would protect it at any price—even if that price meant Oregon lost some jobs in the short run.

McCall counted on the power of his argument and of his persona to convince business that Oregon was not hostile to new industry. McCall could already point to American Can, the new Willamette River pulp mill built under tough restrictions, as proof that his doctrine worked. He also bet that American industry, in seeking livability for their workers, wanted to locate in unblighted areas of the country.

McCall first introduced his doctrine to a large audience in Los Angeles during a March 1969 business recruitment tour. During an Oregon-hosted luncheon, the California businessmen listened as McCall waxed eloquent on Oregon's natural beauty. McCall's speech quickly evolved from passionate to stern, however. The invitation, he declared, was not open to everyone. "We have a high standard of prohibition against industry which will pollute our air, water or scenery," McCall said. He acknowledged that such an attitude could repel the very industry he appeared to be courting. In fact, McCall said, it had. At least $11 million of industrial investments, he said, had recently gone elsewhere because Oregon's standards were too high. He did not mourn the loss.

> Oregon has not been a lap dog to the economic master. Oregon has been wary of smokestacks and suspicious of rattle and bang. Oregon has not camped, cup in hand, at any affluent doorstep.
>
> Oregon has wanted industry only when that industry was willing to want what Oregon is.

His remarks angered many of the Oregon businessmen who had made the trip with him and who believed a governor's commitment to bringing in industry should be unconditional. At a reception following McCall's speech, two Oregon executives griped that McCall should not bother with industrial recruitment tours if he was going to talk about Oregon's high environmental standards.

"He's telling them to bring their plants and not their people," said one. Added the other, "He wants businesses without business problems."

However, McCall's point had not been lost on one of the California executives invited to the speech who overheard the Oregonians' conversation. "If [McCall] can get it all and still have a worthwhile place to live," the Californian told them, "more power to him."

Despite the criticism from Oregon business leaders, McCall did not relent or retreat. Six months later, on a September 1969 recruitment tour to Texas, McCall repeated his warning about Oregon's attitude toward polluters. He said that he stood as guardian of the state's quality, and that polluters should fear him. Then he made it clear that he was not the guardian that industry should fear most.

> When you live in Oregon, you realize how carefully the public watches its heritage.
> Let any speculator attempt to move in the shadows and the voice of the people thunders through the governmental halls. Oregonians care very deeply about the Oregon country.
> And this is a good thing.

When not talking before business leaders, however, McCall was likely to tip the balance even further in favor of the environment. At such times, his break from business and the corporate line was clear. A few weeks after his Texas speech, he took a less tolerant view before an environmental conference in Salem:

> So massive is our degradation, so overwhelming our pollution, so intemperate our demands upon nature and nature's world which sustains us and makes our life possible, continuing our present course threatens disaster.
> Too long we've been dominated by a Gross National

Product syndrome. What is really needed is an index of livability, a measure of performance of how well we're bal-
ancing our demands on the environment with protecting that
environment.

The shift of message from business to environmental audiences was
subtle, but the latter was becoming McCall's prevailing message, a vision of environmental peril that reached beyond Oregon's borders.

The message started with his doctrine, but McCall needed a symbol
of Oregon's commitment to livability. To Oregonians, McCall himself
was becoming that symbol. What the state needed, though, was an enduring action that signaled its dedication. The answer lay waiting, not in
speeches or regulations, but scattered amid the litter along the roadsides
of America.

13

No Deposit, No Return

RICHARD CHAMBERS HATED POLITICS. He had no use for government and cared nothing for the people who ran it. Politics, he said, meant compromise. Richard Chambers was never one to compromise.

But Chambers hated something else more than politics: litter. On his long hikes across the Cascades or along the coast, he cursed the sight of the trash left behind by others. He returned home with bags of garbage that he had picked up during his hikes, and he would sort through the litter, as if seeking a clue to why people cluttered Oregon with their refuse.

One day in 1968, Chambers discovered a clue—and that led him to do what he swore he would never do. He entered Oregon politics. And when he did, Richard Chambers changed Oregon.

Today, Chambers' name appears in no Oregon history books, nor on any monument. Except for a few newspaper articles written about him just before his death in 1974—articles he resisted and wished had never been written—his name never appeared in print. His memorial, however, is any Oregon trail, beach or roadside that is free of litter. It is a memorial he earned with an idea so simple, so humble, so obvious, that many politicians thought him eccentric. They were right. His idea, however, had a power greater than anyone realized.

In Oregon, that idea was called the "Bottle Bill" and its target was litter, the millions of throwaway bottles and cans strewn along beaches

253

and trails and roadsides each year. The bill outlawed these containers, which made up most of the litter Chambers picked up, hauled home and studied.

Designed simply as an anti-litter measure, the Bottle Bill ended up meaning much more. Its enactment showed the nation that Oregonians could be innovative and aggressive when it came to protecting their state from blight. Years later, the bill set an example for recycling efforts intended to reduce the flow of garbage and to conserve increasingly precious energy.

More than any other piece of legislation during Tom McCall's tenure, the Bottle Bill favorably changed the behavior of Oregonians toward their environment. The ensuing attention it brought to Oregon showed the state's leaders they could set new environmental standards for the country.

Over time, Tom McCall became the Bottle Bill's greatest champion and eventually accepted credit for the idea, all of which was fine with Rich Chambers. However, his family, worried that Chambers would be forgotten to history, urged him to write down the story of how he passed the Bottle Bill. Chambers refused. "It's nobody's business what I did," he would boom, "and nobody needs to know."

Chambers' story, however, is a testament to Oregon's own story: the story of a state in which a single man—a logging equipment salesman without political power or money, only a manic drive and stubbornness—could change history. He was a loner who defeated the lies and distortions and bribes of billion-dollar industries. Rich Chambers entered politics, but he did not compromise. Nor did he want publicity, fame or money. He wanted the Bottle Bill. He wanted nothing more.

RICHARD CHAMBERS, his brother, Douglas Chambers, recalled, "was always a solo guy." Born in 1921 in Salem, the square-jawed Chambers was a marvelous athlete, both burly and quick. He disliked team sports, choosing instead handball, a sport that made him alone accountable for success or failure.

After one year in college, Chambers joined the navy to travel the world. His military career ended after a naval officer scolded Chambers for not following regulations. Chambers knocked out the officer with

Richard Chambers, the true father of the Bottle Bill. Chambers shunned publicity and instead worked relentlessly for the bill's passage. Chambers is pictured here receiving an environmental award from McCall in 1974. (Courtesy of the Chambers family, Joseph V. Tompkins photo)

one punch. Chambers insisted the navy give him a dishonorable discharge, but instead he was allowed to quietly resign. His wanderlust unsatisfied, Chambers joined the merchant marine and rode a tramp freighter to the world's ports.

He eventually returned to Salem, married, had three children and joined his father's meat packing business. When that business failed, Chambers traveled the world again, this time as a salesman for a local equipment company. As always, Chambers refused to follow convention. While other salesmen traveled in their business suits, clutching briefcases, Chambers wore a workman's jumpsuit and carried his gear in a duffel bag.

Chambers never stopped seeking adventure. He swore he would climb every mountain in the Cascade Range, kayak every river in the Pacific Northwest, and hike every mile of the Oregon coast. "And I believe," said his wife Kay Chambers, "he managed to do it all."

Chambers usually set off alone, not only because he was independent, but because few could keep up with him. His daughter, Victoria Berger, remembered Chambers hiking long stretches of the coast with his family huffing and puffing behind. On one stretch of beach, a weary Victoria asked her father, "Isn't this beach just like all the others?" "Maybe," Chambers replied, "But I have never seen this beach."

When his family gathered at their coastal cabin in Pacific City, Chambers bounded out of bed long before dawn, worked for a few hours, then drove off in search of a new trail, returning as his wife and children were waking up. "He would have already spent," Victoria recalled, "what for a normal human would have been a day's worth of activities." Often times, Chambers ignored established trails, striking out through the wilds and roaming wherever the glens and valleys led him. Kay might drop him off at one spot in the mountains, only to receive a call from him days later, asking to be picked up far from where he started. She sometimes thought of asking where he was going, but she never did. "That was just Rich," she said. "He wouldn't know where he was going even if I did ask him. He just went."

Wherever he wandered, Chambers returned with bags of litter he had picked up along the way. "Litter drove him wild," his daughter said. "He'd come back with these bags and wave them and say, 'Why do people have to do this?' It perplexed him to no end. Knowing my father, he might have been worrying about how to solve the litter problem for ten years and never said anything about it."

On a sweet, cool Sunday morning in the summer of 1968, that changed. Chambers had returned from his morning walk on Nestucca Spit and had just opened his morning newspaper. "That's it!" he yelled suddenly. "That's the answer!" His family watched him rush out of the house and into tiny Pacific City, where the town's only pay telephone sat at the town's only intersection. There, before 8 A.M., Chambers called Paul Hanneman, the local state representative, whom he knew well. "Paul, you've got to get down here right away," Chambers said. Hanneman sensed an emergency and rushed to Pacific City. There, Hanneman found Chambers standing at the intersection and pointing to litter in the street. "There was paper and crap all over the intersection like someone had lost a load of garbage," Hanneman said. "I looked at Rich and said, 'You got me up at this hour to look at garbage'?"

"Look at this mess," Chambers replied. "We can stop this."

Chambers then showed Hanneman the newspaper, pointing to a small news item about a lawmaker in British Columbia who had proposed banning non-returnable bottles and cans. "Don't you see?" Chambers said. "Most of this garbage is bottles and cans. All we have to do is put a deposit on those bottles and cans and people will bring them back to the stores."

Hanneman looked around, then he looked at the hulking Chambers, his eyes wild with excitement. "What could I say?" Hanneman said. "I told him I'd introduce that idea at the next legislature."

WHEN HANNEMAN FIRST SUBMITTED CHAMBERS' BILL, he did not yet understand the breadth of the problem Chambers had identified.

For decades breweries and soft drink companies had sold their products in returnable glass bottles. The returnable bottle was a way of life in America, largely because bottling companies found it cheaper to collect and wash old bottles than buy new ones. That standard changed in the late 1940s when the steel and aluminum industries—booming after World War II—started to promote the metal beverage can. Before that time, beverage cans were rare, yet the economic benefits became clear to the industry. Making cans was cheap, and that meant the used cans did not have to be shipped back to the beverage companies. Cans as a result became "throwaways," a result the metal companies enjoyed. Unlike returnable bottles, cans required more manufacturing and more business for the aluminum companies. Glass companies saw the trend and pushed to ban the returnable bottle as well.

Throwaways also gave national bottlers and breweries a new competitive edge against small operations. In 1949, more than 400 breweries operated across the United States, most of them small operations serving local markets. In the beer industry especially, national breweries—Anheuser-Busch, Schlitz, Miller Brewing—often had trouble competing with local brands. One reason was cost. The national brewers paid high costs for shipping used returnable bottles back to their central plants, often clear across the country. Throwaway bottles and cans changed that. Because national brewers only had to ship bottles and cans one way, they could undercut the prices of the local brands.

The strategy had an enormous effect on the industry. Beer consumption nationwide had declined until 1958, and the beer industry credited an economic turnaround to the price advantages gained with the disposable bottle and can. By 1958, nearly half the beer shipped came in throwaway cans.

Unable to compete, many local breweries went out of business. The total number of breweries nationwide shrank to about 160 in 1968, putting more than 27,000 workers out of jobs. Soft drink companies also consolidated, changing from local bottlers to larger regional plants. During that same eighteen-year period, the number of soft drink plants fell from 6,600 to 3,000.

Initially, beverage companies, and metal and glass makers showed little concern for the growing litter blight. In Oregon, beer and soft drink companies alone accounted for 173 million bottles and 263 million cans, most of which by 1968 were throwaways. Many of these cans ended up in landfills, but many became the bulk of litter.

In 1953, the Vermont legislature had approved the first bottle bill, which banned throwaway bottles in an effort to stop the one-way flow of trash from the American beverage and container industry. Concerned that their growing profits were threatened, representatives from the beverage and container industry descended on Montpelier, claiming the bill failed to stop litter. In fact, the Vermont law targeted only bottles. Cans were exempt, although they were part of the growing litter problem. Rather than amend the law, Vermont lawmakers gave in to industry pressure and repealed the entire act.

The Vermont experiment created a political alliance of vested interests—breweries, soft drink makers, glass companies and the metals industries—determined to prevent another bottle bill from succeeding again, anywhere. To refocus blame, the industries accused the public of creating the littering problem. In 1953, a handful of national businessmen, most involved with the beverage and container industries, formed Keep America Beautiful, a non-profit group designed to promote anti-litter public service campaigns.

The campaigns successfully kept political pressure off the industries. Nowhere in the United States did anyone challenge these industries until Rich Chambers insisted that Oregon try.

CHAMBERS DID NOT WAIT for the start of the 1969 legislature to promote his bill. He knew lawmakers would have hundreds of other bills cross their desk—1,913 that session, as it turned out—and he wanted to make sure they saw his. Alone, he launched a lobbying campaign that lawmakers soon found impossible to ignore.

He started with letters to bottling companies, asking politely for statistics and information about their operations. The companies, unaware of Chambers' intentions, complied. Out of this information Chambers pieced together the history of the throwaway and its effect on bottling companies' profits. At his own expense, he then started his letter campaign, aimed at both lawmakers and potential allies. He brought a special talent to his cause. "In our family business, [Rich's] job as business manager was to open the mail every day," Douglas Chambers said. "He learned that ordinary-looking letters got ignored."

Chambers produced letters that no one could ignore. He had collected odd stationery during his world travels—from a hotel in Zaire or a business in New Zealand. He mismatched the stationery with colorful envelopes. He even made the postage eye-catching. "If it was a six-cent letter, or whatever postage was then," Douglas said, "it might have three or four different stamps—two half-cent stamps, four one-cent stamps, all of them different and eccentric." The combination made a brash sight.

Chambers pounded out the letters themselves on a typewriter that produced large block letters. Sometimes he typed his message in all capital letters, other times he ran the paper through the machine diagonally. When he copied letters for mass mailings, he printed them on paper in bright shades of red or blue or green. "He did whatever it took to get noticed," Douglas said. "Nobody who ever got a letter from Rich Chambers threw it away."

His letters received answers. By the time the 1969 legislature opened, Chambers had aligned an unusual set of allies, including outdoorsmen's organizations, grange halls, garden clubs, and fledgling environmental groups.

Hanneman, who made a living as a fishing guide, had grown to understand the bill's value. Hanneman carried the bill from lawmaker to lawmaker, looking for co-sponsors. Only two of the other eighty-nine legislators signed on. "I was desperate for support," Hanneman said. "I needed something more besides some grange and garden clubs. Other lawmakers saw this bill as halfway between innovative and frivolous."

Hanneman soon realized that he had been overlooking someone who could make the difference: Tom McCall.

The bill, House Bill 1157, as introduced, simply banned all non-returnable bottles and cans used for soft drinks and malted beverages. The bill had everything that appealed to McCall—an innovative idea that promised to directly clean up the environment. But McCall distrusted Hanneman because he had been one of the few stubborn lawmakers to vote against the Beach Bill two years earlier. However, Hanneman won an audience with Kessler Cannon, McCall's top environmental aide. The bill impressed Cannon, who persuaded McCall to overlook his dislike for Hanneman and endorse the bill.

From the start, however, HB 1157 looked doomed. House Speaker Robert Smith considered it trivial and shipped it off to the House State and Federal Affairs Committee, a catch-all panel nicknamed the "Speaker's Committee," that was a repository for bills that Smith could either win quick approval for or ensure a fast death.

The committee's chairman, Roger Martin, a Republican from the Portland suburb of Lake Oswego, was one of two lawmakers Hanneman had convinced to sign on to the bill. Martin agreed to hold a courtesy hearing for the bill, and Chambers and Hanneman rounded up their supporters. Kessler Cannon testified to the governor's support for the bill, and a parade of enthusiastic backers, brought in by Chambers, followed. A river guide told of the enormous amount of bottle and can litter he had found that summer along the McKenzie River; a farmer testified about four of his cows that had died due to eating metal and glass shards left from discarded beverage containers; an attorney pointed out that current litter laws rarely brought fines or convictions. Chambers himself handed the committee members crusty bottles and cans he had picked up on his hikes.

The bill intrigued committee members, which alarmed its foes. During the hearing, lobbyists for companies and groups such as International Paper, the Glass Bottle Blowers Association, the Seven-up Bottling Co. and Reynolds Metals attacked the bill.

Opponents first attacked the idea with studies paid for by their industry and the state Highway Department that showed bottle and can litter to be a small portion of roadside garbage. (Such claims were deceptive. The studies counted every fleck of paper or metal—even dead animals—as litter. As a result, the real impact of bottles and cans amid the roadside trash looked smaller than it was.) Union lobbyists stepped in to spin gloomy tales of job losses in the glass and metal industries if such a bill ever passed.

Noting skepticism among committee members, Hanneman offered a compromise. Rather than ban non-returnables, the bill could require a five-cent deposit as an incentive to return bottles and cans. Hanneman argued that the idea was hardly radical, as it only required brewers and bottlers to operate as they had a few years before. The panel amended the bill as Hanneman suggested.

By this time, however, industry lobbyists had leaned on chairman Martin, who secured promises from five of the panel's nine members to vote to trap the measure in his committee.

Or so he thought. Hanneman had quietly persuaded one committee member, State Representative Carroll Howe, a conservative Republican from rural Klamath Falls and a Hanneman fishing buddy, to change his mind. When Martin finally held a committee vote on HB 1157, he expected to see the bill tabled on a five-to-four vote. To his shock, the panel instead voted five to four—with Howe's turnaround vote—to send the bill to the house floor.

The action set off a panic among Republicans and lobbyists, who geared up their opposition to the measure. Embarrassed, Martin could not explain how the bill had escaped his committee. Smith thought the GOP-run house could still kill the bill, but he could not be sure. The Bottle Bill was now a renegade, and Chambers and his ragtag alliance suddenly had a chance to win.

When the bill reached the floor, Martin asked that the house send it back to his committee. Martin parroted the complaints of industry lobbyists that, as a sponsor, he had never raised before. Martin promised to amend the bill in committee and make it satisfactory to all sides, but Hanneman knew Martin had no intention of keeping that promise. Hanneman rose to defend his bill, describing the behind-the-scenes effort to destroy this simple idea and pleading with his colleagues to save it. When finished, he collapsed in his chair, certain he had failed. "There aren't many bills that escape from the house floor with all the guns firing," he said years later.

Yet the Bottle Bill nearly did survive. Of the house's sixty members, twenty-seven voted with Hanneman, three short of keeping the bill alive. As suspected, Martin, despite his promise, promptly buried the 1969 Bottle Bill in his committee. Frustrated, Hanneman did not know where to turn before remembering the one ally he had not called on.

Tom McCall had remained largely silent throughout the battle over HB 1157. Now, Hanneman thought, another public blast such as the one McCall had delivered for the Beach Bill two years earlier could change the Bottle Bill's fate. He asked the governor's office for last-minute support.

It never came. Instead, McCall delivered a final blow to the bill. McCall's office sent a letter to a bottling company executive saying that the governor now wanted no Bottle Bill this legislative session. The letter, copies of which house Republicans circulated, killed the bill. The letter stunned Hanneman, who had thought he could count on McCall's support to the end. When United Press International (UPI) correspondent Don Jepsen asked McCall about the letter, the governor exploded in a fury that Jepsen had never before seen.

McCall recognized the bill's potential, but he did not think lawmakers were ready for such a bill. During his rant to UPI's Jepsen, McCall complained that controversy over the Bottle Bill now would "blow the cover." In fact, McCall had secretly agreed with the Bottle Bill's opponents to endorse their plans for an anti-littering campaign to begin in 1970, a campaign they thought would douse support for a new Bottle Bill in the 1971 session. However, McCall planned to revive the bill in 1971 after lulling the bill's opponents into a false sense of security. "He was convinced the time wasn't right," Hanneman said. "I thought, 'Why wait?' But he wanted to wait. As time eventually showed, his judgment showed him to be right." McCall had another motive behind his strategy. The bill had been someone else's bill in 1969. In the 1971 legislature he would endeavor to make it his own.

While the bill's death disappointed Hanneman, Richard Chambers shrugged off the setback. "He never thought it would pass the first time," said Kay Chambers. "He always thought it would take years. So when it died the first time, he went right back to his typewriter and started mailing more letters. He never paused, not even for a minute."

14

Red Hat

TOM MCCALL FOUND THAT, over the years, political expediency often clashed with his environmental sensibilities, as it had with the Bottle Bill in 1969. His determination that the environment win out over politics played well with Oregonians, and, in March 1970, he said he would make environmental issues the theme of his re-election campaign.

His choice of theme was timely. That same month, a national survey firm, Louis Harris and Associates, conducted a poll on environmental issues for Pacific Northwest Bell, the area's telephone company. When asked what they considered the most pressing Oregon problem, respondents, influenced by the growing attention to environmental issues, overwhelmingly named "pollution." The survey also found strong sentiment for the tenets of McCall's doctrine. By an impressive seventy-seven percent, the Harris poll found that "[T]he public appears to firmly oppose the new industry which cannot guarantee that it is pollution-free."

McCall sensed these attitudes as he traveled the state. His reportorial style of gathering information had not changed, nor had his determination to keep in touch with Oregonians. Not only Oregon, but America as a whole was becoming more conscious of environmental issues.

The ecology movement of the late 1960s and early 1970s was not triggered by a specific occurrence, such as the 1989 *Exxon Valdez* oil spill in Alaska's Prince William Sound, but by many events: a spectacular oil spill in January 1969, when a Union Oil Co. drilling platform ruptured six miles off the coast of Santa Barbara, California, spilling more than twenty thousand gallons of oil, killing thousands of animals and savaging the area's tourist economy; a major airport threatened Florida's Everglades; DDT poisoned animal life—the bald eagle, the United States' national symbol, was dying off, in large part because of pesticides; in major cities across America, water and air pollution created small-scale scandals as the dirtying of the Willamette River had in Oregon decades earlier.

Out of the disasters, large and small, emerged a picture of a civilization out of balance with the environment. But the images that crystallized the earth's precarious position for many people were those sent back to Earth by the Apollo astronauts. From the dead stone of the moon's surface, millions of Americans were reminded that the Earth was alone in its trip through space, with nowhere to turn for help if its sources of life were extinguished.

Awareness of environmental issues grew into a cultural movement. Plans for "Earth Day" in April called for rallies and marches across the country. Long-time advocates of environmental reform looked on the movement with a mixture of appreciation and skepticism. "The environment," wrote scientist Barry Commoner in 1970 with some irony, "has just been rediscovered by the people who live in it."

Politicians adjusted their rhetoric accordingly. President Richard Nixon devoted much of his 1970 State of the Union speech to environmental concerns: "The great question of the seventies is, shall we surrender our surroundings, or shall we make peace with nature and begin to make reparations for the damage we have done to our air, our land and our water?" Political leaders felt pressure to take action—or to appear to take action. On the federal level, there was a rush of legislation: the National Environmental Policy Act, the Water Quality Improvement Act and stronger amendments to the Clean Air Act. Congress, in 1969, also created the Environmental Protection Agency as a clearinghouse for all the new regulations.

In all the environmental activity, McCall discovered the bigger stage that he wanted. In 1969, Congress created a three-person presidential advisory panel, the Council on Environmental Quality. The panel included an ad hoc citizens committee, the Citizens Advisory Committee on Environmental Quality. The panels, intended to add even more advice on environmental policy, would periodically report to the president on environmental issues of growing concern.

When McCall heard of the citizens' committee, he pressed Nixon for an appointment to it. Nixon hardly owed McCall any favors, but McCall made a nuisance of himself and Nixon relented. McCall's efforts to win the appointment drew sarcastic comments within the White House. In a private 1969 memo, one Nixon aide wrote that he would "inform [McCall] that he is being appointed to a Presidential Commission in accord with his most earnest desire."

McCall again was with tall company. Nixon had also named Laurence Rockefeller, aviation hero Charles Lindberg, and entertainer Arthur Godfrey to the panel. Unlike most of those celebrities, however, McCall brought with him an established reputation on environmental issues.

McCall was grateful to Nixon for the appointment, yet the warmth did not last. Within days of McCall's appointment, the Nixon White House backed McCall into an inescapable political corner, and McCall found his bitterness toward Nixon renewed.

IN LATE 1969, A DEADLY LEGACY of America's military lay buried in the desert a few miles above the Columbia River near Hermiston. Many Oregonians knew that the Umatilla Army Depot, opened in 1941, served as a storage site for tens of thousands of unwanted bombs, artillery shells and weapons. They generally did not know about the nerve gas. Starting in 1962, the army had secretly shipped about six thousand tons of nerve agents to Umatilla. The nerve agents included the deadliest liquids ever developed: GB, an asphyxiating liquid that killed within minutes; VX, requiring only a single drop on the skin to cause death within seconds; and World War I-era HD mustard gas, less sophisticated but as lethal.

The army had been dumping aging casks of nerve gas in depots like Umatilla all over the United States—and all over the world—since 1941. In 1968, however, the secret stockpiling became a political and safety problem. Nerve gas killed 6,400 sheep just outside the Dugway Proving Grounds near Skull Valley, Utah, when a pilot on an experimental gas spraying mission forgot to turn off the plane's spigot, sending a deadly cloud floating off the base. The army at first denied any responsibility, and then confessed that nerve gas had killed the animals.

The army faced an even larger credibility fiasco the next year. Starting in 1963, the army had shipped thirteen thousand tons of gas-filled bombs, missiles, mortar rounds, mines, and rockets to the Chibana Ammunition Depot on Okinawa, the Japanese island under American control since the end of World War II. The storage operation had remained secret, even from the Japanese government, until the Nixon administration began negotiating the return of Okinawa to Japanese control. Then, in July 1969, a leaky bomb exposed twenty-six army workers to GB; all survived without serious injury. Despite the army's efforts to hush up the incident, the *Wall Street Journal* reported the leak, revealing the illicit presence of American nerve gas on Japanese soil.

Japan angrily demanded the United States remove the weapons from Okinawa. Nixon had to move them to placate Japan. He knew no other foreign country would welcome them. So Department of Defense officials scurried to find an American location to dump the nerve gas weapons. On 25 November, Nixon issued a statement denouncing nerve agents as weapons of war. But that same week the Pentagon found the perfect spot to put the Okinawa arsenal: an isolated army outpost accessible to the Pacific Ocean, one accustomed to handling dangerous weapons, in a sparsely populated state where public opinion might matter less.

That place was Oregon.

Nixon approved the secret plan to ship the weapons to Umatilla in November 1969. Army officials knew, however, the actual shipment could not be kept secret. Federal law required the governor of any state hosting a nerve gas shipment be warned ahead of time.

But no one had told Oregon's governor. The Pentagon waited until the last minute to alert McCall of its decision. With the announcement scheduled for 2 December 1969, a Pentagon official called Ron Schmidt on 30 November to ask for a secret meeting between McCall and Thaddeus Beal, under secretary of the army, for the next day. Schmidt gleaned only a rough idea of what the Pentagon wanted, and he urged McCall not to give the Pentagon officials an audience. McCall waved off Schmidt's protests. "I'm going to listen to the Pentagon and do what the government finds necessary," McCall told him.

Beal came to the meeting with two generals and two colonels in tow. He opened the meeting with a patriotic speech about America's defense needs, then read a letter he had drafted for McCall announcing the shipment of the gas through Oregon. "Transportation of this material through your state," the letter said, "is necessary in the interests of National Security." Schmidt watched McCall's nod. "It was as if they knew what buttons to push with Tom," Schmidt said. "The whole flag-waving tone played right to his prejudices."

Like a reporter, McCall took detailed notes as Beal and the officers explained the shipments. Code-named "Operation Red Hat," the shipments would start arriving by ship within a month at the Bangor Naval Base near Bremerton, Washington, move by rail south through Washington, and then east through Oregon up the Columbia River Gorge to Umatilla. Most of the gas would remain in five-hundred-pound bomb shells, all of which were defused. From McCall's notes, it is clear Beal was emphasizing only a rosy view of the potential dangers of the shipments. "Flawless," McCall scribbled as he listened. "Safe."

McCall told Beal he did not like the plan but would go along if the president insisted. Beal said the president would insist, and he and the officers left.

Schmidt shut the door behind them and whirled around to face McCall. "You can't go along with this," he said. "You have to oppose this."

"I have no choice," McCall said. "My hands are tied." He reminded Schmidt that the army had authority to move the shipments into Oregon whether the governor liked it or not. Schmidt disagreed. McCall did not have to accept the army's plan. He could at least seek a way to stop the shipments.

McCall paced around the room, wondering out loud what the president would think if Oregon opposed him. McCall had already given Nixon grief during the election by refusing to endorse him. Now, after his own pleadings, Nixon had granted him the spot on the environmental panel that McCall had coveted. How could he cross the president of the United States now?

Schmidt said McCall should not care what Nixon thought. "Since when does party loyalty matter to you?" Schmidt asked. "Why can't we take on the government?" Schmidt then laid out a plan to wage the fight. He described a strategy for blocking the shipments—an all-out political campaign. Within hours, Schmidt said, he could activate the McCall organization and turn it into an anti-nerve gas machine. McCall—with a bold, outraged declaration against the shipments—could generate the momentum.

Schmidt soon realized that Beal's patriotic pitch had worked on McCall, and McCall wanted to hear nothing more about defying the commander in chief. Still, Schmidt did not give up. The two argued back and forth for the next four hours. McCall refused to budge and grew enraged at Schmidt's defiance.

"I'm not going to be part of this," Schmidt finally yelled. "And if you proceed with this then I quit."

"You can't quit!" McCall boomed.

"Why the hell not?" Schmidt asked.

"Because you don't have a job anymore!"

And on the argument went. McCall saw no need to fight a losing battle. Schmidt insisted that the battle was the point. After midnight, his voice growing hoarse and his stomach aching from the yelling, Schmidt surrendered. Before he did, however, Schmidt reminded McCall of why he had come to work for him in the first place: McCall's inspiring 1964 speech before the Jaycees convention.

"You told all of us we could make a difference," Schmidt said. "That's why I came to work for you. This is the chance you have been waiting for. This is the chance for you to be the Tom McCall Oregonians voted for, the Tom McCall who said he would protect this state. You were made for this kind of fight. And now you won't fight." Schmidt then grabbed his coat and left.

The next day, McCall left for Washington, D.C., for a meeting of governors. His fight with Schmidt had disturbed him deeply. He had barely slept, nagged by self-doubt. During a stopover in Denver, McCall telephoned Schmidt.

"Are you mad at me?" McCall asked him. Schmidt could hear the little boy in McCall—wanting to be loved, heartbroken at rejection.

"Not mad," Schmidt said, "Just hurt."

Increasingly troubled, McCall stole away from the governors' conference to meet again with officials from the army and the Department of Health, Education and Welfare, the agency charged with reviewing the army's plans for the shipment's safety. The briefings lacked the flourish of patriotism surrounding the meeting the day before. McCall started to view the shipments through a prism of concern and alarm. If the army does not need this poison, McCall thought, then why not destroy it? And why store it in the wilds of Oregon, where in the event it were needed, it would take weeks to reach a battle zone? Remembering what he had learned the day before—that one drop of the gas could kill a human—McCall did his own math. Using long division and filling scratch paper with numbers, McCall calculated that the nerve gas bombs headed for Oregon contained more than seven billion drops of deadly liquids—more than double what it took to kill every human on earth.

Twenty-four hours after the Portland meeting with McCall, the Pentagon announced its plans for the Red Hat shipments and assured Oregonians their governor had approved of the plan. But no one had checked the announcement with McCall. By that time, McCall—overwhelmed by doubts and sobered by Schmidt's disappointment—had changed his mind.

"Listen," McCall said in a call to Schmidt later that day, "put together a plan to fight this thing." Schmidt thanked McCall and hung up. He had, in fact, already done so. While sincere in his promise to quit, Schmidt had believed McCall would change his mind. He had already launched the public relations campaign he had described to McCall the day before. Schmidt said later:

> He wanted to say no to the shipment. This is what McCall wanted to do. He didn't want to just make headlines. He wanted to stop the sucker. This meant going up against the entire Pentagon, against the president of the United States. He wanted to do it. But he didn't have the confidence to pull it off. He had always talked about taking on a fight like this, but he never had before. This was to be his first great war with the establishment.

McCall returned to Oregon on 5 December to launch his attack on Red Hat. Had he decided to fight the shipments earlier, he might have deflated the Pentagon's publicity with a preemptive critique for the Oregon media. But the army had already announced its plans. McCall quickly wired Nixon—and promptly gave reporters a copy of the telegram—to say he had changed his mind about supporting the shipments.

> To say that the citizens of Okinawa . . . should not be subjected to the proximity of these inherently dangerous and frightening chemicals is an incredible statement when you go on to say that it is all right for the citizens of Oregon to suffer this same proximity. . . .
>
> May I suggest that rather than bring these weapons from Okinawa to Oregon that you take a further step as evidence to the world that America means business in moving away from this heinous concept of war?

The "further step" McCall advocated was the destruction of the weapons.

McCall was not alone in his opposition. Senator Mark Hatfield had denounced the plans, as had most of the congressional delegations from Oregon and Washington. Their concern caused the Pentagon to suspend its plans for immediate shipment.

McCall's blast at Nixon became national news and page-one headlines throughout Oregon. His loud defiance soon caught national attention. "I can't recall an issue I've faced as governor as disturbing as this one," he told a reporter for the Los Angeles Times. "It's a terrible problem for me because I'm a strong supporter of President Nixon but I had to do what my conscience told me."

Schmidt had sensed Oregonians would overwhelmingly oppose the shipments. He was right. He had also guessed that without one of their leaders in the forefront, Oregonians would lack a clear channel through which to voice their anger. So McCall quickly became the focus of Oregonians' hopes. Several citizens groups, including one called People Against Nerve Gas, sprang up in Oregon and Washington. Petitions and letters accumulated in tall columns on McCall's desk, and Schmidt kept a tally. By early January, McCall had received 16,350 protests—through messages or petition signatures. At the month's end the number had grown to 23,000. "We need poison gas here in Oregon like Custer needed more Indians," said one letter. Added another, "We expect you to do all in your power to prevent such foolishness."

What were McCall's powers? In deciding to fight the army, he was leading Oregonians to believe that he could truly stop the shipments, yet he had no practical way to do it. McCall suggested the state sue the army, which would allow him to appear as if he were taking some bold action against Red Hat. State Attorney General Lee Johnson and McCall's own legal counsel, Robert Oliver, reported that the president's authority to order the shipment overrode any power McCall had to refuse it. "I conclude (reluctantly)," Oliver wrote McCall in mid-December, "that any effort by the state to block shipment of the gas into Oregon is foredoomed to failure in the courts."

The president had never responded to McCall's first telegram. Instead Nixon had had Defense Secretary Melvin Laird write a reply. On 8 January 1970 Laird wrote admitting that the army did have defensive needs for the nerve gas—a point the Pentagon had been loathe to admit earlier. "[T]he President renounced the use of lethal biological agents and weapons, and all other methods of biological warfare. . . . Our national security requires, however, that we have the capability to deter the first use of lethal chemical weapons against our forces. We can only do this by maintaining a limited deterrent stock under strict safety precautions."

Angrier than ever, McCall released Laird's letter to reporters to reveal the falsity of the Pentagon's claims. As he handed out the letter at a press conference, McCall vented his frustrations.

> By the Army's own definition then, [the nerve gas] was sort of a garbage—a very lethal but non-essential garbage—looking for a home. Since it frightens the Okinawans, let's dump it in Oregon. . . . These terms ought to be unacceptable to Oregonians—and the fact that they are unacceptable is supported by the tremendous wave of revulsion that has swept across the state.

By February the number of signatures on the petition to stop the shipments had reached 62,000. Such a count may have looked small to the Pentagon, three thousand miles away, but by local measurements, the message was extraordinarily strong. Organized campaigns to place initiatives on the statewide ballot required far fewer signatures and took several months to accumulate. McCall had collected the signatures within a matter of weeks.

McCall returned to Washington, D.C., in late February, carrying the petitions to show the White House his opposition was not symbolic. Refused a meeting with Nixon, McCall was brushed off on Secretary of the Army Stanley Resor. The meeting was disastrous. Resor spent the meeting talking past McCall, while the governor's temper burned. Finally, McCall gave Resor the petitions collected from Oregonians and insisted they be given to Nixon. Resor refused and said he would send them only to Laird.

McCall flew home furious and, on 4 March, again wired Nixon. Resor, McCall told the president, "was more implacable than ever in his avowed determination to ship the controversial munitions from Okinawa to Oregon." McCall pleaded with the president to tell him personally why the shipments were justified. Then McCall noted that State Treasurer Robert Straub had said that, on the nerve gas shipments, "I believe Tom McCall has done all he can do." McCall ended his message to Nixon in the third person: "Even though McCall has done all he can do," he told the president, "McCall cannot give up."

BY THE START OF APRIL 1970, four months after the Pentagon had announced its plans to ship nerve gas, McCall's battle had become one the public could not ignore. The *Wall Street Journal*, for example, described the controversy in a long, page-one story. McCall could not have written a better lead himself: "Can the Republican governor of a Republican state successfully oppose the Republican Administration in Washington on an issue wrapped in the mantle of national security?"

McCall had never heard from Nixon personally. "We were naive," Schmidt recalled years later, "to think that we could with public opinion change the Nixon White House's mind on this. They were ready to roll over Tom McCall in the same way they were rolling over so many other people with this plan."

Confidential White House memos show that Nixon's aides were painfully slow to realize how public opinion had lined up against the nerve gas shipments. On 11 April, four months after McCall announced his opposition to the shipments, Brigadier General James D. Hughes, Nixon's military aide, boasted to White House aide John Erlichman, "Governor McCall has reluctantly agreed to support us if, in fact, the President will not change the order to store the gas at Umatilla." The White House clearly was not paying attention to McCall's message.

Through it all, McCall remained a lone voice of opposition. Certainly, members of Congress from Washington and Oregon opposed the plan, yet none took such a forceful position as McCall. As the Pentagon delayed its plans, many politicians opposing the Red Hat shipments toned down their complaints. For a while, many state officials thought the Pentagon would quietly drop the idea.

McCall knew better. The army had sent him a classified copy of the shipment plans, and the details were harrowing. Though the army controlled the shipment, it insisted Oregon and Washington be responsible for the safety of their citizens. The plan required the states to prepare for a disaster of a monumental scale. In Washington, for example, the army had told Governor Daniel Evans to prepare for evacuating 1,300 square miles and 150,000 people should anything go wrong with Red Hat.

The nightmarish precautions mocked all the soothing assurances from Pentagon officials about the shipment's safety. The description of the security plan did serve one useful purpose, however. It sent politicians elbowing past McCall to voice their renewed opposition. Evans, who had been silent until now, was one of the quickest to speak out. "Our previous information was that any spills of gas would be localized and easily dissipated," Evans told reporters in Olympia. "The plan for widespread evacuation simply does not square with that statement." Now accustomed to the deceptions, McCall described the army's claims about safety more succinctly: "It was hollow talk."

McCall was pleased the details of the army's plans had set off more alarms. But the shipments were still coming.

AS THE DATE FOR THE RED HAT shipments neared, on 22 April, the United States celebrated its first Earth Day. In hundreds of cities, and especially on school campuses, protestors demanded an end to America's polluting ways. More than ten thousand people marched in Washington, D.C., and another hundred thousand attended a rally in Manhattan. Everywhere people joined in the ecological symbolism. Students rode bikes or roller skated to protest smog-belching cars; in San Francisco, protestors dumped motor oil into a fountain outside the offices of Standard Oil Co. to symbolize the damage done by off-shore drilling; colleges and high schools held "teach-ins" on ecological issues.

McCall spent Earth Day touring schools across the state, delivering his main speech of the day at the University of Oregon. The speech marked a turning point in his public statements about the environment. His doctrine for Oregon was, by nature, parochial. His message on this day, however, was far broader, although he acknowledged that his immediate mission was to protect his own state.

> In Oregon, we use the phrase, "We still have time. . . ." If we are to succeed in saving our planet the battle will be won or lost at the local level, right in the streets and fields of Hometown, America, the project works or fails. It is not an issue anyone will be able to back away from. . . . Oregon is the key state in the Domino structure of North America. If we fail, pollution marches on.

His own work on environmental issues had started as an assault on pollution in a single site, the Willamette River. He now saw problems in a far greater scale, and he expressed his concerns with characteristic drama.

> It will take drastic and continuing efforts to stave off mankind's suicide. . . . There is no longer anything sentimental about trying to save a tree or protect an old swimming hole. The heyday of "grab and go" is all over.
>
> For the first time men are beginning to realize that there are measurable limits to his living environment. There isn't unlimited air space. There isn't land enough for everything. Mankind is supportable by a finite world. There is just so much air, so much earth, and so much water. . . .

Although it was human nature to quickly blame the faceless corporate polluters for the world's environmental problems, McCall said, human nature itself was the culprit.

> Man has fouled his nest. Man has squandered his resources. Man has treated his environment with cavalier abandon as if it were his to have and hold—as if it were within his power to make better balances than nature has already designed. . . .

For the first time in his career, McCall made the issue of personal sacrifice tantamount to the demands he was placing on polluting industry.

> Everyone wants electricity but no one will support dams or nuclear power plants. We want Kleenex and paper towels and Handi-wipes and disposables of all kinds but we don't want the pulp and paper plants. We want the standard of living that ample harvest of forest products make possible, but we don't want the wigwam burners, the logging trucks on the highways, the rafts of timber in our waters or the clear cutting of forest areas. We want abundant foods, but don't use the chemicals that make them possible. . . .
>
> It's obvious that a change in attitude is vital, and a first desirable change would be the realization that the problem of environment and pollution is not the other fellow's, but the responsibility of everyone. It is not, "What are you going to do about it?" nearly as much as it is, "What are we going to do about it?"

Most of all, McCall worried that Earth Day would be a fad that passed before change took hold.

> The lobbyist for pollution is indifference. As long as the average citizen washes his hands in the bowl of Pontius Pilate so will he continue to give tacit approval to the crucifixion of this particular human society.

The world doesn't need us—we need the world. When everyone knows this [and] faces it honestly and thoroughly, we may have not the death of man, but the transfiguration of man.

The speech marked McCall's first strong call for a change not just in how America produced, but in how it consumed. And the speech marked his departure from the singular concerns of how Oregon stops pollution, to how the world prevents it.

In a final irony, however, McCall's message never extended beyond his college audience of two thousand. During a question and answer session, a student asked about the Western Kraft paper mill near Albany. For years, the mill had spewed its rotten-egg stench near Interstate 5, making it an infamous landmark for travelers. McCall's answer reflected the popular frustration with the mill.

"What is going on in Albany," he declared, "is a stinking cancer on the broad, green bosom of the Willamette Valley."

Rather than note McCall's speech, the Oregon press instead grabbed on to his racy quip. Once more, McCall's flair had overshadowed his greater message.

THE PROSPECT OF OPERATION RED HAT hung over Earth Day in Oregon like a toxic pall. With the army intent on making the nerve gas shipments, McCall's remaining hopes were left with the non-military agencies that had the power to rule the shipments unsafe and halt them. The person whose review carried the most weight was Surgeon General Jesse Steinfeld, a Nixon appointee who would decide for the Department of Health, Education and Welfare if the shipments should proceed.

McCall appealed to Steinfeld in a letter, asking him to consider the dangers now exposed in the army's own warnings. Steinfeld disagreed that the shipments constituted any public danger and on 1 May he approved the shipment plans. The army set the shipment date for 23 May.

With one last, lonely cry, McCall turned to an old friend, Spiro Agnew, the former Maryland governor now Nixon's vice president.

I have remonstrated until I am hoarse and my writing arm is
aching [McCall wrote Agnew on 2 May]. There are no con-
ceivable circumstances that would obligate us to use nerve
gas. It is almost incapable of safe movement. It is a weapon
without purpose, unless that purpose might be the alarming
of Americans. . . . For heaven's sake, Ted, give the feelings
of Oregonians a little consideration and ease up on the bull-
headedness that is forcing so many supporters of the administration to the wall in Oregon!

Agnew's reply read as if a Pentagon publicity officer had drafted it.

With no other avenue left, McCall finally convinced the state's
lawyers to sue the federal government. Joined by Washington's Governor Evans, McCall's suit charged that neither state could meet the onerous security and safety requirements for the shipments imposed by the
army.

The lawsuit provided the bold action McCall wanted. The newspapers played it up as he thought they would. McCall understood from his
private legal advice the suit could not stop the shipments, only delay
them further. However, the suit never got that far. As McCall's lawyers
had predicted, a federal judge quickly tossed out the case. The ruling
was the final defeat in a battle McCall had wanted desperately to win.

As Red Hat drew nearer, public outrage about the shipments grew.
Protestors in Seattle held a "die-in," falling to the streets in mock death.
Other groups laid plans to physically block the Red Hat train as it moved
south through Washington toward Oregon.

The two states' congressional delegations also turned up the heat.
Washington senator Warren G. Magnuson introduced, with Oregon senators Mark Hatfield and Bob Packwood's endorsement, a resolution to
block the army's funding of Red Hat and all future nerve gas shipments
into the United States. Even if the bill had passed, it would have come
too late to stop the shipments.

Throughout the debate over Red Hat, all but one of the members of
the Oregon and Washington congressional delegations had opposed the
shipments. If that one member had also opposed it, the Pentagon would
have never proposed the shipments. When that one member changed
his mind, it made all the difference.

Senator Henry M. "Scoop" Jackson was a hawk's hawk, a cold war veteran and Democrat who for thirty years had represented Washington in Congress. A liberal on social and environmental issues, Scoop Jackson had never wavered on support for the nation's defense establishment. His seniority on the Senate Armed Services Committee gave Jackson enormous clout in the Senate. While other Democrats bristled at the thought of supporting Nixon, Jackson and the president shared a kinship over the Vietnam War. Nixon, as a result, trusted Jackson. When he wanted to test the political mood of the Pacific Northwest, Nixon looked to Jackson as much as his GOP allies in the region.

From the day the Pentagon announced plans for Red Hat, Jackson, alone among congressional members from Oregon and Washington, stood up for the administration, parroting the Pentagon's claims the nerve gas should be preserved rather than destroyed on Okinawa. Jackson's support for Red Hat alone would have preserved the Pentagon's plans, but his support abruptly disappeared. At any other time, Jackson would have stood firm. In 1970, however, Jackson was running for re-election.

Jackson's popularity in Washington appeared to guarantee his re-election in November. Yet when he returned to campaign in April 1970, he discovered hostile voters almost everywhere with only one thing on their minds. They wanted the nerve gas shipments blocked. Jackson tried to explain his position to angry Washingtonians, but every time he did, voters shouted him down. Jackson knew that his support for Red Hat might not cost him the election, but it was proving too embarrassing for him to remain a supporter of the shipments.

So he did what any politician—especially one determined to hold power—would do. He changed his mind.

In late April, Jackson told Nixon he was changing his position on the shipments. As a cover story for his fast change of heart, Jackson held up the National Environmental Policy Act, a law he had sponsored the previous year. The law required that shipments such as the one proposed under Red Hat be reviewed under the tenets of that act. They had not been.

Had the Pentagon remained committed to Red Hat after Jackson's opposition, the military would have complied with the law and had the shipment reviewed. The sight of Jackson turning on the nerve gas issue, however, told Nixon and the Pentagon that it was time to cancel the shipments.

"It was a near-perfect political approach," noted Jackson co-biographers, William W. Prochnau and Richard W. Larsen. "If the shipment had to be stopped, then it would be better to have it halted by a Jackson bill."

On 23 May, Nixon called Jackson, then on a campaign tour of central Washington, to tell him personally the shipments had been cancelled. Jackson gleefully called a press conference and took credit as the man who had stopped the shipments. "I was the only one who went to the president personally," Jackson claimed later.

Indeed, Jackson was the only one who went to Nixon personally because he was the only one Nixon agreed to see. The president completely ignored the one person who had tried to reach him the soonest and the most often: Tom McCall. The White House made certain that Jackson—and only Jackson—had official confirmation of Red Hat's cancellation. When rumors of the cancellation reached McCall, he called the White House for his own confirmation. His call was never returned.

The White House's snub infuriated Ron Schmidt. After months of work, he wanted the credit for McCall. "Tom wasn't mad," Schmidt said. "After the bloody fight we had waged, he expected it from the Nixon White House. He shrugged it off."

Nixon may have sought to deny McCall credit, but other leaders knew the truth. Washington governor Daniel Evans said Jackson would not have acted without the public outrage stirred by McCall. "McCall," Evans said, "deserved better."

Still, McCall was relieved. He told reporters later that his fight against the shipments had been a "tedious six-month battle toward reason."

"Let this be proof," he added, "that the system does work; that the White House does and must listen; that the Pentagon ultimately is compelled to obey the citizenry."

McCall had not wanted a fight with the Nixon White House. He had lacked the stomach for it. Yet he had waged the fight anyway, guided by instincts and an innate sense of what Oregonians wanted. His skepticism about Nixon soon turned into suspicion. From Red Hat he learned that the president was willing to treat McCall and his state like pawns when the ends required it. It was a lesson that guided him through the next crisis that promised to consume Oregon, a crisis already swirling around him.

15

Vortex

B Y MAY 1970, when the nerve gas shipments to Oregon were
halted, most of McCall's first term had slipped away, and he
faced a re-election campaign. What had McCall to show for his
three years in office? He had promised to create a new doctrine for Oregon to protect the state against ravishing growth, yet he had made only
small steps toward fulfilling his promise. Those small victories had
often been bumped from the limelight by the problems that had dominated his first term: the Nestucca Highway, failed tax plans, a prison
riot, nerve gas, and his son, Sam.

His former opponent, State Treasurer Robert Straub, had announced
he would again challenge McCall in 1970. McCall's political sense
might have put him at ease; polls showed that the public still thought
well of him. Yet those same polls showed that his personality alone
would not be enough to guarantee him a second term. In April 1970,
the *Oregonian* had published a poll showing the McCall-Straub rematch
was a dead heat.

Straub commissioned his own poll and discovered why. "Our surveys showed substantial numbers of people saying, 'McCall's weak,
he's wishy-washy, he's on the fence'," Straub aide Ken Johnson recalled. "We knew Tom was an accommodating, fair person. He would
wring his hands over issues in public. He hated to make decisions that

were going to hurt somebody. It was either black or white, and he'd always go with gray. And that left the impression of weakness."

Pounded by events and slowed by his own missteps, McCall had little time to overcome his image as an equivocating governor. In the spring of 1970, McCall wished only for a stretch of peace during which he could collect his wits. Instead, his administration was overcome by a potential crisis he could not avoid—a crisis that offered him his greatest invitation for calamity, but gave him his deliverance.

IN THE THREE YEARS since McCall had taken office, in 1967, a new icon had appeared in America: the war protestor. Young, loud, long-haired, questioning authority—protestors did not fairly characterize their generation, but they did help define it. They had opposed the United States' involvement in Vietnam since the mid-1960s; through the decade the anti-war movement had increased, especially on college campuses. By 1970, Americans had become accustomed to televised images of students marching against the war.

In Oregon, the war protests reached their peak between 1968 and 1970. The University of Oregon, in Eugene, was the state's center of protest, with student leaders holding angry marches on issues ranging from the Vietnam War to grape boycotts.

The protests tore McCall in two directions. As a former journalist, McCall instinctively felt that the protestors' First Amendment rights needed to be defended, no matter their message. "Without the right of dissent, all of the newspapers, magazines and broadcast agencies would be grinding out government pap, a grisly gruel of bureaucratic jargon designed to cement the status quo," McCall said. "When your rights are gone, it makes very little difference to the prisoner exactly who it was that threw away the key." Yet when University of Oregon student organizations included profanities in their protest publications, McCall, erstwhile freedom of speech defender, grew livid.

Although McCall might defend their right to free speech, the protestors' message grated on his patriotic soul. "Americans," he said about the anti-war demonstrators, are "fed up to their eardrums and eyeballs." In a harsh letter to the university's acting president, Charles E. Johnson—a letter that McCall gave to the press before Johnson could read it—he insisted "that this kind of depraved mischief be stopped."

Overall, McCall worried about the divisiveness of the era. "We are in danger of becoming a society that could commit suicide," he said, "a society that sometimes seems to be ripping itself apart just for the masochistic pleasure of seeing the blood."

Oregon schools, however, had largely avoided the violence plaguing other campuses. McCall's chief of staff, Ed Westerdahl, had insisted that the state, not local police, oversee crowd control on campuses, and he convinced McCall to allow him to handle campus disorders. "He was a hothead when it came to protestors," Westerdahl said. "He realized he would not think logically when it came to handling these crowds."

By early 1970 the anti-war tension had eased. Nixon, who had inherited the war from Lyndon Johnson, had promised a "peace with honor" and had steadily withdrawn American troops from Southeast Asia. However, Nixon was only changing how the war was fought. While pulling troops out, Nixon launched titanic bombing campaigns over North Vietnam. Then on 30 April, Nixon ordered an invasion of Cambodia, which the Communists used as a base and supply route. Americans saw suddenly that, after eighteen months in office, Nixon was not ending the Vietnam War but was widening it with savage initiative.

As elsewhere, the waning anti-war movement in Oregon exploded with new fury in reaction to the invasion. Marchers became violent at the University of Oregon; at Portland State University (PSU), protestors blocked downtown streets at rush hour; even at placid Oregon State University (OSU), considered the state's most conservative university, the ROTC headquarters was firebombed.

At Kent State University in Ohio, where Governor James Rhodes had pledged to "eradicate" protestors, on 4 May, five days after the Cambodian invasion, the local National Guard unit opened fire into a crowd of student protestors. The bullets struck fifteen students. Four died.

Anti-war protestors responded to the Kent State killings with renewed intensity. In Eugene, a thousand-student throng stoned the ROTC building. At PSU, protesters called a strike, again blockaded downtown streets and took control of the student center. On 7 May, PSU president Gregory Wolfe closed the campus for a cooling-off period. For the next

four days hundreds of protestors vandalized campus buildings and oc-
cupied the South Park Blocks, the narrow, tree-lined swath running
through the PSU campus.

McCall was torn over the local and state events. Privately, he supported the Cambodian invasion. Soon after Nixon had announced the invasion McCall had written Nixon to endorse the president's policy on
Vietnam. McCall had also telephoned Vice President Spiro Agnew to
repeat his support. But for the first time, McCall sounded impatient with
Nixon's handling of the war. "The president is on notice," he told
Agnew, "that the nation will not stand for our straying into a new bot-
tomless quagmire in Southeast Asia."

Sensing the volatility of the moment, McCall remained silent about
Nixon and Cambodia until campus protestors marched to the Capitol
on Monday, 11 May. His staff urged McCall to send a representative to
face the protestors, but McCall himself walked out to meet the crowd of
seven hundred that had gathered on the building's front steps under pal-
lid, misty skies.

Student leaders insisted he denounce the Cambodian invasion. Mc-
Call walked up to a microphone, flashed a peace sign with his fingers,
and said, to jeers, that he thought Nixon was "on the right track." He
then criticized the students for shutting down the campuses. "One percent of the students are throwing bricks and lighting fires, while ninety-
nine percent are throwing out ideas," he told the crowd. "When you
close the classrooms you compress the jugular of a free society."

Later, he escorted protest leaders to his office, listened patiently to
their complaints, and refused again to denounce the Cambodian invasion. When one student leader complained about McCall's stubbornness over Vietnam, McCall replied, "You wouldn't want me to say what
I don't feel, would you?"

McCall's appearance on the Capitol steps had diffused the tension of
the gathering. As he spoke in Salem, however, the relative peace on
Oregon campuses shattered. After a weekend of chaos at PSU, student
leaders still maintained a foothold in the South Park Blocks on Monday
morning. Over the weekend protestors had barricaded streets and
erected large tents, for which they had obtained permits from the city.
The permits had expired that morning, however, and Mayor Terry

Schrunk, who oversaw the police, and City Commissioner Frank Ivancie, who oversaw city parks, ordered the protestors cleared.

Under any other circumstance, Westerdahl would have overseen crowd-control operations at PSU. But he was out of the state on business, and the Park Blocks belonged to the city. Besides, city officials wanted to send a brutal message to protestors, and they sent one. Shortly after noon, a one-hundred-man police riot squad moved in on the Park Blocks, where they found about one hundred students milling aimlessly in the park. With little warning, the police moved in, attacking without provocation. (Police officials claimed they acted in self-defense, but an independent investigation later found that their claim had no foundation.) The officers clubbed and punched anyone in the park not wearing a police uniform. No one was spared—officers even bludgeoned a student already on crutches. Thirty-one protestors, many with head and face injuries, later required medical care.

The police attack sickened McCall and only added to his sense that events around him were beyond control. In campaign speeches around the state, he listed the problems he faced—budget troubles, the nerve gas shipments, failed tax plans, and now campus violence. "It has not been," McCall sighed drolly, "a Victorian lawn party at the Capitol lately."

Meanwhile, resentment brewed among protest leaders at PSU, and a small group of students leaders talked of a retaliatory march—payback for the police beating suffered in the Park Blocks. The talk spread, first from impromptu conversations in coffee shops to meetings in students' homes. No one had a plan, really, but anger and frustration reigned as people started to hatch a scheme—a "confrontation," in their words. The plans grew when Portland newspapers announced, on 25 May, that in September, at the national American Legion convention, Portland would play host to the war protestors' greatest nemesis: Richard Nixon.

IN LATE JUNE 1970, agents of the Federal Bureau of Investigation (FBI) arrived in the governor's office for a meeting with McCall. The agents had been secretive about the topic of the hastily arranged meeting. McCall soon learned why. The agents said they had discomforting criminal intelligence about anti-war protestors in Oregon. Said McCall later:

Not long after Kent State, I received word that Oregon
seemed destined to be the next battleground. . . . According
to the U.S. Justice Department, some 50,000 young people
calling themselves the People's Army Jamboree were planning to descend on Portland. Some of the group's members
openly welcomed a riot. I could envision our state being
pulled apart before the world's television cameras.

Shortly after that it was announced that Nixon would give the keynote
address at the national convention of the American Legion, the country's largest veterans' group, the FBI had opened a routine security file
and had begun filling it with reports from informants on the PSU campus.
The agents told McCall their sources had suggested that anti-war protestors planned to disrupt the American Legion convention. Given the
recent violence at PSU, McCall found the FBI information chilling.

The Portland FBI office had sent the same information to its Washington headquarters. In a previously classified FBI memo, Portland
agents, on 18 June, reported: "[R]adical 'New Left' element in the Portland area is planning major disruptive operations during the [Legion]
convention." In another memo, also dated 18 June and addressed directly to FBI director J. Edgar Hoover, the Portland office warned: "Although at this early date the disruptive planning of the dissenters is only
in its formative stage, Portland is well aware of the possibilities involved and the volatile conditions that might develop with the presence
in Portland of two, very large, polarized groups. . . ."

Hoover thought the quality of the original intelligence reports was
quite low. After receiving the two classified memos in June, he wired
the Portland office to say the report was unconvincing and needed more
proof to back up its warnings.

The Portland office would not be dissuaded, however, and responded
with a dispatch stating, "all current information indicates that thousands
of dissidents, hippies, anti-Vietnam and anti-military protestors, and
other individuals generally bent on bringing down society, the government, and all its representatives will be gathering in Portland. . . ."

McCall never doubted the dire tone of the FBI report. He thought
highly of the FBI and the agents he had known in Portland. His personal

FBI file included a 1966 profile describing him as "pro-Bureau." The next year, a Portland agent, writing directly to Hoover, said that Mc-Call was "a great admirer of the Director, of the FBI and of this office." McCall's faith in the FBI led him to fear for Portland's security.

What the FBI was predicting in June 1970, after all, was entirely consistent with the times and the violent protests that had erupted across the country: the 1968 Democratic Convention in Chicago; Kent State; and even Portland State a month earlier. "We couldn't run the risk that the FBI wasn't right," recalled Ed Westerdahl, who sat in on the initial briefings. "When the major law enforcement agency in the United States says you're going to have fifty thousand people invading your city, you go on the basis it's going to happen. . . . It was moot whether they were right or wrong. In the climate of the times, we thought it was very likely they were right."

How accurate was the FBI in its warnings? Declassified FBI records and interviews with protest planners show that the bureau's alarm was greatly exaggerated. Many of the intelligence sources the FBI cited were actually newspaper clippings culled from the PSU newspaper, the *Vanguard*, and one of Portland's major dailies, the *Oregon Journal*. One *Journal* article quoted a student leader predicting as many as seventy thousand protestors would descend on Portland. The reports also cited rumors passed along by students serving as FBI informants on the PSU campus.

The truth was that the People's Army Jamboree in June and early July was a hapless group of hippies too contentious to agree on the basic planning for a protest. Rather than energize protestors, the PSU riot had actually alienated and exhausted many of the local anti-war movement leaders. Others activists refused to take part in a protest certain to draw more police violence. "People were just burned out," recalled Peter Fornara, one of the Jamboree's early leaders. "It was hard to get anyone interested."

Then what had convinced the FBI that fifty thousand protestors planned to come to Portland? "We had heard that the Legion expected to bring twenty-five thousand people to Portland," Fornara said. "So we just doubled the number, made it up out of thin air. The number meant nothing. It wasn't real. It was just talk."

WHAT TRULY WAS AT WORK in the summer of 1970 was not fact but fear. "There was a feeling of surprise in the warnings, but not necessarily skepticism," Sidney Lezak, then the United States attorney for Oregon, said years later. As Lee Johnson, then Oregon's attorney general, recalled, "More important than the intelligence was that [the FBI's prediction] was being printed in the papers. . . . I had the distinct impression that this thing was going to come together because all of these people would just show up here."

By early July, word of the FBI's warnings about the Jamboree had leaked to Portland's two daily newspapers. Both cited the fifty-thousand number as gospel, as if the protestors had already made reservations. "Pretty soon," Ron Schmidt said, "there was a legitimacy to that number."

The predictions by law enforcement officials about the Jamboree's size and scope surprised no group more than the Jamboree leaders themselves. They laughed when they read claims by police in the newspapers that fifty thousand people would show up, and they used the outrageous numbers to wheedle concessions out of city officials. "We exploited it," recalled Robert Wollheim, one of the organizers. By doing so, Jamboree leaders made the FBI's warnings self-fulfilling prophecies.

Portland's newspapers made the Jamboree and its leaders front-page news as they applied to use Washington Park, located in the West Hills overlooking downtown Portland, as an encampment for protestors. Soon, local Legion officials swaggered before television cameras to declare they would confront anti-American protestors. With this happening two months before the convention, Oregonians soon had an inescapable impression: violence in the streets of Portland was a certainty, and only its intensity remained unknown.

By July, however, McCall had started to doubt the credibility of all sides in the affair, even the FBI. By then, the bureau was claiming to have more specific intelligence that representatives from the Black Panthers and the Seattle Liberation Front, a militant group with alleged ties to the radical Weather Underground, planned to use the Jamboree to incite violence. The FBI also claimed that convoys of hippie protestors appeared headed for Portland from around the country.

It began to seem as if federal officials were not interested in keeping the peace. "The Nixon administration kept warning us about violent confrontations," Schmidt said. "Tom believed that a violent confrontation was exactly what the White House wanted. It would have fit into their scenario of what they would have liked to have happened—these 'commie peace protestors' put down for their opposition to America's war."

McCall urged Nixon to cancel his Portland trip, hoping to defuse the situation. Nixon did not respond, and McCall vented his frustrations to his staff. "They're going to play this for all that it is worth," McCall fumed. As Schmidt recalled, "Tom was well aware of what their game plan was. He saw that he was caught in the middle. Both sides wanted to make a violent point. And Tom did not want Portland torn apart for the White House's political advantage."

McCall was in an impossible position. He could not sit idly by while Portland burned, yet no one seemed interested in preventing a confrontation. He had no escape—until two hippies came to his door.

LEADERS OF THE PEOPLE'S ARMY JAMBOREE had believed that every counterculture group in Portland would rally behind their plans. Many groups did follow, including the Students for a Democratic Society and some Vietnam veterans organizations that opposed the war. By July, however, the Jamboree's following was in shambles. The increased public attention the group was getting in the press only made matters worse. As city and law enforcement officials talked more of violence, Jamboree leaders became more strident.

During one July meeting, many of the one hundred or so people gathered to hear Jamboree leaders left in frustration and disgust. Several people retreated to a coffee shop to talk, and the talk turned to creating an alternative event that would take place outside of Portland. Someone suggested the event be a rock concert, like Woodstock, the New York festival that had attracted a half-million people only the year before.

The idea caught on, and the group began calling itself the "Family," dubbing its alternative event the Clear Creek Festival of Life. The festival would be free: admission, food, music. The Family even issued a crude press release calling the festival "a peaceful coming together." One of the Family's members—no one recalls who—called the festival a vortex of peace. The name stuck, and the group soon called its festival "Vortex I."

Two of the group's members, Robert Wehe and Glen Swift, took the plan to city officials and found no one willing to listen. They then visited the governor's office, where they were referred to Ed Westerdahl. Westerdahl had spent weeks grappling with the Jamboree problem. He was not sure what two hippies could offer him, and at first he refused to meet with them. After they had returned twice over the next week, Westerdahl relented and agreed to listen.

The meeting created an odd scene: Westerdahl in a crewcut and suit, his two long-haired visitors on the other side of his desk. Westerdahl remembered thinking that one of the hippies looked like Jesus Christ himself. As he listened, McCall's chief of staff saw logic in their idea. "They identified the right way to deal with the problem," he recalled. "Decrease the numbers in Portland, give these people an alternative. It was very practical."

Westerdahl quietly scouted the state for a place to hold such a festival and decided on McIver State Park, a two-year-old, 847-acre park in rural Clackamas County, about thirty miles southeast of Portland. He then called in Ron Schmidt and Robert Oliver, McCall's legal counsel, to describe his plan.

Vortex, Westerdahl explained, was the solution to their problems. With the city of Portland denying the Jamboree park permits, the tens of thousands of protestors that the FBI predicted would descend on Portland had nowhere to stay. Once protestors moved to Vortex, lured by promises of the music festival, they would stay put, contained within the park. The Jamboree would be denied the throngs it needed to disrupt the American Legion and Nixon's visit.

Westerdahl added that the plan would only work under two conditions. First, the state would not only condone Vortex but actually run it. Second—and most controversial—law enforcement officials would close their eyes to whatever might happen inside the festival. Woodstock had become famous for its open drug use and nudity. Westerdahl argued that the state had to tolerate the same activities at Vortex. A police presence in the park could inspire people to flee the festival and return to downtown Portland.

Schmidt and Oliver liked the plan, but no one knew what McCall would think of it. The three aides presented the scheme on 5 August, and the governor's blood boiled. "Westerdahl, are you crazy?" McCall screamed. "Are you out of your goddamn mind?"

In the face of McCall's ire, Westerdahl listed the benefits. McCall calmed down and thought about the idea. Given his experiences with his son Sam, McCall could not accept the idea of open, unrestricted drug use in the state park. Westerdahl explained that state police would ring McIver Park for security. If police moved inside, however, the peace inside the park would collapse.

Frustrated by his narrowing choices, McCall turned to Schmidt and Oliver. They told him they agreed with Westerdahl. McCall then asked Schmidt a question that no one had yet considered. "Ron," McCall said, "you're the political man. If I make the decision to do this, what happens?"

Schmidt shook his head. He noted that the election followed the American Legion convention by only seven weeks. "Whether it works or not, Governor," he replied, "it's very likely you'll lose the election because of it."

McCall fell silent. He looked solemnly at Schmidt, and then at Oliver and Westerdahl. He then sat up in his swivel chair, spun the chair around and faced the wall behind him.

THE DILEMMA MCCALL FACED was inescapable. From the FBI's reports, he had no choice but to assume the throngs of protestors were coming into Portland. McCall believed violence in Portland was now inevitable, whether initiated by Jamboree protestors, outside anarchists, drunken Legionnaires or out-of-control police. In this deepening morass he had found he could trust few people—not Jamboree leaders, not the White House, not the Portland police. The only people he could trust were his closest aides. And they had brought him a plan that he could not stomach.

He trusted Westerdahl's analysis and recognized the boldness in his plan. He also trusted Schmidt's analysis: no matter the result—whether he allowed violence to erupt in Portland, or if he pandered to hippies— McCall could expect to lose re-election.

McCall was, above all else, a gambler. Gambling, he had said often, was in his genes. As a gambler, he had found comfort in certain defeat, as he had in sinking his last nickel into slot machines years earlier. Politics was indeed different, and the American Legion convention far more serious, yet McCall's spirit was the same. And so much already seemed lost: peace in Portland, his second term, and hopes of finishing his work as governor.

He spun his chair around to face his aides. "I've made my decision," McCall told them. "And I've just committed political suicide."

IN AUGUST 1970, Lieutenant Eugene Doherty had already served more than a decade as a sworn officer of the Oregon State Police, proud to serve as a defender of the law. His superiors knew Doherty to be a faithful officer willing to obey orders, so he did not find it surprising when Oregon State Police Superintendent Holly Holcomb asked Doherty to join him in a walk from police headquarters across the street to the governor's office.

Doherty asked what the governor wanted to talk about. "You'll see," was all Holcomb would say.

Holcomb and Doherty entered the governor's private office and found Tom McCall and Ed Westerdahl waiting for him.

"What do you know about rock festivals?" McCall suddenly asked Doherty.

Doherty paused for a moment. His mind flashed to images of the jumbled masses of young people he had seen on television. "You mean like Woodstock?" Doherty asked.

"Yes," McCall replied, "something like that." Doherty replied he did not know much about rock festivals.

"Well," McCall said, "now you have a chance to learn a lot more."

Westerdahl described plans for Vortex as Doherty listened in shock. Then McCall cut in. "We're putting you in charge," he told Doherty.

"Governor," Doherty protested after a moment, "what you're asking me to do is condone a lot of unlawful activities. I'm a sworn officer and I can't do that."

McCall looked around the room and shrugged. "Well," McCall said, "if you feel that way, as of now you're no longer assigned to the state police. You're assigned to my staff. You work for me now. And you can do as I tell you. If I tell you to ignore the law, you do it. It's as simple as that."

Doherty understood instantly what was going on. McCall had chosen a risky plan. Now nothing would go by the rules.

The scene was symbolic of what the next six weeks of planning by McCall's office would be like. Westerdahl had to prepare to house, feed, and entertain tens of thousands of young people at McIver Park. Not a single state dollar was allocated for such a purpose. So Westerdahl made his orders to state agencies clear: If the rules interfered, change or bend them. If that did not work, break them.

McCall kept arm's length from the entire operation. Initially, he wanted to call a press conference to announce and explain Vortex. Westerdahl vetoed the idea, deciding the governor needed to be insulated if something went awry. So Westerdahl, flanked by the two hippies who had brought him the Vortex idea, appeared before reporters 6 August to announce the state would endorse plans for the McIver Park festival.

At first some of the reporters did not believe him, and when the news went out, many Oregonians could not believe the announcement, either. The plans particularly outraged residents of Estacada, a logging town a few miles from McIver Park. "[McCall] should get the chair for this," sneered one resident after hearing the news. McCall himself related one story of an Estacada woman who called him in outrage. "We're not going to put up with it," she screamed at the governor.

"Then what would you propose to do in this confrontation?" McCall asked her.

"Goddamn it," she snapped, "shoot 'em."

Other state and local officials were publicly convulsed at the announcement. "You're telling these people, 'You can get stoned at this state park . . . but please don't do anything violent. We will exempt you from our laws and rules'," said Portland City Commissioner Frank Ivancie, the most vocal city official against Vortex.

The state's newspapers took a surprisingly reserved stance, but those which attacked the idea did so with vigor. "Government officials would be naive and misled if they believe that merely providing 'bread and circuses' for these young people will avert confrontations," intoned an *Oregon Statesman* editorial.

McCall also had problems among his own supporters. "A number of the people on the campaign committee thought I was a certified loony and turned McCall into one as well," Westerdahl said. But he, too, was worried by now about pulling off Vortex as planned. So he turned to the one person he knew could make the difference: Glenn Jackson.

As the Transportation Commission chairman, Jackson had authority over the state park system. With Jackson's approval, Westerdahl ordered tens of thousands of dollars in public funds spent to prepare the rock concert. When public money ran short, Jackson shook down his business friends for $50,000 in cash and materials to cover the state's needs.

Throughout the planning, no one knew how Robert Straub, McCall's opponent, would react. When Straub heard about Vortex, the thought of naked, drug-using teenagers romping through a state park offended him. He dashed off a press release lambasting McCall, but his aide Ken Johnson grabbed the release and tossed it in the trash can. He told Straub that the dynamic of panic and violence had gone beyond politics and that the plans for Vortex had changed everything in the campaign. If Vortex failed to prevent violence in Portland, Johnson said, McCall's hopes for re-election would be ruined anyway. Privately, though, Johnson recognized the brilliance in what McCall had done and realized the reverse was just as true. If Vortex worked—or, what was more likely, if it only appeared to have prevented violence that was not inevitable after all—the race for Straub was lost.

MEANWHILE, LEADERS OF THE JAMBOREE protest effort found their support drying up as many people who had been planning the marches decided to work on the Vortex festival instead. Their attitude was "[L]et us use dope, get all the sex we want, play music and do anything as long as we leave the politics to them," said one Jamboree organizer in frustration. Added Jamboree leader Peter Fornara years later, "You didn't have to be a genius or a hippie to know that opening a park and having some music would draw a crowd in 1970. It was a conscious and very clever use of [McCall's] power."

McCall narrowed the Jamboree's support even further by putting up a tough front. He activated the Oregon National Guard and sent selected divisions to Fort Lewis, Washington, for riot training. As the American Legion convention approached, Westerdahl, who had McCall's approval to direct troop movements, told Jamboree leaders he expected to have ten times as many troops as the state would really have on hand. Westerdahl then kept jeeps and soldiers moving around the city to make the National Guard's numbers appear far greater than they were.

The National Guard's maneuvers in Portland both chilled the Jamboree leaders and heightened the alarm in the city. A rumor control center was flooded with calls: "Will the streets be closed?" "Are the Hell's Angels really coming?" One local headline read, "Citizens Urged to Be Cool as Youth Invasion Forecast."

The American Legion president, arriving in Portland early, did nothing to calm fears, declaring that the National Guard should be armed and prepared to fire. "Until we treat [protestors] as common criminals," he declared, "we will never solve the ills of this country."

The riot plan devised by McCall's office banned the use of loaded guns. Instead troops would physically separate war protestors from Legionnaires if scuffles did break out. One provision—dreamed up by Schmidt—even called for helicopters to sweep in low over protestors. Instead of dropping tear gas, though, the helicopters would shower the streets with rose petals as loudspeakers played a tape of McCall asking for peace.

Publicly, however, signs of peace were scarce. Downtown businesses boarded up their windows. Multnomah County gave the sheriff the equivalent of martial law powers in certain sections of Portland. The city and county emptied their jails, sending inmates to the state penitentiary to make room for mass arrests.

However, the People's Army Jamboree had failed miserably to recruit throngs to Portland, and by this time the FBI realized its predictions had been off—way off. Intelligence reports of traffic heading toward Oregon showed no unusual activity, and bureau officials secretly slashed their official estimates of protestors from the original fifty thousand to ten thousand. Three days before the convention opened, the Portland office admitted in a classified wire to Director J. Edgar Hoover, "Outsiders are filtering into the city daily but to date not in the large numbers predicted by PAJ [Jamboree] leaders."

No one made the diluted predictions public, however. The fears that had been ignited were allowed to burn.

TOM MCCALL SEIZED THE MOMENT, on 25 August, to deliver an extraordinary statewide address about the tensions facing Portland. The speech was unprecedented in that it was carried by sixty-seven television and radio stations across Oregon. In his speech, McCall revealed the revised FBI estimates, saying, "[I]ntelligence sources have advised me that the tide of young people coming to Portland for confrontation may be waning." However, McCall stuck that information deep inside a speech that judiciously conveyed a sense of crisis, conviction and—most of all—compassion.

> Great numbers of the young people attracted to Portland are not coming to riot, burn or kill. They are coming to peacefully exercise their constitutional rights. However, some will seek to manipulate the others as pawns to trigger serious and possibly violent confrontation.

He defended his plan to sponsor Vortex as an "alternative to milling madness" and then implored that each group—the Jamboree, the American Legion, and the citizens who had become simple bystanders—behave themselves.

> Violence—no matter who perpetrates it—will be put down, vigorously, promptly and with absolute certainty. . . . Whatever the future has to say about our preparations, it cannot fault the fact that we have built with painstaking care against the imponderables of this fortnight.

The speech was classic McCall and one of his finest ever: dramatic, lyrical and strong. He embraced the protestors' First Amendment rights—in which he strongly believed, and which he alone among political leaders was willing to defend—while threatening to squash the anarchists the state imagined lurked within the city of Portland.

McCall drove from the television studio to the Portland Hilton and

McCall delivers a televised statewide address before the start of the controversial
1970 American Legion convention, hosted by Portland. Law enforcement officials
warned of a violent confrontation between Legionnaires and anti-war protestors, and
McCall pleaded for calm. The peace symbol, a prop for another television show, was
an ironic touch. (Courtesy of the *Oregonian*)

entered Room 2020, where the state had set up a command center. As
they had for the past year, events were sweeping McCall's administration along beyond his control. The coming days were to be no different.
All he could to was wait, his knuckles turning white.

THE DAY MCCALL GAVE HIS SPEECH, a small, little-noticed story in the
Oregon Journal reported that law enforcement officials along the west
coast saw no evidence of any sort of a youth "migration" toward Oregon. However, the next morning, few Oregonians were paying attention to any news other than Tom McCall's rock festival.

No one knew how many would show up at McIver Park. McCall guessed the park's population would hit fifteen thousand. However, by 26 August, the day after McCall's statewide address, and two days before the festival started, more than two thousand people had already poured into the park's single entrance. Vehicles of all kinds—motorcycles, pickups, vans spattered with Day-Glo paint—created a long caravan toward the park. When the festival officially opened Friday, 28 August, Vortex's population rose to five thousand. The next day all roads leading to Vortex were clogged with cars, and traffic was backed up for twelve miles on State Highway 224, leading to McIver Park. Thousands of cars filled nearby farmers' fields, leased by the state for use as parking lots; many people heading for Vortex abandoned their cars and walked. By the end of the day, more than thirty-five thousand people jammed the park.

The days were clear and hot, and inside McIver, Vortex blossomed into a gigantic, peaceful gathering. Many people at Vortex were local folks who had come to the park simply to see what a rock festival looked like. They saw what they had expected to see: young people openly smoking marijuana and strolling around naked. Hundreds of party-goers splashed in the Clackamas River, prompting a flock of local voyeurs into the area. So many private airplanes and helicopters circled overhead to give their passengers an aerial view of skinny-dippers, that the Federal Aviation Administration finally had to issue a formal warning that the airspace above McIver Park was too crowded to be safe.

Thirty miles north, another festival, called Sky River by its organizers, had drawn twenty thousand more people. Held in Washougal, Washington, just across the Columbia River from Portland, the Sky River festival had no official sponsorship. As Saturday night fell, more than fifty thousand revelers were camped at the two festivals. At McIver Park, campfires glowed as music and drums pounded through the night.

So far, McCall's ploy had worked. But the American Legion convention was scheduled to start the next day, Sunday, 30 August, and Westerdahl worried about keeping the masses peaceful and within the park. Then Sunday morning, officials in Portland heard sobering news: people were leaving both festivals in great numbers.

The Sunday exodus set off alarms especially with the FBI. "Any movement out of both festivals," the FBI office in Portland alerted J. Edgar Hoover by wire, "is regarded by law enforcement agencies as a disquieting development inasmuch as the first People's Army Jamboree parade is scheduled for 2:30 P.M."

By Sunday afternoon, the population at Vortex had fallen sharply, from thirty-five thousand to eight thousand. Back in Portland, more than twenty-five thousand American Legion members had arrived, and Jamboree protestors intended to confront them.

To McCall, the worst possible scenario had begun to take shape. He had taken great political risk in sponsoring Vortex. Now an estimated twenty-seven thousand people were pouring out of McIver Park just as the Jamboree planned to assemble its major protest march in Portland. In the Hilton Hotel suite, McCall feared the throngs would rush into the city and ignite violence after all.

He stood at the tall windows of the command center and peered down twenty stories to the Portland streets, imagining how the violence might look—rushing crowds swarming amid clouds of tear gas.

And then, nothing happened.

The Jamboree initiated its march and the protestors moved north through downtown. No more than a thousand people fell in behind. The protestors walked into the city, chanted their anti-war slogans, and peacefully marched back out.

The next day, Monday, 31 August, ten thousand Legionnaires took to the streets for their own star-spangled parade. It sparked no incidents. Fewer than a hundred Jamboree protesters showed up. When a few protestors jeered the Legionnaires, a contingent of Portland police officers drew their billy clubs and moved in. The police stopped when an elderly lady pushed herself in front of the officer in charge. "Go back, you police just make trouble," she said, shaking her finger at him. "Why, you even incense me." The police withdrew.

On the third day of the convention, a second Jamboree protest march barely mustered eight hundred people. And on the final day, news leaked that President Nixon had backed out of his scheduled appearance, and Vice President Spiro Agnew arrived instead to speak at the Memorial Coliseum. Outside, no confrontation occurred. Only three hundred protestors showed up to hold signs outside the meeting hall. Agnew gave a toned-down speech and left town without incident.

It was over. No hordes, no bombings, no riots, no shootings, no injuries. In the city predicted to become the next battlefield of the anti-war movement, total damage amounted to a single broken window.

After three months of swelling tension and fear, the threat posed by the American Legion convention of 1970 deflated overnight, and city and state officials proclaimed success. McCall accepted praise and credited Vortex for releasing the pressures that otherwise might have built up in Portland and led to a crisis.

THAT TOM MCCALL'S ROCK FESTIVAL saved the city from certain violence soon became conventional wisdom in Oregon. But the events of the time, cooled by the passing years, tell a different story.

Without question, the era smelled of fear and violence. Fear alone might have been enough to incite confrontations between anti-war protestors, Legionnaires, and police during the last hot week of August 1970. However, much of the fear generated had its roots in the FBI's alarming predictions.

Today, the FBI's on-going censorship of its records makes a complete review of its intelligence in the summer of 1970 impossible. The agency will release less than one-third of its three-thousand-page file related to the People's Army Jamboree and the records it will release are heavily edited. However, what little has become public shows conclusively that the harrowing predictions were based on not much more than rumors and paranoia. "The Legion convention," United States Attorney Sidney Lezak said years later, "showed that the official estimates that fifty thousand people were coming had been bullshit."

The Jamboree had first fooled the FBI, and then fooled itself into believing fifty thousand people would arrive from around the country to jam Portland's streets. Because so many had believed that number, in the Legion convention's aftermath, city and state officials pointed to the thousands who had jammed Vortex and Sky River festivals as proof the crowds had indeed been diverted from Portland.

Yet the fifty thousand people enjoying rock music, drugs, and the sunshine during that weekend were not the fifty thousand the FBI had ex-

The American Legion parade marches up Broadway in downtown Portland. While there were protestors, the numbers and severity of the confrontation had been overestimated by both the media and the FBI. (Gerry Lewin *Statesman-Journal* photo)

pected and feared. The people who rushed out of Vortex and Sky River, sending law enforcement officials into a panic, were not heading into Portland to commit violence. They were just going home.

The Vortex crowds were not bought-off protestors. They were local kids who had no interest in political marches, but were interested in a party. The FBI itself, in fact, later conceded in classified memos that Vortex was made up of local "weekenders," not out-of-state radicals. "We knew going in ninety-eight percent of the kids going to Vortex would be local kids," Westerdahl acknowledged years later. "We feared they would be in downtown Portland, only adding to the crowds."

In that sense, Vortex had its intended effect. But the myth that Vortex drained off thousands of people who would have rampaged through downtown Portland still lingers.

The McCall-supported alternative Vortex gathering outside of Portland provided a major distraction for young people. McCall gambled politically by endorsing the rock festival. (Gerry Lewin photo)

Nonetheless, Tom McCall had wagered his political career believing the predictions of violence. His decision to hold Vortex was one of the boldest ever made by an Oregon governor, even if, in the end, its impact was exaggerated.

Although Vortex may have had only mythical influence in averting violence in Portland, it did have one very real result. With his decision to sponsor the rock concert, McCall had swiftly destroyed doubts Oregonians had about his courage and leadership. And he knew it. Eugene Doherty, the state police lieutenant assigned to oversee Vortex, recalled meeting McCall only hours after the American Legion convention ended.

"Hell of a job," McCall told Doherty.

"You know, Governor," Doherty said. "I don't think you're going to be too hurt by this."

For the first time in weeks, Doherty saw McCall smile. It was a knowing, wise smile at that.

"Gene," McCall replied, "I don't think so either."

In the months prior to the American Legion convention, polls had shown Oregonians thought McCall was indecisive. That had changed forever. "And the turning point," Ken Johnson said, "was Vortex."

"If [Vortex] hadn't happened," Robert Straub said years later, "there was a chance [McCall] would have lost the election. At the beginning of the campaign he and I were neck and neck." After Vortex, Straub said succinctly, "I was through."

The crisis that never happened dominated the 1970 campaign for the governorship. Straub questioned the need for Vortex and charged McCall with giving in to the blackmail of hippies. "They smoked marijuana widely, used other kinds of drugs openly, they broke the law in personal conduct in an obscene and public way," Straub said indignantly about the Vortex crowds. "This was going on while policemen sworn to uphold the law stood helplessly watching." For peace in Portland, Straub said, "The governor paid a ransom that is too high a price."

No one seemed to care. McCall had proven himself innovative, bold and brave. "If I had to do it over again," he said during an October speech, "I would do it precisely the same way."

The Oregon press asked few tough questions about the need for Vortex and the panic created over the American Legion convention. "If the press had really wanted to do McCall in, this would have been the time," said Lee Johnson, Oregon's attorney general. "But the press never wanted to do him in." Instead, newspapers across the state endorsed his actions, recognizing he had made a difficult decision without the benefit of hindsight. "McCall showed courage and ingenuity," the *Oregonian* said, "in risking his political future in an election year by turning over beautiful McIver State Park for an unrestricted week-long hippie encampment."

Nothing else Straub hurled at McCall—criticism about his management, lack of progress on pollution issues and tax reform—mattered in the campaign. Not even a lousy debate performance by McCall in a televised appearance with Straub on 12 October seemed to matter.

The momentum gave McCall a rare confidence toward his own elective fortunes. "Straub," McCall told reporters in late October, "is going to lose the election as badly as anyone ever did in a major race in a two-party state in fifty years." McCall's confidence was so concrete, in fact, that he even agreed to campaign with his mother.

During one late October morning, Dorothy Lawson McCall led her son and a dozen reporters down the sidewalks of northwest Portland with all the spirit of the eighty-two-year-old grande dame she was. "I'm his mother," she would declare to passers-by. "How would you like to shake my hand?"

Delighted to see the television stations had brought their cameras down to see her, Dorothy drew from her purse a copy of her memoir, *Ranch Under the Rimrock*, and held it up for the cameras to see. "That's enough promotion," McCall grumbled to his mother. "We're supposed to promote me, not the book." Unperturbed, Dorothy insisted that the reporters follow her through a local grocery store where she stood before the dairy case and began a long speech about her favorite brand of milk. "Goddamn it, Mother," McCall finally interjected, "Knock it off." Dorothy then marched out, with the reporters and TV cameras in tow, and the governor far behind. One of the grocery checkers looked at the mayhem and said to McCall as he left, "Well, you've got nothing to lose."

"No," replied McCall, "Only the election."

MCCALL TROUNCED STRAUB on election day by collecting just under fifty-six percent of the vote, a margin only slightly larger than his 1966 win.

Victory freed him as never before. After months of tension and crisis, and his second term secured, he unleashed his tongue again, and he did not do so idly.

McCall had been forced to the brink of crisis in Oregon with the American Legion and the People's Army Jamboree. Angry as always at anti-war protestors, however, McCall had seen the Nixon administration as the true agent of violence and division that summer.

The month after the election he went to Sun Valley, Idaho, dark and cold in the winter months, a fitting setting for the vanquished. Republican governors had scheduled their annual meeting at the ski resort, and the mood was grim: eleven GOP governors joining McCall at Sun Valley had lost their re-election efforts; many blamed the heavy-handed law-and-order rhetoric of Nixon and Agnew during 1970 for their losses.

Agnew was the guest of honor at the governors' meeting. The vice president was no longer the moderate, friendly Ted Agnew of Maryland whom McCall had befriended three years earlier, and McCall made no secret of his distaste. At a December press conference in Salem, a reporter had asked McCall what he thought of Agnew. McCall replied that Nixon should consider dumping Agnew from the Republican ticket in 1972, calling Agnew Nixon's "hatchetman . . . a triggerman," stalking about the nation "like a man with a knife in his shawl."

McCall's remarks made national headlines and reporters flocked immediately to his side when he arrived in Sun Valley. "The press would set me up on cue a while because they knew I'd give them something peppery if they framed the question right," McCall said years later. "Agnew's gutter tactics and demagoguery made such questions unnecessary." McCall volunteered acid thoughts about Agnew and repeated his "knife in his shawl" quote for any reporter who might have missed it.

As soon as Agnew arrived in Sun Valley, he asked for a meeting with McCall to forge a truce. As McCall recounted their meeting, Agnew was visibly agitated. He fixed McCall a drink and then said, "Tom, I'm mad as hell at you. What happened? We used to be great friends. Why have you changed?"

"Why have you changed?" McCall replied. "You used to be one of the party's leading moderates. Now you're just another win-at-any-cost politician."

The two seemed to make peace, and for a moment, McCall believed Agnew might have a change of heart, but his hopes soon vanished. At a closed-door meeting with governors, Agnew defended the administration's tactics and negative attacks on its "enemies."

"There's only one way to campaign, and you're very naive if you don't recognize it," Agnew, according to McCall, told the governors. "There's only one point to campaigning and that is to chew your opponent's nuts out before he chews out yours."

No prude about crass language, McCall grew angrier than ever at Agnew's attitude. Sensing McCall was about to explode, Agnew tried to have him kept quiet. That night, 15 December, Agnew planned to give a dinner speech to the governors. Just before the speech, he asked New Mexico governor David Cargo to implore McCall not to criticize him or

Nixon that night. Cargo agreed, and went to the dining hall and sat down next to McCall.

"Tom," Cargo said, "the vice president asked me personally to appeal to you not to make any adverse comments about his speech. I've got the rest of the governors to agree to leave him alone. If the press wants to take him apart, let them."

"Fine, fine," McCall replied.

Cargo relaxed and turned his attention to Agnew. Agnew's speech at first sounded conciliatory. He said he had come to the governors' conference "to reaffirm our personal friendships and relationship and mutual trust." Once said, however, Agnew used militaristic rhetoric to defend his slashing style. The defeated governors, he said, had "fallen in political combat."

> What they do not need, those who have fallen in the political wars, [Agnew said] are excuses and rationalizations for their defeats. What is not needed is the assessment of blame. . . . The assignment of blame—even though it may be labeled as a constructive criticism—is an opinion exercise which may very well, if taken seriously, mandate changes in strategy which could be conducive to further weakening.

Sitting only a few feet away, McCall seethed as Agnew spit out each word. "When you read the speech, it wasn't so bad," recalled Robert Davis, a McCall aide who heard the speech. "But when you heard the inflection and tone of his voice, it really dripped with venom."

Making matters worse, McCall believed—accurately or not—that Agnew stared directly at him. As McCall described it, Agnew's "smoldering eyes would burn right through me."

> Nothing is more unreasonable [Agnew continued] to me than the cries of "Mr. Vice President, you are dividing the country." What is an election if it is not an attempt to divide the voters . . . ? I have said to people who have constrained to label my partisan attempts during the last campaign as divisive, "Have you ever run against an incumbent?" . . . I say

to those governors here tonight that if you have never run
against an incumbent, perhaps you don't know what it is to
be partisan and divisive. But when you have to fight the establishment or an "in" vote there is only one way—attack.

McCall whirled his head around and looked at Ron Schmidt, who sat
nearby. "Is that son of a bitch saying what I think he's saying?" McCall
said loudly enough for several people nearby to overhear.

"You're listening to it, too, Governor," Schmidt replied.

McCall jumped up from his table and stormed out an exit and onto a
snow-covered veranda. Schmidt followed and found McCall stomping
in the snow, clouds of steam churning from his mouth and nostrils into
the cold Idaho air. "I can't believe he said what he did!" McCall roared.
Schmidt tried to calm McCall, but it was no use. Reporters who had
seen McCall's furious departure quickly surrounded him, and someone
asked him what he thought of the speech. McCall unleashed a string of
profanities and then composed himself.

"There was," he said, "the most unbelievable, incredible misunder-
standing of the mood of America in that rotten, bigoted little speech."

McCall aide Robert Davis rushed up to the governor and patted his
tall shoulders.

"Listen, Tom," Davis said, "now is the time to be cool. Let's be
statesmanlike about this."

"Well," McCall replied, watching reporters close their notebooks,
"that's going to be a little hard to do now."

Meanwhile, back at McCall's table, David Cargo looked up to find
McCall gone. The New Mexico governor could see reporters and television cameras surrounding McCall outside. Cargo shook his head,
knowing he had failed. Moments later, a waiter handed Cargo a note
sent from the front table by the vice president. "David," Agnew had
written, "thanks for helping me with Tom McCall."

By the next morning McCall's characterization of Agnew's "rotten,
bigoted little speech" was front-page news across America. After a year
of Agnew's bombast, another Republican had finally said what many
Americans had been thinking. Other Republican governors chimed in

behind him. Only California governor Ronald Reagan called Agnew's speech "fine, right and proper."

The next day, McCall had to face Agnew again during a closed-door meeting with the governors. Furious, Agnew shook a copy of a news story, reporting McCall's quote, at Oregon's governor.

"Tom, I can't believe you said this!" Agnew screamed before the group.

"What does it say?" McCall asked innocently, knowing full well what the newspaper said.

"I can't believe you called it 'a rotten bigoted, little speech'."

McCall looked up and replied, "I don't think I said *little*."

AFTER THAT, MCCALL SAID, "The wind roared in my ears." Never one to seek the comfort of the Republican party, McCall had finally turned against it. The GOP of Richard Nixon was not that of Tom McCall, just as the conspiring Republican party of Massachusetts had not been that of Samuel Walker McCall.

His denouncement of Agnew had been in character, but a change had clearly come over him, a change in both the way Oregonians viewed him and the way he viewed himself. "Tom's impression as a wishy-washy leader went away and never came back," Ken Johnson said. "And it wasn't just the perception that changed. It was reality that changed."

Vortex had changed it. His bold decision, made amid crisis, had pulled him from certain defeat and given him a profound new sense of courage. His years as governor had included other acts of bravery, but too often his impetuousness and nerves had overcome him. In that way, Vortex did not simply change the fate of the 1970 election. It changed Tom McCall—and Oregon's history as well.

So much of the work that defined McCall's years as governor came during his second term. A McCall loss in 1970 would have sent Oregon on a far less bold—and probably forgettable—course. Even a weaker victory might have left McCall tenuous.

But that did not happen. Vortex gave an emboldened McCall his second term, and gave Oregon a new future.

PART FOUR

16

Visit, but Don't Stay

HE WIND NEVER AGAIN stopped howling. By standing up to Agnew, McCall once more surfaced nationally as a courageous politician. The crises McCall had faced at the end of his first term had not been lost on national journalists already fond of the outspoken governor. McCall relished the attention, but he wanted it paid to Oregon as well.

By the time McCall took his second oath of office in January 1971, he had pieced together a respectable environmental agenda. No other state had tried all that Oregon had: protecting beaches, statewide zoning, aggressive clean-ups of major rivers. But McCall wanted more. He wanted Oregon to have a lasting image as a state that put livability above all else.

A few days before his second term began, McCall, now fifty-seven years old, granted an interview to CBS News reporter Terry Drinkwater. Drinkwater's piece focused on the environmental gains Oregon had made. McCall said that he was determined Oregon would not be overrun like California, or become the victim of the pollution and decay found in eastern states. Oregon—as McCall had said before, in speech after speech—wanted growth, but a steady, smart growth.

How do you stop people from coming in? Drinkwater asked. McCall lifted his head and said the words that would become a new slogan for the state:

Come visit us again and again. This is a state of excitement.
But for heaven's sake, don't come here to live.

For four years, McCall had searched for a way to articulate his new
Oregon doctrine. He had wanted the nation to take notice. With a single
quip, he had accomplished it.

McCall said years later that he knew immediately the statement was
"impugning Western hospitality, which is equated with God and moth-
erhood." He did not care. The statement promised to shock people, and
that was what McCall wanted to do.

The interview aired 12 January 1971, the day after McCall's second
inauguration. Across America, people heard Oregon's governor pro-
claim he did not want anyone moving into his state. Immediately, the
mail poured in from around the country. Some letters—sent by people
who had never intended to visit Oregon at all—scolded McCall for
being inhospitable. "The personal freedom to live where we choose,"
groused one Californian to McCall, "remains a cherished privilege."

Most letters, however, were from Americans who understood his
message clearly. "How refreshing it is," read one letter from Indiana, "at
a time when most states still compete in the insanity of quantity, to hear
the head of at least one state speak of quality and stability." One Vermont resident said he sympathized with McCall's declaration because
"we here are currently under siege from New York, Connecticut, Massachusetts, New Jersey and other assorted uninhabitable places." Another letter, this one from Wyoming, put it simply: "You are the first
person I've ever heard to place the environment above economics."

The sight of a governor closing his state's doors caught the immediate attention of the national press. McCall found himself explaining his
statement to reporters, answering charges that people were not welcome
in Oregon. He had not said people were not welcome at all, he told them,
just that he wanted people to go home after their visit.

Still, McCall could not shake from the statement its inhospitable
tone. Taken out of context—as it would be countless times over the next
decade—McCall's declaration of "visit, don't stay" grew out of control. Newspapers across the United States and Canada—and even Europe—repeated McCall's statement. The Los Angeles *Times* followed

up with a balanced report on Californians' eager migration to Oregon and Oregon's concerns about planning for such growth. However, the subtleties were lost in a page-one banner headline that declared in two-inch high letters: "Oregon: Keep Out."

McCall had to defend the statement almost everywhere he went. When a Brookings resident—recently transplanted from California—complained about McCall's tone, the governor replied flatly, "I think you yourself would not have wanted to move to Oregon if it didn't have the very qualities that could be destroyed by overpopulation."

The comment especially enraged leaders of Oregon tourism industry, who feared it would discourage people from even visiting. "Absolute hogwash," McCall growled as he stared down a convention of miffed tourist executives in April 1971.

> An office holder would have to be a political basket case to publicly scream for closure of [tourism]. What a paradox. The entire nation is now justifiably a-babble about environmental threats. Everyone is shouting, "Stop talking and do something." Oregon does something, and gets blasted for being inhospitable at worst, provincial at best—or is it the other way around?
>
> . . . We are continuing to woo new industry. We have to have it. But we are not willing to take any industry at any price. The industry must come here on our terms, play the game by our environmental rules, and be members of the Oregon family. We lose some this way—and we want to lose that kind of company.

McCall was as unapologetic on the business recruitment tours that followed. In fact, he used his "visit, but don't stay" remark as a marketing tool. On a 1971 recruitment tour to New York City, he told Manhattan executives during a showcase luncheon for Oregon:

> I think I might be able to anticipate your first question. "Did you say what the New York *Times* said you said?" . . . Yes. I did say it. And I continue to say it. And I mean it.

. . . [W]e aren't being hostile or provincial. We are being
prudent. It is not our intention to lure anyone to a promised
land that becomes, instead, an environmental disaster.

We are being realistic. We know we cannot . . . support a
human tidal wave of migration. We haven't the jobs for that
kind of onrush—we haven't the facilities—and we are determined to maintain our magnificent environment. . . .

It may sound presumptuous, or immodest, but the context in which I pitch to you is this: Oregon is accepting a few
applications for location of branch offices by a carefully
screened set of corporations with reputations for honoring
the sanctity of the environment.

The "visit, but don't stay" comment brought him fame and derision
for the rest of his life. It gave Oregon the lasting reputation as a state
willing to protect its resources, even if it meant isolationism.

McCall, of course, did not want isolation. He simply hoped to protect
the qualities that made Oregon, Oregon. To do that, McCall began by
completing unfinished business.

RICHARD CHAMBERS HAD NEVER LOST FAITH that McCall would finish
work on the Bottle Bill. After Republicans, in the 1969 legislature, had
squashed the bill, Chambers had returned to his typewriter. During the
long interim between sessions, when most politicians forget about new
legislation, Chambers continued to pepper lawmakers with letters and
reminders about his bill.

When McCall had walked away from the Bottle Bill in 1969, he had
sponsored formation of a private, non-profit group called Stop Oregon
Litter and Vandalism, or SOLV. The organization had quickly launched
a public education campaign about littering that Chambers thought was
intended to kill momentum for a Bottle Bill. "He thought SOLV was a
bunch of crap," his daughter, Victoria Berger, recalled. "He thought they
could say, 'Why do we need a Bottle Bill now that we've got SOLV'?"

With its do-good image, SOLV appeared to be just a front for the Bottle Bill's opponents. The *Oregon Times*, a Portland news weekly, and
the *Oregon Journal* in March 1971 reported that SOLV had collected

nearly three-fourths of its budget from companies and organizations dedicated to killing the Bottle Bill. Those opponents secretly funding SOLV included the Northwest Glass Container Manufacturers, the Carbonated Beverage Container Manufacturers Association, the Brewers Institute, and the Oregon soft drink industry. McCall, his private correspondence shows, knew of these interest groups' financing of SOLV. In addition, the non-profit organization later received another $32,000 in state funds.

As far as McCall was concerned, Stop Oregon Litter and Vandalism was only a diversion, however. McCall had sponsored SOLV to keep the Bottle Bill's opponents busy. He wanted the container industry groups to believe he would support whatever alternative they offered to the Bottle Bill. Although he had been timid in his support of the Bottle Bill in 1969, in January 1970, he launched a determined publicity campaign of his own for the Bottle Bill. His first major statement on the issue came when he told a Salem civic club he had not caved in to industry pressure, and that he would fight for the bill. "I want to make it very clear that there will be no quid pro quo in the form of a relaxation of my commitment to put a price on the head of every beer and pop can and bottle in the United States."

With this announcement, Tom McCall did what he had done so many times before: grabbed an idea, made it his own, and then fought for it with all his will.

Bottle Bill opponents were stunned, especially as McCall had a scheduled appearance before the Oregon-Washington Bottlers Association the next month. With some glee, McCall stared down bottling executives and—with shifting metaphor—scolded them for their selfishness.

> The environmental crisis towers over us like a massive cresting wave. If we establish standards and hold to them, we resist engulfment and save ourselves—and business—from inundation, ocean to ocean, by bottles and containers. . . .
>
> What happens in Oregon is going to set a precedent for the rest of the nation. We are the key state in what I feel will be a domino reaction—and, as the key domino, the way we move will set off a chain reaction.

McCall with Bottle Bill supporter, YWCA leader Mrs. Joe Rand, one day after McCall called for putting a "price on the head of every beer and pop can and bottle in the United States." (*Oregon Journal* photo; OrHi 012697)

That was just what the national companies did not want—a chain re-action, with states across the nation following Oregon's lead. Similar container-deposit laws had already passed in British Columbia, Finland and Norway. Stopping Oregon from becoming the leader in a nation-wide trend was imperative for the bill's opponents.

Now that they had McCall's support, backers of the Bottle Bill set out to disprove opponents' claims. Grocery stores, for example, had com-plained about being the receptors of all the returned bottles and cans, claiming the financial strain of processing the returned containers could bankrupt small stores. It took only one businessman to destroy the claim that the bill was unworkable and expensive. John Piacentini, owner of Plaid Pantry, a local chain of convenience stores, offered a half-cent for any soda or beer bottle turned in to his stores. "I hope," Piacentini said, "that [Oregonians] bury me in litter." They did. Within two weeks more than 150,000 cans arrived at Piacentini's sixty stores. McCall ordered National Guard troops to haul the bottles and cans away.

The success thrilled Richard Chambers, but he quickly learned that his infectious idea had brought him enemies and unwelcome attention. "The companies were highly suspicious of Rich and what he was doing," his wife, Kay Chambers, said of the industry lobbyists. "They couldn't believe that he wasn't backed by somebody." Indeed, Chambers had paid for his crusade with his own money. Yet Chambers discovered that at least one group opposing the Bottle Bill—he never said if he knew which one—had hired a private investigator to tail him and scrutinize his finances. "My father was not a paranoid man," said Victoria Berger. "He learned from good sources there were people digging into his background. He wouldn't tell us any more than that—only just enough so that we would be aware."

Bill opponents soon found that they were up against more than one man, however. With McCall's bold endorsement, several groups stepped in to promote the Bottle Bill. One fledging group, called the Oregon Environmental Council—later a large force in the state's conservation movement—organized a citizens' lobbying campaign. Meanwhile, an interim legislative committee spent the summer of 1970 drafting a new Bottle Bill that would be as tough against littering as Chambers had first imagined. The Oregon Bottle Bill, officially House Bill 1036, called for outlawing non-returnables and setting a minimum five-cent deposit on all soft drink and beer bottles. Soon, every member of the interim panel would claim some degree of authorship. "By the time the 1971 legislature opened," one lawmaker recalled, "the Bottle Bill was a train speeding down the tracks with everyone aboard."

The opponents—a coalition of glass and metal companies, bottlers and unions—did not concede easily. Preparing for a fight in the Oregon Legislature, the Bottle Bill's opponents sharpened their tactics in nearby

Washington, where Initiative 256 on the November 1970 ballot sought to enact a similar law. Bill opponents outspent proponents, their campaign spreading fears of widespread job losses. The fear tactics worked. After leading in the polls with seventy-nine percent approval, the measure in the end lost, fifty-one percent to forty-nine.

Meanwhile, glass, metal and bottling companies lined up their defenses in Salem. Some groups, such as the American Can Co., took out full-page ads to debunk the need for a Bottle Bill. Other opponents drafted a bill calling for tougher littering laws rather than the proposed deposit law. Lobbyists from New York, Chicago, Los Angeles and New Jersey flew in to fight the bill. The coalition of opponents also hired Oregon-based lobbyists who knew how to work the state's legislature. In the end, more than twenty major corporations sent lobbyists into the legislature to oppose the Bottle Bill.

When the bill first came up in the house, House Speaker Robert F. Smith appeared ready to order a dismal repeat of 1969. He sent the bill to the House State and Federal Affairs Committee, again chaired by State Representative Roger Martin, the combination that had killed the bill in 1969. But it did not work this time. Although Smith offered the opposing lobbyists a compromise, they refused, saying the bill's death was their sole interest. Smith refused to kill the bill and within weeks the house had approved it fifty-four to six.

Stunned by their quick defeat, the opposition lobbyists rushed to the state senate. However, most of the lobbyists did not understand how the Oregon Legislature worked. Accustomed to the high pressure tactics employed in other states, the lobbyists succeeded only in offending Oregon lawmakers. "They did the most awful job," said Betty Roberts, a Democratic senator from Portland and chairwoman of the Senate Consumer Affairs Committee, which dealt with the Bottle Bill. "It was like, 'Here we are from back in the East, and this is little dinky Oregon.' That was their attitude: 'You don't understand this bill. Trust us'."

With the condescending attitude of the eastern lobbyists came rumors of bribes. At least one meeting took place between the out-of-state lobbyists and those hired from Oregon to kill the bill. The lobbyists put it bluntly: Who must we pay off to have this bill killed? Within days rumors spread throughout Salem. Unsubstantiated stories of lobbyists carrying bags of cash were heard in all the Capitol hallways. When lobbyists found they could not get their way with a direct appeal before Roberts' panel, opponents resorted to outright trickery. Roberts fell victim to one trick that nearly killed the bill.

As a goodwill gesture, Roberts accepted an amendment from one opponent to help define "beverage"; the amendment essentially loosened the bill to include almost any liquid. Only after the bill reached the senate floor did Roberts see the trap. The few senators hoping to kill the measure had brought in hundreds of bottles of all kinds: milk, wine, cooking oils, even the squeezable lemon juice container shaped like the fruit itself. As the debate began, the opposing senators held up the odd-shaped bottles. "Is this bottle covered in your bill's definition of 'container'?" they asked in mocking tones.

Opponents had succeeded in demonstrating one of their claims—that the Bottle Bill was too vague. Roberts asked the senate to send the bill back to her committee. She watched chortling lobbyists file out of the gallery, believing they had killed it. Roberts quickly rounded up selected members of her committee. In one swift motion, she convened the panel, changed the bill to its original form and adjourned. Opponents never knew what happened until the bill appeared on the senate schedule a second time.

The emergence of the repaired Bottle Bill started a second panic among its opponents, and the rumors of bribes turned into reality. The night before the senate vote, Roberts received a telephone call about the bill. She recognized the caller, although she has never named him publicly. The voice was direct. "If you can kill this bill, there will be plenty of money for Democratic candidates in the next election." Roberts realized she had just been offered a bribe. She cut off the caller and hung up.

Another senator, Portland Democrat Ted Hallock, received a call from a distraught George Brown, the former lobbyist for the Oregon AFL-CIO. Brown was one of the lobbyists hired by a collection of metals companies to defeat the Bottle Bill. He pleaded with Hallock to help him stop the measure. Hallock refused. Brown finally revealed that he was authorized to offer $5,000 in campaign contributions to any senator who voted against the bill. Hallock was less diplomatic than Roberts, cussing out Brown before he slammed down the receiver.

The next day, 27 May, the drama peaked as Roberts took to the senate floor and detailed the bribe she had been offered. Her speech destroyed any further plans of foul play. The senate approved the Bottle Bill twenty-two to eight.

McCall happily signed the bill into law, calling it an act "to turn us away from use and waste to a positive program of reuse and save." In time, the Bottle Bill became Tom McCall's own calling card as he lobbied for it in other states. As with his "visit, but don't stay" remark, the bill helped define him in the nation's mind.

As the Bottle Bill's success helped forge McCall's reputation, it ushered out of politics a quieter man. Richard Chambers had watched his idea as it took each step through the legislature. On that final day, as the senate clerk read the results, Chambers stood and left the gallery. He held no parties to mark his victory nor did he call a press conference. He did what he always said he would do when he won. He went home.

Three years later, Richard Chambers was dead. He died as quietly and anonymously as he had worked the Capitol, as quietly as he had changed Oregon history. When his friends learned Chambers was dying of cancer, they successfully urged McCall to award Chambers the state's new Clean Up Pollution Award. In 1974, at a small ceremony virtually ignored by the Oregon press, Chambers declined to give an acceptance speech. A few days later, he consented to the only newspaper interview he ever granted about the Bottle Bill. "I am in no way qualified for this award," he said.

Other people asked him to fight for the Bottle Bill in other states. His family urged him to tell his extraordinary story before he died. But Chambers always refused. "I accomplished what I set out to do," he said. "I don't give a shit what the rest of the world has done with its litter, because now Oregon has this bill."

Richard Chambers had been an eccentric, hulking, rebellious man with a simple wish: to walk the trails and beaches of Oregon and not return carrying bags of bottle and can litter. He lived to see that wish fulfilled. He wanted nothing more.

ASIDE FROM THE BOTTLE BILL, the 1971 legislature, later dubbed the "ecology session," added more environmental laws to the books than any session before it. The state had the authority to control air pollution by permit, in the same way it controlled the wastes going into rivers. Until 1971, the state had to seek criminal charges against a polluter. Lawmakers made it easier to go after polluters by giving the state power to levy civil fines, and vesting the governor with the power to shut down polluting industries on an emergency basis. Finally the state had the power McCall thought it had always needed to slap any industry that broke the toughened rules.

Business leaders did not accept these steps gladly. Many saw the measures—from the Bottle Bill to the new pollution permit system—as affronts to their ability to turn a profit. McCall offered no solace. He insisted the state had a duty to lay down strict rules, and most companies followed. A few companies expected to get a break now and then. McCall offered none. "The 'captains of industry' never grew comfortable with him," James Faulstich, the state's director of economic development, recalled. "They were always made uneasy about McCall. They couldn't buy him off. He wasn't one of them. That's putting it mildly."

McCall's "visit, but don't stay" remark had hardened corporate dislike for him. Faulstich had to soothe many business leaders who called frantically to complain about the poor image McCall's remark had given the state. However, rather than repelling business, McCall's statement proved to be intriguing to outsiders. "Oregon suffered from a total lack of recognition on the national scene," Faulstich said. "At the time our major enemy was indifference. Wherever I went, people wanted to know, 'What's so special about Oregon'?"

In years to come, many business leaders—and the politicians they later bankrolled—charged that McCall had burdened Oregon with a negative image. What was overlooked was that these business leaders themselves often soured Oregon's image by loudly proclaiming that the state was a bad place to do business. Some of them aired reasonable concerns that McCall was inhibiting normal economic growth. "We've got to have a little balance between utopia and practicality," one U.S. National Bank of Oregon official told the *Wall Street Journal*. Others, however, were apoplectic at McCall's environmental agenda.

One such leader was Robert Pamplin, Sr., chairman of timber giant Georgia-Pacific Corp. Pamplin vented his anger about Oregon's environmental ethic in a way the nation's business leaders could not miss. He told the New York *Times* that Oregon was plagued by environmentalists whom he called "the woodsy witch doctors of a revived nature cult." Oregon had ruined its business climate, Pamplin said, with its "current environmental hysteria, the state's tax structure, inflation, labor unrest, fiscal irresponsibility, monetary mismanagement and escalating welfare schemes."

Pamplin was not alone in his attacks. One of McCall's loudest critics was Associated Oregon Industries (AOI), Oregon's most powerful business lobby. In 1971, the group's president, Phil Bladine, a newspaper publisher from rural Yamhill County, accused McCall and the legislature of environmental "overkill." Bladine said a protected environment and healthy economy could not co-exist—a myth McCall had tried to dispel in "Pollution in Paradise" nine years earlier. "Add it all up and it's going to cost you businessmen, and if businesses are hurt it's going to hurt all people in all walks of life," Bladine said.

Bladine was also spokesman for the Western Environmental Trade Association (WETA), an organization he helped create. The group, forged with both corporate and union backing, complained in the New York *Times* that Oregon had fallen victim to "hysteria" and "environmental McCarthyism."

As criticism of his environmental policies increased, McCall directed the state to keep up the pressure on polluters. In 1969 lawmakers had created the Department of Environmental Quality (DEQ) with close co-operation of the very businesses facing the tighter regulation. The DEQ's budget had grown from one million dollars in 1965-67, when it was still called the state Sanitary Authority, to $39 million eight years later. As with many agencies, the DEQ had a citizens panel, the Environmental Quality Commission (EQC), overseeing its operations. The agency continued the old Sanitary Authority's policy of negotiation over confrontation. The DEQ now had much more leverage—authority to yank permits, the power to levy large civil fines—and so was much more effective in its negotiations than it had been in the past.

Still, McCall thought the agency lacked fire. He wanted corporate polluters to fear the DEQ. He wanted Oregonians to understand—and believe—that the agency carried out his environmental will.

To make such a gesture, in 1967 he had named himself to run the Sanitary Authority. In 1971, he wanted someone with as much determination and bluster as he commanded. He found someone who had even more.

That person was L.B. Day, and no one who ever met his ferocious stare ever forgot his intensity. But it was his voice people remembered most of all, not for how it sounded but for how it felt. Without the volume raised, Day's voice rattled, it shook, it pounded. It was the very tone Tom McCall wanted for his top environmental official. Reflecting on Day, McCall once said, "You have to understand L.B. He starts negotiations at the death struggle."

L.B. Day never knew what the initials of his name stood for. He even doubted that his father, with whom he shared the initialized name, knew. A native of Nebraska, Day was born in 1932 to a prominent family; L.B., Sr., was a Nebraska Supreme Court justice. Day attended law school in Oregon, but quit to work for the Teamsters, a union under fire for its ties to organized crime. Day saw his role as a crusader helping to clean up the union. "He had a talent for persuading people," Frank Day, L.B.'s brother, recalled. "I asked him once why he would join the Teamsters. He said, 'Goddamn it, they need someone like me'." Painfully honest and opposed to the crooked leadership, Day quickly rose from union organizer of cannery workers to secretary-treasurer of the local.

A few years later, Day won a seat in the Oregon House, where he was a master of intimidation. When he walked, he hunched and cocked his head to the side, like a raptor scanning for food. His eyes often held a wild look, as if he was on the verge of an outburst. Often, he was. In committee hearings, he berated witnesses, seemingly at random.

"L.B. was a bully. And he enjoyed being a bully," said one McCall aide. "'Vicious' does not begin to describe L.B. at times," recalled Robert Oliver, McCall's legal counsel. "He could be extremely abrasive toward people he didn't like." Most often the people he did not like were those who surrounded government—the bureaucrat, the lawyer, the engineer, the consultant—people he saw interfering with the public's business.

Day served six years in the Oregon House, converting from Democrat to Republican in mid-career. His reason was simple. The Republicans were in charge of the house and L.B. Day wanted to win.

In the legislature, Day had advocated many of McCall's proposals, especially land-use planning. In 1970, Day became the Pacific Northwest's liaison to the Department of the Interior under Secretary Walter Hickel. When President Nixon fired Hickel, Day returned to Oregon. McCall soon gave him the helm of DEQ and ordered him to exert his will over the state's polluters.

Day generated controversy from the start. He argued with the Environmental Protection Agency (EPA). When the federal regulators told Oregon to accept federal pollution standards, Day launched a loud public feud with the agency. Oregon's standards were higher, he said, and he refused to negotiate. Eventually, the EPA backed down.

McCall's staff later learned that Day had quietly worked out a deal with the EPA beforehand, then threw his tantrum for the publicity—a knack McCall could appreciate. "Sometimes it seems as if I'm shouting and ranting for no purpose," Day said. "But there's always a purpose. I look for 'grabbers'—you know, something that will stir up the pot."

Once finished with the EPA, Day turned on the Army Corps of Engineers. Presented with evidence the Corps' dams were killing salmon runs, Day launched a virulent and merciless campaign against the agency and soon proved he was as quotable as his boss. "If the Corps of Engineers is environmentally concerned," Day raged during one public tirade, "then Dracula was a vegetarian." Day was not finished with the federal government. The Federal Bureau of Mines had announced that it intended to honor pumice mining claims in the Three Sisters Wilderness area, one of the most pristine regions in Oregon. Day knew the state had no power to stop the federal agency but that it could impose stiff regulations over the mining process. The company could mine, Day said, but only with "a pick, a shovel and a mule."

Day's antics made many state officials uncomfortable. "There was always a feeling," said B.A. "Barney" McPhillips, an EQC commissioner, "that L.B. was more interested in his own image than the work of the agency." Yet McCall never flinched from his support of the DEQ's head. He understood—and admired—Day's talent for bombast. It gave the DEQ exactly the tenor McCall wanted.

When business leaders came to McCall, in early 1972, to register complaints about Day, McCall promptly shut them out. Soon, WETA called for Day's resignation. McCall groused in front of reporters that

WETA was dedicated "to getting rid of the governor and L.B. Day" because of McCall's "militancy" toward the environment. "We are going to continue to be militant," McCall said flatly.

AMID THE CRITICISM, Tom McCall asked L.B. Day to do a giant job that remained unfinished.

Ten years earlier, the Willamette River had slogged through its valley burdened with municipal and industrial wastes. Fish suffocated in the tepid waters. Oregonians contracted diseases from going near its shores.

In 1972, however, the Willamette had changed. Oxygen levels rose, salmon returned to the river, and the clean-up became a national example of environmental success. "Recognizing the ecological ills infecting other states, Oregon acted before time ran out," said *National Geographic* in June 1972, in an issue that featured the Willamette River on its cover. "Now chinook spawn even below once-deadly outfalls. Little untreated waste ever enters the stream. Transgressors have learned that laws won't bend."

The key to the Willamette's turnaround had been the reins on the pulp mills. Every mill along the Willamette now treated its air and water wastes at least once and met the state's firm standards. That is, every mill except for one. That mill, owned and operated by the Boise Cascade Corp., sat in downtown Salem only blocks from the Capitol. The pulp and paper plant employed six hundred fifty people and provided a large boost to the city's economy.

The Boise Cascade mill was an environmental blight, and its central Salem location did not help. Unlike other pulp mills, located away from large cities, the Boise Cascade mill allowed its rotten-egg odor to leak across Salem. The company attempted to dissipate the smelly pall with expensive air pollution filters and blowers, but the hulking machines failed. Although the air quality problems held the DEQ's attention, Day directed the agency to investigate the water pollution oozing from the mill.

Five years earlier, the Sanitary Authority had given Boise Cascade five years to stop dumping raw waste into the Willamette River. At the time, Boise Cascade, like other mills along the river, dumped its wastes

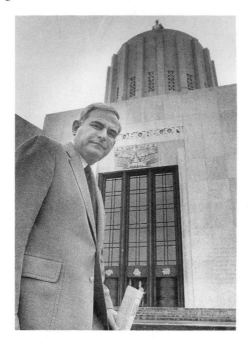

L. B. Day, who spearheaded
much of McCall's environ-
mental agenda. (Gerry Lewin
photo)

into open lagoons. When water levels rose, the mills flushed the lagoons
into the river.

While the other mills had acted early to install anti-water pollution
devices before the 1972 deadline, Boise Cascade had dawdled. Then, a
few months before the deadline, the company hurriedly installed new
equipment. The equipment soon failed and raw waste poured directly
into the river. In March 1972 DEQ officials found Boise Cascade even
further behind the clean-up schedule, and, according to one internal DEQ
memo, the company was "showing little concern for the slippage from
schedule."

In July, Boise Cascade declared the problem solved. Skeptical of the
claim, Day ordered another investigation. The DEQ officials found the
plant dumping 145,000 gallons of waste daily into the river, fifteen
times what its permit allowed. The inquiry also determined that the
company dumped another 400,000 gallons of waste every day into a

nearby slough. To make matters worse, Boise Cascade's air pollution controls were still failing.

The plant's operations so close to the Capitol brought intense attention. Newspapers chronicled each new problem. Citizen complaints by the hundreds poured into DEQ and even to Day's home.

Believing Boise Cascade had deceived him, Day decided to use the DEQ's authority to shut down the plant entirely. First he checked with the governor. McCall's reaction was direct: Why the hell did it take you so long? With that mandate, Day, on 19 July, said he would close the plant if Boise Cascade failed to abate the high levels of air pollution, close all waste water pipes leading directly to the river and halt dumping of waste into feeder streams. Boise Cascade declined to follow the order. Day in turn had DEQ's attorneys draft a court injunction against the company.

Before the injunction could be filed, however, Boise Cascade, on 25 July, shut down the plant on its own. As it turned out, equipment failure prevented the plant from operating that day, but that was not the story workers heard. As the six hundred fifty employees showed up for work, some company officials told them—incorrectly—that DEQ had ordered the closure. In fact, the DEQ did not file for an injunction until the next day.

The closure sparked rage among the plant's workers, who thought McCall and the DEQ, not equipment failure, were to blame. The following morning, the Boise Cascade workers' union organized nearly three hundred employees in an angry march to the Capitol. The employees carried placards attacking McCall and Day for their stringent environmental stands. McCall heard about the march that morning and ordered Day to join him in facing the protestors.

When McCall emerged from the Capitol's front doors, the protestors surged forward. Some of them screamed "Hitler!" at the sight of Day and McCall.

"They're referring to you, L.B.," McCall said to Day.

"No, Governor," Day replied. "The honors are all yours."

Some protestors appeared to applaud the shutdown, but Boise-Cascade workers dominated the scene, heckling McCall as he attempted to reason with them.

McCall defended the state's environmental enforcement before angry Boise Cascade
workers put out of work when the company shut its Salem plant in May 1972 rather
than comply with environmental rules. "They're using you as pawns," McCall told
the workers. (Gerry Lewin photo)

"Why should one company—one company—get to break the law
and ruin the river?" McCall bellowed over the noise.

"Are you more interested in the river or us?" one woman shouted
back.

"They're trying," someone else said of the Boise Cascade officials.
"What the hell do you want?"

"We've fairly well fixed the responsibility where it belongs," Mc-
Call responded angrily. "It's with the management. They're using you
as pawns."

McCall and Day then led the crowd back to the Boise Cascade plant,
where they confronted company officials, and the officials backed

down. "No one denied that the state's pollution fighters made a much more dramatic scapegoat [than the equipment failure], so we were used," McCall said.

The DEQ pressed forward with its injunction. Boise Cascade agreed to the state's terms within hours.

The Boise Cascade confrontation had been unnecessary. Yet the incident made for great political theater in the newspapers and on television. McCall relished the images of himself and Day confronting the managers of a polluting plant. More importantly for his doctrine, McCall had stood unwaveringly behind his bellicose DEQ director.

FROM THE BOTTLE BILL to the Boise Cascade episode to McCall's continuing "militancy," Oregon's reputation as an environmental haven grew mightily at the front end of his second term. It is necessary to note, however, that McCall's environmental policy had its limits.

Two areas in which McCall did not allow environmental policy to interfere with Oregon's economic growth were profound: development of nuclear power, and high timber harvests. McCall supported both, making it clear he was not the anti-business monster his enemies portrayed. But McCall's views on these issues underscore that his environmental foresight had its failings.

In the quest for environmental balance, no other area pitted McCall's principle against expediency as did timber. Timber ran the Oregon economy. For decades, management of the state's timberlands had fallen largely to the federal government, which controlled fifty-seven percent of the forests in Oregon. In 1972, one of every eleven workers made a living directly from the timber industry. In many towns nestled against the rainy Cascade Range entire economies relied on the wet, sheared logs carried out of the woods each day by rumbling trucks.

The federal government purported to manage timber harvests on the basis of sustained yield, cutting no more than the forests could handle. McCall subscribed to the theory, as did most politicians of the day, and he had faith the United States Forest Service and the Bureau of Land Management followed their cutting standards. Many times, though, he asked for higher cuts than the federal agencies wanted to deliver. For

McCall, timber was strictly an economic issue, not an environmental matter, and he stuck with that view even as more environmentalists concentrated on protecting the nation's forests.

For example, in its initial Wilderness Act in 1964, Congress set aside eleven million acres in the country, of which about 662,870 acres were in Oregon in nine new designated wilderness areas. In 1972, conservationists pushed for expansion of the Wilderness Act, and in Oregon that meant protecting several large tracts of prime timberland.

Also, the 1971 legislature approved the nation's first law governing the methods used by timber companies to clear the land. Some environmentalists questioned the use of clearcuts in which, rather than selecting certain trees from a land sale, timber companies simply mowed down everything in the tract. The companies claimed clearcutting offered the only economical method of tree harvests. By 1972, however, opposition to the practice had grown large. Clearcutting destroyed the forest itself—replanted trees became a tree farm, not a new forest, environmentalists charged. In addition, the road building and soil erosion accompanying the clearcuts often led to landslides, which in turn damaged or destroyed creeks and rivers. As a result, the spawning beds of salmon—another valuable resource for Oregon's economy—were being wiped out.

On preservation and cutting practices, McCall sided with the timber industry. He wanted cutting restrictions and practices limited no further. In 1971, when several western governors attempted to place a moratorium on clearcutting because of the environmental damage, McCall opposed the move.

McCall often opposed expanding wilderness designations that would affect the timber base, including a proposal by Senator Mark Hatfield to expand the Eagle Cap Wilderness in northeastern Oregon. McCall proposed protecting the area only so that logging could not be seen by visitors. His concern was with the scenery, not with preservation.

McCall's concern for the Oregon economy also led him astray from most environmentalists in another area: nuclear power. Throughout his career, McCall had supported private utilities. Moreover, he believed that Oregon and the Pacific Northwest soon faced an energy shortage. McCall opposed the other major energy alternative, namely, building more dams across the Columbia or other major rivers.

As early as 1967, McCall had favored alternative forms of energy, including solar and wind. In 1970, however, those energy sources remained largely science fiction in theory and inefficient in practice. For that reason, McCall declared in October 1970 that nuclear power was "the wave of the future."

McCall supported nuclear power because he saw it as the only workable solution of the moment—no matter how expensive or dangerous. He rationalized his stand with what he later called his "Tarzan" theory. "When swinging through the energy forest," McCall would say, "never let go of one limb until you have hold of another."

Today, only one nuclear power plant, Trojan, stands in Oregon. It is owned and operated by Portland General Electric (PGE), which first won construction approval from the Atomic Energy Commission in 1971, during McCall's administration. It opened in May 1976 and ran until November 1992, when PGE closed it. At the time Trojan was approved, Oregon had no standards for such a plant, and McCall was reluctant to impose new rules on the siting. Officials from PGE repeatedly assured McCall and his staff of the safety of the 1.1 megawatt plant, to be built by Bechtel Inc., along the Columbia River forty-two miles downstream from Portland. However, unlike the timber issue, nuclear power already had a vast research base to underscore its dangers. Many critics were troubled that Portland General Electric would store radioactive waste at the Trojan site. No one knew for sure what might happen if the cooling system failed and Trojan's core had a meltdown.

McCall's authority to halt the plant was doubtful, but he did not to try to stop it. Some other state officials, feeling the withering pressure from PGE to allow the plant to move forward, ignored critical information about the plant's site. A state geologist's report raising concerns about a fault running under the site, for instance, was quietly buried.

Eventually, laws passed by the legislature beginning in 1971, which regulated siting of future nuclear plants, effectively ensured no more were built in the state.

McCall, in the early 1970s, was indeed a progressive environmental leader. However, for all of his foresight, he could not predict shifting environmental attitudes, either on nuclear power or Oregon's number one business, timber. Environmental groups had not yet sued to protect native forests, which later became standard practice. Even if they had, it is

doubtful McCall would have changed his mind. Still thinking like a reporter, McCall acted only on what he could see. He had seen polluted
rivers, littered highways and consumed farmlands. He had not seen how
clearcuts destroyed wildlife habitat, nor had he seen a nuclear accident.
In these cases, where he saw the economy of his state directly threatened, McCall sided with jobs.

None of McCall's positions stood in conflict with his doctrine of wise
land use and protection against pollution. Unlike the image portrayed by
his enemies in later years, McCall was not a preservationist in the classic sense. He was strictly a conservationist. He did not believe in preserving the environment intact for all time, but in conserving resources
for future use. McCall never swayed from his beliefs, even in future
years, as the environmental movement he helped launch shifted further
away from him.

17

Once a Commentator,
Always a Commentator

NEXT TO THE BOTTLE BILL, the biggest debate during the 1971 legislature centered on legislation to thwart migrant farm workers' attempts to form labor unions. Oregon's influential agricultural interests had demanded the bill. Each picking season farmers hired migrant workers from Mexico, paid them pathetically low wages and provided them with housing that was often ramshackle and dangerous. Led by activist César Chávez and his United Farmworkers Union, migrant workers were beginning to organize so they could demand better wages, decent housing and protection against the pesticides used in the fields. Under considerable pressure from the farming industry, the legislature passed a measure that prevented the workers from striking during harvest seasons and outlawed negotiations over critical issues, such as the use of pesticides.

Once the bill passed, rural legislators and agricultural groups inundated Tom McCall and demanded that he sign the bill. During the debate, McCall had not committed his support to the farming interests, but had said nothing that indicated he would not go along. McCall remained silent about his intentions—even to his aides—until the deadline for signing the bill approached. When the day came, he picked up his pen and said simply, "I'm going to veto that son of a bitch."

And he did. The Oregon Farm Bureau and other agricultural lobbying groups, believing they had won their fight against the migrant work-

If anything, McCall's public persona grew during his second term. McCall knew almost no bounds when it came to a publicity shot: He jogs (left) at the Salem YMCA (Gerry Lewin photo), makes a point with grade schoolers (opposite above), and soaks in the tub at the new home of Japanese Consul-General Keisuke Ochi (opposite below). (Gerry Lewin photo. Roger Jensen photo courtesy the *Oregonian*)

ers' unions, exploded in fury. Legislators declared McCall had betrayed them. Some never forgave him. McCall did not care.

Once again he had shown he was not the governor of powerful interests but of all those who lived and worked in Oregon. That included the migrant workers who lived amid poverty and who had no one in Oregon government to speak for their concerns. McCall spoke for them.

Emboldened by Vortex and his re-election, McCall, in his second term, acted with a sharpness and clarity so often obscured by his hand-wringing of earlier years. He was fifty-seven when he began his second term. His well-known face with the jutting chin had turned softer with age; his dark hair had grown thin and silver. But he remained as vigorous and as ambitious as ever, and he still cherished the attention the governorship granted him.

The press gave him all the attention he could want. Reporters from all over the country discovered what the Oregon press had known for years: McCall was a great story.

"He had a very good public relations sense," recalled Jules Witcover, then the national political reporter for the Baltimore *Sun.* "He knew from his newscasting experience what made news. His quotes were usually irresistible."

After his public break with Nixon and Agnew, McCall showed reporters a courage of which most American politicians were incapable. "He was his own man, a dying breed of real liberal Republican," Witcover said. "Some people thought McCall was a loose cannon. But I never thought he was. When he shot off, he did it with a purpose. He thought there should be some fresh air blowing through the Republican party and he provided it. He was canny about it all. He was a very volatile guy, but he was also very careful that his volatility hit."

However, McCall's candid comments sometimes gave his staff headaches. McCall and his staff developed subtle techniques to protect him from his own mouth. During phone interviews, Ron Schmidt sat nearby, his finger near the receiver button. If McCall grew too reckless in his comments, Schmidt would jab the button. After counsel from Schmidt, McCall would call the reporter back, apologizing for being cut off. If McCall went astray while talking to reporters in person, the aide standing closest to him was charged with stepping on McCall's foot. The job usually fell to Schmidt or Audrey, who found they needed to jump on McCall's large feet for him to notice the signal. The warning was supposed to shut him up. Sometimes it did. Many times, however, McCall simply ignored it—all to the press' delight.

In 1971, for example, McCall had barely stepped off the plane in Jackson Hole, Wyoming, to attend a governors' conference before reporters surrounded him. The conference was set to discuss the federal welfare program and the trouble the states had with how the Nixon administration managed it.

Usually loathe to cover such dull affairs, reporters waited eagerly for McCall's arrival. McCall happily greeted the reporters and began to ramble on. At one point the San Francisco *Chronicle* reporter told McCall that there was not much news. McCall said he would help out.

"For beginners," McCall replied, "how would it be that we allege Governor Reagan is holding the president hostage?"

The reporters wrote frantically in their notebooks and he expanded.

McCall had grown tired of Reagan's conservative demagoguery. Reagan, for one thing, had always brandished his Eleventh Commandment in McCall's face: Thou shalt not speak ill of another Republican. McCall considered this pompous hogwash. Reagan frequently attacked Republicans—liberal Republicans like McCall himself. A few months earlier, Reagan had sided entirely with Agnew in the Sun Valley showdown.

So, as reporters scribbled, McCall delivered his story. Reagan, McCall alleged, was holding up his political support for Nixon, who was gearing up for re-election. In exchange, the Nixon administration was giving California hundreds of millions of dollars more in welfare payments than the state was due.

Nixon was being "squeezed unduly" by Reagan, McCall declared, adding, "I resent any governor holding a president hostage." His comment had a rich irony—as if he really cared that anyone was squeezing Nixon.

Meanwhile, across the tarmac, Audrey McCall looked up and saw her husband talking emphatically to reporters. She walked over and belatedly stomped on his foot.

McCall's broadside shocked the White House into a response. "Apparently Gov. McCall is not aware of the good relations we have with Gov. Reagan," Nixon's press secretary, Ron Ziegler, told reporters. Nixon, as it turned out, was at the time staying at San Clemente, his California retreat. The coincidence gave Reagan a quip to fend off reporters' inquiries about McCall's charges. "The president is a guest in California, not a hostage," Reagan said. "He is free to come and go as he pleases."

The press interest in McCall intensified. The next day, McCall awoke to find reporters and a NBC News camera crew waiting outside his chalet. As McCall walked toward the meeting hall, he saw Reagan and his entourage. McCall called out to Reagan, who pretended to ignore him. McCall rushed up and called out again. As McCall remembered the exchange:

> When I said "Hi, Ron!" for a second time, he couldn't avoid
> me. So he drew me into his contingent as we hurried along

and said, "Damn it it all, Tom, why couldn't you have called me? I'd have told you there wasn't any sort of irritation or pressure between the White House and Sacramento."

"But, Ron," I said, "if I'd done that, there wouldn't have been any story."

"Which," as McCall noted later, "is something he overlooked."

McCall never overlooked the odds for a story. Had he made up the claim just to get headlines? McCall said later he had had a hunch that California was getting more than its share of federal welfare money. Later, press reports suggested McCall had been right. That had only been half of McCall's motives. He had hooked reporters' attention onto welfare—the otherwise drab topic of the conference.

As McCall put it later, he saw it as "the necessity of saying something once in awhile—not to cause a lot of people's guts to boil—but to add reason for the national press corps to come to these meetings and pick up something solid about governors along with the political froth which [reporters] cherish so greatly."

"People forget," he told the New York *Times* after his remarks about Reagan and Nixon, "that once a commentator, always a commentator. [Reporters] ask what I think and I tell them."

At that same governors' meeting, McCall let fly another comment that had strong resonance back home. A reporter asked him idly what his own political plans might include. McCall said he intended to challenge Oregon's senior senator, Mark Hatfield, the following year.

Like so many McCall statements, his comment surprised almost everyone. Those people who understood the bitter relationship between Hatfield and McCall, however, had known some kind of confrontation was inevitable.

THEIR YEARS APART—Hatfield in Washington, D.C., and McCall in Salem—had done little to soothe their prickly relationship. Each possessed deep political ambition and jealousies, and they goaded each other constantly. Considering their stature, the battles often grew petty. In 1968, for example, Hatfield and McCall had agreed to give each other

California governor Ronald Reagan with Oregon's governor. McCall thought Reagan and his conservative rhetoric were divisive forces that drove the Republican Party too far to the right. (OrHi 90680)

wide berth at the Republican National Convention, scheduled for Miami. Traditionally, a state's governor served as delegation chairman, which meant appearing on national television to announce the delegation's votes, as Hatfield had twice before. Under a gentleman's agreement, Hatfield had told McCall that it would be McCall's turn to be delegation chairman. As the convention approached, however, Hatfield learned his name had been added to Richard Nixon's list of possible vice-presidential nominees. Wanting as much of the spotlight as possible, Hatfield quietly organized state GOP leaders in his favor and against McCall. Oregon's delegate to the Republican National Committee, George "Bun" Stadelman, asked Hatfield why the senator had gone back on his agreement. "Things have changed," Hatfield replied.

When time came to select the delegation's leadership, not only did McCall lose the chairmanship, Hatfield made certain McCall held no position of influence at all.

Burning with anger, McCall waited until he appeared at a state Republican meeting held three days before the start of the national convention to lash out at Hatfield. The banquet schedule called for McCall to simply introduce the guest speaker, Massachusetts governor John Volpe. But McCall had drink after drink while sitting at the head table. When he stood to introduce Volpe, McCall launched into an angry speech denouncing Hatfield for his opposition to the Vietnam War. He first spoke of his son, Tad, who faced assignment in Vietnam. "I would feel safer," McCall snarled, "if Dick Nixon were president of the United States standing behind that boy than if Mark Hatfield or Wayne Morse were president of the United States."

McCall then attacked an anti-war plank that Hatfield wanted in the national GOP platform. He called the proposal a "yellow, chicken kind of resolution." Added McCall, "When you've got a boy over there, then you begin to count the cheating and weaseling when it comes to what do you have to say about Vietnam. . . . We've been a weaseling, two-faced party on the war."

The Republican audience sat stunned. The next morning, a sobered McCall apologized for his tone, but not his attack on Hatfield. He said the attack had been "seething inside of me for the last four years."

Later, Floyd McKay, reporter for the *Oregon Statesman,* described the political wreckage McCall left behind. McCall, wrote McKay, "told friends that he was glad he had made the spontaneous comments—that it was something he had to say. That is the simplest, and probably the most accurate, explanation of the McCall remarks, for that is the sort of man McCall is."

McCall went to the national convention as an exile within his own delegation. Hatfield had arranged to have McCall sitting in the middle of a row, away from the aisles where reporters worked. Anxious to get his name in print, McCall later moved back a few rows, to the Michigan delegation behind Oregon's, so he could have an aisle seat and access to the press.

Most of all, McCall watched with mixed disappointment and glee as

Despite the public smiles, jealousy between McCall and U.S. Senator Mark Hatfield often created an icy relationship between them. (OrHi 90679)

the dovish Hatfield chased the hawkish Nixon in hopes of the second-place spot on the ticket. "Hatfield," McCall observed later, "threw himself at Nixon." A few newspaper reports named Hatfield as Nixon's choice. Southern Republicans, still loyal to the Barry Goldwater ideal of conservatism, however, warned Nixon they would block Hatfield's nomination. Nixon went on to pick Agnew instead.

After the 1968 convention, the Hatfield-McCall feud intensified. Although the two men's staffs worked quietly together on state business, the governor and the senior senator spoke to one another only when necessary. "Whenever you saw them together, you could just see the chill," said a friend of both men.

For his part, Hatfield played the innocent victim, wronged by McCall's uninvited attacks. Hatfield, however, was more subtle. He knew McCall's soft spots and stabbed them when he could.

Late in 1969, when McCall visited Washington, D.C., Hatfield invited McCall to a private lunch. There, Hatfield attacked him. He was tired of McCall's public criticism of him, he said. He had never second-guessed McCall's performance as governor. Why could McCall not do the same for him? McCall apologized, and that angered Hatfield even more.

"I am tired," Hatfield said to McCall, "of your public tantrums and private apologies."

McCall left the lunch humbled. Two days later, he picked up the Salem newspaper to see an account of the lunch, leaked by Hatfield and written by A. Robert Smith, a Washington, D.C.-based columnist for several Oregon newspapers. Smith gave Hatfield all the sympathy, portraying the senator as a beleaguered soul who was innocent in his efforts to maintain his patience with McCall. Smith, responding to Hatfield's strategy, went on to label McCall a "garrulous ex-broadcaster."

McCall exploded. He grabbed a typewriter and furiously dashed off a response to Smith. Blackened by errors and scribbled corrections, the letter is a portrait of typographical fury. Just as Hatfield's leak shows his disrespect for McCall, the letter reveals the depth of McCall's spite for Hatfield. McCall wrote Smith:

> I thought initially it was as cruel and vicious a thing as you ever put on paper about a fair and friendly soul. I patiently explained to my harried loved ones of all ages, "That's the way you have to write in Washington to show that you're as deft a nut-cutter as the next cynic in punditry's capital."
>
> That shrank their tears down a few acre feet—enough to let them ask, "But isn't it obvious from the writing that Mark O. leaked it, massaged it, pushed it and shaped it through a more than willing conspirator?"
>
> "No comment" is my reply. It's not that I don't mind telling them it was the most transparent plant since Drew Pearson's last expose. It's just that I don't want to be accused again of garrulity. . . . Come out and see—see some of the very best speeches, the big dialogs on every issue, 'cause we haven't ducked a single one. Then if you still want to use your stiletto, fine. But you use it—not the owner of that stealthy white hand who used you last week.

TWO YEARS LATER, McCall was talking of a direct challenge to Hatfield. It was not a far-fetched idea. In mid-1971, early polls showed Hatfield had fallen from Oregonians' graces, just as McCall had risen steadily. A survey performed by a Republican group showed McCall had a two-to-one edge over Hatfield in a hypothetical Senate primary. A few weeks later, the *Oregon Journal* reported another poll showing McCall with an even bigger edge—sixty-two to twenty-four.

McCall found no mystery in Hatfield's decline in popularity. He felt Hatfield was pursuing personal fame at Oregon's expense. After missing the vice presidency, Hatfield had parlayed his opposition to Vietnam into national celebrity. With Senator George McGovern, a South Dakota Democrat and later Democratic presidential nominee, Hatfield sponsored an amendment giving Nixon a deadline to end the Vietnam War. Hatfield also pursued a vigorous, nationwide public speaking schedule. And stories of Hatfield's own presidential ambitions had resurfaced.

When reporters asked, McCall happily gave them his analysis of Hatfield's woes. "The criticism of [Hatfield], whether it is true or not, is that he is not so interested in the state as he is in being president of the United States," McCall said, gloating. "That's it in a nutshell." Even in his effort to be civil, he could not resist digging at the senator. "I wish 95 percent of the people were for him," McCall said, "but they're not. He just hasn't done a very good job."

McCall's desire to challenge Hatfield came from more than simple vengeance. It came, as much of his ambition did, from his family roots. He never forgot the disappointment suffered by his grandfather, Samuel Walker McCall, over losing the Senate seat to Republican dealmakers. When first talking about his own ambitions to Schmidt and Westerdahl eight years earlier, McCall had confided that the Senate remained his goal. As McCall recounted years later, "There was always a disappointment that [Samuel Walker McCall] had not realized his senatorial ambition. . . . I thought of myself as a very pale carbon copy of grandfather McCall and looked upon the Senate as an opportunity to succeed at the one level he had failed."

In the summer of 1971 McCall was certain he would challenge Hatfield, and by August, McCall had told several people he intended to make the race. The prospect put Hatfield on edge. "Tom was a very unpredictable person," Hatfield said years later. "It depended on what condition he was in—mad, happy, pleasant or whatever—what he might do. I took it seriously."

So, too, did the Nixon White House. Nixon held no particular love for either Hatfield or McCall. Both Republicans had caused his administration grief and poor publicity. Nixon, however, came to Hatfield's rescue. Nixon, who himself trailed in several national polls, assumed any Republican dissent in Oregon could hurt his own chances in the state, and he began to work quietly to get McCall to drop the challenge. McCall later reported that Kansas senator Robert Dole, the Republican national chairman, pressured McCall to stay out of the race. Oregon congressman Wendell Wyatt, a Republican who got along with both McCall and Hatfield, also carried Nixon's message to McCall.

McCall told both Dole and Wyatt that he would probably not run against Hatfield, and on 6 October, he told reporters the same thing. Still, McCall resented the pressure and suspected Hatfield's hand at work. His anger toward Hatfield grew and he renewed talk of a Senate race. He saw the Senate race as a grudge match, not as a means to an end.

But Hatfield understood how to play McCall's emotions to his own advantage. In February 1972, McCall and Hatfield appeared as guest speakers at an awards banquet for Glenn Jackson, who had helped both men's careers. Before the festivities, Hatfield initiated an exchange that may have changed McCall's thinking for good about the Senate race.

Hatfield pulled McCall aside and asked him what his plans truly were for the Senate. McCall started talking as if he intended to challenge— and defeat—Hatfield in the Republican primary. Hatfield watched as McCall grew more agitated and heated. Then Hatfield cut him off. "Fine," Hatfield told McCall. "Come into the race if you want to. But I want to say one thing. I'll shred you."

McCall fell silent, stunned at Hatfield's icy response. Hatfield knew that his comment had struck home. As Hatfield said ten years later of the exchange, "[Tom] knew I would. Tom's not a man who really wanted to get into the arena, bare-knuckling it. I can meet people on that basis if I have to."

The warning laid a permanent chill in McCall's spine. In the abstract, the thought of being called "Senator McCall" was very attractive. The stark prospect of facing Hatfield on the attack, however, made McCall's thin skin curl.

Soon after the confrontation with Hatfield, McCall said he would announce his plans for the Senate race in late February. His staff knew by then he had no intention of making the race, but McCall understood the valuable suspense the delay built in the press and the Republican party. He waited until the Dorchester Conference, the annual Oregon Republican meeting held at the coast, then hinted his speech to the meeting would contain an important announcement.

With dozens of reporters present and a packed Republican house waiting for his decision, McCall delivered a short, mundane review of issues facing the state. He said nothing of the Senate or Hatfield.

When he finished his prepared text, McCall looked at his audience and smiled. "All in all," he said finally, "this has been a pretty mild speech for a McCall to give."

Then, gripping everyone's attention, McCall dove into a subject that he had hastily added to his speech text. He declared Oregon must provide its citizens with a new right: the right to death with dignity.

Silence fell over the room. McCall watched the audience as, he remembered, "Suddenly, eyes popped wide."

He had been thinking, he said, that anyone who wishes to end his or her own life should have a right to do so. He noted that many people lingering on, in comas or with terminal illnesses, may choose to have their lives ended.

"It's an unclear right that somehow must be clarified and made legally available," McCall said simply. "Death with dignity in one's advanced years, as opposed to death as a vegetable."

In 1972, when McCall let loose his ideas about death with dignity, few in America had given the issue much thought. McCall made his observations three years before the controversial national debate on the question first opened over the celebrated case of Karen Ann Quinlan, a New Jersey woman left in an irreversible coma whose parents wanted her life-support systems shut down, and two decades before the national debate about doctor-assisted suicide. "That just shocked the shit out of everybody," said Clarence Zaitz, the United Press International reporter covering the speech. "That was something governors didn't talk about. Hell, nobody talked about it."

No one knew what inspired McCall. Later, he said he had been thinking about the issue for months and at a moment's notice decided to fling it out before the Dorchester audience. McCall had hastily typed out the "death with dignity" comments and tacked them onto his prepared speech.

McCall again proved his eloquence and mastery of political timing. "He said what he thought without stopping to think about the political consequences," said Zaitz. "But he was so goddamn popular, he could say almost anything and it didn't hurt him very much."

Meanwhile, the Senate question still stood unanswered. McCall directed Schmidt to draft two announcements—one declaring his challenge to Hatfield, the other explaining why he instead intended to finish his governorship. On 7 March, he delivered the latter, as many people expected by this time.

As much as he liked the sound of "Senator McCall," he knew the 1972 campaign would not be his last chance for the Senate. He also knew that a mid-term campaign could upset work on his environmental programs. If he won, who could he trust to finish his agenda? He worried more about losing, however, and the nasty campaign Hatfield had promised. Defeat to Hatfield, McCall confided to two friendly newspaper editors, "could turn me into a lame duck who really limped rather than one who still could quack to beat Hell."

McCall never reconciled himself with his decision to pass up the Senate, although he took some comfort believing he might have beaten Hatfield, without ever committing to do so. Still, the notion of giving up on his dream and allowing Hatfield a free ride gnawed at him. He continued to taunt Hatfield with threats to enter the race as an independent. On 25 May, the day after the GOP primary, McCall issued one such threat. The press treated the declaration with skepticism. Associated Press reporter Paul Harvey wrote, "When McCall was asked . . . to explain what he meant, the governor said he didn't want to discuss it anymore without thinking about it. The implication was that the governor didn't do much thinking before he made the first statement."

McCall stood by wistfully as his rival won re-election in 1972. The

After his early broadcasting jitters, McCall was to become one of the masters of the publi forum. He was comfortable and often eloquent when confronted by an array of microphones. (OrHi 90693)

dalliance with the Senate race made McCall more contemplative of his own future. He loved the spotlight more than the battle, and, barred by state law from running for governor for a third term, the spotlight would dim in only two more years. However, McCall drew from the experience what he cherished most—a sense that he stood atop politics in his state. He also walked away remembering why he had first become governor and what work still remained unfinished.

MCCALL WAS SOON OVERCOME by a fear that time was, indeed, running out. In September 1972, McCall underwent a routine doctor's examination at the University of Oregon Medical School in Portland. McCall had been complaining privately about a urinary infection, and his doctor decided to take a biopsy from McCall's prostate gland.

The results chilled McCall. The doctors found the early roots of a growth in McCall's prostate and thought they had discovered cancer. The growth was too small to determine its threat, and McCall's physicians decided to treat it with powerful antibiotics. McCall and his staff agreed that the discovery and the antibiotics, which brought on wooziness, merited a long rest for McCall. He and Audrey sneaked off to the Carmel Valley in California for two weeks. Contrary to McCall's usual candor, his office kept the trip's true reason quiet, telling the public only that McCall had left the state to recover from a bladder infection.

In California, the thought suddenly hit McCall: What if it is cancer? And if it is, why am I whittling away my time? He could not simply sit still, and did not allow himself to rest as the doctors had ordered. After a week under the medication's haze, McCall jumped up and played eighteen holes of golf and three sets of tennis.

McCall returned home to better medical news. His doctor declared the growth had diminished, and he decreased McCall's medication. The brief scare had stiffened McCall's resolve to finish his work. Time was slipping away.

18

Among the Grasping Wastrels

ALTHOUGH HE RARELY REPEATED his "visit, but don't stay" line, McCall found that by 1973 the quip had helped define his governorship. He joked that the statement was better known than he was, and that every newspaper except *Pravda* had repeated it. When a local humorist wrote about a wall Oregon intended to build around the state, a citizen sent McCall the article with a note attached, reading, "You didn't!"

"We can't," McCall wrote back, "but sometimes I wish we could, don't you?"

McCall conceded that the attention his statement had drawn to Oregon was actually inspiring more people to move in, not stay out. Between 1970 and 1972, Oregon's population had jumped nearly five percent. "Oregon's leadership in fighting pollution with the emphasis on livability has made the state an appealing place to live," he said early in 1973. "The better job we do the more people want to come—that's the irony of it. . . . It's just a matter of time before we're swamped."

Despite his famous rhetoric, McCall, of course, could not slam the gates of Oregon against immigrants or new business. Instead, he believed Oregon should wisely prepare for generations of growth. Although the public and the press grew angry about polluting industries, litter and unprotected beaches, McCall saw that all those concerns were interconnected. They all depended on the way in which Oregon managed its land.

McCall had tried to introduce a system to protect against misuse of the land when, in 1969, the legislature had approved the statewide zoning law he wanted. The law, as he envisioned it, set aside land for new homes and industry, while locking away valuable, irreplaceable farm and forest land. Oregon would then have room to grow without attacking its underlying economic values.

Although the law required that all 277 local governments complete zoning plans by 1971, the deadline had come and gone and few local governments were in compliance. Cities and counties claimed the law was too vague, and many local officials had waited for the state to help pay for the zoning project. Lawmakers had promised the money, but never delivered.

Four years later, little had changed. Development was rampant, with little or no planning for services. Most newcomers moved into the burgeoning Willamette Valley where the loss of farmland continued. By 1972, fifteen thousand more acres of Willamette Valley farmland had been paved since SB 10 had been passed in 1969.

As land speculation increased, scenes like the one in Progress, a quiet Washington County community twenty minutes from downtown Portland, became more common. Near Progress, the new Washington Square shopping complex sprawled, inviting even more development around its edges. In late 1972, one Progress farmer saw the inevitable. "I'd like to hold on to my land," he sighed. "Farming's all I know. But they're squeezing me out. I figure I can last another year or two, then I'll sell for a good price and retire early."

The spreading development moved so quickly that local governments could not keep up with services. The problem was especially dire when developers moved to areas far ahead of population growth. Emblematic of this so-called "leapfrog" problem was the 477-acre Charbonneau housing development, located along the Willamette River near rural Wilsonville. Charbonneau's owner, the Benjamin Franklin Savings and Loan, had plunked down its two thousand home sites fifteen miles from the nearest suburb. The development promised to spike the values of nearby farms and to stretch tiny Wilsonville's ability to provide services.

The development caught McCall's attention and he asked an aide to investigate. The investigation's results underscored McCall's fears about out-of-control growth. Despite its potential problems, the report noted, Charbonneau's developers had broken no rules because even for such a gigantic development, no rules existed. "The system hasn't failed," the report concluded. "There is no system."

The reform in land-use planning that McCall wanted could not occur from within his office alone. He needed dramatic changes in Oregon law. With his second term nearing its halfway point, McCall had only one more legislative session as governor. If he failed in the 1973 legislature, it meant his doctrine of land use and livability would be left vulnerable to erosion and attack.

Unlike a polluting factory or a threatened beach, however, land-use planning rarely got lawmakers' attention. In 1973, McCall needed more legislative champions to win sweeping land-use changes.

McCall had one such champion from the start.

Hector Macpherson for years had run his family dairy near Corvallis in rural Linn County. He had no intention of surrendering his land to the new development that, even in the early 1960s, he saw crowding his farm. Other farmers, however, were cashing out for what looked like princely sums. "Scratch a farmer," Macpherson often said, "and you'll find a subdivider."

Macpherson, whom one historian described as a "raw-boned and somewhat cerebral dairy farmer," struck out to solve the land-use problems in his county. As early as 1963, Macpherson had founded a county planning commission and had proven to be an uncommonly eloquent proponent for greater planning. "Visualize the alternative," Macpherson said in 1967, years before such notions were popular. "A valley where neighbor encroaches upon neighbor, a land unproductive agriculturally where hunger and want must surely follow, a land defiled and unsightly, a monument to man's greed and shortsightedness."

Macpherson won an Oregon Senate seat in 1970 and immediately set to work on land-use planning, but he found no one wanted to listen. "Oregon had this environmental wave building up," Macpherson recalled. "But this land-use planning idea was so controversial that people in the legislature didn't want to touch it."

Near the close of the 1971 legislature, however, Senate President John Burns allowed Macpherson to oversee an interim land-use study, although Macpherson received no money or staff to conduct his study.

He soon found kindred spirits among McCall's staff. By late 1971, McCall had recognized that the statewide zoning law was failing and had directed his staff to seek a new land-use proposal. Macpherson joined in as if he were a member of McCall's staff, not a lawmaker. Together, Macpherson and the governor's office drafted their ideal land-use bill.

Because local zoning remained vulnerable to local pressures, Mc-Call and Macpherson's new land-use bill placed final control in the state's hands. The bill formed fourteen planning districts. Within each district, cities and counties had to zone the land as they saw fit. Then, over the zoning, the planning district would place a comprehensive plan that set out growth policy for the entire district. Zoning could not be changed if it violated the district plan. The district plan could not be changed if it violated the state's land-use rules. In other words, the state would place a protective coating over the use of the land. The bill went even further, including language that could block construction of new nuclear power plants and protecting several specific scenic locations throughout the state.

McCall understood the political implications of the bill. Before he had been elected, the state had ceded control of land-use decisions to local authorities. McCall now wanted the state to strip away local control if state standards were not met.

"I knew nothing would get done at the local level even if the local officials were top notch," McCall remarked years later of the rationale behind his plan. "I could take the heat, I could push for preservation of farm lands and urban growth boundaries to stop sprawl, where 80 percent of the locals would be bounced out on their fannies for trying to do this."

McCall believed that lawmakers would find little incentive to approve such a controversial change in state policy. However, he also knew lawmakers bent under the force of the public will. So, beginning in 1972, McCall started to make the public aware of the advantages of land-use planning.

During the year, McCall's office launched a public education campaign about land-use concerns. At its heart was what McCall dubbed "Project Foresight," a task force charged with studying the demands of population and industry on the Willamette Valley. The project panel produced two scenarios of four decades of future growth. One portrayed a Willamette Valley unshielded from the blast of population and development, a valley clogged with traffic, stripped of farmland and hemmed in by housing tracts. The second showed a well-planned valley, one in which the state had carefully directed four decades of growth. Land was set aside for development, other land stood free for forestry and farming, and highways and mass transit worked together.

The Project Foresight task force paraded these two scenarios before 275 civic groups and town hall meetings. When lawmakers convened in 1973, McCall's scheme had already generated widespread support among local government officials. Then McCall used his greatest weapon—his own power to inspire.

"[McCall] threw a great deal of public attention on land-use problems," Macpherson said. "Tom was a master with words. . . . He was not a nuts-and-bolts man. . . . But this is the kind of thing we needed. He prepared the public for the legislators back home and helped create that groundswell."

McCall launched a statewide tour of speeches, ending with a land-use congress he sponsored in November 1972. McCall brought in national planning experts to study Oregon's problems and debate solutions, but McCall headed the list of speakers. Despite the dry topic, the Oregon press flocked to his speech.

"We need growth," McCall said, "but not the chain-letter type that leaves future generations with an empty mailbox." He warned that land-use opponents would wield such emotional phrases as "due process" and "freedom of choice." Still, he said, he did not pity developers and builders who consumed Oregon's land without regard for the needs of the whole.

> The phrase "land-use planning" is well understood by speculators, and that's why they don't want any of it. There are those who want our money so badly they will break the spirit

of our laws. . . . Their interest is in their pocketbook and they intend to rule by misdirection. They have rewritten the Golden Rule to say that he who has the gold makes the rules. . . .

Oregon should not be a haven to the buffalo hunter mentality. . . . We must stop those so interested in money they rape the land and worship the dollar.

His speech received prominent press attention statewide, and McCall appeared to have completed his message to Oregonians. But several weeks later, McCall issued an even stronger address to the 1973 legislature. His speech was one of the most memorable of his career.

There is a shameless threat to our environment and to the whole quality of life—unfettered despoiling of the land. Sagebrush subdivisions, coastal condomania and the ravenous rampage of suburbia in the Willamette Valley all threaten to mock Oregon's status as the environmental model for the nation.

We are dismayed that we have not stopped misuse of the land, our most valuable finite resource. . . . The interests of Oregon for today and in the future must be protected from the grasping wastrels of the land.

With that, McCall sent his plan forward into the legislature, where the buffalo hunters and grasping wastrels waited.

AS MCCALL SUSPECTED, lawmakers balked at the reform he had prescribed. And as State Senator Hector Macpherson surmised, he found few people willing to sign on to the land-use bill, Senate Bill 100. But he did find one formidable ally, State Senator Ted Hallock, a doctrinaire liberal Democrat from Portland.

The profane and volatile Hallock swung from extremes—insightful and cunning at one moment, raving and fearsome the next. McCall and Hallock had been friends since the 1950s—Hallock had also been in radio but as a disc jockey—and they shared a crusading streak and raging impatience. As Hallock observed, "[Tom] had the same distaste for dumb people that I do."

Hallock took up SB 100 in his Senate Environment and Land Use Committee. He wanted to jam the bill quickly through the senate, however, the senate's new president, Democrat Jason Boe, was a conservative who disliked the bill. Boe had stacked Hallock's committee against the bill, so that the panel, as one writer noted at the time, ranged "from unconvinced to hostile." Still, Hallock and Macpherson, who also sat on the panel, pushed on. Hallock held hearing after hearing, attracting hundreds of onlookers who crammed the small committee room. Environmental groups—now including concerned farming groups—found themselves supporting the bill across the table from the opponents' big guns: lumber giants, such as Georgia-Pacific and Weyerhaeuser; private utilities, such as Portland General Electric and Pacific Power & Light; the Oregon Home Builders Association; and the corporate interest group Associated Oregon Industries.

McCall saw that the weight of this opposition could crush SB 100 despite Hallock's best efforts. So McCall stirred up even more public pressure.

The existing law gave McCall the authority to grab emergency zoning powers. Although he saw this authority as unwieldly, he thought it could prove effective when used with precision. He used it to create public outrage.

Four years earlier, state inspectors had discovered severe health problems resulting from poor land planning in coastal Lincoln County, the site of booming growth for years. In some cases, sewer lines from subdivisions went nowhere, leaving open septic pools. In late 1972, McCall quietly ordered another investigation. As hearings on SB 100 began, McCall released the damning results of the Lincoln County study.

The new investigation had found more serious health and environmental problems stemming from Lincoln County's failed planning system. The study identified thirty-eight sewage outfalls running from new subdivisions directly onto public beaches. In addition, Lincoln County had repeatedly violated its own zoning standards in allowing the unsanitary housing projects to proceed.

McCall unleashed a savage attack on Lincoln County when he re-

McCall delivers one of his most famous speeches, admonishing the 1973 legislature to approve statewide land-use planning to protect Oregon from the "grasping wastrels of the land." (Wayne Eastburn photo, courtesy of the Eugene *Register-Guard*)

leased the report to the press and brandished an executive order halting all new construction in the county. "My first thought was that King Tom had declared martial law in Lincoln County," one coastal lawmaker grumbled.

His real ability to stop construction was dubious, but McCall's action made for perfect theater. His outrage was translated, as he knew it would be, into the outrage of Oregonians. Lawmakers again saw floods of letters demanding something be done to stop sewage on their beaches.

McCall then gave his land-use campaign even greater exposure. He arrived in Washington, D.C., in February to testify before the Senate Interior Committee in favor of a national land-use planning bill sponsored by Washington senator Henry Jackson.

Already worried SB 100 might fail, McCall told the committee that the federal government had to step in and support land-use planning. "There is a valid public interest in directing growth and development, and in preventing misuse of land and sprawl of suburbia, knowing that unlimited and unregulated growth leads inexorably to a lowered quality of life." When western senators suggested that a federal bill would usurp states' rights, McCall showed that he still believed in the expanding role of federal government. More "intrusion" was inevitable, he said, if for only one reason: In protecting the land, "There are no tomorrows."

Despite the exposure, SB 100 still languished. Lawmakers found it too complicated and controversial an issue to approve so easily. Many lawmakers wanted to delay the issue two more years, if not more. McCall, facing retirement, could not afford the delay.

Worried and frustrated, one day McCall sought solace in the Capitol press room. McCall sensed that the statehouse reporters had assumed land-use planning was a dead issue for the session and would stop writing about it. When McCall arrived, reporters scurried for their notepads. "Whenever Tom was around [reporters] would fall all over themselves because you never knew what the man was going to say," said the Eugene *Register-Guard*'s Henny Willis. Willis recalled, however, that on this day McCall did not have a catchy phrase or specific story he wanted to plant. Instead, said Willis, "He came down to spill his guts. He sat on the edge of a desk and talked about land use and how important it was, and that Oregon had to be the first state to set some sort of standard, because we cared about our environment." A few reporters tried to change the subject but McCall was not diverted. Willis recalled the quiet passion in McCall's eyes during the half-hour session. "You see, he had the sense that he was losing this issue, and that it was very dear to him," Willis said. "It was one time Tom didn't want us to do a story. He just wanted us to know how he felt."

Privately, McCall feared the entire effort would fail. He told Hallock he could patch together a statewide land-use plan out of existing laws but needed new funding to do so. "If you can't pass the bill," he told Hallock in exasperation at one point, "just get me $500,000 and I'll do the son of a bitch myself."

Hallock, however, thought the plan still had a chance. He told McCall he planned to set up a special committee, made up of lobbyists and land-use planning advocates, to write a compromise bill. McCall and Hallock agreed that the strategy could produce a meaningful bill only if this special committee had as its leader someone outside of the legislature, someone with strong environmental credentials, someone as fierce as the two of them combined.

To run this special committee, Hallock appointed L.B. Day.

Day had recently ended his fiery tenure as director of the Department of Environmental Quality. He lunged at the chance to forge a new land-use bill. To form his committee, Day took the list of the land-use bill's major opponents and gave them all places on the panel. The panel members included the representatives of the League of Oregon Cities, timber giant Georgia-Pacific, and the Home Builders Association. Calling everyone into a closed-door meeting, Day calmly invited everyone to have a seat.

After the door slammed shut, Day raged until he was hoarse, staring at each member with his wild, cross-eyed glare. His baritone voice resonated, vibrating the bones of everyone on his committee. As one participant, Home Builders Association lobbyist Fred Van Natta, recalled:

> The first meeting consisted of L.B. haranguing individually and collectively everybody there, until we weren't sure it was even worth our time to come to the next meeting. He was loud, aggressive belligerent, threatening—"You're not going to stand in the way of this bill. This is good for the interest of the state"—that kind of an approach. By the time he's done with you, you figured, "Well, I better ask for the bare minimum." And that's what we got.

As Day beat down opposition to SB 100, he constructed a compromise plan. He dumped the language that would designate specific scenic spots off limits to development. The private utilities dropped their opposition when Day exempted the siting of nuclear power plants from land-use decisions. Rather than create fourteen new planning districts, Day gave control to the thirty-six counties. Most importantly, though, Day changed the means of land-use planning. The standards that guided care of the land would now be set not by bureaucrats, but by Oregonians themselves through a series of hearings. "We're talking about planning that basically comes from the bottom up, not from the top down," said Day.

Hallock grabbed the compromise bill—which had turned many opponents into supporters—and rushed it through the senate on an eighteen-to-ten vote. Hallock and Macpherson then delivered the bill to the house, now under control of liberal Democrats. Hallock feared that opponents of the bill had pulled back on their opposition when confronted by Day, but might still hope to kill the bill in the house. "I told them not to change that bill," Hallock recalled. "Not to change a fucking period." Unaltered, SB 100 sailed through the house and landed on Tom McCall's desk.

Even as McCall signed SB 100, he fretted about the new law's stewardship and the price of compromise. "Senate Bill 100 is tremendously hedged," he said soon after signing the bill. "In fact, it's got so many hedges I'm not sure it's going to get done." The prospect of leaving the land-use undertaking to another governor clearly worried him. "We have just really got to pay attention to this," McCall said "and make sure it doesn't drift away."

Statewide land-use planning became the cornerstone of Oregon's environmental work. The new agency created to oversee the reforms, the Land Conservation and Development Commission (LCDC), adopted fourteen new land-use standards, called "goals," in late 1974, but it took nearly ten years before every county and city met its planning requirements under the law.

No other act in McCall's administration left such a profound impact on Oregon, nor was any other as controversial. Land-use soon became a booming business for lawyers as local governments and private interests fought the new law in court.

In the end, Oregon's land-use laws accomplished all that McCall hoped they would. Oregon had a plan for growth, no matter how painful its enforcement. McCall spent the rest of his life making sure the intent of land-use planning did not "drift away." Quietly, solemnly, McCall promised himself he would fight to preserve Oregon's new planning laws for the remainder of his life, even if it meant fighting through his final days.

In the end, it did.

MCCALL MIGHT HAVE STOPPED THERE in 1973. He had set out all he had wished for to protect Oregon. Yet his sights on the future had been grounded in his care for the land and its rivers. He wanted another kind of legacy, however, that no other governor had left behind: tax reform.

McCall's lonely fight to change the Oregon tax system was more than one man's fight for fairness. The entire episode epitomized all Mc-Call had become. He was driven to reform government—indeed, to transform it. No governor in recent times had had the courage to try to completely change the tax system. McCall intended not only to try, but to succeed. He believed he could do it with the force of his own will and popularity.

In 1973, Oregonians, per capita, paid among the highest income tax and property tax rates in the country, because there was no sales tax to share the tax burden. The increasing property tax especially victimized local school districts, which depended largely on the locally controlled tax. As a result, school districts varied widely in wealth and quality; in 1973, $600 was spent per student in the poorest district, $2,500 in the wealthiest. Schools in Portland, for example, sat comfortably on a regular tax base and could count on fat budgets year to year. Many other school districts, however, had no property tax base and went begging each year to local voters for a levy simply to keep school doors open. A school district without a property tax base could have one comfortable year, followed immediately by a barren year, the quality of its education careening at the whim of local voters.

Already, a few populist leaders had talked of a property tax limitation—cutting off the tax at a restrictive level, and forcing state government to come up with the money to pay schools. McCall wanted to believe Oregonians would never cut off their schools so cruelly. Yet he understood the resentment over property taxes—and he understood that the resentment had to be extinguished before Oregon faced fiscal disaster.

McCall proposed a way to solve both the school funding problem and property tax escalation at once. He knew that, in 1973, the state of Oregon's budget paid for about one-third of local schools costs. Most of the remaining funding came from property taxes. McCall wanted to hike the state's portion of school support to ninety percent—the highest level of such support in the nation. In turn, the state would then freeze property taxes, making permanent the property tax relief delivered through state funding of schools.

The switch would come with a severe price, however. To pay for schools, he proposed a steep income tax increase, thirty percent overall, making Oregon's income tax the nation's highest. To protect those less able to pay, for whom a tax increase would be a financial hardship, McCall proposed shifting the income tax burden away from the middle class and onto the rich. In a single stroke, Oregon's tax system would become the most progressive in the nation—truly based on ability to pay, funded most by those who could best afford it.

McCall gave the proposal his name—the McCall Plan—and sent it to the 1973 legislature. The plan was virtually the same as the one he had given lawmakers in 1967. Then, too, he had demanded action, only to see Republicans leave it to rot.

Times had changed. Lawmakers once could ignore Tom McCall. But now he represented a force few wanted to test. No politician in Oregon needed a pollster to point out McCall's soaring popularity. McCall virtually controlled the Oregon press, and, in turn, the imagination of Oregonians.

Taxes, though, proved a much different problem than the ones McCall had solved before. One tax plan after another had died at the polls. Voters had not approved tax reform since they had approved the state income tax in 1930.

Bolstered by his ego, however, McCall believed he alone had the answer to Oregon's tax riddle: Tom McCall. In his mind, his tax plan and all the pride welling within him hardened into a single core. Much of what he had already accomplished as governor also had been called impossible. He would accomplish this task, too. After all, he was Tom McCall. How could he fail?

"Tax reform was the one issue that no one had ever been able to accomplish," recalled Doris Penwell, McCall's assistant. "Tom felt that if anyone could have done it, he ought to be able to do it. He was the most popular governor in decades. And he knew it. He thought if Oregonians loved him, they could trust him as well."

McCall's plan emerged from the legislature, but not without a struggle. Democrats now controlled both chambers, but McCall had never built partisan walls, and the Democrats rewarded him with more loyalty and honor than legislative Republicans ever had. McCall and the Democrats, as one reporter wrote at the time, "get along like two long separated brothers meeting at a family reunion." When the senate's Democratic tax committee chairman held up the bill, Senate President Jason Boe stripped him of his chairmanship and finished the work himself.

Democrats could not deliver all the necessary votes for his plan. McCall ensured them he could deliver the necessary Republican votes, but the senate GOP caucus voted to defeat the plan simply to embarrass McCall. "They screwed Tom," Boe recalled. "They resented his politics and his popularity. The Republicans in the senate were saying, 'Up your ass, governor'." Boe kept the tax bill alive, three Republicans changed sides, and it limped out of the senate by a single vote.

The McCall Plan's narrow escape warned of tougher times. By shifting the burden to the rich, McCall's tax plan promised to provide tax relief for four of every five Oregonians. However, those people destined to pay a greater share often controlled the state's biggest corporations—banks, timber companies, utilities, insurance companies, and so on. Corporate Oregon, already angered at McCall, lashed out at the tax plan with fury. "It gored everybody's ox," McCall said. "It was more personal. That was resented [among business leaders] more than anything else I did."

The corporate opposition saddened McCall, who saw short-term concern over wealthy Oregonians' income tax rates overshadowing protection of the state's school system. Speaking before one business group after another, McCall candidly asked corporate executives for personal sacrifice. Is not a stable school system worth it? he would ask. Most often, he received cold stares in reply, pin-striped arms folded in disgust.

McCall believed that he alone could convince Oregonians to overhaul their tax system. Preparing for a 1 May vote, he started a lonely campaign for his measure. McCall traveled the state, following a schedule as exhausting as a race for the governorship itself. Before civic groups of all sizes, McCall spoke each day until he grew hoarse. The message was essentially the same: fairness. In the Portland suburb of Milwaukie, McCall blasted corporate greed represented in the opponents' campaign.

McCall conducting a band at the kickoff for his tax plan campaign. He linked its success with Oregonians' love for him, and its defeat was crushing. (Gerry Lewin photo)

> Some opponents treat tax reform as if it were like the new educational toy on the market. No matter how you put it together, it's wrong. What they're saying, of course, is that they like things as they are, and well they should. Many big corporations have gotten tax benefits for themselves in the past, and now they're opposing a new system that would benefit the middle-income majority of Oregon.

"The school finance program offered to you will make our corner of the world a better place in which to live," McCall told his audiences, then added dramatically, "and for that I promise you my word."

His plan won support from most of Oregon's Democratic leaders and grass-roots organizations, such as the Oregon Grange, to unions, such as the AFL-CIO. Still, the supporters' organization, Tax Relief Now, could barely keep up with the barrage of paid advertising attacks backed by Republicans and corporations.

McCall took the tax plan campaign directly to the voters, appearing here with Portland mayor—and future Oregon governor—Neil Goldschmidt. (Bruce McCurtain photo, courtesy of the *Oregonian*)

Even so, surveys showed the McCall Plan was running well ahead in the polls, due to McCall's own stature. Experience, though, told him tax measures often started with leads only to fall victim to voter skepticism and fear.

Throughout April he abandoned his other duties to campaign across the state. Wayne Morse, the aging former senator, traveled from his Eugene farm to campaign for the bill. Portland Mayor Neil Goldschmidt worked the city's sidewalks with McCall. For the most part, however, McCall carried this burden alone. Each day he headed off by car for a new round of speeches, or, despite his fear of flying, flew off to distant sites in a small airplane.

The rigors of the campaign pounded away at his aging body, and, as in campaigns past, his patience burned away. One night, while eating in a Eugene restaurant, McCall overheard a man at the next table complaining about the tax plan. The man, a doctor who had just moved from California, complained that McCall's tax plan would cost him an extra

$800 a year in taxes. McCall—guessing the man made more than $60,000 a year—jumped up and towered over his table. "You son of a bitch," McCall roared, "if you don't care any more than that about the schools of Oregon, why don't you go back to California?"

McCall reached election day near exhaustion. Haggard and pale, McCall spirits soared when he thought of his accomplishment. The vote would prove him right after all. He had welded his pride to his tax plan, his reputation to the hopes of victory. After all, he had given Oregonians his soul, McCall thought. How could they give him anything else but victory?

On election night, McCall hosted a party in the governor's house to watch the returns. No other issue or candidate shared the ballot that day.

Last-minute polls showed the vote could go either way, and McCall boldly predicted it would win. The early results showed otherwise, however, running three to two against the plan. As the night wore on, the margin narrowed slightly, then stopped. The governor had had his routine number of martinis during the party. He had several more as the results showed on the television. The guests silently watched McCall approach a breakdown. When it became apparent that the bill had gone down to defeat, McCall gasped, "The people have rejected me."

"He was personally wounded," said Elizabeth Myers, wife of then-Secretary of State Clay Myers, who was there that night. "Everything that he did was personal. In this he was anguished. There was an anger as well as anguish, as well as misery, unlike anyone had ever seen before."

McCall motioned to Ron Schmidt and the two men walked outside into the cool spring night. McCall hurried along Winter Street, the Capitol glowing only a few blocks ahead. Schmidt rushed to keep pace with McCall's long, agitated strides.

"I'm resigning," McCall said suddenly. "I can no longer be governor of this state. The people have told me tonight I am no longer their governor."

Schmidt listened patiently. "Voters only rejected your plan, not you," he said after a moment.

"No," McCall said. "They rejected me. I'm through."

Schmidt did not know if McCall was serious, but he saw how deep the wound went. Forever childlike in his yearning for praise, Tom Mc-

Call had placed all of his pride in this single vote. The results had smashed his giant heart.

Schmidt worried that McCall would abruptly announce his resignation that night. With Clay Myers, Schmidt stayed until nearly dawn, coaxing McCall to think over his decision.

McCall slept only an hour that night. Waking early, his eyes hard and dry from the gin, he reached for his bedside note pad and scribbled his thoughts. "Feeling of hopelessness," he wrote. "Big business has simply bought the election." He walked solemnly to the Capitol.

Schmidt greeted him with word that a press conference had been called for that morning. McCall could announce his resignation at that time. Now sober, McCall balked at his earlier declaration. Soon, the phone started ringing. Calls from McCall's friends poured in. Many calls were spontaneous. Others had been prompted by Schmidt, who had frantically dialed everyone he could think of, often rousing them from sleep, to explain McCall's heartbreak and the desperate need to buck him up. "Once he started getting the calls from people lauding him, no more was said about the resignation," Schmidt recalled.

Later, McCall entered the morning cabinet meeting and collapsed into his chair. No one in the crowded room moved.

McCall spoke slowly, softly, describing the merits of the failed tax plan, as he had hundreds of times before. McCall grumbled that he understood that the complicated plan was a tough sell. Why had so many selfish people stood in its way? His words grew more tortured and strained. Then he stopped speaking. In that flash of silence, McCall rose, wadded up his long fingers and slammed his fist onto the table.

"Goddamn it," he roared, the table still rumbling under his furious hand, "it was for the people!"

McCall dropped back into his chair, his jutting chin falling flat against his chest, and he began to weep. One by one the staff members stood. Uneasy and awkward, a few clapped their hands. Others joined in. Soon, a thundering, solemn ovation filled the room. An aide stood up, took McCall by the arm and led him away. "McCall disappeared," one witness recalled, "as a giant, sobbing, moving without a will."

19

Energy and Power

M CCALL'S SPIRITS SANK after the tax plan's defeat. He refused to separate the loss from his own self-esteem, even though his popularity remained high among Oregonians. "Tom aged visibly that night [of the tax plan election] and a lot of the joy of political combat seemed to leave him for a time," recalled Jason Boe. "There was a profound change in Tom McCall that lasted for a long time."

As always, his feelings emerged more readily when he was drinking. During a wedding reception for a niece, McCall spotted Forest Amsden, a KGW-TV executive who had aired a commentary that had opposed the tax plan. Clearly drunk, McCall swaggered over to Amsden and loomed over him. "You defeated my plan," he boomed. "I'm not going to be governor much longer, but for years to come I'll be a very important person in this state, and I'm going to get you." Amsden stood looking at McCall in disbelief until the governor walked away. Then McCall walked back to repeat the threat. The incident dramatized not only how drinking could change his moods, but the depth of the pain he still felt about the loss.

McCall never shook the bitterness, but he soon found consolation. The nation was starting to take notice of him and his work.

TOM MCCALL STOOD OUT IN AMERICAN POLITICS in 1973 for all the reasons he stood out in Oregon: his refreshing candor that spoke of com-

369

mon sense, not obfuscation. While other politicians excelled at simply identifying problems, McCall had gone a long way toward solving the problems facing Oregon. Through it all, he had delivered a consistent, rational vision for the future of the state. Most of all, McCall showed that government could still work when government elsewhere appeared to crumble. And in 1973 the federal government appeared to be crumbling from the top.

In mid-1973, Richard Nixon's administration was beset by the revelation of campaign espionage, money laundering and obstruction of justice that collectively became known as Watergate. The Nixon White House's illegal operations had been going on for some time, but the public awakening had come on 17 June 1972, when Washington, D.C., police arrested five burglars breaking into the Democratic National Committee headquarters in the Watergate Hotel. Investigations of the break-in quickly tied the burglars to White House officials and employees of Nixon's re-election campaign.

The break-in was only a small part of a money laundering and dirty tricks operation Nixon's campaign had run to discredit opponents. Within a few weeks, the *Washington Post* had linked illegal contributions to Nixon's Committee to Re-Elect the President to a bank account of a Watergate burglar. The congressional General Accouting Office (GAO) disclosed that as much as $350,000 in campaign funds had been transferred illegally, much of it to one of the burglar's bank accounts. In October, the *Post* reported that former Attorney General John Mitchell, who had then been running the re-election campaign, had had control over the secret slush fund.

The White House denied any connection with the break-in, and Nixon, on 7 November 1972, was overwhelmingly re-elected. But over the next six months, the Watergate scandal continued to unravel. In the spring of 1973 a special Senate committee began to investigate.

At that time, most Americans thought it unlikely that the president of the United States had ordered felonious activity or had covered it up later. McCall, however, took a different view. For years, the GOP had made him feel, as McCall put it, "the bastard at a family reunion." So while Republicans nationwide scrambled to protect Nixon from his growing critics, McCall lashed out at the president.

Two days after the tax plan's defeat, McCall left for a nine-day trip to Israel to help celebrate that country's twenty-fifth anniversary. The trip provided McCall with much-needed rest. He traveled throughout the country and in Kafr Kana he dedicated a grove of trees in his name. During his trip, McCall received the attention afforded an international dignitary, for he was the only United States governor attending the Israeli ceremonies.

As usual, reporters sought out McCall. During a 9 May stop in Cana, a reporter asked McCall what he thought about the broadening Watergate scandal and the congressional investigation.

McCall was already looking past the investigations. He privately suspected Nixon had known about the crime or had launched a cover up. So, out of the blue, McCall said he thought Nixon's impeachment might be in order—a step that at the time sounded extreme. Impeachment hearings alone, he said, would "simply clear the air. . . . [I]t might be a healthy thing—a purge for the country."

The comments, coming as they did from a prominent Republican, ricocheted around the world. The next day, while in Tel Aviv, McCall learned his words had been carried on the international news wires. Reporters mobbed him seeking more quotes on Watergate. McCall happily obliged. When asked if he thought that Nixon knew about the Watergate crimes beforehand, McCall said, "He would be a sloppy president not to have known . . . but that's a lot better than having been one of the crooks. One is misfeasance and one is malfeasance. You teeter between sympathy and revulsion for [Nixon]."

In Oregon, McCall's comments had created a furor. He came home to overtures from Democrats who saw great popular appeal in McCall. His old foe, Congresswoman Edith Green, and Texas senator Lloyd Bentsen, the Democrats' National Senate Campaign chairman, begged him to switch parties.

Did he dislike his party so much that he would abandon it? He felt the same way he had ten years earlier when, in 1963, Edith Green had asked him to become a Democrat before running for governor. "As far as changing parties is concerned," he had told her, "your party has no more heroes and just as many whores and cheaters as ours."

McCall had become a Republican as a result of the tradition established by his grandfather, Samuel Walker McCall, who once also had been besieged by GOP extremists. Samuel McCall, however, had stayed within the party and fought for its principles rather than quit out of convenience.

Tom McCall's independence, too, rose above the labels and the baggage that came with party membership. "As a maverick soul, tuned only to the public need and enhancing Oregon's natural loveliness, it makes no practical difference which party I claim as my own," McCall told reporters on 13 June. "The McCalls have been in the Republican party for generations, and it has worked out fairly well; so I think I'll just stay put."

ALONG WITH THE INSTITUTION OF THE PRESIDENCY, the American way of life also appeared to be crumbling due to the short-sighted consumption about which McCall and other conservationists had long warned. In 1973, the United States was faced with an oil crisis.

Since the end of World War II, Americans had had access to cheap, plentiful oil with which to run their cars, trucks and trains, and with which to heat homes, schools and businesses. This energy dependence left the nation's oil companies in a unique position of power. The companies soon sought to find out just what kind of price America would pay to keep itself running.

In 1960, the United States imported only ten percent of its oil. By 1973, thirty-six percent came from foreign sources, primarily in the Middle East. These mostly Arab countries supplied more than sixteen million barrels of oil daily to the United States. The profits for the Arab states and the oil companies came through the sheer volume of oil sold, allowing the countries to make fortunes with only a small mark-up on their crude.

A dramatic change occurred in 1971, however, when a Libyan army colonel, Mohmar Quadaffi, led a successful coup and nationalized the oil companies' operations in his country. The companies continued doing business with Quadaffi, who insisted on tightening controls over the flow of oil.

The portent of national oil shortages in America had already been foreshadowed by shortages that many people thought were planned by the companies themselves. The shortages began in the winter of 1972-1973, when supplies of heating oil appeared to run low. Factories, businesses and schools across the Midwest closed, unable to keep their buildings warm. Grain shipments sat rotting without the fuel-generated heaters to dry them. As demand soared, Nixon eagerly agreed to oil companies' demands that he lift federal price controls on oil. The Nixon order, on 11 January 1973, sent prices immediately upward.

A quick victim of the rapidly increasing prices was the independent filling station. The major oil companies, hoping to shut down all but the stations they controlled, squeezed out the independents with the higher prices and low supply.

The international dynamics of big oil and the lack of an emerging energy policy had sharp ripple effects in Oregon because the state had a larger than average share of independent gas dealers. When their gasoline supplies dried up, the shortages in Oregon became far more acute than in other parts of the country. Months before the nation felt the oil shock in 1973, gas stations in Oregon were struggling to keep up with demand. The state's distance from shipment sites and its large proportion of independent stations meant that by the fall of 1973, gas stations across Oregon had begun closing on weekends.

Oregon had other energy problems, too. The Pacific Northwest depended almost entirely for its electricity on the hydroelectric dam system along the Columbia River basin. Rain and snow melt from Montana, Idaho, Washington, British Columbia and Oregon ran into the Columbia through tributaries, and washed through the great dams from Grand Coulee to Bonneville producing power. Since the dams had gone up, the winters had always provided ample water to power the generators.

However, in 1973, a dry winter left reservoir levels precariously low. At Grand Coulee Dam in Washington, reservoir levels reached their lowest point in thirty years; in other reservoirs, water levels fell below records set a century earlier. The low levels meant the region could quickly run out of its major power source. "It's like losing the entire generation of a Bonneville Dam," said one federal energy spokesman. The Bonneville Power Administration (BPA)—the federal broker of the region's electricity—warned of spring brownouts and summer blackouts.

McCall works by lantern light. He staged this photograph in his private study in the Capitol to help dramatize Oregon's efforts to save energy. (David Falconer *Oregonian* photo; OrHi 90701)

So in May 1973 McCall faced a double energy crisis in Oregon, one of oil and one of electricity. But he was far better equipped to understand it than most of his fellow governors. Earlier that year, McCall had allowed his staff to use part of the office budget to start an energy study group. Operating from the Capitol basement, the small energy staff had analyzed how Oregon's growth could deplete its energy resources, and had proposed a range of energy conservation steps to soften the effect of growth on those resources.

When the energy office opened, no one had talked about energy supply as a problem. The dams always lit the region, and gasoline was still cheap and available. Many people dismissed the governor's energy office as another McCall eccentricity.

That changed, though, when the BPA warned of the impending energy shortages. Relying on his energy office's research, McCall, on 31 May, put the state on an "energy alert." Echoing the BPA's warning about potential blackouts, McCall issued a statement that had a familiar ring: "The fact remains that we face a blatant mismatch between usable energy supplies and expected demands."

McCall's warning was essentially the same one he had been issuing for years about America's over-consumptive habits, but his statement was in a stark contrast to the attitudes of other national leaders. All over the country, politicians were demanding the nation seek more oil and other energy sources, yet here was Tom McCall saying the nation actually needed less energy. In Oregon, even the state's press was unusually skeptical. The *Oregonian* dismissed McCall's warnings as hyperbole: "[McCall] overstated his case and perhaps generated unnecessary apprehension among Oregon residents."

McCall reacted to this criticism by asking Oregonians to take voluntary energy-saving steps—dropping their highway speed to fifty-five miles per hour, reducing home thermostat settings, and staggering working schedules. McCall considered the ideas modest, yet he understood they were certain to "raise the hackles of nearly everyone in the state."

McCall's attitude toward conservation was particularly notable in the stance he took toward building new dams. In 1954, McCall had entered politics backing construction of the private Hells Canyon Dam on the Snake River. That debate was over who was to own the dam, but McCall and the rest of the Pacific Northwest's political establishment had never doubted that the dam should be built. Now, McCall openly opposed a new dam on the Snake River, which was still tied up in legal battles. "I think we can look first to less environmentally devastating ideas. . . ." McCall said pointedly. "Do we have to build [the dam] to air-condition office buildings?"

McCall's was also one of the voices asking why the federal government did not act to cut energy use. President Nixon, clearly distracted by the unraveling Watergate scandals, had issued an inadequate energy message in April 1973. Instead of calling for conservation steps, Nixon wanted rollbacks of the nation's new Clean Air Act and approval of the Alaskan oil pipeline.

In light of Nixon's lack of leadership on the issue, McCall on 3 June took his pleas for energy conservation to the national governors' conference at Lake Tahoe. A few Democratic governors took to his ideas. Most, however, listened politely and declined to act.

Throughout the rest of June and early July, McCall fretted about the state's energy problems. He wanted to take bold action, as he had done repeatedly on environmental issues, to drive home his concerns about conservation. However, McCall was soon distracted by his troubled health.

A MONTH AFTER HE RETURNED from Lake Tahoe, McCall one day doubled over in pain. The ache in his groin that he had suffered nine months earlier had returned. He remembered his doctor's requests to return for regular check-ups. He had not done so, consumed as he had been with the fight for his tax plan. McCall sheepishly returned to his doctor, Ralph Purvine, on 14 July. Four days later Purvine diagnosed a swollen prostate gland. The diagnosis was unmistakable: cancer. Three days later McCall checked into the University of Oregon Medical School in Portland for a check-up. Thirty-six hours later, a biopsy fulfilled McCall's worst fears. The cancer was malignant.

McCall immediately underwent surgery to have the prostate removed. He remained in intensive care briefly after the successful surgery and then rested for four days in discomfort. McCall's height meant he hung off both ends of the hospital bed. An *Oregonian* reporter heard his first public comments about the operation. "I've been in the rumpus room," he said, "and my rumpus is sore."

Later that week, on 6 August, McCall left the hospital for a month of recuperation at his beach cabin near Lincoln City. Walking pained him, so he sat by the cabin's window and watched the ocean lap the shore. Five nights later, a raging fever swept through him. The state police rushed him to the hospital in Portland, where doctors diagnosed an infection of McCall's urinary tract.

Four days later, a nurse discovered a nitroglycerin bomb hidden in a restroom one floor below McCall's room. Police rushed McCall out of the hospital and into hiding at Salem Memorial Hospital. (Police never determined whether McCall was the target of the bomb.) McCall's fever quickly receded and his urinary tract infection cleared, but doctors worried about a recurrence of the cancer. The day before his scheduled release, 20 August, McCall underwent surgery again. This time surgeons removed his right testicle, believing a drop in the level of hormones produced by the testicle would aid McCall's healing. A gaunt, shaky McCall received his final hospital release on 29 August with strict instructions to rest and limit himself to one martini a day.

As with all else in his career, McCall chose to be candid and open about his bout with cancer. Rather than hold back the delicate details of his operations, McCall authorized Schmidt to tell the press all about his surgeries. The resulting candor in the newspapers left McCall himself a little embarrassed. "The prostate," he said later, "is hardly a subject for chitchat over teacups." The *Oregonian* provided the most detailed coverage, prompting one disgusted reader to complain that he found it "distasteful to have the Governor's glands for breakfast in a family newspaper."

As time passed, McCall found the whole subject ripe for humor. He started calling himself "One Ball" McCall and worked more tasteful quips into speeches. When a broadcasters' association gave him an award, McCall told the group dryly, "I just want you to remember you are holding up as a model an imperfect person. And after my last two operations, I'm also incomplete."

Although McCall joked, the cancer had been an inescapable warning. Tom McCall was sixty years old. He had ignored doctor's warnings and a malignant cancer had spread inside of him. He had always been a man charging at life, but now he was uncertain how much life he had left before him. He had so much left to do, and he could not begin to charge again soon enough, nor fast enough.

AS HE RECOVERED from the cancer surgery, McCall turned his attention to the state's energy dilemma once again. Already in Oregon an estimated 3,000 fuel industry employees had lost their jobs. Another 1,500 workers in the aluminum manufacturing industry, which was heavily reliant on electricity, also faced layoffs. Even before he was fully recovered, he insisted on pressing forward with new conservation measures. From his hospital bed, McCall on 22 August fired off another energy warning.

Jobs are at stake and it could be yours, or your neighbors'. . . .
We've gotten the idea that energy in abundance would forever be at our fingertips. We've gotten careless. We've
installed all the modern conveniences, used them without regard to energy supply, and now the piper must be paid.

He followed the warning with an executive order declaring an energy emergency in Oregon. McCall wanted a ten-percent cut in energy
use statewide and decided to use his own administration as a model. He
imposed sixteen conservation measures on state government. He banned
the use of air conditioners and exterior lighting on state-owned buildings. All water heaters in state buildings were turned off. (The "hot"
knobs were actually removed from many washroom sinks.) McCall directed that all state buildings close by 6 P.M., and that no state car be driven over fifty-five miles per hour or with fewer than two people riding
inside.

Most ideas were simple, some ingenious. All were a bold departure
from the action taken by other governors and the Nixon administration.
Yet when McCall returned to his office on 4 September, his staff reports said the state had managed only a two-percent drop in energy use.
Amid the get-well cards, McCall found letter after letter from citizens
doubting an energy crisis really existed.

Many people pointed to the commercial display lighting of motels,
restaurants, used car lots, and billboards that burned through the night.
"People wouldn't believe there was a crisis with the Golden Arches
blazing away," McCall later said. "Underlying the comments, though,
was the feeling that the people are fed up with garishness. They feel assaulted by blinking, flashing, rotating, ostentatious waste."

McCall took the complaints to a staff meeting where someone suggested he order businesses to turn off their lights. McCall blinked, and
then smiled. He waited until the following week, when he expected
eleven other western governors to arrive in Oregon for their annual conference on 23 September. McCall welcomed the governors to the Salis-
han resort at Gleneden Beach, then gathered up the national press corps
for a surprise press conference.

Describing the Pacific Northwest's potential power shortages with dire phrases such as "risk of catastrophe . . . the making of a calamity," McCall brandished a new executive order that shut off the lights. Specifically, McCall's order banned what it called the "wasteful practices" of illuminated display advertising, and building and landscape lighting. McCall acknowledged that many businesses might be hurt by the ban. "But as a hard fact of life" he said, "we will simply have to look more carefully at what is open, and what is not."

Did he have the power to order businesses to turn off their display lighting? McCall assured reporters that he did and, with characteristic gusto and hyperbole, said he would have issued the order even if he did not. "That danger to a governor is far less grave than would be a vacuum of leadership," he said of a potential legal challenge to his order. "Political leaders cannot lie fallow when the economic and social harvest of the citizens is itself in peril."

His statement artfully ducked the question, but McCall knew the real answer. He did not have the legal authority to order the lights out. But he also knew that, for businesses reluctant to comply, defying Tom McCall would be difficult.

The Oregon press helped by applying pressure. In Salem, the *Oregon Statesman* listed on its front page businesses that had violated the lighting ban. Meanwhile, McCall anxiously sought a business to take to court to test his authority, but every violator he challenged backed down. In Eugene, state police served a surplus store with a summons for failing to respond to the governor's order. The store turned its lights off twenty minutes later. When businesses complained, Robert Davis, McCall's chief of staff since Ed Westerdahl had resigned, begged them to sue McCall, hoping to force a test case into court. Fearing the negative publicity such a case could bring a business, no one sued.

However, one large Salem motel appeared ready to test McCall's ban. McCall himself told the story, perhaps apocryphal, of why the owner backed down. As McCall told it, "[W]hen the motel owner went to the hospital to see his mother who was dying of cancer, she said: 'I've been reading the paper, son. You obey the governor'."

As the ban took hold, the state's biggest cities—Portland, Eugene and Salem—went dark at night. The office towers of Portland, as *Time* magazine described it, "loom like abandoned hulks, their silhouettes illuminated only by a handful of office lights and the winking red beacons that warn aircraft the buildings still stand."

Enthusiastic about his success, McCall went one step too far. He suggested in October that Oregon's 1,300 public schools close for four weeks during the winter to save energy. Parents across the state protested and, two weeks later, McCall admitted he had made a mistake.

In early December, McCall lifted the business lighting ban, but noted that concern about conservation had led to the cancellation of Christmas lighting contests all over the state. "Somebody claimed the order was issued," he said,"because I didn't even want Santa Claus to visit, much less stay."

McCall's energy concerns were consistent with his concept of the wise use of resources. But the energy crisis added a new dimension to his doctrine of livability. McCall had once said he would slam the doors of Oregon against any business that did not meet the state's standards for preserving environmental quality. At the time that meant business must be non-polluting. Now it meant the business must be energy efficient as well.

In 1973, the region's aluminum companies consumed eight percent of the region's power. McCall could do nothing about energy consumption of the existing plants. Most aluminum companies had special electricity contracts with the BPA, which was out of McCall's jurisdiction. He could, however, discourage more plants from coming into Oregon. In 1972, the Department of Environmental Quality had given approval to the AMAX Aluminum Co. to build a new plant at Warrenton, at the Columbia River's mouth. The plant would employ eight hundred people—a number equal to half the population of Warrenton itself.

McCall's energy office counted up the jobs promised by AMAX on one ledger and then looked at the resulting energy cost. By its estimates, the office guessed the energy burned by the proposed AMAX plant would light and heat ten thousand homes for a year. Moreover, the office estimated that the 240,000 kilowatts required for the plant could potentially cost other industries 1,500 jobs, or twice AMAX's economic benefit to the state.

One year earlier McCall had backed the plant's construction. In 1973, however, he changed his mind and declared his opposition to AMAX.

"We cannot invite industry that consumes electricity far in excess of those with greater job-producing potential," McCall said of his decision. "It is wrong from that standpoint, and it is wrong psychologically. . . . A governor had only one way to go on this one, unless, of course, he decided to be reckless to the point of disaster."

His change of direction jarred AMAX and officials in coastal Clatsop County, where the plant would have been located. In the end, beset by other potential environmental problems, AMAX cancelled its plans to build its Oregon plant.

McCall never regretted his decision, or the negative message it sent to business. Once again he had shown he was committed to the right kind of growth—clean growth, and, now, energy-efficient growth.

OREGON'S CONSERVATION EFFORTS remained largely ignored until October 1973, when world events again scrambled American energy concerns. On Yom Kippur, the Jewish holiday of atonement, Arab countries launched an invasion of Israel. The United States sided with Israel, which finally pushed back the invading countries. Angered by American military support for Israel, the Organization of Petroleum Exporting Countries (OPEC) placed an embargo on oil going to the United States.

The oil embargo lasted from October 1973 to March 1974. Gas shortages appeared imminent as oil companies hoarded their stocks and waited for the inevitable price increases.

Hoping to avert public panic, President Nixon emerged from his Watergate haze to issue another energy message. Unlike his earlier calls for more energy development, Nixon, for the first time, asked the public to take conservation steps and proposed many of the ideas already at work in Oregon. As specific energy savings actions, Nixon extended daylight savings time and lowered the speed limit to fifty-five miles per hour.

As the result of Nixon's prompting, within days, governors across America who, five months earlier, had ignored McCall's conservation pleas at the Lake Tahoe conference, started following his example by banning outdoor display lights, ordering thermostats turned down, and staggering working hours. Overnight, McCall found himself and his conservation policies at the center of national attention. Once again, the national press descended on Oregon to see how McCall had solved problems other states could not. McCall cheerfully told the New York *Times* he was paying a personal price for energy conservation. The *Times* headline read: "The Governor Has a Cold, or How Energy Savings Goes in Oregon." McCall also reported that because he kept the thermostat low at home, even his dog had the sniffles.

In November, McCall's prophetic energy leadership made him the star attraction at the Republican governors' conference in Memphis, Tennessee. Happy to again be the center of attention, McCall lashed out at the president and his energy plan. Buried within the president's proposals, Nixon had again insisted that new anti-pollution laws be curtailed in the name of energy conservation. McCall saw this as a ploy to help industry shirk their environmental responsibility in the pursuit of more oil and coal.

McCall warned his fellow governors not to mix the urgent calls for energy savings with excuses to undo their small environmental gains.

> The public is—or can be—convinced of the need for a heroic effort. People all over this country are up in arms over the suggestion that environmental standards be relaxed in the name of an energy crisis. . . . The growth addicts ought to stop blaming everything on the environmentalists.

The pulse of McCall's warnings pounded louder than ever before, if only because the man McCall targeted with his comments—Richard Nixon—was on hand at the Memphis conference.

The president was there to get the support of the Republican governors, as he had lost the public's confidence. That month polls had shown that the number of Americans disapproving of Nixon's conduct as president outweighed those who favored it, the first time during his presidency that had happened.

The televised Senate hearings into the Watergate scandal and the revelations they had produced had eroded Americans' faith in Nixon's veracity and credibility. Former White House Counsel John Dean had implicated Nixon in the cover-up. The president's "enemies list" had been made public. And the country had discovered that Nixon routinely recorded Oval Office conversations and telephone calls. The prospect that the full extent of Nixon's involvement in Watergate might be revealed in the tapes changed the investigations. Despite a Senate subpoena, Nixon refused to release the tapes. His actions only fueled speculation that he was covering up illegal White House activities. By the time Nixon attended the governors' conference, the United States House of Representatives had introduced bills to initiate impeachment proceedings against the president.

To counteract the revelations, Nixon had initiated a public relations blitz, called "Operation Candor," designed to show he played no part in the cover-up. It was during this effort that Nixon told reporters in Orlando, Florida, "People have the right to know whether or not their president is a crook. Well, I am not a crook."

The GOP governors at the Memphis conference went along with Nixon's strategy to improve his credibility. They proposed a resolution supporting Nixon and applauding the president's handling of Watergate. McCall refused to go along. "I won't be a party to a knee-jerk exercise in adulation," McCall sneered when reporters in Memphis asked him about the resolution. "We just don't buy the fact [Nixon] has come all the way back. We will not be housemen for the White House, and we are not going to whitewash one of the saddest episodes in American history. He has to earn his way back from this morass of misery in which he finds himself." When asked what the governors should do instead of pass the resolution, McCall suggested that they tell Nixon he had to be "more credible, more human."

Once again, McCall was virtually alone among his GOP brethren. The governors passed the resolution over McCall's objections.

The next day, 20 November, Nixon arrived in Memphis. During his hour-long meeting with the governors, Nixon was very persuasive, apologizing for the trouble and embarrassment the Watergate scandal had caused other Republicans. "If I have added to your burden," Nixon said, "I am sorry for it."

While other governors softened at this remark, McCall opened up with a barrage of questions, as if he were again a working reporter.

"Are we going to be blindsided by any more bombshells?" McCall asked.

"If there are any more bombs, I'm not aware of them," Nixon responded.

Nixon's answer calmed McCall and the other governors as well. "All of us are going home feeling better," California governor Ronald Reagan said at the convention's close.

The calm lasted only for twenty-four hours. The next day, on 21 November, United States District Court Judge John Sirica, overseeing Watergate prosecutions, disclosed that a critical White House tape—one that included Nixon's discussion of the Watergate break-in three days after it occurred—contained an unexplained eighteen-and-a-half-minute gap. History has shown that Nixon had known about the gap when he had assured McCall that no more bombshells existed.

McCall raged at the news. He had been lied to as the nation had been lied to. When the press called, McCall spoke of the betrayal. He predicted—nine months before Nixon's eventual resignation—that the president was through. "[Nixon's] insensitivity to what a bombshell is saws at his credibility," McCall told the New York *Times*. "You're already in a morass of problems, and here disaster stares you in the face in the form of this tape, and you don't even recognize it. I just don't see how they're ever going to crawl out."

HIS HANDLING OF OREGON'S POTENTIAL ENERGY SHORTAGES drew more press attention to McCall as 1973 ended. He had one more year in office, and he wanted to make sure the attention continued. Shortly before Thanksgiving 1973, McCall told a *Newsweek* reporter that he wanted to run for president of the United States—not as a Republican, nor as a Democrat, but as leader of an independent political movement he named the "third force."

McCall's surprise announcement, which *Newsweek* carried in December, echoed across an American political wasteland left by Watergate. He knew—quite correctly—that his remarks would invite a renewed flood of media attention to himself and Oregon.

He wanted to tell the Oregon Story and had only one year to do so. And this time, he was certain, America was watching.

20

The Oregon Story

A FTER SEVEN YEARS, Oregonians understood well how Tom Mc-Call worked. Now, the nation was learning. As 1974 opened *Newsweek* declared, "Energy crisis, drugs, pollution, population growth, the lack of candor in government—a fairly inclusive list of what most Americans would regard as major problems to be handled as someone thinks of a solution. But in Oregon, a clear sense of satisfaction hangs in the air along with the perpetual damp. The state . . . has simply been tackling each problem as it arises, with an apparent minimum of special pleading and a maximum sense of the general good. And so far, anyway, the Oregonians don't seem to have come across anything they can't handle." Above this enthusiastic review of Oregon's Tom McCall years, the magazine placed this headline: "Where the Future Works."

The *Newsweek* story initiated a pilgrimage of reporters from the national media into Oregon. In one of nearly forty national newspaper and magazine stories appearing about McCall in 1974, *Newsday* of Long Island, New York, described the phenomenon simply: "All of [his work] finally reached the attention of the national media. The result: Tom McCall at what normally would be considered the tag end of a political career is suddenly a hot item."

The year that followed brought McCall more fame than he would ever see again in his life. He seized the chance to publicize what Oregon had accomplished during his administration, as well as to delight in the blinding spotlight. He called his tale the Oregon Story.

"People are yearning to hear some success stories out of government," McCall told reporters. "The Oregon story could be a catalyst for a third force capable of attracting 50 million independents and disgruntled Republicans and Democrats who are looking for the positive and hopeful in a country that deserves spirited leadership."

In 1974, the United States had anything but spirited leadership. The Watergate scandal dragged on toward resolution with McCall calling for Nixon's resignation. Vice President Spiro Agnew had resigned in the face of a criminal investigation into allegations that he had accepted $30,000 in a contract kickback scheme while he was governor of Maryland.

What troubled McCall was the way in which both political parties reacted to Watergate and Agnew's resignation. Republicans deluded themselves over Nixon's fate while Democrats recklessly cheered on the collapse of the presidency. McCall watched with disgust the damage inflicted by both sides. He told the reporters making their way into Oregon, "There has got to be a better way than this two-party system which is not getting to anything. You've got to have a spirit that doesn't worry about politics to lead America."

A government without politics. That was McCall's ideal. Public service should be the noble pursuit his grandfather Sam McCall had championed. McCall was trying to say what he thought he heard Americans saying: Why can our leaders not simply do what is important and what is right?

It sounded naive—but coming from McCall, it sounded hopeful as well. He knew he represented in Oregon a leadership that transcended politics. The national press agreed.

McCall began to flesh out his ideas into what he called a "third force," a movement beyond party label. McCall soon found himself on a crusade for a new way of political thinking and action. "I'm mapping out the creation of a third force which makes a striking power," McCall said at one point, "a power which would insist on standards to clean up politics as it is now and set guidelines for a new kind of politics in this country. . . . No more $150-million dollar campaign kitties. We need an open government, a free press, and we need to get rid of the windbags and find the right people for office who care about the country—who will be stewards of the land."

When he took a short vacation on Maui in early December, the press followed him everywhere. Clare Booth Luce, widow of *Time* founder Henry Luce, invited McCall for dinner during his trip. In awe of such a legendary woman, McCall gushed with joy as Luce (as McCall told the story) urged on his third force idea. "Governor," she told him, "go back to the mainland and announce you're starting a new party."

While often repeating the story, McCall carefully explained he was not starting a new political party. "It's no political bandwagon I'm building," McCall said. "It's a lot more like a pink cloud."

McCall's third force idea raised his profile even higher in the national media. Soon after the Hawaii trip, McCall flew to New York for an appearance on NBC's "Today Show." To interviewer Bill Monroe, McCall described the "great disillusionment" in America and added: "The Oregon story is a hopeful force. I think it shows that the system can work and that people respond if there is leadership with imagination and guts."

Upon his return McCall found his desk covered with hundreds of letters from all over the country that urged him on. "I was amazed," he said after reviewing the mail. "I thought everybody would laugh me into the Pacific Ocean."

More stories followed, including glowing profiles in the New York *Times*, the Boston *Globe*, the Philadelphia *Inquirer*, the Washington *Star*, and the Los Angeles *Times*. Bill Moyers of PBS devoted an entire show to McCall. Two more stories were done at NBC—a lengthy piece by David Brinkley, and a second appearance on "Today," for which the camera crew strapped a wireless microphone on McCall and followed him for several days. McCall, for once, found the microphone too candid. "How d'ya shut this thing off when you go to the john?" he asked the technicians.

Each story was filled with positive accounts of McCall's tenure and style. "Oregon's Gov. Tom McCall is a throwback to the era when governors were the most exciting characters in American politics," the Philadelphia *Inquirer* declared. Added the Boston *Globe*, "McCall can hardly be described as a fresh young voice on the national stage. But his is indeed the voice, Boston-flavored and described as Ivy-League barn-yard, which minces no words. The candor for which he is famous does not necessarily qualify him or anyone else as president of the United States. But it certainly makes him an attractive candidate in a field where ambiguity is one of the staples."

McCall knew he had no serious plans to run for president. "There's no point in being coy about it," he said when asked in early 1974. "Yes, I'd like to be president. Hell, yes." But he never did more than talk about the possibility. Instead he would add, referring to his cancer operation, "It may be that I'm running for the mortuary."

McCall had started talking about running for president only as a way to draw more attention to himself and to Oregon—it was what reporters call a "hook." As more national press representatives came to Oregon, McCall directed their attention to the litany of Oregon's achievements: the Willamette clean-up, protection of the entire Oregon coast, energy conservation, land-use planning, the nerve gas blockade.

Of all the innovations, the Bottle Bill won special attention. The idea was an infectious one. Thirty-five other states were busy trying to pass their own bottle bills using the Oregon model. "It has challenged the people," McCall said of the bottle bill during his Hawaii visit. "[Litter] just violates [Oregonians'] consciences, and as a result we have 2.2 million citizens all deputized in their own hearts against litter. It has produced a new esprit de corps while at the same time provided a good mechanical device for keeping our streets clean."

As if the journalists needed more fodder, McCall gave the nation yet another answer to the growing energy crisis.

The Arab embargo of oil to the United States, followed by the oil companies' desire to hold back reserves, had worsened the gas shortage. The federal government had begun overseeing shipment quotas to the states to ensure even distribution of gas supplies. But Oregon's gasoline and oil quotas seemed unreasonably low. McCall at one point called out the National Guard to deliver heating oil to one central Oregon town. By Christmas 1973, Oregon had come to a virtual standstill. Nine out of every ten gas stations in the state had shut down. In the 110-mile stretch of Interstate 5 between Eugene and Portland, only a half dozen stations offered fuel. Those stations that remained open had instituted some form of rationing, either by limiting purchases or selling only to regular customers. Some stations in Portland sold gas only by appointment. Even these stations ran out of gas within a couple of hours. The shortages caused panic buying, which only made the lines and shortages worse.

Why had Oregon come up short of gasoline? "Was it true, as many Oregonians claimed," author Robert Sherrill later wrote, "that the oil companies were making an example out of Oregon because it had some of the nation's toughest environmental laws?" McCall privately suspected retribution from the federal government. However, Oregon's large percentage of independent stations, which had all but been cut off by the major companies, was perhaps the leading reason for the state's shortages.

While the federal government mulled over a rationing plan to ease the shortages, McCall instituted one of his own. One January evening, Don Jarvi, the chief of McCall's energy information office, was driving to Portland for more meetings on the gas shortages. He wondered how the state could avoid waves of panic buying and the erratic shortages that panic buying caused. As he drove, Jarvi kept his eyes focused on the license plate of the car ahead of him—and he got an idea.

Back in Salem, Jarvi laid out his idea to McCall's staff. The governor would declare that people be allowed to buy gasoline only on certain days, and the last number on their license plate would determine the days. McCall loved it. The next morning, 3 January 1974, McCall announced what became the "odd-even" rationing plan. Cars with odd-numbered plates would get gas on odd-numbered days, even-numbered plates would get gas on even-numbered days. Stations would also fly flags—red, yellow and green—to signal fuel availability. The plan was magical in its simplicity—voluntary gas rationing, without coupons, bureaucracy or black market sales. The state's gas dealers at first complained, and then gave in to McCall's persuasion. That evening, Jarvi watched his idea broadcast on the national network news. "I sat there watching it, this idea that I'd had only a few hours earlier being announced on TV, feeling amazed at how fast McCall could make things happen," Jarvi recalled.

McCall threatened mandatory rationing if the plan did not work. But it did work. Within a week, gas station lines all but vanished as the panic buying eased. Within days, other states followed with similar rationing plans.

The odd-even plan brought another rush of news stories about Oregon. Of all of them, none was more illuminating and thorough than E.J. Kahn's "Letter from Oregon" published in *The New Yorker* magazine on 25 February. Kahn had arrived in the governor's office in Salem and found McCall bundled up in a cardigan. The room temperature was set at an energy-saving sixty-three degrees, five degrees below the maximum allowed.

Kahn's profile was one of the best pieces written about the McCall years, for it captured the spirit that McCall had infused in the state: "That the state of Oregon, with two million people, or roughly one percent of the national population, should have got the jump on most of the rest of the country in perceiving an energy crisis does not especially surprise Oregonians. In the last seven years, they have become accustomed to all sorts of innovative and bizarre goings on."

ALL THE FAME brought McCall much joy, but it also inspired the old Lawson melancholy. Barred by law from seeking a third consecutive term, McCall knew his ride would end within a few months. He was not ready to retire. What he wanted was another platform, a position of power, to continue his crusade. The incumbent in Oregon's First Congressional District, Republican Wendell Wyatt, planned to step down after 1974. Wyatt urged McCall to take his place. With his popularity, McCall would swamp any opposition and surely win the congressional seat. However, McCall saw the House of Representatives as a step backward. He wanted something bigger. He wanted the Senate. However, McCall faced three acute obstacles in accomplishing what his grandfather had never been able to achieve.

One problem was his health. His doctors had not yet pronounced him cured of cancer. The second was the incumbent senator, Republican Bob Packwood, who had defeated Wayne Morse six years earlier. Morse had been a vicious campaigner, but Packwood had been far more ruthless. While McCall had animosity for Hatfield, he liked Packwood personally, although he did not respect him. Packwood was the kind of politician McCall was denouncing—self-centered and self-serving, an opportunist who shifted with the political winds. Packwood's strong campaigning skills were another reason McCall shied away from considering a challenge to the freshman senator.

McCall's third problem was that he had given Packwood his word in mid-1973 that he would not run against him. Now, however, McCall found himself averting his eyes from the brightness of his own ambition, lit by the flash of media attention. Despite his pledge to Packwood, McCall drew near a decision to run. His aides witnessed McCall's common sense battle his pride. He would start by belittling Packwood in a rousing self-inspired pep talk. "Can you believe he's a United States senator?" McCall would say "I can beat him. I could, couldn't I? Yeah, I know I can. Can't I? I think I can." One aide, Ken Johnson, recalled a golf game with McCall during this time. After the game McCall headed straight for the clubhouse lounge and polled the golfers there. "All of them thought he should run against Packwood and could beat him," Johnson said. "He liked that. He liked that a lot." During the car ride home, McCall grinned from the praise, only to turn somber quite suddenly. "You know," he said, "just because you can beat somebody doesn't mean you ought to run."

So it went, up and down for weeks. In early March, not long before the filing deadline, two things happened to sway McCall's decision. Two polls provided by private sources—one of which was probably Glenn Jackson—showed McCall had a substantial lead over Packwood. The lead far surpassed any margin of error, convincing McCall his prophecy that he could defeat Packwood was true. Then, on 5 March, his doctor delivered thrilling news. The cancer, as far as tests showed, was gone.

The day he received the medical news, McCall flew with Audrey and Ron Schmidt to Washington, D.C., where he was scheduled to attend a governors' conference. While there, he planned to press federal energy administrator William Simon for larger gas quotas. By the time he had landed in Washington, McCall had decided to run for the Senate. He told no one—not even Audrey or Schmidt. Once in Washington, McCall learned that Packwood had invited him to his home for dinner. Believing McCall posed no threat to his re-election, Packwood had actually planned the dinner in McCall's honor, inviting Simon and other VIPs.

As the guests gathered, Packwood was gracious and warm, praising McCall and offering a toast. McCall stewed. He had promised Packwood he would not run against him. Now he had convinced himself to do exactly that, and there he was, attending a dinner held by Packwood in his honor.

Distressed, McCall gulped down several martinis before dinner. "It was a few more martinis than he would normally do," observed Schmidt later. "It was at least one martini more than one should have." When Packwood went into the kitchen to make another batch of drinks, McCall rushed in after him. Sensing something wrong, Schmidt followed.

In the kitchen McCall confronted Packwood. "You should know, Bob," McCall stated flatly, "that I intend to run against you for the Senate."

Packwood froze. Schmidt, who through the years had heard McCall say any number of outrageous things, felt as if he were about to fall to the floor.

"Tom," Packwood said after catching his breath, "do you recall when I came to you prior to my running in 1968 and asked if you wanted to run for this seat?"

"Well, yes," McCall said.

"You said no, that I could run for it," Packwood said. "I wouldn't have gotten into this, I wouldn't have run for this seat, had you not given me your blessing. I certainly intend to stay here now."

"But it's my seat," McCall blurted out.

"What?" Packwood gasped.

McCall's rationale spilled out. He claimed that he had only encouraged Packwood to run because he had never imagined that Packwood would actually beat Wayne Morse. McCall had expected Packwood to lose, leaving him a shot at Morse's seat in 1974. Therefore, as the drunken McCall now explained in Packwood's kitchen, he had always considered the Senate seat as his own.

"Well, Tom," Packwood replied coldly, "if you thought it was your seat, you should have run for it."

"But you weren't supposed to win," McCall said again. "So it's my seat."

Packwood realized he could not argue with McCall's logic. "He had it all figured out in his mind," Packwood recalled. "I simply turned out to be not just an interruption but an absolute roadblock to what he had planned out in his mind."

McCall strode back out to the Packwoods' living room and announced to the guests that he would soon declare his candidacy against Packwood.

"This," McCall noted later, "made a mess of the evening."

Schmidt grabbed their coats and led McCall and Audrey out the door, leaving the stunned dinner party behind. William Simon turned to Packwood in disgust. "I can't believe what I just saw," Simon said. "I'll do whatever you want to help you." A few days later, Simon announced Oregon's gas allocation would increase. He did not credit McCall, who had pressed for months for a higher gas quota. He gave full credit to Packwood, whom McCall doubted had done anything to help.

The snub angered McCall. However, the ambitious angst that the martinis had liberated in Packwood's kitchen soon haunted him. Word of the disastrous dinner party had leaked to the *Oregonian*. The paper quoted a "highly reliable Republican source"—probably Packwood himself—as saying McCall had announced his intentions to run at Packwood's home two days earlier. McCall returned to Oregon on 11 March and dodged the questions of reporters waiting for him at the airport.

Now that he had blurted out his intentions, and the blurtings were all over the Oregon newspapers, McCall wanted a sober assessment of his chances against Packwood. Schmidt delivered a grim picture. McCall had already promised not to run against Packwood. He could break that pledge, but that would threaten his prized credibility. McCall's assurances that he would not run had freed many financial backers to fall in behind Packwood. He could not jump in now without alienating them. And what were the issues? McCall and Packwood agreed on many issues. Timber companies were now angry at Packwood for becoming a zealous advocate of wilderness areas. How could McCall exploit that and carry on as an environmentalist too?

Most of all, Packwood promised an ugly, mean battle, the kind that McCall dreaded. And Packwood made sure McCall knew how nasty he would get. He started by publicly boasting that his style of politics would "make the shootout at the OK Corral look like a duck pond pic-

U.S. Senator Bob Packwood (right) threatened to expose details of McCall's drinking and Sam McCall's drug habit if McCall challenged him in 1974. (David Swann photo the Bend *Bulletin*; OrHi 90694)

nic." Then he began spreading word that he intended to drag details of McCall's private life into public view.

McCall's thin skin had toughened somewhat over the years, but he could not stomach what Packwood threatened. Packwood announced to associates that he intended to make an issue of McCall's drinking habits. But what worried McCall most of all were Packwood's threats to drag McCall's son Sam and the issue of his drug addiction into the race.

Schmidt first heard about Packwood's threats through mutual friends—people Packwood had told probably knowing that they would rush back and tell McCall and Schmidt. At first glance, a threat to bring up Sam's drug addiction seemed prone to backfire against Packwood. After all, the McCalls had been public about Sam's problems. But

Schmidt saw the significance. Packwood, or someone working on Packwood's behalf, was preparing to leak to reporters the stories about McCall's staff's efforts to hush up Sam's crimes. More damaging to McCall, however, would be the story of the governor accepting thousands of dollars raised in 1967 by Glenn Jackson and others to pay Sam's medical bills.

Schmidt heard this threat from a businessman who claimed to have talked to Packwood and, as it turned out, was one of those who had helped pay Sam's medical bills. The donations for the medical bills had remained secret for seven years. Now, the possibility of its exposure could create severe problems for McCall. After all, the money was ultimately to McCall's personal financial benefit. If he were dealing with the Oregon press, Schmidt knew he could control the story, portraying McCall as a compassionate father trying to help his son. Outside of Oregon and in the Watergate era, however, the national press was casting about for any hint of scandal. Schmidt knew that the media's love affair with McCall would sour at the first whiff of fund-raising efforts for Sam. He feared the headlines: "McCall Covers up for Law-Breaking Son," or "McCall Accepts Secret Payments." The press that had made McCall a star might as easily rejoice in tearing him down.

Packwood later denied making plans to smear Sam or Tom, although others have since confirmed Schmidt's account. "Even the suggestion of the smear," Schmidt said later, "had its desired effect on the desired targets: Tom and Audrey. Its release might damage Packwood, but it would in turn obliterate McCall emotionally, wound Audrey and possibly send Sam off the deep end one more time."

Schmidt conferred with McCall about Packwood's threats, but on 12 March, McCall told his family he was running. The next day, he called a hasty press conference to say he was not running. "My electoral successes tempted me to seek election to the Senate, and not many politicians could resist the pull of the Potomac," McCall said. "But I must resist."

Jean McCall Babson, Tom's youngest sister, recalled hearing the news with some shock. "Tom had told me the night before he would run against Packwood," she said. "Later he said that Packwood intended to use the whole matter with Sam, of him accepting money from Glenn Jackson and others. He couldn't bear the pain, and didn't want the scandal. It was the only thing that stopped him."

AFTER MCCALL REJECTED a run for the Senate, his staff saw his mood darken. "It was sort of a pathetic thing," said Robert Oliver, McCall's legal counsel. "He thought his power was slowly slipping away."

McCall found some solace in the continuing demand for his presence from across the country. That year he gave about thirty speeches, to groups ranging from John Deere Co. employees in Moline, Illinois, to the American Institute of Planners Conference in Denver. The awards also rolled in from environmental groups. The National Audubon Society, for one, honored McCall for his environmental work with its highest citation, the Audubon Medal. He flew to Huntington, West Virginia, to accept it, noting his environmental doctrine was really quite simple.

"Nobody is being asked to stop the world—it's only a matter of taking stock and acting to assure that the earth remains a decent place to live." McCall then noted some of the other environmental awards he had received in his career, adding, "There is nothing yet from the strip-mining people, the land speculators and the clearcutters."

His ongoing talk of his third force in politics continued to get attention. McCall, by then, had better defined his talk about an independent movement. He wanted strict controls on campaign fund-raising, national initiative petition and primary systems, and an end to the archaic selection of party nominees. The third force platform put consumer protection second only to an aggressive effort to protect the American environment.

"Regeneration, damn it, that's what it is," McCall said in describing his ideas. "Candidates are only as important as their sensitivity in recognizing what the issues are and in finding alternatives."

The deeper Nixon's troubles became, the more attention McCall and his reform ideas received from the national media. Of all the admirers, *Washington Post* columnist Nicholas Von Hoffman gave McCall's ideas the strongest endorsement. Von Hoffman, a doctrinaire liberal, saw McCall's candor as balm for the oozing wound of Watergate.

As governor, he's done what we say we want our politicians to do, although when they do it we usually don't vote for them [Von Hoffman wrote]. He's been unmistakenly forthright about every public issue. . . . That President McCall would spin us around and send us off in marvelously new directions is more than history teaches we should expect. But what we would get from him is the example of modesty, simplicity and openness we are so desperate for.

Von Hoffman was realistic about McCall's slim chances at the presidency.

But then in 1936, when McCall graduated last in his college class of 600, his chances of becoming governor weren't much brighter. . . . McCall does have the gift of hope and the virtue of persistence. . . . His simple emergence as a national political figure should remind us of the difference between a big man and a big shot.

Understanding the media's power, McCall knew that the flood of newspaper and network news stories boosted his image, but did little to fully establish his third force ideas. He thought he had finally stumbled upon the breakthrough, however, when "60 Minutes," the popular CBS-TV news magazine, planned to devote a long segment to McCall and his ideas for a new political movement. A camera crew followed McCall for a week. One of the show's correspondents, Mike Wallace, flew to Oregon to interview Tom and Dorothy Lawson McCall. The segment was set to air in July 1974, only to be inexplicably delayed and re-scheduled for 14 August.

Before then, however, McCall had seen the legs knocked out from under the third force.

On 24 July, the United States Supreme Court voted unanimously that Nixon had to comply with all subpoenas for the White House tapes. Three days later, the House Judiciary Committee voted twenty-seven to eleven to approve articles of impeachment. The affirmative vote included six Republicans.

After months of hounding by federal prosecutors, Richard Nixon, on 5 August, released a second batch of White House tapes, and the contents were devastating. One set in particular, made 23 June 1972, six days after the Watergate break-in, revealed Nixon ordered his aides to keep the FBI off the trail of the Watergate burglars and their connections to his re-election campaign. It was an effort to obstruct justice, pure and simple, the so-called "smoking gun," proof Nixon had known about the connection of his campaign to the crime months earlier than he had admitted. The final tapes told Republicans in Congress they could do nothing more to save their president. On 8 August, Nixon announced his resignation.

McCall applauded the resignation but knew it had doused his own career. "60 Minutes" cancelled its segment on him. With the president's resignation, McCall said, came "the CBS management decision that the Third Force had overnight lost its timeliness. Twenty-five million people would have learned about the Third Force had the CBS program been aired. There's little doubt that it would have been well launched had President Nixon somehow stuck it out."

McCall was clearly rationalizing, and doing what he loved to do—imagining his own greatness couched in many "what ifs." He had done it with the Senate races he had never made, and now he was doing it with his third force idea that would never fully bloom.

THE OREGON PRESS looked on in amusement and curiosity at McCall's fame. Between May and September, the *Oregonian* alone published five articles that chronicled, analyzed or attacked McCall's fondness for the national limelight. "What is Tom McCall doing out there?" asked one *Oregonian* columnist after the Von Hoffman piece. McCall's reply: "I'm having fun." One writer speculated in print about the propriety of McCall's barnstorming, noting, "It is an open question in fact, how much McCall has enhanced Oregon's image and how much Oregon has enhanced McCall's." Another writer said of McCall's Oregon Story: "Oregonians, beset by field burning smoke in the Willamette Valley, crime in Portland, a depressed lumber industry and Californians at the border, might dare call it fiction, but McCall's out-of-state audiences apparently called it gospel." Other reporters paid attention only to the speaking fees

McCall collected during the year—$26,250 plus expenses for sixteen talks, in addition to his $35,000-per-year salary as governor.

The critiques held a strange irony for the Oregon press, however. For ten years the press had fallen over itself to praise McCall. Now, as McCall had lifted his own sights beyond Oregon's borders, the press rarely reported his expanding message.

No speech better expressed McCall's beliefs during this time than one he delivered on behalf of the National Aeronautics and Space Administration (NASA), which had signed McCall to deliver seven lectures for its Earth 2020 program. McCall was the keynote speaker of the program, which looked at the environmental and scientific challenges of the next century. The Oregon press noted only that NASA had agreed to pay McCall $10,000 for the speeches and had given him free trips to California and Hawaii, where the programs were held.

Most important to McCall, though, was the speech in which, after fifteen years of environmental work, he summed up all that he had learned, not only about conservation and growth, but about human nature as well. In his travels, McCall had seen environmental problems on a global scale. The appeal of the Oregon Story was not that a single, small state had done so much good work. The appeal was that its accomplishments could be exported. The key, however, was in McCall's belief that human beings still had the ingenuity and desire to stop the earth's degradation.

> The title of my address [McCall began]—"One More Step to the Styx"—seems to come from the doom-and-gloom school. It seems to imply that unless we change our ways we'll soon be through the gates of perdition, stumbling through the fire, tripping over the brimstone.
>
> In a less literal sense, that's the thought I intended to convey. I'm not insisting that we're one step away from the end of the world, that man's survival is truly in imminent jeopardy. Man is too innovative and creative to preside over his own funeral. We'll find a way to survive as a species, but I'm concerned about the quality of life that will be attached to survival.

McCall warned that American habits of consumption threatened to paralyze its economy and way of life. In doing so, he hit on his long-held theme of conservation of all kinds.

> In the chase for unreasonable profit, sound land use theories are trampled, making some of us wonder if we might awaken someday to find we don't want to live here anymore. We see so many things manufactured for one-time use that we might eventually find ourselves competing with the rats at the land-fills for materials basic to economic survival. . . .
>
> Unless we restrain our demand, [electricity] rate increases will be piled upon rate increases. People already resent pay-ing more in order to live no better than before. And they came to government with their resentment and we have an alternative to offer: Reduce your use of electricity.

McCall said that the lessons of conservation already were there for Americans to see, and that they would pay dearly for ignoring those lessons.

> I had hoped the shock of the energy crisis would implant forever in our minds the truth that humanity has begun to exceed the earth's ability to provide. But once the gasoline supply situation eased many Americans resumed their habits of flying down the freeway—wasting oil and wasting gaso-line. . . .
>
> The oil companies advertise on television that it sure costs a lot to get oil these days, but they say they are getting it for us—which is a public relations way of saying that the price will be high, but we'll still have all the oil and gas we want. . . .
>
> The Gods of growth continue to feed on the sacrificial lamb. They continue to spout their homily that "In every cri-sis there is opportunity to make a fast buck."

Consumer desires, corporate greed—all of it seems basic to a capi-
talistic world, McCall said. Yet he was convinced those same forces,
left unaltered, would destroy the nation's livability.

> Our standards of living—as defined by us—became the
> highest in the world. But in our rush to riches we should take
> a gander at the precipice ahead. Using up finite resources of
> this country and others only to make money for now is to
> shoplift from the future. . . .
>
> Most of us have made the assumption there always has
> to be rapid growth and we have to have more of the same. It
> isn't necessarily true. We do have to have growth. . . . But it
> is [not] an increasing population that is responsible for
> bringing us closer to environmental poverty. It is our ap-
> petite for a second home and a second Cadillac. It is our no-
> deposit, no-return ways of waste.

The theme echoed McCall's 1970 Earth Day speech. Despite this
outward pessimism, however, McCall fell back to his earliest beliefs of
human nature. Even as a child at Westernwold, while his siblings had
brooded over their family's lost fortunes, Tom was cheerful, sunny and
hopeful. At age sixty-one, at the end of the political career he had hungered for, McCall still recognized the optimism he believed everyone
shared.

> Perhaps our leaders have aimed too low, and at the wrong
> goals. Perhaps there hasn't been enough integrity, vision and
> truth-saying to convince us of the folly of eating up tomor-
> row.
>
> We have treated our world with cavalier abandon. But it
> has always been Tom's First Rule of Thumb that we have a
> greater capacity for love than to destroy. And because we
> are in love with the world, we will not be able to resist the
> temptation to make it better.

IN 1974, THE WILLAMETTE RIVER, once a 187-mile gutter choked with industrial and municipal waste, ran with life. In 1965, the fall salmon count, as measured in the Oregon City locks, reached fewer than one hundred fish. In 1973, the total reached twenty-two thousand. Sewage treatment plants and manufacturing sites still emptied wastes into the river, but now, under the muscle of the state, those plants first treated their wastes until they were all but benign, based on the standards of the era. The Boise Cascade mill in Salem, the closure of which had sparked a Capitol steps protest, operated for ten more years within the boundaries of the state's environmental laws. It eventually closed for economic reasons.

The glistening Willamette, once a highway for typhoid and hepatitis, now invited boaters, skiers and swimmers. Its shoreline fell under zoning control of the state to protect it against overdevelopment. The Willamette Greenway was far from what Robert Straub had first envisioned—a long public park running the river's length—but with added parks and landings, Oregonians had more access to their clean river than ever before. In downtown Portland, where a freeway had once run along the river's seawall, McCall initiated a long waterfront park. Suddenly, Oregon's biggest city had access to the river that coursed through its center. After his death, the city of Portland named the park for McCall.

But McCall's reward had come much earlier. The house that he rented from the state sat along Mill Creek in Salem, and from the lawn he peered down at twenty-pound salmon spawning in the stream—a sight that would have been unimaginable ten years earlier.

In 1974, the Oregon coastline stood free of development and ruin. The 1967 Beach Bill had been upheld by the Oregon Supreme Court and augmented by a 1969 measure carefully delineating the boundary of public control over the beach. Nestucca Spit, where Glenn Jackson had wanted a four-lane highway, became a state park, eventually named for its protector, Bob Straub.

In 1974, Oregon's streets and beaches lay clean because of a single innovative law. When McCall toured the nation, few accomplishments caught Americans' fancy as did Oregon's Bottle Bill. McCall unabashedly championed the idea, rarely stopping to note his own caution toward the bill when it was first introduced in 1969. By 1974, Vermont, which saw its own bottle bill enacted and repealed in the 1950s, reintroduced the law. Meanwhile, more than thirty-five states tried in vain to pass the bill, only to see the metals, glass, plastics, beer and soda pop industries crash down upon their lawmakers. In Oregon, the Bottle Bill's success remained unchallenged. Once considered an anti-littering measure, the bill introduced a recycling mentality into the daily life of Oregonians. In 1973, ninety-five percent of bottles and cans purchased in Oregon—385 million containers in all—were returned for a refund rather than sent to landfills or strewn along the state's roads and beaches. (Nonetheless, opponents did not give up. A group of brewers and container makers sued the state, charging the law was unconstitutional. The Oregon courts rejected their pleas.)

In October 1974, the Land Conservation and Development Commission (LCDC) went into effect. The LCDC launched a two-year effort to define its statewide land-use goals and compel every city and county in Oregon to produce plans for growth. The land-use work was only one of many environmental efforts McCall had to leave to others as he left office. To ensure the agency did its job to his own standards, McCall installed the bombastic L.B. Day as LCDC chairman.

In 1974, 2.26 million people called Oregon home, an astounding population increase of slightly more than twenty-five percent during the eight years McCall had been governor. He had declared that outsiders should "visit, but don't stay" in 1971, but it seemed as if no one was listening. McCall could not turn away the tide of immigrants seeking a new Eden. Rather, like the nineteenth-century promoters who had inspired the westward migration in 1843, McCall had been the best publicist Oregon had ever had. His declaration of his intent to protect Oregon had only made the state more attractive. The final irony of his administration was that his flamboyant pride for his state ultimately brought Oregon more growth, testing the very environmental protections of which he was so proud.

In 1974, no one in Oregon could remember a leader like Tom McCall. No Oregon politician had done so much for his state, and in so little time. Newspaper editorials mourned the limitations on the number of terms a governor could serve, wishing McCall could stay in office indefinitely.

Convinced that no one could live up to her son's standard, Dorothy Lawson McCall threatened to run for governor to succeed him. Only those familiar with Dorothy knew it was not just a publicity stunt. In Lawsonian fashion, she was refusing to let loose of the fame Tom had returned to the family. Dorothy remained nothing but enthusiastic about her candidacy. After calling a press conference to announce her plans, she called her son to tell him it had been a success. "How do you know?" he asked. "Because," Dorothy replied, "some of the reporters stayed so long they had to go to the bathroom." McCall finally talked his eighty-five-year-old mother out of making the race.

In 1974, Tom McCall was sixty-three years old. He had been fifty-one when first elected to office, with three-fourths of his life already behind him. To give McCall's spirits a final lift, his friends threw a party for him unlike the state had ever seen. More than a thousand people filled the Portland Hilton, and hundreds of thousands more watched the banquet, which McCall's aides turned into a roast, as it was broadcast live over Portland television.

At the banquet, McCall laughed and drank at the head table, reveling in the tribute. During his own speech, however, he turned somber. He clearly worried about his legacy, and the way in which Oregonians would remember him and the work he had started. As he closed his farewell speech, McCall offered his own epitaph:

"He tried, oh Lord, he tried. There was no final victory. But did he not point the way?"

NOT LONG AFTER BEGINNING HIS SECOND TERM, McCall had met with an eleven-year-old girl in his Capitol office. The girl had faced heart surgery the previous summer, and McCall, after hearing about her operation, invited her to visit him when she recovered. The two talked for a long time before the girl asked McCall a favor. Her fifth-grade class had learned of her trip to the governor's office and compiled a list of questions for McCall. Would he take time to answer them? McCall agreed and looked over the questions: "What's it like to be governor?" "Do you think taxes are too high?" "Do you get paid enough?" McCall smiled and took out a pen and began writing out his answers.

The last of his finest days, 14 January 1975. Photographers capture McCall as he signs the final document of his administration, minutes before he relinquished office. (Courtesy Eugene *Register-Guard*)

McCall eventually reached this question: "How will you feel when you're not governor anymore?"

He thought for awhile and then wrote a short reply:

"I will feel both relief and sadness. Nothing will ever be as interesting again."

For Tom McCall, nothing ever was.

PART FIVE

*Show me a hero and
I will write you a tragedy.*

F. Scott Fitzgerald

21

The Once and Future Governor

THREE YEARS AND ONE MONTH after saying farewell, Tom McCall asked Oregonians to once again elect him governor. He had left office in January 1975 hopeful and exuberant, popular and revered. But he loathed the day he returned to private life. "I hate to find myself at only sixty-one, and with an enthusiastic following, relegated to the political boneyard," he said.

From the day he left the Capitol, he thought about little else except how to return. State law allowed him to run again for governor after four years, and despite the pleadings of his closest advisers and friends, he did not resist trying once more.

He had realized that at first the transition to private life would prove difficult. "I will never be content with the role of disinterested elder statesman," McCall said. "I hope to stay creative as a writer and as a political theorist. I really don't know the meaning of the word 'retirement'." Indeed, he faced up to retirement poorly. Rather than spending his days moving forward with life, McCall reached backward, his hands grasping to recapture something lost, his fingers closing around only emptiness.

He had welcomed his successor, Democrat Robert Straub, with great warmth. He had all but endorsed Straub for election the previous fall, and refused to back the Republican nominee, State Senator Victor Atiyeh, a member of what he called the GOP "wrecking crew" that had opposed so many of his ideas. He had left office feeling that with Straub, with whom he agreed on so much, Oregon was left in good hands.

He tried to fill the void of retirement by staying busy, and the flurry of activity into which he threw himself satisfied him temporarily. McCall remained in demand as a speaker and jetted from San Diego to Maine reciting updated versions of his Oregon Story. Awards, too, rolled in, from the National Resources Defense Council, which threw him an impressive banquet in Manhattan, to Florida's Collier County Conservancy, which also held a dinner in his honor.

The job offers flowed in. The Smithsonian Institution offered him a fellowship. Linfield College, a private liberal arts university in rural McMinnville, offered him its presidency. (He declined, believing the job too comfortable.) Major environmental groups—the Conservation Foundation, the Center for Growth Alternatives, the American Farmland Trust—committed to protecting land from unwarranted destruction, appointed him to their boards. The *Oregonian*, the state's biggest newspaper, signed him to do a weekly column. A Portland radio station, KEX-AM, put him back on the airwaves, doing three commentaries a week. Oregon State University (OSU) founded a Tom McCall Chair of Communications and Public Affairs, a teaching position with a $30,000-a-year salary that McCall himself would hold; the chair was funded by Glenn Jackson and a dozen or so other major contributors. McCall received a $50,000 grant from two New York-based organizations, the J.M. Kaplan Fund and Faigel Leah Foundation, to open an institute dedicated to studying energy conservation.

Amidst all of this, McCall started to write an autobiography, with national publishers waiting anxiously to bid for its rights. He even made a short film appearance, a cameo role in "One Flew Over the Cuckoo's Nest," filmed at the Oregon State Hospital in Salem during mid-1974; he played a television news anchorman whose face and voice appeared over the television playing in the mental hospital ward.

All of these activities paid him handsomely. The columns and commentaries alone paid him about $2,000 a month, and he immediately collected $25,000 of the energy grant as a salary. The money more than made up for the $35,000 governor's salary.

By mid-1975, McCall had roared off in too many directions, usually without a destination. He missed the guidance of a staff to focus and discipline him. Soon, many of his early enterprises failed, if only because McCall's heart was not in any of them. The energy conservation foundation, called the Institute for Applied Energetics, sputtered. His hopes of writing a best-selling memoir also foundered when New York publishers winced at his melodramatic retelling of his life and when he refused their requests to replace his chosen co-author, Steve Neal.

The thought of holding a professorship buoyed him briefly, until he started teaching. "I thought the teaching and the contact with young people would be very stimulating," he said. "It was too static. Static means you gave your best speeches and they never clapped." He left OSU after teaching one class and one term.

Soon, the speech offers tapered off, and, eventually, the Oregon press, which had reported McCall's every move since his retirement, lost interest in him. "The winding down process," he confided at one point, "is terribly difficult."

In July, McCall received the first offer to truly engage his soul. Tom Dargan, his former boss from the KGW-TV days, had moved to Portland television station KATU-TV. Dargan offered him a contract to serve as the station's news analyst, and McCall eagerly accepted. As in the old days, he could speak directly to Oregonians again. The station paid him a nearly $37,000-a-year salary plus syndication bonus, more than he had made as governor. With the additional $13,000 he earned from his radio spots, McCall and Audrey bought a new home in Portland's fashionable West Hills.

For the next year, McCall clicked through his days with solemn resolution. He wrote his radio and television commentaries on his old manual typewriter, punching each word out with his two-fingered typing technique. His doctors said he was free of cancer, and he burned his new energy playing golf and tennis, and swam a few times each week. He and Audrey took their first trip to Europe.

As busy as he was, McCall said, he felt useless. "The whole point is," he said, exasperated, "I'm overworked but under-used."

Everyone around McCall knew he had not made peace with private life. As governor he could pound his fist and change the state. As a commentator, McCall found that even the wisest broadcast would change nothing. Ron Schmidt, now running his own advertising firm, sought a bigger challenge for his old boss. In early 1976, Schmidt thought he had discovered the angle McCall needed. President Gerald Ford that year was waging a desperate campaign to win election in his own right after ascending to the presidency upon the resignation of President Richard Nixon. Soon after taking over the presidency, Ford was in trouble. He had pardoned Nixon, which had angered many Americans, and he faced a conservative challenge from former California governor Ronald Reagan. Meanwhile, former Georgia governor Jimmy Carter, an old McCall friend, led all Democratic candidates for their party's nomination. As the Oregon primary approached, both Ford and Carter recognized McCall's continuing popularity and sought his public endorsement.

Privately, McCall preferred Carter, and Schmidt quietly negotiated with the Carter campaign. He hoped an endorsement could translate into McCall "writing his own ticket" after the election—namely, McCall's appointment as Secretary of the Interior.

McCall's mind raced at the notion. As Secretary of the Interior, McCall could preach his doctrine from a cabinet-level pulpit. But even as Schmidt laid out the scenario, McCall balked. Endorsing Carter would cost him his KATU-TV job with no guarantee of a White House appointment later. Privately, he fretted again that the revelations about his son Sam, which had kept him out of the Senate race, would surface if he faced a Senate confirmation hearing. He dismissed the whole deal as an impractical long shot, and for once, the gambler in him abstained.

MCCALL RETURNED TO THE CAMPAIGN TRAIL in 1976 to promote Oregon's environmental agenda, starting with the Oregon Bottle Bill. Few doubted the success of the measure in Oregon, and the law's opponents—the beverage companies, the glass and metal manufacturers—had conceded defeat in their efforts to repeal the deposit law after losing an Oregon Supreme Court case on the issue. Opponents now chose to fight the bill in the other forty-nine states, spending $20 million to squelch the container deposit idea nationally. "They've decided to isolate Oregon, let us have our little victory and set their sights on keeping this fine measure from spreading across the land," McCall said.

With such fierce opposition, debate about bottle bills always lacked objectivity. In late 1974, for example, the Oregon Legislature hired Applied Decisions Systems, Inc., (ADS) a Massachusetts-based consulting firm, to produce an independent report on the bill's economic effects. Soon afterward, Jerry Uhrhammer, an investigative reporter for the Eugene *Register-Guard*, revealed that ADS was consultant to American Can, Continental Can, Coca-Cola, Schlitz and Owens Illinois—all plaintiffs in the suit to overturn Oregon's Bottle Bill. Despite Uhrhammer's revelations, the report went forward, and legislators later found the study was not independent enough; ADS had relied heavily on statistics provided by industry. Even so, the report had found a decrease in litter in Oregon.

Container manufacturers then launched a national advertising campaign that slandered not only the bottle law, but Oregon itself. In late 1975, aluminum giant Alcoa produced a campaign dubbed "Trouble on the Oregon Trail." Distributed by the Aluminum Association, pamphlets and advertisements charged that the Oregon Bottle Bill had cost consumers more money and actually increased litter. Aside from the bogus claims, the ads carried an unmistakable message: Oregon is an inhospitable place to do business. "Oregon has almost become a four-letter word," the campaign quoted one federal official as saying, "and the possibility of a national mandatory deposit law has caused fear for survival of the industry."

Oregon officials fought the claims without success. Oregon senator Bob Packwood asked the Federal Trade Commission (FTC) in July 1976 to investigate Alcoa's advertisements, citing seventeen statements "which seem to be either deceptive, patent misrepresentations of data, or misleading." Cowed by industry pressure, however, the FTC refused to investigate.

Pressure to douse enthusiasm for the bill appeared elsewhere. The Environmental Protection Agency (EPA) issued a report that gave rousing support for the Oregon Bottle Bill, then tempered it when labor unions complained. Oregon senator Mark Hatfield had struggled since 1973 to bring a national bottle bill to the Senate floor. When he succeeded in 1976, the industry pressure prevailed—the measure lost sixty to twenty-eight, and never came up for a full vote again.

The industry opposition encouraged McCall to campaign for the bill in other states. Forty-five states by then had considered similar laws. Only two states, Vermont and South Dakota, had enacted the laws. In 1976, however, four more states—Michigan, Massachusetts, Maine and Colorado—all placed bottle bill measures on the November ballots. McCall spent the fall traveling to those states to campaign for the measures. In each state, though, he saw the expensive campaign mounted by the opposing industries. In Michigan, the opponents' campaigns—in addition to the old warnings about high prices and lost jobs—described the long lines in Oregon grocery stores caused by the law. Another lie, McCall said. "The pluses are absolutely so numerous and so impressive that it's a crying shame you're probably not going to win," he told reporters in Lansing, "because this is the most stacked deck you'll ever run into." He flew to Boston to campaign for the bill with Massachusetts governor Michael Dukakis, then went on to Maine, where he told reporters that Oregonians "are incredulous when I go home and tell them that other states are apparently not accepting this thing that works so well." Michigan and Maine later approved bottle bill measures, while voters in Colorado and Massachusetts rejected theirs.

Back home, McCall had another campaign to run.

McCall considered the state's new land-use laws his greatest achievement as governor, the imprint that would last for decades, shaping and controlling the growth that threatened Oregon's livability. Land-use planning had barely been in effect two years, however, before its opponents tried to repeal it.

The law had been under fire since the day it was enacted. The state Land Conservation and Development Commission (LCDC), the agency charged with carrying out Oregon's land-use policies, had pleased no one. Instead it had helped divide Oregon politics into two distinct camps: those who advocated a strong central planning role for the state, and those who sought to dismantle McCall's vision for sensible growth.

Frustration with the LCDC came largely because everyone involved underestimated how long it would take the state to make the program work. The commission faced the daunting task of compelling local governments to designate use for the state's twenty-five million acres of private property, most of which was agricultural land. The job seemed politically impossible, considering the varied Oregon landscape and the near-sacred tenets of private property ownership. "There's no way that land-use planning can make everyone happy," said one planner reflecting on the Oregon system, "because it involves many having to give up individual rights to do as they please with their property for the overall good of the citizens of the state."

Because McCall wanted the LCDC to have the same high profile he had given the Willamette River clean-up, he named L.B. Day as the LCDC's first chairman. Day grabbed the unpaid chairman's position with full force. The commission's first job was to establish a set of land-use principles, called "goals," that planners had to follow. Day wanted to slam through the set of goals already on the books, but other LCDC officials argued the state needed fresh goals. So Day threw open the goal-writing process, and the commission held dozens of hearings and listened to thousands of witnesses before approving the fourteen goals in late 1974.

The goals covered controls on farm and forest lands, which were protected to ensure that they were not quickly developed into industrial parks or subdivisions. But urban sprawl emerged as the most important issue to the commission, which insisted that each city and county in Oregon—277 in all—submit a blueprint for its future growth. These "comprehensive plans" had to meet the LCDC's new goals. The commission gave local governments a January 1976, deadline to comply with the goals.

That was how it was supposed to work. But the LCDC was vague about its standards, and many local governments dragged their heels, which only irritated Day. When one county official asked for an extended deadline, Day said flatly, "Over my dead body."

Privately, Day admitted that delays were inevitable. "Why so slow?" McCall asked him about the LCDC's pace in 1976.

"You can't move any faster than the people will let you move," Day replied.

Opponents' anger at the LCDC and the entire planning system also grew because of the emergence of a simple special interest group: 1,000 Friends of Oregon, an environmental organization whose purpose was to serve as watchdog over the state's land-use laws. McCall had helped form the group just before leaving office, and others, including Glenn

Jackson, contributed heavily to get 1,000 Friends up and running. Staffed with aggressive lawyers, 1,000 Friends frequently succeeded in challenging the LCDC on its own standards. With no comparable group on the other side to oppose it, 1,000 Friends won several legal precedents on the side of conservation and preservation in the new land-use laws. Meanwhile, opponents believed the group was succeeding only in halting development.

So in 1976, land-use opponents gathered enough signatures to place on the fall ballot a measure repealing most of the LCDC's regulatory powers. Day, fearing the measure was directed at him, resigned the commission in hopes of taking pressure off the land-use program. McCall insisted that Day had not been the issue. The ideal of statewide land-use planning needed a champion.

He had always played that role, and he did so again in 1976. Despite his position as an objective broadcaster, McCall campaigned wholeheartedly against the ballot measure, reminding Oregonians of the foresight he had provided as their governor. "If there's anything that characterizes Oregon as a leader," he said at one appearance, "it is the sense of stewardship Oregonians have to the land." His campaign appearances showed he still had the knack, and his derision of the arguments of land-use opponents was withering. "Some people would subdivide the village graveyard if they could make a $50 profit," he said. After one of McCall's campaign speeches in Eugene, one local land-use foe stormed toward the podium and tried to hand McCall anti-land-use fliers. "I've seen all that crap," McCall snorted, to the audience's delight.

As election day 1976 neared, McCall worried that his idea lacked popular support. However, voters treated the issue as a referendum for McCall's policies and trounced the measure, with fifty-seven percent saying they wanted to keep Oregon's land-use policies in place.

THE SIGHT OF MCCALL CAMPAIGNING AGAIN fueled press speculation about his political future—namely, a McCall comeback in the 1978 governor's race. When asked about the possibility, McCall smiled sheepishly. Publicly he continued to wish his successor, Robert Straub, all the best. "I hope he hacks it," McCall said at one point, "and I don't feel the pressure to run. But I do miss it terribly."

Privately, of course, he thought about little else besides running again. Even when McCall tried to forget about a comeback, the media would not let him. Only a few months after Straub had taken office, newspapers began commissioning polls to test a 1978 McCall-Straub match-up. To no one's surprise, the polls gave McCall a whopping lead over Straub.

McCall knew the polls reflected the impossible task inherited by his successor. Few politicians in America had the talent to follow McCall's performance, and Straub was not one of them. Straub was a big-hearted man deeply committed to the conservation issues he and McCall had championed twelve years earlier, but he lacked McCall's charisma and charm, and still struggled to string together two graceful sentences. Straub had also been given the thankless job of making the McCall programs—namely, land-use planning—actually work.

McCall had first refused to criticize Straub's performance, but soon, in his television commentaries, he started comparing Straub to himself. Meanwhile, he could not take his eyes off the polls. In February 1977, a new *Oregonian* poll showed him with a commanding lead over Straub. Two months later, McCall broke his silence about running in 1978. "I must say I haven't decided if I will run again," McCall told a reporter. "But if I do, I already have my campaign slogan. . . . 'Let's put Oregon back on the map'."

AS HIS POLITICAL AMBITION SURGED, McCall faced mounting personal troubles. He learned in 1976 that the Internal Revenue Service (IRS) had taken a keen interest in his personal finances. The IRS pressed McCall about the $12,000-a-year expense allowance the state provided its governors. McCall had used much of the allowance to pay his rent on a state-owned home in Salem. Internal Revenue officials at that time had told him the allowance was tax exempt. Now, the agency had changed its mind and demanded back taxes. After months of digging through state records, IRS investigators also found one discrepancy in his expense account: a 1973 advance of $1,000 in expenses for which McCall had not accounted. He had taken the expense money the day he had left for a governors' conference, and he had either failed to file his receipts for the trip or the records had been misplaced. Altogether, the IRS told

McCall in 1976, he and Audrey owed $21,150.33 in back taxes, interest and penalties.

McCall refused to believe Internal Revenue's sudden interest in his finances—coming as it did with renewed talk of his re-entry into politics—was a coincidence. "Our CPA is at a loss to explain it," he wrote Schmidt about the audit. "We are forced to believe the tempo—and the whole proceedings—[is] politically motivated." McCall never said who he thought had interested the IRS in his affairs. He did not believe Straub could be responsible, but believed an anonymous "political satrap" from either party had brought the IRS down on him.

Most troubling of all, however, his son Sam remained a dangerous and unpredictable presence.

Twenty-eight years old and still a drug addict, Sam lived at home. Tom and Audrey's efforts to help him make it on his own had always failed. He still had scrapes with the law. He was arrested in August 1976 by Salem police for disorderly conduct and criminal activity with drugs. Prosecutors dropped the charges in exchange for sending Sam back to the state mental hospital. Such episodes triggered in McCall a mix of frustration and compassion in his feelings toward Sam. In a letter to a friend that September, he called his son "a poor dear creature, so lovable, but so beaten up . . . because God left some vital connection out of his warning system." Despite their love, the toll on Tom and Audrey was inescapable. McCall called it "our frightening battle against despair."

After his release from the state hospital, Sam tried to start fresh in Spokane, Washington, Audrey's hometown. Tom and Audrey felt great relief, but it did not last. In March 1977, Spokane police charged Sam with a felony, obtaining drugs by fraud, after he had tried to get Valium by telling a local hospital that he was an epileptic. With those charges pending, police again arrested Sam in June when he tried to steal Valium from a local pharmacy. Sam eventually pleaded guilty to the fraud charge.

Tom and Audrey flew to Spokane to testify on their son's sentencing, and McCall took the witness stand. Haggard and sad, he recounted Sam's troubled life and asked the judge for mercy. "This has gone on a long time," McCall told the judge. "There's been a lot of screaming and misery. There's been inordinate expense. It has broken our hearts."

In Oregon, Sam McCall had been protected as the governor's son, but in Washington, authorities considered him nothing more than a thief and drug addict. Spokane County Superior Court Judge Willard Roe declared Sam had been coddled long enough. "I can sympathize with the underprivileged. But this isn't any deprived boy like I see so often in this court," Roe said to Sam, as Tom and Audrey listened. "If you're going to make it, you're going to make it on your own, your own free will, with what you have, from here on out, without looking backward for any excuse."

Roe gave Sam a three-year suspended sentence and put him on probation back in Oregon, where McCall and Audrey would again be responsible for him. The probation carried stiff rules, including a prohibition against drug and alcohol use. Sam only waited until he reached the Spokane airport before violating the rules. He drank on the plane and, once in Portland, stole the family car. Within a few days he was under arrest again, and police finally put Sam in the Multnomah County Jail for probation violation.

Tom McCall saw the ghastly cycle beginning again. "The governorship had always been an escape for Tom," one of his close friends said privately. "When Sam acted up, he could always immerse himself in his job. Now, there was no escape."

"I WILL FEEL," McCall had said of leaving the governorship, "great relief and great sadness." Sadness seemed to be the greater emotion now. In late 1977, Audrey confided to friends, "Tom would just die if he couldn't be governor again."

His first problem in launching a political comeback was money. He was sixty-four years old and still had no financial security. McCall was earning $52,000 in 1977, and he would have to give up his broadcasting jobs if he ran for office. However, he needed the money to pay Sam's legal and medical bills, and the IRS, which, after demanding more than $21,000, had agreed to settle for $12,230. In the end, McCall turned to two out-of-state friends he had met through environmental organizations, and they agreed to loan him $35,000 to live on during the campaign.

He also worried about his health. His doctors had said he was free of cancer, as far as they knew, but he lacked his old vigor, often ran short of breath and had trouble concentrating for long periods of time. Given the polls, though, he anticipated an easy campaign—not too much traveling or speaking, he hoped—and he thought he could find a reasonable pace.

He had assumed his old team would rise up with him to recapture the governorship, but he was wrong. Far from being enthusiastic about his plans, his closest advisers—Ron Schmidt and Ed Westerdahl in particular—urged him not to run. Westerdahl warned that McCall might not even win, despite what the polls said. Schmidt told him that, even if he won, he would not enjoy the job he once loved. "He wanted to recapture all that was grand about being governor," Schmidt said. "I told him he couldn't recapture it. He couldn't go home again. I pleaded with him to let it go." Another former aide, Robert Davis, agreed, noting that nothing would be as it was before. If you run, Davis told McCall, "You'll get your heart broken."

These men had been McCall's most trusted advisers, but they were not giving him the answer he wanted, so he sought counsel elsewhere. Even the opinions of passers-by on the street who urged him to run suddenly carried more weight with McCall.

Public speculation about his comeback increased when, in late 1977, a Portland publishing company released his memoir, *Tom McCall: Maverick*. The book, originally titled *Visit Oregon—But Don't Stay*, provided the first full-length portrait of McCall's life, even though it ignored embarrassing subjects, such as his support of the Nestucca beach highway, and exaggerated others, such as the McCall-for-Mayor movement in Moscow, Idaho. The book was largely superficial and filled with potshots at other politicians, including Mark Hatfield and Bob Packwood, revealing a certain pettiness in McCall's nature. "If all the people McCall has wronged in his book wanted to sue," grumbled one victim of McCall's prose, "we could have a class-action suit."

Amid the crescendo of press attention accompanying McCall's return to politics, *Oregon Magazine* writer Tom Bates, in late 1977, visited McCall at his Lincoln City beach house. As McCall gulped his drink—a rum and tomato juice mix he dubbed a "Maverick"—he talked continuously about his future. Bates' resulting article, "The Once—and Future(?)—Governor," heralded the inevitable McCall comeback. It was also one of the finest portraits ever of McCall, a proud, wistful man nagged by physical pain and the loss of fame.

During one interview the two men took a long walk along the beach, and McCall spoke as if he had no choice but to jump back into politics. "Can you see a politician with all that daylight to run and not running at it?" he said.

As McCall wandered toward the ocean, a large wave heaved a log up onto the sand and nearly on top of McCall's legs. Bates called out to him, and McCall, startled, lumbered away from the rolling log.

McCall looked back at the gray water, and Bates heard McCall mumble something under his breath.

"What did you just say?" Bates asked.

"I said," McCall replied, "'You're dead a long time.'"

"WHEN I ANNOUNCED I WAS GOING TO RUN," Tom McCall said in early 1978, "it was like opening the cage and letting the bird out. If I hadn't run, I would have gone to my grave regretting it. And I may go there regretting that I did."

He waited until 14 February 1978, Oregon's 119th birthday, to officially announce his comeback. The Oregon press trumpeted McCall's return with bold headlines, and pundits looked ahead to what greatness a new McCall administration might bring Oregon.

He had, to his own satisfaction, thought all of the issues through. He had money to tide him over and public support behind him. But he had failed to settle one lingering issue. He was running as a Republican.

After years of talking about running as an independent, McCall's decision to hang onto his old party label was inexplicable. Not long before running, McCall had mused about the possibilities of an independent candidacy. "Just having conventional party hacks all frothing at each other and running against each other," he said, "and then you take the middle right out as an independent and leave them sidelined."

Yet he still stuck with the GOP. Later he said he had done so out of loyalty to his grandfather, Samuel Walker McCall. Old Roman did not abandon the party, McCall said. He would not either.

His oddly sentimental decision boxed him into an impossible situation. He had no organization or campaign money, and he faced a three-way Republican primary only a hundred days off. Meanwhile, his two opponents had sharp, well-funded operations already running. His first opponent was Victor Atiyeh, the Oregon Senate GOP leader from Washington County who had lost to Straub four years earlier in the race to replace McCall. The second was Roger Martin, the Republican leader of the Oregon House. Both men were conservative, old-fashioned politicians linked closely to the state's business community. Yet neither generated much excitement, and McCall's entry overpowered them at first. "Hopefuls Stand in McCall's Shadow," read one headline.

Martin and Atiyeh thought their candidacies would split the conservative vote and give McCall an easy victory—a result neither wanted. So they concocted a strange deal that was supposed to lead to one candidate's withdrawal. Martin and Atiyeh asked a three-person panel of Republican businessmen to judge which one had the better campaign strategy and organization. The loser would agree to drop out. The panel chose Martin, but Atiyeh refused to stick by his agreement and remained in the race. The deal never became public.

Conventional wisdom had McCall as the winner, as the polls suggested, yet even those polls held a clue to his fate. After four decades in the public spotlight, virtually every Oregonian recognized him, and few people would be changing their views on him before election day. McCall recognized the problem. "The legend always grows bigger than the guy ever was," McCall said at his announcement, speaking of himself in the third person. "Tom McCall is at his peak as a public figure. Political observers will conclude that I have peaked eight months before the general election—and the only way for McCall to go is down."

For the next three months, all McCall had to do was hang on to the popularity he had. He at first assumed he could do that by simply being Tom McCall. "He really wasn't geared for a tight, well-organized campaign," said Atiyeh later. "I've described it as an actor jumping on the stage and saying, 'tah-dahh,' and waiting for everyone to applaud. And he did this—tah-dahh—and everybody didn't applaud."

As a result, McCall ignored the basics of a campaign: the need for money. "[McCall] was shitty in raising money," said Ted Hallock, who, despite being a Democratic state senator, worked to elect McCall again. "He thought money would flow in to him. He didn't think he would

McCall and his 1978 Republican primary opponents: the eventual winner State
Senator Victor Atiyeh of Beaverton (left) and State Representative Roger Martin of
Lake Oswego (center). (Courtesy of the *Oregonian*)

have to ask for money. So he wouldn't ask for money, and the money
didn't flow to him."

What McCall also lacked—and what he had always needed—was
someone to impose discipline. His organization consisted of earnest but
inexperienced campaigners who lacked the skills to run a statewide effort and who lacked experience in dealing with the emotional candidate. As a result, as McCall campaigned, his message veered erratically,
and he acted at times as if he were trying to ruin his own chances.

Without the discipline he needed, McCall also had trouble controlling the publicity that he had once mastered. Many of the reporters who
had fawned over him in the earlier years were gone. In their place came
a younger flock who, after Watergate, looked upon all politicians with
skepticism.

In early March, McCall heard that reporters were chasing rumors spread by his opponents' campaigns that the IRS had investigated a "slush fund" he had controlled as governor. Doug Yocom, an *Oregon Journal* reporter McCall knew well, asked him about the rumors. In a burst of characteristic candor, McCall, as if in a confessional, blurted out everything. He disclosed the IRS audit and the settlement he had paid. He then described a travel fund paid for by Republican businessmen in the late 1960s. He had never controlled the fund—Ron Schmidt had—but the money, totalling $12,152, had allowed him to take political trips and not charge taxpayers.

Then, suddenly, McCall bared even more. For the first time, he talked publicly about the financial assistance Glenn Jackson and other businessman had given McCall to pay Sam's medical bills.

Once finished, McCall released a giant sigh. "You could tell all of this stuff was bothering him and eating away at him," Yocom said later. "He wanted to let it all out, probably before his opponents did. You could just see the relief on his face."

Yocom's story reverberated through the press and made the national wires. The *Oregonian* followed Yocom's story with its own about the slush fund, and the secret payments for Sam's medical and psychiatric bills. The stories prompted a rash of critical editorials—"Tarnished Image for McCall?" read one headline.

To the average voter, the sudden rush of news about McCall's finances was confusing and troubling. No one had accused McCall of illegality or wrongdoing, but the stories seemed to suggest that McCall—with one of the cleanest reputations in Oregon politics—was not above question.

McCall might have fought off these negative stories if he had been able to clearly answer one simple question: Why did he want to be governor again?

McCall fumbled for the answer. He pledged to "reinspire the team that has written the Oregon Story so well." But the Oregon Story, as McCall retold it, offered no fresh ideas, no talk about the future, only the past. And talking about the future was the one thing McCall did so well; it was what voters expected of him. However, the time away from government had distanced him from the day-to-day problems Oregonians wanted to hear a candidate talk about: taxes, schools, and crime. McCall instead talked of global issues. The drifting speeches left his staff and supporters wondering if McCall had the mettle to govern the state again.

As his campaign staff scheduled event after event, McCall showed resentment toward the enterprise. He still loved people, but the pains of age had slowed him, and the fire for victory that had once burned in him had grown faint and cool. Atiyeh and Martin were younger men whose groomed, well-financed organizations had speakers working for them all over the state. McCall's campaign had only McCall, a man who, with puffy eyes, thinning silver hair, and a sagging face, made voters weary just to look at him. Ted Hallock attributed much of McCall's woeful spirits to a drinking habit that finally had worn down his edge. "I just think he was fuzzy," Hallock says. "It's that simple. On issues, on announcing what he would do as governor, his thinking was fuzzy. The drinking diminished his acumen."

Perhaps as a result of this fuzzy thinking, McCall fell victim to campaign traps laid by his opponents that he should have recognized. Traditional strategy dictated that McCall, as front-runner, should avoid any forum that gave his opponents equal footing and publicity. When, in early March, Atiyeh and Martin issued a joint debate challenge, McCall made the politically wise choice to turn it down. "[W]hy should I rent the hall, pull the crowd so that lesser known people can use me as a dart board?" he said.

A few negative editorials followed McCall's refusal, as he might have expected. "Too arrogant to debate?" asked the *Capital Journal* in Salem. "Let McCall stand up so we can measure him," said another Salem paper, the *Oregon Statesman*. Rather than letting the criticism pass, McCall exploded. In earlier days, Westerdahl or Schmidt would have succeeded in buffering him in his anger, but his young staff, urging him not to accept the debate challenge, had no such hold on him. Without warning, he suddenly announced he had changed his mind. "I felt completely out of character," he said. "Logic may be on [the campaign staff's] side, but logic doesn't apply to me."

The decision to take part in the debates proved disastrous. Both Atiyeh and Martin knew that to beat McCall, they had to tear him down. "It was obvious," Martin said later, "that unless somebody really went

The toll of his failing comeback campaign was apparent on McCall, speaking here in March 1978. (Courtesy Eugene *Register-Guard*)

on the offensive against McCall—and that was me—[a McCall victory] would happen that way."

The shredding started in earnest in Eugene on 28 April, when McCall shared a stage with Martin and Atiyeh for one of their debates. The simple sight of McCall on stage with his opponents diminished him. "Tom looked tragic," Hallock recalled. "There were three people on the stand and, God almighty, here we have an 11-foot-tall giant looking miserable." Hallock said McCall seemed to shrink physically, hunching forward as if he were melting. "Here was a hero," Hallock said, "and it was as if he was saying to himself, 'These two guys are not as good as I am. What the hell are they doing here? Why am I here'?"

Martin pulled out the first knife in hopes of peeling back McCall's thin skin. "We knew that if he got mad he might say things that would hurt him," he recalled. Martin opened the debate with a sneering broadside: "Unlike Tom McCall, I don't think Oregon needs a king. I don't believe Tom is the only person possessing a divine right to be governor. Unlike Tom I'm not preoccupied with national titles or beauty contests. Tom's love affair with the LA *Times* won't solve [Oregon's] problems." Atiyeh joined in, albeit without the ruthlessness. He questioned McCall's record of helping business in the state and doubted McCall had the ability to lead Oregon again. Atiyeh knew when to hold back, and wisely promoted himself and let Martin throw the punches. "It was a very clever conspiracy," McCall would remember with bitterness. "[Martin] would just wreck me, knife me, rip me, and that was his whole campaign. Atiyeh went floating around like an angel . . . but the dirty work he needed to be done to dispose of me was done by somebody else."

Rather than respond with a characteristic outburst, McCall simply took the punishment and held his temper, as if the attacks were beneath his dignity. Henny Willis, the Eugene *Register-Guard* political reporter who had covered McCall for eleven years, watched in horror, stunned that McCall showed no willingness to defend himself. "I said to myself, 'That's not Tom McCall running up there. That's some Republican candidate'," Willis recalled. "Tom was so placid. Tom did not campaign as Tom. He tried to be a Republican. And it was forced and phony. In the old days he would have banged his fist on the podium and said, 'This is where I am'."

The Eugene debate became the pattern for later debates. Audiences arrived to see the legendary McCall and two men they did not know at all. They found a weak, uncertain ex-governor bewildered at the attacks unleashed on him.

"It was sad," Willis recalled. "It was just so sad to watch."

MERCIFULLY, THE DEBATES ENDED. The attacks did not.

In speech after speech, Martin and Atiyeh charged that McCall had wrecked the Oregon economy with his environmental gospel. Atiyeh especially accused McCall of putting up barriers to business by telling the world Oregon did not welcome newcomers. Martin, for his part, charged McCall with hypocrisy for "wearing two hats," one as an environmentalist and one as a booster of Oregon's economy.

McCall listened to these attacks with disbelief. Oregon's population and economy boomed in the McCall years and after. More than two hundred thousand people had moved into Oregon since McCall first said "visit, but don't stay." Certainly, he had been no concubine for corporate Oregon. He had tongue-lashed polluters and greedy executives who resisted his tax reforms. But he also had supported a wide range of programs to encourage business, including low-interest loans and bonds to companies expanding or moving into Oregon. He had even helped recruit a major high-technology company, Hewlett Packard, starting a trend toward a state computer industry later dubbed the "Silicon Forest." McCall had even passed the ultimate corporate litmus test of the 1970s: support for nuclear power.

Most of all, McCall saw environmental protections as being in the best interest of Oregon's business, as well as in the best interest of the state's citizens. He thought the land-use system was not stringent enough, and that tougher enforcement was needed to stop the "jungle of neon" and prevent planning decisions made by local officials "over a cocktail at the Elks Club." Was land-use planning not supposed to protect farm and forest land, and in turn, the state's biggest businesses? Were pollution controls not supposed to keep Oregon livable, so that businesses would want to move here?

No matter what McCall thought, business leaders did not see him as one of their own. Corporate money flowed into the Atiyeh and Martin campaigns, while McCall received only a trifle of support from Oregon businesses.

Battered by these attacks from pro-business opponents, McCall sought solace by turning to his old friends, the leaders of the state's environmental groups that had sprung to life during his years as governor. When he did, many of those very environmental groups shunned him.

In the decades since McCall's policies had launched an active environmental movement in Oregon, the rules had changed. The environmental movement had moved far beyond him. By 1978, the environmentalists' tests of loyalty were not just support of clean rivers and land-use planning, but opposition to nuclear power and herbicide spraying, support of expanding wilderness areas and lawsuits against the federal government to stop the harvest of timber.

McCall no longer met the environmentalists' tests. He considered the new environmental agenda often too extreme. In his years as governor, McCall had offered a clear doctrine to protect Oregon's land and beauty. The resources—its water, trees and land—were not supposed to be locked up under his doctrine. They were to be used, carefully, deliberately, prudently. "[Mine] is a pragmatic environmentalism. It's not treehouse environmentalism," McCall would say. "After all, you've got to eat." The "treehouse" environmentalists, McCall said, had discouraged Oregonians from "thinking as keenly about the environment. . . . They [the groups] can go into court and in 24 hours bring everything to a halt." Such tactics, he said, were "willful, childish, temper-tantrum" tactics.

His criticism brought a firestorm from environmental groups, who had thought of him as their ally. But he did not fully understand the wrath of environmentalists until he made a campaign stop in Eugene in mid-April. The trip was nostalgic for him. At the University of Oregon campus eight years earlier, McCall had launched the first Earth Day in the state with a passionate plea for environmental controls.

The audience had cheered then. It did not cheer now.

As part of his campaign speech, McCall told the Earth Week 1978 rally that nuclear power was a necessary evil until new sources of energy could be developed. He repeated his "Tarzan" theory of energy planning: "Never let go of one limb until you have hold of another." He warned that, without nuclear power, the region faced "brown out, black out, cold houses and cold food for children."

A few people started to boo him. McCall looked up, stunned. When a few people heckled, he lost his temper. "Damn it," he screamed at the hecklers, "I'm just telling you the tradeoffs!"

"Candidate Tom McCall appears to want to rewrite the Oregon story of which he seemed so proud in its unexpurgated version," one journalist reported of the mood among environmentalists in 1978. "Trouble is, environmentalists who used to be his strong supporters don't like the way he's editing it. . . . If he believes that responsible environmentalism stops with the Bottle Bill, I'm not going to like the epilogue to the Oregon story."

McCall understood the political attacks from Atiyeh and Martin, bankrolled as they were by Weyerhaeuser, Boise Cascade and other companies that had learned to hate him. The attacks from environmentalists, however, broke his heart.

Lonely, vilified by the corporate interests, considered a sellout by environmentalists, McCall was accused by everyone of changing, because each side remembered a Tom McCall who had never existed—a Tom McCall who wanted to turn back the clock and stop growth, or a Tom McCall who would protect Oregon's environment no matter the cost. But Tom McCall had not changed, only the times had.

Beyond the spiteful rhetoric of the 1978 campaign, he was beginning to see this change and his future—as short as that might be—and the sadness it would hold.

MCCALL REALIZED THE CAMPAIGN WAS OVER on 14 May, nine days before the election. That day, the *Oregonian* published a poll showing him holding a fourteen-percentage-point lead over Victor Atiyeh. An old hand at analyzing politics, McCall saw the meaning in the poll's fine print. The fourteen-point spread was among all Oregonians, not just among Republicans who would be voting in the primary. Among Republicans, McCall held just a slim six-point edge over Atiyeh. He could see that Atiyeh would soon pass him.

His young campaign staff rejoiced at the poll, however. "We thought we were where we should be," said aide Phil Keisling. "We didn't understand what the numbers meant. But he knew. You could see it in his eyes."

McCall had slipped in the polls because he had been campaigning as if speaking to the whole of Oregon, but the only voters that mattered in May were Republicans. He had not faced a contested GOP primary since he had beaten Homer Angell in his 1954 congressional race. He had won that race by showing himself to be more conservative than his opponent. Now, he was the liberal, the outcast—the bastard, as he had said before, at the GOP family reunion.

By then, McCall's campaign was in shambles and broke. His opponents would spend nearly $390,000 to McCall's $87,000. "Six months out you were supposed to worry about the money," said Hallock. "Six weeks out the money was a dribble." In his frustration, McCall lost his charm and exuberance, angrily berating his young campaign staff and drinking more than he should have.

Meanwhile, the press had hardly given Oregonians a warning that the legendary McCall was anything but a cinch to win. Election night, as a result, provided Oregon with an enormous shock. From the time the polls closed at 8 P.M., the returns looked to many people as if they were inaccurate: McCall trailed Atiyeh. As the night wore on, Atiyeh's lead held.

McCall had seen the result coming yet was unable to face reality that night. In the ballroom of the stately Benson Hotel in downtown Portland, McCall took the stage to cool applause and refused to concede. The closest he came to admitting defeat was an offhand comment to reporters, "I may have run once too often."

Across town, Atiyeh claimed victory. Tradition had it that the winner wait patiently for congratulations from the loser. But Atiyeh could not wait. He marched over from his party at the Mallory Hotel to the Benson. He said later he was going to comfort McCall, but to McCall, seeing Atiyeh walk into the Benson lobby, it seemed Atiyeh was trying to smugly extract a concession. By coincidence, as Atiyeh arrived, McCall was crossing the lobby, television cameras trailing him. McCall spotted Atiyeh in his hotel and turned on him. The cameras, Atiyeh learned later, were live, their pictures going directly out to viewers across Oregon. McCall loomed over him, chewing him out for his campaign of attacks and innuendo. Atiyeh meekly defended himself, but McCall glared down at him. "I'm not going to bicker with you," he said. "You've apparently got enough votes to win the Republican nomination." Finally, he allowed the squirming Atiyeh to slip away. The television cameras followed McCall as he walked into an elevator, eyes averted. The elevators doors closed, and he was gone.

McCall was never reconciled to his defeat or the mistakes that had driven him toward a comeback. In a matter of weeks, Tom McCall the Oregon political legend had been reduced to a second-place finisher behind a legislator he despised.

In the end, Atiyeh collected forty-six percent of the vote, aided greatly by the lowest voter turnout for a GOP primary in more than thirty years. McCall finished with thirty-three percent, and Martin—his more personal, negative attacks on McCall backfiring—crawled in with seventeen percent. The next day McCall issued a conciliatory letter to Atiyeh, although he refused to endorse him.

Although McCall knew that the Republican primary had not been a referendum on his popularity, in his heart he felt exiled from the state he loved. After all the years of success and the accolades for all he had done for Oregon, he saw himself reduced to what he had been after his 1954 race: a loser in a sure-win campaign, and a loser again buried in debts.

He faced tens of thousands of dollars in debts—a $35,000 second mortgage that had financed him through the campaign, medical bills for Sam—with no income. Although KATU-TV offered McCall his job back, he was not allowed to resume his duties until the general election concluded five months later.

Faced with financial ruin, Tom McCall did what for all of his life he had refused to do: he put his name up for sale.

McCall first lent his name to a fledgling company that wanted to lease state campgrounds and turn them into RV parks. The offer of five thousand shares of the company stock sounded lucrative and he lunged at the offer from the firm's promoter. The company went broke, leaving McCall with nothing but embarrassing news stories that questioned his connection to the dubious scheme.

The next time he sold his name again, it was for real money.

The Oregon ballot in November 1978 included an initiative measure intended to make it easier for public utility districts to form. Private utilities—with a virtual monopoly in the state since the 1930s—fought the measure with enormous bankrolls. Ron Schmidt's advertising firm handled the campaign for the utilities, and Schmidt arranged to pay McCall a $10,000 fee for appearing in ads that denounced the measure. His appearance opposing the public utility measure caused outrage in the press and among environmentalists. McCall tried to dismiss their response. "I wasn't bought," he grumbled. "I was borrowed."

On election night, 7 November 1978, Oregonians saw that McCall's bitterness had only intensified. He had not commented on the governor's race between the Republican Atiyeh and the Democratic incumbent, Governor Robert Straub, except once to tell a reporter he considered it a race between "Governor Blunderbuss and Senator Milque-toast." But on election night, McCall had his first chance to speak out, when KATU-TV welcomed him back on the air as a news analyst.

That night, McCall watched regretfully as Victor Atiyeh over-whelmed Bob Straub to capture the governorship. On the air, McCall first showed signs of conciliation. Then, the anchorman, Paul Hanson, asked McCall for his thoughts on the outcome of the governor's race.

Hanson had expected a few quips or insights from the former gover-nor. Instead McCall turned toward the camera, vengeance in his eyes. Without a script, McCall lunged into a rambling commentary, punctu-ated with spite. He wanted the last word on the election that should have been his own. He condemned Atiyeh for the state senator's petty attacks on McCall's legacy. He lashed out at the Republican party for its failure to anoint him.

Finally, appearing uncharacteristically out of control before a televi-sion camera, McCall spoke of Straub. Straub had failed as governor, McCall said, not for lack of talent, or lack of will, or lack of sincerity. "Bob Straub," Tom McCall said, "could never move out from under the shadow of Tom McCall."

McCall halted, his chin high, showing no regrets. The camera panned back to an ashen Hanson, speechless at the sudden fury that had just poured out over the airwaves on a cold November night.

SEVERAL DAYS LATER, as the Oregon press surveyed the 1978 elections, Don Bishoff, a columnist for the Eugene *Register-Guard*, felt compelled to study McCall in defeat. McCall's acceptance of the $10,000 fee from the utilities especially disturbed Bishoff, an admirer of McCall. He called the former governor to ask him why he had taken the money. During forty emotional minutes, McCall swung from regret to humbled reflection to heated ranting over his fate. He had needed the money, he told Bishoff. He did not want to sell his name. He did not have a choice.

Bishoff told McCall that, because of all that McCall represented, he had an image to uphold, and that he had let a lot of people down by doing it.

At that, McCall exploded in a singular outburst that bared his bruised pride. His defeat in the 23 May primary election had separated him from the state he loved. He had entered the race because he thought he owed more service to Oregon, but he had been wrong, for he now believed the state he loved no longer wanted him.

"Tom McCall was emancipated on May 23, finally," McCall said, "and he doesn't have to be a legend anymore, damn it."

22

Reckoning

NO ONE IN KINZUA believed the town's lumber mill would close forever. Like most mills in Oregon, the Kinzua plant would halt temporarily during slow times, but when demand for pine lumber grew again, the mill would reopen, and its blades would whine all night, slicing the giant logs harvested from the nearby hills. That was how the lumber business worked, not just in Kinzua but all over Oregon—boom to bust to boom again. Mills closed but always reopened, and the hills always had plenty of trees to cut.

Kinzua was one of the last company towns in Oregon, built in 1929 by the Kinzua Corp., which owned the sixty thousand surrounding acres of pine forest. The company owned the land, the homes, the store, and even the barber shop. Only one hundred fifty people lived in Kinzua, about the same number of people who worked in the mill. The stark beauty of the place made up for the isolation. The town, located in central Oregon's remote Wheeler County, was nestled near Thirtymile Creek and surrounded by ridges laced with scrub and pine.

The pine trees in the hills around Kinzua had been the source of the town's prosperity for three generations. Yet in all that time, few people had seen a year as good as 1978, when Oregon produced 8.2 billion board feet, the highest production level since 1950. The reason for the demand was simple: Americans, worried about inflation, anxiously built new homes to stay ahead of soaring housing costs. Demand for new homes meant a demand for lumber, and Oregon delivered.

Despite the boom in 1978, however, the Kinzua Corp. announced that the mill and the company town would close, not just for awhile, but forever.

The closing of Kinzua seemed to make little sense during those heady days for the timber industry. But boom times required two parts to the equation: demand for lumber and trees for cutting. For Kinzua, there were too few trees left to cut.

Overcutting of private forest lands in the 1950s and 1960s had left timber companies few places to find the logs they needed. They turned to the only source left—the federal forests.

The federal government owned millions of acres of virgin forest in reserve, managed by either the United States Forest Service or the Bureau of Land Management (BLM) under the practice of sustained yield. Federal law required the agencies to manage the lands prudently. The federal lands, were never intended to be the timber industry's chief source of logs. As a result, the number of trees the federal agencies could sell was strictly regulated. Yet in 1978, with the demand for lumber soaring, the industry was howling for more logs. What timber the federal government could sell went for record prices.

Like many other timber companies that had relied on private lands, Kinzua could not afford to compete with the frantic bidding for federal timber. Amid a feast, Kinzua starved to death.

The Kinzua mill ran for the last time on 26 May 1978. The company later dismantled the mill and tore down the empty buildings. A few newspaper stories noted Kinzua's passing, treating the company town nostalgically. None of the stories looked into the reasons for Kinzua's closing or asked what the town's demise meant for Oregon. It would have been an unfathomable leap of logic to suggest that the passing of Kinzua was a sign of things to come.

But Kinzua—once resilient, now flattened into rubble—was exactly that.

THE SCARCITY OF PRIVATE TIMBER and the high price of logs soon claimed more victims after Kinzua, and the victims were not small companies. The Champion International Corp. shut down its Roseburg stud and planing mills in May 1979. Located in Douglas County, which produced more lumber than any other county in the nation, the mill had provided seventy-five jobs. The next month, another timber giant, Georgia-Pacific, closed down its plywood mill in Coos Bay, a coastal port town west of Roseburg, and put two hundred more people out of work.

Americans continued to demand more new homes despite rising mortgage interest rates—ten percent in March 1979. Usually, when interest rates rose, home building slowed. But the demand remained high, and timber companies kept signing contracts for expensive federal timber, blind to the reality that bust always followed boom. "We had an artificial economy," one Oregon lumber executive recalled. "We were fat and sassy."

Then in October 1979, the government agency that controlled the supply of money, the Federal Reserve Board, undertook an aggressive new strategy to control inflation, which had reached thirteen percent that year. The Fed planned to tighten the money supply to make each dollar worth more. The result, in theory, would mean less inflation. Even if the strategy worked, however, it spelled economic woes in the short run. Milton Friedman, a pioneer of the monetary theory that the Fed was now following, admitted as much: "The alcoholic who goes on the wagon suffers severe withdrawal pains before he emerges in the happy land of no longer having an almost irresistible desire for another drink. So also with inflation." When, on 6 October 1979, the Federal Reserve Board tightened banks' access to money, the besotted economy began to dry out—and dry up. Mortgage interest rates climbed to fifteen percent by early 1980, and the rate of borrowing collapsed. No loans meant no new houses, and that meant less demand for Oregon's lumber.

Timber companies found themselves trapped. They had committed themselves to paying extraordinarily high prices for logs from federal lands just as demand for lumber vanished. Unable to sell the lumber to pay off their contracts, one company after another shut down. Six large mills in Oregon closed during the first week of April 1980, a time when mills should have been firing up their blades in anticipation of a new cutting season. In timber-rich Douglas County, mill closures within the month cost eight hundred more people their jobs.

By the next month, a staggering ninety-three mills had shut down and another seventy-three had slowed production. In less than a year, 13,519 timber jobs—one out of every seven timber jobs in Oregon—had vanished. The crisis spread beyond Oregon as well. The Western Wood Products Association reported that 44,000 lumber-industry workers had lost their jobs in twelve western states.

To many in the timber business, the downturn seemed like just another bust period, albeit a rougher one than most. Company and union officials refused to believe things would stay bad, even though the evidence was troubling. "Companies are operating on a week-to-week basis," one befuddled union official said. "Plants that have never shut down before are closing down now."

The mills kept closing—and they did not reopen. In towns where generation after generation had seen difficult times come and go, the realization that an era had ended did not sink in easily. When it did, however, it often left town residents devastated.

In Willamina, population 1,400, when Champion International Corp. shut down the mill that kept the town's economy afloat, few people worried. "It was like a vacation," one union official recalled. "Everybody went fishing." Time passed. Days and months came and went, and unemployment benefits ran out. At first the people of Willamina showed a granite resolve. "You don't even see them in the bars," said one local minister. "Most of them are staying home and brooding. You ask people how they're doing and they say 'fine.' It's not considered proper to admit that you're hurting."

Slowly, the resolve eroded. Willamina had always been a tough town, occasionally a bit rowdy, as timber towns tend to be. But by late 1980, a few months after the Champion mill closed, the town's normally friendly character darkened. Out-of-work men who once stayed away from local taverns returned to the bars with despair. Local police broke up more drunken brawls than ever before, and other alcohol-related incidents and crimes jumped by half. Although at first people had kept their problems to themselves, a local pastor and a psychologist soon reported a flood of townfolk coming to talk about their growing depression. "These are salt of the earth people," said one local counselor. "Not only do they feel they are displaced persons, but they have no other skills that they can translate."

In the port city of Coos Bay and the neighboring town of North Bend, together home to 24,000 people, three out of every four jobs were tied to the timber business. In mid-1980, 1,200 area mill workers sat idle. At the Port of Coos Bay, 500 longshoremen also had no work. Timber companies had been shipping raw logs overseas rather than milling them in Oregon, but the logs were now too expensive to ship.

For Coos County, it was as if everything that could go wrong did. Even the crab and salmon seasons were poor enough to force many out of business. Stores and smaller companies that relied on money spent by the local timber company employees began to close.

The human toll grew as well. Crime of all kinds increased, especially burglary. A local crisis center for battered women saw its caseload jump by five times in one year. Virtually all the cases were alcohol-related and involved out-of-work husbands or boyfriends, dazed and angered by economic circumstances they could not control.

Willamina and Coos Bay were only two towns stunned by the timber crisis. Similar scenes were repeated all over Oregon. In a state once proud, nothing looked the same anymore.

In March 1981, Oregon's unemployment rate hit 9.6 percent. By the end of 1981, it was up to 11.4 percent, well above the national rate of 8.9 percent and the highest ever in Oregon since records were first kept in 1947. In rural counties, the rate of joblessness was often twenty percent. The official number of Oregonians out of work reached 154,500. Another 15,000 had been unemployed so long they had disappeared from the rolls. Some 27,000 jobs in the Oregon timber business had vanished, and most would never return.

The cold statistics did not tell the entire story. For every job lost, a family faced bankruptcy and two more people in the community felt the effects. In time, the fortunes of timber towns in Oregon might reverse, but the torn fabric of a fading way of life could not be easily repaired.

Oregon had always held a promise for a better life. The Movers had come for that reason and so had generations that had followed. In late 1981, however, researchers at Portland State University (PSU) announced that Oregon's historic population growth had ended. In fact, the population of Oregon was dwindling as people fled the state.

The residents of Oregon's mill towns did not need big-city professors to tell them that news. They had seen their communities abandoned, one house at a time. "These suddenly jobless people still have children in school, bills to pay," one union official said. "And their only hope for another job is to pull up their roots and move elsewhere." In Coos Bay, the manager of the area's U-Haul rental trailer chain reported seven moving trailers leaving town for every one that came in.

Scores of Oregon communities had once survived as one generation after another carved a life out of the woods. That life had disappeared, and the next generation felt betrayed. "We raise [our children] believing it's never going to die, that the trees will always be there," said one woman who had lost her mill job. "Then they see it crunch up under them."

Added a union official who watched the sad migration out of Oregon, "They tell their friends that it's only temporary, but in a lengthening recession like this, Oregon may have lost them forever."

WHEN HE TOOK OFFICE in 1979, Victor Atiyeh could not foresee the economic calamity that was coming. The 1979 legislature allocated $3 billion for the next two years, an all-time spending increase for state government. Lawmakers even turned $70 million back as tax refunds, leaving almost nothing in the state's rainy-day fund as a hedge against stormy times. When jobs started to disappear, so did the income tax revenue to run state government. Lawmakers had to convene for an extraordinary budget-cutting session in August 1980 and cut $127 million out of the state's budget to keep it in balance.

The Oregon media made the state's woeful economy their top story. Unemployment statistics, once buried deep in the financial section, jumped to page one, as the Oregon press monitored the jobless rate like a doctor watching the heartbeat of an ailing patient.

Corporate leaders took the opportunity to bemoan the state as a whole. Oregon was unkind to business, they said. Taxes were too high and environmental rules were too tough. "Oregon should be more pro-business than the average state," said the chairman of Georgia-Pacific, just before his company moved its headquarters from Portland to Atlanta.

Although Atiyeh echoed the sorrowful chorus of complaints by Oregon's corporate and business leaders, he understood what was driving the economy down: the outrageous cost of new homes, the high price of lumber, and mortgage rates hitting fifteen percent. Atiyeh hoped to revive Oregon's economy, and he launched an economic development crusade to recruit new and diverse industries. However, of all of Oregon's problems, Atiyeh concentrated on the state's image.

The image of Oregon, he said, had been badly damaged over the years by its "visit, but don't stay" reputation. How can we lure new industry with such an image? he asked. He declared Oregon "open for business" and pledged to change the state's image for the better.

The notion that Oregon's image was to blame for the state's titanic recession soon became part of the conventional wisdom. Few journalists or politicians paused to question the dubious idea that changing Oregon's image could solve the state's problems and lure new business.

Blaming Oregon's image, however, was an easy excuse for the state's leaders. Oregonians in the throes of a economic crisis did not want to hear long-winded explanations, anyway. People wanted something, or someone, to blame, someone who could be held responsible for Oregon's problems, both real and imagined. They soon found that person. They found Tom McCall.

AS 1979 OPENED, Tom McCall was still coming to terms with his election loss the previous spring. "I was thrown out trying to stretch a double into a triple," he said. He also saw the folly of having run as a Republican. "Damn fool!" he exclaimed. "I was stupid to get caught with all those moneybags against me." In defeat, he finally did in 1979 what he had always threatened to do while in power: he quit the Republican party and became an independent.

Despite the election loss, his appeal remained high in and out of Oregon. He remained a popular fixture delivering commentaries for KATU-TV, and received many speaking requests from around the country. He campaigned for bottle bills in the capitals of neighboring states: Olympia, Washington, and Sacramento, California. "It is the most demonstrable bridge we have between a wasteful and a husbanding society," he said of Oregon's Bottle Bill. "Its features include so many values we must learn to embrace [in] this coming age of new economic realities and conservation." Most of all, McCall still championed Oregon itself. "We're the lead domino in the domino theory," McCall said. "How many innovations would have died aborning, perhaps never to be heard of again, if the domino called Oregon had been an easy pushover?"

In May, environmental groups in Colorado invited McCall to talk about land-use planning. Colorado's governor, Richard Lamm, had recently reacted to citizen pressure to curb sprawl in his state and belatedly called for tough land-use laws such as Oregon's. McCall arrived, surveyed the political scene and concluded that Lamm—like so many other politicians McCall had seen—had acted too late. The sprawl around Denver, McCall told his Colorado audience, would make land-use laws like "nitpicking over how to dress a corpse."

The most disturbing experience on the road for McCall in 1979 was in Cleveland. Ohio had put its first container deposit law on the statewide ballot for November and, as usual, the beverage and container industry, McCall said, was spending millions to spread lies. Before the Cleveland City Club, McCall debated a vice president of Continental Can, one of the bottle bill's most ardent corporate foes. At one point, the corporate vice president declared: "Gov. McCall, don't you try to foist the Luddite ways of the people of Oregon on the people of Ohio."

The remark confirmed for McCall what he had suspected all along: the anti-bottle bill campaign was being used against Oregon itself. "The Oregon Bottle Bill laid the seeds of trouble in powerful corporate board rooms around the country," McCall said later. "They are trying to get us by running down our reputation. In the rarefied atmosphere of right-wing boardrooms, there is some resentment."

The attacks on Oregon frustrated McCall. If he were governor, he said, he would be fighting back. But he was not governor, and no one else stood up to take on the fight.

MCCALL'S PERSONAL TROUBLES INCREASED when his brother, Samuel Walker McCall II, died in his home in Bakersfield, California, in February 1979. Sam was the youngest son of the McCall family, and by most accounts, the warmest, the sweetest and the smartest of all the McCall children. He became a respected history professor at Bakersfield College, yet he had never escaped the wrath of his mother, who bad-gered him relentlessly. He died at age fifty-nine. Doctors said it was due to a heart attack. His twin sister, Jean, however, thought Sam's early death was due to his drinking.

Sam's death meant more than the loss of a brother to Tom. A few years earlier, the family had transferred Westernwold's title into Sam's name to avoid the inheritance taxes on the ranch when Dorothy died. Everyone had assumed Sam would live the longest. Now the McCalls faced the inheritance taxes on Sam's estate. No one wanted to sell Westernwold, least of all Dorothy, now ninety. She still swept through the chilly house, ignoring the sagging beams and worn carpets, seeing only her father's glory. Nonetheless, in September 1980, the ranch went up for sale for $2 million. Almost two years later, the ranch sold for just $450,000. A final irony: the family that bought the ranch was moving in from California.

AS THE 1970S CLOSED, McCall despaired at what he saw happening to the state he loved. "I've never seen so much doubt and suspicion as I do now," McCall told a reporter in late 1979. "We have gone from believing all the best of the future to believing all the worst. We have to stop thinking in terms of crises; a job or a mission is thinkable, a crisis is not."

Author Studs Terkel visited McCall in 1979 to interview the former governor for his upcoming book, *American Dreams: Lost and Found.* Terkel, who had visited McCall four years earlier, found him melancholy.

"I'm sort of shattered, but I'm still useful," McCall sighed to Terkel. "I'm just living day to day, making speeches, and challenging the know-nothings and trying to tell the people that they're being heard again. And wondering, where is the glow of yesteryear? Wondering where the heroes went. Gosh, I don't know how long ago they left."

The notion of heroes stayed with McCall for a moment.

"Heroes are not giant statues framed against a red sky," he said. "They are people who say: This is my community, and it's my responsibility to make it better. Interweave all these communities, and you really have an America that is back on its feet, a comfortable nation to live in again."

"I think," Tom McCall added, "we're gonna have to reassess what constitutes a hero."

IN SEPTEMBER 1980, McCall received a high and unexpected honor. Dr. Rene Dubos, a renowned scientist and environmentalist, invited him to serve as executive chairman of a new center to study the relationship of man and technology to the earth. Dubos was the seventy-nine-year-old Pulitzer Prize winner whose writing on the environment had helped inspire the United Nations, ten years earlier, to hold its first environmental conference. Dubos' work in bacteriology had led to the development of antibiotics, but he had turned his attention to broader concerns. In his books, including *So Human an Animal* and *A God Within*, published during the 1960s and 1970s, Dubos was a leading critic of society's growing worship of technology, and he decried the decay of the environment. He established the Rene Dubos Center for the Human Environment at Rockefeller University, where he taught. On a 1980 trip to Oregon, he met McCall. The two found they had much in common, not the least of which were their environmental views and their relationships with the Rockefeller family. As executive director of the center, McCall would remain in Portland, but would help direct the center's forums.

A year or two earlier, McCall might have attacked the new job with his usual vigor. But for all his spirit, he was, at age sixty-seven, aging quickly. His hair had turned all but white and he tired easily. He complained often of pains in his back, and his right knee, first injured when he was in high school, hurt intensely. McCall might have slowed down, just a little, but he could not afford to. His KATU-TV commentaries and his speeches paid the bills.

McCall's speeches of 1981 had a familiar target: Ronald Reagan, now president. McCall may have been disappointed by Jimmy Carter's environmental record, but he knew Reagan too well to expect anything but a weakening of purpose. Speaking to a conservancy group in Pine Mountain, Georgia, in February 1981, one month after Carter had left office, McCall said that Reagan "cannot hold a candle to Jimmy Carter as an environmentalist."

Time proved McCall right. Reagan appointed as his Secretary of the

Interior James Watt, an anti-environmental activist who proposed opening federal land preserves for oil and gas exploration. In April, addressing an audience at Washington State University (WSU) in Pullman, McCall labeled Watt "Dirty Water Jim" and a "crafty exploiter of the public resources." With his appointment of Watt, McCall said, Reagan had "thumbed his nose at the entire environmental community and Tom McCall in particular."

The WSU speech revealed his growing bitterness. He lashed out at his audience, telling them they were incapable of protecting their land as Oregon had. "You just don't have the attitude to do it," he grumbled.

Something in McCall's mood that night suggested that he was more than simply irritable, however. He was clearly in pain, grimacing as he sat down, wincing when he stood up. On 27 April, a few days after returning from Pullman, McCall entered Good Samaritan Hospital and Medical Center in Portland for tests. The local press gave McCall's admission into the hospital big play, however, McCall remained uncharacteristically quiet about his ailment.

The word soon leaked out. The cancer had returned.

The cancer had reappeared along his spine, a small, malignant tumor clinging to his fifth vertebrae and causing McCall severe pain. Doctors suggested that he could reduce the cancer's growth by reducing the hormones in his body, so on 29 April, McCall underwent a fifteen-minute surgery to remove his remaining testicle. As usual, his surgery became big news in Oregon, and he later remarked on the public nature of his most intimate operations. "I don't ever expect to read again about my testicles on page one," he told reporters as he left the hospital.

McCall remained outwardly upbeat. However, weakened and disheartened, he struggled through each day, collapsing in exhaustion each night under the burden of his work and declining health. "They say take it easy," McCall said, "but they never tell you how."

He saw that he could not rest, however. The final assault upon his work had begun.

The attacks began anonymously and slowly, so slowly that McCall did not awaken to them until they had overwhelmed him.

At first, he could not see the source of the attacks. News stories examining Oregon's economic woes began citing the state's image problems, hinting that they dated back to McCall's "visit, but don't stay" statement. Many stories cited it ironically while noting the ongoing flight of Oregonians from their state in search of work. Soon, the press and politicians began generally noting McCall's statement as a cause of Oregon's image problems. "People throughout the country still view Oregon as not welcome for business," said Atiyeh's economic development chairman at one point, although he did not offer any evidence to support his claim.

Eventually, the whisper campaign struck at McCall directly.

He first waved off the charges as idle talk. But when talk continued, he was flabbergasted. He had not even been governor for six years. How could he be blamed for powerful economic forces outside Oregon, or the dwindling supply of timber? Moreover, Oregonians had embraced his doctrine and cheered his "visit, but don't stay" declaration. Now, by the press and state leaders, Oregonians were being told the doctrine had ruined the state's economy and that McCall had been anti-business. How could his famous statement, taken out of context of the times, be used so cruelly against him?

One of the few publications to address the charge was *Oregon Business* magazine, which granted McCall a long interview in September 1981. In the interview, he deftly defended his record and his policies, and he cited the state's economic strength during his years as governor despite his "visit, but don't stay" slogan.

> My famous speech, that one, was that we just don't like rattle, bang, grime and dirt. We don't have any astonishingly tough rules in Oregon that you have to obey. You join our club and we'll welcome you with open arms. But if you're a polluter then pollution control ought to be part of your business. At the same time, you can't eliminate the last pinch of stink. The last pinch of pollution is unreachable economically. You see? I wasn't mad or zany.

The interview underscored, once again, that times had changed and McCall had not. He believed that the doctrine he had introduced as governor could not be followed only when convenient or popular. The protection of Oregon's land and resources had to be toughest at times such as these, when pressure mounted to trade livability for jobs at any price.

In the *Oregon Business* interview, McCall had tried to defend himself with logic and facts. Rather than bolster his side, though, the magazine interview triggered a new round of stories assigning blame. "Is Fiscal Slump McCall's Legacy?" asked the Eugene *Register-Guard* in a headline in October 1981. The newspaper offered no evidence, nor did it quote any accusers willing to step forward and be named in the blaming exercise. McCall alone defended himself, and his patient tone started to dissolve.

"I've been called a lot of things over the years," McCall said, "but being called a no-growth guru is the one that hurts the most. I've never been no-growth. I just insisted on measured, prudent growth." McCall insisted Oregon's image had been damaged not by him, but by the slander of Bottle Bill opponents. The problem, he added, lay not in his record, but in the current cowardice of Oregon's leaders. If he were governor now, McCall then ventured, he would disregard the "Reagan bootlickers."

His protests could not halt the tide of accusations, though, and soon national newspapers that had once been eager to tell the Oregon Story joined in. The *Wall Street Journal* in October 1981 helped heap blame by quoting an unnamed state official as saying, "We have an image problem." The paper went on to report: "That image was shaped under former Gov. Tom McCall, who invited outsiders to visit briefly and then get out, lest they ruin the place." The New York *Times* in March 1982 dramatized the depths of Oregon's recession in timber-dependent communities, and then added: "This has happened in a state where a governor, Tom McCall, took pleasure 10 years ago in making a speech that included such lines as, 'Come visit us again and again, but for heaven's sake don't move here'." Neither paper had asked McCall for his defense.

He fought back from KATU-TV's commentary desk as best he could. But fight back at whom? He swung at vapors, and he saw the futility in the battle.

In November 1981, Atiyeh declared a state of disaster in Oregon's timber industry. Nearly half the mills in Oregon were closed or slowed to a crawl. As 1982 began, and Atiyeh stared at a campaign for re-election, things were much worse. State financial analysts told him Oregon was running $237 million in the red. By the time he called the legislature in for an emergency session, the analysts admitted they had underestimated the deficit by another $100 million. All told, the state's deficit equaled ten percent of its total budget. On 18 January, Atiyeh declared Oregon was in an economic crisis.

Lawmakers spent thirty-seven angry days in special session quarrelling over how to cut the budget, only to have to return twice more that year to do more cutting. McCall could only watch the goings-on with despair. When asked about the condition of Oregon, McCall replied, "I cry for it."

THE ONSLAUGHT WAS CRUEL in its timing, as McCall tried to defend himself, sick as he was. His home life grew worse at times, too. After seventeen years of coddling a drug addict son, McCall thought troubles with Sam could grow no worse, but they did. Sam McCall was thirty-four years old and still completely dependent on Tom and Audrey. His drug binges increased, eroding McCall's will and reserve. One day while in the KATU-TV newsroom, co-workers noticed McCall was especially worn and distressed. He explained he had awakened the night before and found Sam unconscious on the floor, overdosed. He had called for medical help and, in the morning light, regretted his decision to do so. "Why did I have to wake up?" McCall asked, his eyes suddenly filled with tears of guilt and anguish. "If I hadn't awakened, you see, he might be dead, and all of this might be over now."

The greatest fear of the McCalls' friends had always been that Sam would lash out violently and injure or kill his parents. Finally, in late 1981, the violence took over. On 21 November, McCall appeared in public on crutches. He told a reporter he had been in the hospital for a knee injury, then gave a convoluted account of how he had hurt himself slipping on an ice cube while in the kitchen. His story might have been true, but friends and family said later that Sam had assaulted his father. On the very day McCall appeared on crutches, he and Audrey asked a Multnomah County judge to grant a restraining order against Sam. In a sworn affidavit, Tom and Audrey said they "at times have been victims

Tom McCall at work in his study, 1981. He tried to defend himself against growing attacks on his legacy, but early on underestimated their intensity. (Courtesy of the Eugene *Register-Guard*)

of abuse committed by Respondent [Sam] in that Respondent has caused bodily injury to them."

Amid the pain of his public fate, McCall had finally faced a horror at home he could no longer bear.

ON 2 APRIL 1982, McCall received another reminder of his own mortality.

At ninety-three, his mother, Dorothy Lawson McCall, had still demanded the world's attention. She had never lost the Lawson flamboyance, never for an instant. She had not stopped her late-night phone calls, oiled as they were with her evening serving of Manhattans. Her health remained good, except for an increasing deafness that made her usually one-sided telephone conversations even more so.

Even as Tom's fame grew tarnished, Dorothy, always the proud mother, loyally clipped out news stories about him and pasted them in her scrapbook. The stories about his failing health were tucked neatly away in a separate envelope. On the first day of April, she had clipped a story about the Natural Resources Council of America giving McCall an achievement award for his environmental work.

The next day, Dorothy, alone in her apartment, reached for the telephone. Before she could finish dialing, her heart stopped. When they found her, Dorothy Lawson McCall was dead on the floor.

The proudest Lawson of all, Dorothy had fought to preserve her father's greatness, her son's fame, and her own place in it all. She had done so for years with the bombast taught her by Thomas Lawson. The telephone had been her weapon and her death was fitting: when they found her body, the telephone receiver was gripped tightly in her hand.

FOR DOROTHY'S FUNERAL, McCall returned to Westernwold, which had not yet been sold, where his surviving brothers and sisters had gathered. In quiet moments, he roamed about the old house, physical pain evident on his face, his breathing labored. He stopped at the shelves in the living room and pulled down the dusty books Dorothy had read with such flourish at the fireside each night sixty years earlier. These books had given him his power of words, his love of language, and her tales had told him of his family's force and strength. Where was that force now? Where was that strength?

When he returned to Portland, his doctors grew concerned about his increasing pain. They found the tumor in his back had grown, although they found no sign that it had spread. He re-entered the hospital and began cobalt treatments to shrink the tumor and take pressure off his back.

No sooner had the latest sapping of medical treatments begun than he faced another blast: "Does McCall Quip (Visit but Don't Stay) Still Hurt?" asked the *Oregon Journal* in a blaring headline. "[T]he seemingly innocent McCallism has come back to haunt Oregon in the hard economic times of the 1980s," the story said. Unlike previous pieces, the *Journal* story actually named two of McCall's accusers: Governor Vic Atiyeh and Senate President Jason Boe. "It would be unfair to say that Tom did not work for economic development," Atiyeh said cautiously. "But it's strange how that phrase stays on and becomes larger than life when you're trying to get industry to locate in Oregon." Boe seconded that, but offered no anecdotes to support his claim.

The *Journal* also quoted former governor Robert Straub, his longtime rival and compatriot, in McCall's defense. "[Tom] is misunderstood and maligned by people who don't know the facts," Straub said.

McCall's own response—buried at the bottom of the story—lacked the vigor of his previous responses. "There's always in time of recession a lot of scapegoats," he said.

McCall had tried defending himself with logic and patience, but the time for logic and patience had passed. It was, as he said, a time for scapegoats.

Finally, the attacks on Tom McCall went one step too far. On 5 April 1982, while McCall buried his mother in Redmond, a group calling itself Oregon Citizens for Fair Land Planning announced plans for a statewide initiative campaign. The ballot measure the group put forward would, if passed, abolish the state's powers to control land use.

McCall had seen repeal efforts launched against Oregon's land-use planning laws before, and seen them all fail. His friends told him not to worry, that this measure would fail, too. But he knew better than anyone how the times had changed. Where compassion had once ruled, fear and panic now set in.

With the news of the assault on the state's planning laws, the one achievement he hoped would live on, McCall abandoned hopes of his own recovery. He poured the strength he needed to survive his cancer into a final battle, for he feared his legacy for Oregon, once strong, was dying, just as he was.

23

To Smite a Few More Bastards

OREGON HAD ENTERED a dangerous time. In the third year of recession, the state's vital signs flickered. More than 150,000 Oregonians, nearly one out of eight, officially were without work. Outside Portland, the level jumped to one in six. Although the rest of the nation knew pain as well—interest rates hovering at sixteen percent, home sales plummeting to forty percent below 1978 levels, bankruptcies hitting levels as high as any since World War II, and nearly ten million Americans out of work—Oregon had sunk earlier, faster and deeper. "Oregon is as green and beautiful as ever this spring," wrote *Washington Post* columnist David Broder in May 1982, "but there is a climate of fear that seems alien to this setting."

McCall sensed the fear, and he knew that fear had a ravenous appetite.

He considered the passage of Senate Bill 100 his greatest single achievement as governor, and he championed the way in which the bill allowed for both growth and the protection of the state's precious lands for the future. When he had introduced land-use planning to Oregonians, he had heard protests and grumbles, yet Oregonians had supported it—voting twice to sustain it at the polls.

When the new initiative to repeal Oregon's planning laws first surfaced in April 1982, McCall recognized that the transformation of the state meant the land-use laws were not safe. Early polls in 1982 showed that McCall's instincts were correct: Oregonians by a two-to-one margin told pollsters they favored abolishment of the Land Conservation and Development Commission (LCDC) and the planning laws the agency oversaw.

He recognized that many Oregonians were actually voicing frustration at the bureaucracy, not at the intent of the planning laws. Reasons for their frustrations abounded. Nine years after the passage of SB 100, the LCDC had yet not finished its basic work and local governments still had not completed their plans for growth. McCall understood the pressure on local officials—and the state's role as their backstop. "These local officials are playing with the hottest fire out there and it's up to the state government to give them some support and to set some standards for them," he said.

The state, however, proved painfully picky in reviewing the plans submitted by local governments, in large part because the watchdog group McCall had helped form, 1,000 Friends of Oregon, kept up the pressure. No other group had a more dramatic effect on land use in Oregon. Its director, Henry Richmond, saw that land use was a blank slate and that zealous efforts by 1,000 Friends could tilt the laws toward conservation. Without comparable opposition from developers, 1,000 Friends chose its battles carefully, filing cases that set precedents. "If it hadn't been for us," Richmond boasted years later, "land-use laws would have been interpreted into mush."

Meanwhile, 1,000 Friends, the LCDC and other land-use proponents were losing the public relations battle. Opponents—namely, timber and real estate companies that wanted no restrictions on the way they could exploit land—pointed to the snarl of court cases and legal challenges as proof land use was an unworkable nightmare. The complaining had a receptive audience: Oregonians in a statewide poll had recently placed unemployment far at the top of their day to day concerns, well above concerns for the environment.

McCall saw that the program needed an image boost. He criticized former governor Robert Straub for utterly failing to champion the program. And he questioned 1,000 Friends' zeal, albeit not the group's motives. "Henry," McCall pleaded with Richmond at one point, "we all have a little schlock in our hearts. You need to allow for a little schlock now and then."

The debate surrounding the LCDC never answered the key question, however: Was land-use planning working?

So much energy had been spent fighting over plans that no one yet knew if the system worked. Growth had yet to put pressure on the local plans or the laws. To the average Oregonian, the state's grand experiment in planning had devolved into a jumble of rules and legal follies in which only lawyers seemed to profit.

McCall saw that land-use planning's image, just like Oregon's image, was under attack. Governor Victor Atiyeh soon gave McCall the opportunity to start to fight back.

Although Atiyeh earnestly believed that Oregon had to reverse the state's image as unfriendly to newcomers, not everyone apparently agreed. A prankster in southern Oregon erected a sign on the Oregon-California border warning that locals would shoot every seventh Californian coming into the state. Local residents took down the sign, but not before a photograph of it had run in newspapers statewide.

When he saw the photographs, the taciturn Atiyeh exploded in a rare, visible fury. He demanded at a cabinet meeting that the state take immediate, dramatic action to counteract this terrible publicity. Atiyeh then remembered the official state border sign welcoming Californians on Interstate 5. The sign read, "Welcome to Oregon, We Hope You Enjoy Your Visit." To Atiyeh, the sign implied that Californians—or anyone else—were not welcome to stay. It was then that Atiyeh said the state should blow up the sign—literally—by rigging it with dynamite.

Atiyeh settled on blacking out the words "We Hope You Enjoy Your Visit." He planned a media event at the sign and took the extraordinary step of inviting McCall to appear at the ceremony, as Atiyeh said later, "to be the speaker at the funeral of his own prose."

McCall quickly accepted. When he told Ron Schmidt of the event, Schmidt said that Atiyeh was setting him up for more embarrassment and ridicule. "Vic thinks he's trapped me," McCall replied. Schmidt then realized that McCall had plans of his own.

It was there, at the border of California during July 1982, that McCall made his stand. He made the painful flight to Medford and suffered the drive down Interstate 5 to the border sign. He waited patiently while

Atiyeh made his colorless remarks about Oregon being open for business, and when the television cameras panned to him, he turned the tables.

He started by mocking Atiyeh's event and the governor's original plan of igniting dynamite under the sign—"Wouldn't a little paint be more reasonable?" he said he had counseled Atiyeh. "A little less like Arafat?" Atiyeh, appearing pained at McCall's side, remained silent.

Then McCall defended his image and his work for Oregon.

> There's been a lot of bad mouthing about "visit, but don't stay." It served its purpose. We were saying "visit, but don't stay" because Oregon, queen bee though she is, is not yet ready for the swarm.

If Oregon's image was really the issue, he asked, then how could anyone forget the fame the state had enjoyed under his leadership? The "visit, but don't stay" comment may have appeared inhospitable, but it also had provided the state with an allure that McCall cautioned should not be abandoned.

> I am simply saying that Oregon is demure and lovely, and it ought to play a little hard to get. And I think you'll all be just as sick as I am if you find it is nothing but a hungry hussy, throwing herself at every stinking smokestack that's offered.

As if waking from a stupor, Oregon listened to words it had not heard for so long, and heard a voice that, like a recurring dream of years past, was sweet and familiar. If Oregonians had forgotten what he stood for, he now had reminded them. And he had alerted them that the fight was on.

ON 3 AUGUST, McCall was suddenly overcome with dizziness and again entered Good Samaritan Medical Center. Doctors believed he was suffering from an inner ear infection that had affected his equilibrium, but further tests produced mortal news: the cancer on his spine had gone on an unexpected rampage through his body, marching around his chest, into his ribs, and scaling his spine to the base of his skull. Doctors guessed he had six months to live.

Why now? He had only started to fight back. He tried not to despair, and soon accepted his lot for what it was. His physician, David Rosencrantz, suggested McCall slow down and try an easier schedule. That request, Rosencrantz admitted, was "like talking to the wind."

Upon his release from the hospital, the press declined to report the obvious, that his cancer was terminal. They left the mortality of the news for McCall to announce. He was not yet ready to do so, however, recognizing the power such an announcement could carry and wanting to wait for the right moment to unleash it.

Instead, as reporters greeted him as he left the hospital, he told them how he felt. "I'm restless," he said. "I may be headed for Valhalla like a bat out of hell."

THE CAMPAIGN TO ABOLISH OREGON'S LAND-USE PLANNING laws had won an early battle. Supporters of the measure had collected the fifty-four thousand signatures required to place their initiative, Ballot Measure 6, before the voters in November. Land-use opponents had also employed cunning language to confuse matters. The measure asked, "Shall the state's land use authority and goals be advisory only. . . ?" Only upon close, careful inspection was it clear that the answer "yes" meant abolishing the LCDC and erasing McCall's dreams.

Once the measure reached the ballot, the true face of the land-use opponents became public. The group was not just a collection of anti-government landowners. It included the most powerful players in corporate Oregon. Associated Oregon Industries, the state's strongest business lobby, came down hard for repeal of land-use laws. So did Associated General Contractors, the state's largest development group. The list of timber companies that followed with giant financial contributions was a who's who of Oregon corporate power: Boise Cascade, Georgia-Pacific, Louisiana-Pacific, Publishers Paper, Weyerhaeuser. At least twenty-six timber and lumber firms joined together to try to pass the measure—a bitter irony considering the industry's track record toward land-use planning and the overcutting of Oregon's woods.

To his credit, Governor Vic Atiyeh resisted the enormous pull to join the campaign to repeal land-use planning. While opposing the measure, Atiyeh nonetheless criticized the LCDC as a collection of "nitpickers" and agreed the program needed reform. He ordered a blue-ribbon investigation of the agency. The resulting report found much of the problem lay in the way his own administration ran the agency. The report also issued a firm conclusion: Despite the nightmarish claims of the repeal advocates, no evidence existed that land-use planning laws hurt Oregon's economy.

A new generation of corporate power agreed. High-technology giants, such as Tektronix, Hewlett-Packard, and athletic shoemaker Nike, all fought the measure, believing that land-use planning helped the economy by identifying land for commercial development and by reinforcing zoning around their business sites. Atiyeh recruited companies such as these—cleaner manufacturers and businesses that diversified the state's natural resource-based economy.

Supporters of land-use planning soon formed "Citizens to Defend Your Land" and commissioned a poll in September to see where they stood. The results were grim. After nine years of support, Oregonians had turned against their land-use laws—and done so with a vengeance. A whopping fifty-one percent of Oregonians said they were likely to vote for abolishing the LCDC. "Almost everyone who wanted to repeal land-use planning was firm in their convictions," said Tim Hibbitts, the campaign's pollster. "No one was about to change their mind. This was a solid majority willing to tear it all down."

The campaign turned to other numbers in the survey to seek reassurance. They found little. Only twenty-five percent of voters said they would vote to save land-use planning, and that support was soft. The campaign had only sixty days—and little money—to reverse the trend against the planning laws.

Hibbitts' poll revealed one small glimmer of hope, however. He had asked voters whom they would trust to talk about land-use planning. Overwhelmingly, Oregonians had named Tom McCall. "Having McCall as a spokesman on the issue will substantially increase the visibility of the measure, and alert the voter to just how much is at stake," he wrote in a strategy paper for the campaign.

"We realized we had to get Tom involved," Eldon Hout, one of the campaign's organizers, recalled. "As if we could have kept him out."

Indeed, McCall wanted in. Everyone knew he would play a role. But what would it be? His employer, KATU-TV, vetoed his proposed appearance in campaign commercials, and McCall, burdened with medical bills, could not risk losing his job.

But he knew he did not need to make a commercial. His standoff with Atiyeh at the California border had rekindled public interest in him, and the press had started to follow him again. In late September, the Oregon Shores Conservation Coalition gave McCall the Oswald West Memorial Award, named for the governor who had first protected the state's beaches. Rather than giving a polite acceptance speech, McCall delivered a harsh attack against Ballot Measure 6, recalling the passion he had raised among Oregonians in 1967 when public ownership of the beaches had been challenged. "They want us to give up the gains we've made," McCall boomed, "to turn our backs and let the speculators build wall-to-wall condominiums."

It was the old McCall again, and the press loved it. "No matter how momentous the victory is," McCall said, "no environmental milestone is secure."

IN SEPTEMBER, McCall had undergone cancer treatments in an experimental program at Virginia Mason Hospital in Seattle. The treatments had had little effect, and he knew he must make careful choices about how to use his time. He was scheduled to appear with William Reilly, president of the Conservation Foundation, at a dinner for opponents to the land-use repeal measure in early October. McCall was supposed to simply introduce his friend Reilly, but he told the campaign staff to tip the state's media. He planned to say a few words. No one in the press should miss it.

On 7 October, sixty supporters crowded into a basement room at the University Club in downtown Portland. The campaign had invited John Hayes, an *Oregonian* reporter, to record McCall's words, and the campaign had provided for a film crew. McCall went to the microphone, and his haggard appearance struck many people. He hobbled as he walked, and his eyes had the look of a weary man searching for a distant rest.

He had not yet publicly acknowledged he was dying. He had waited for the right moment. Now, he had found it.

"I haven't much time left," McCall began. "This is my last chance to talk to you about this."

His familiar voice rose as if he were a long-neglected conscience looming over Oregon. In all that he said that day, McCall offered courage to the state he loved. He found none in its current leaders, trembling in the face of crisis. The lack of courage—courage that he had once given Oregon—had now left the state adrift.

> I see people wringing their hands over what an awful image we have. Well, I want to know what the hell happened to the image I left. I'm upset that the power structure around here has become the "cower" structure. We are whipped by the economy judging by the extent we are groveling in apology for our business image. . . .
>
> I do resent the decline in Oregon's self-esteem and the scapegoating of the McCall years as somehow to blame eight years later. It would be a poorer nation and world if people no longer have Oregon to rely on for the pioneering of imaginative ideas.

His frustrations vented, McCall moved quickly to the issue that concerned him most.

> There is no brighter jewel in the Oregon diadem of innovations than [land-use planning]. If you really want to signal to one and all that Oregon is down—that we can't even agree on what we are doing, that we are ready to quit—just pass Measure 6 and totally repudiate the Oregon mystique.

He looked into the sad eyes of those in the audience, and he barely paused.

You all know I have terminal cancer—and I have a lot of it. But what you may not know is that stress induces its spread and induces its activity. Stress may even bring it on.

Yet stress is the fuel of the activist. This activist loves Oregon more than he loves life. I know I can't have both very long. The trade-offs are all right with me.

But if the legacy we helped give Oregon and which made it twinkle from afar—if it goes, then I guess I wouldn't want to live in Oregon anyhow.

He finished and looked away. No one moved; no one spoke. Few in the room could keep from crying.

The words of the dying Tom McCall appeared the next day on the front page of the *Oregonian*, and then flashed across the state and nation, unleashing a flurry of stories, columns and editorials praising McCall's candor and courage that had been long absent in Oregon.

"Now is the time to plan for growth, not abandon the state's goals until what Oregonians cherish is paved over," wrote one columnist. "If Oregonians cannot hold onto the livability they boast so much about, who in the world can?"

"Oregon owes Tom McCall something better than the repudiation of his dream for the state," the Salem *Statesman Journal* declared a few days later. "To throw this all away with passage of Measure 6 . . . would be to blind ourselves to the vision of Oregon's great future which motivated—and motivates—a Tom McCall."

THE POLITICAL SURVEYS taken in September 1982 were categorical: Oregonians wanted land-use planning cast aside. The September survey taken by the measure's opponents had shown the measure passing by twenty-six points. Another, conducted by Bardsley & Haslacher for the *Oregonian* in early September, showed a twenty-one-point lead.

The *Oregonian* had commissioned a new poll, and the survey was in the field when McCall gave his impassioned speech. The results, published 19 October, startled even the experts: support for the measure had disintegrated. The survey found only a four-point gap, a sign opposition to the measure was surging.

"We had done almost nothing in the way of campaign against the measure," said Tim Hibbitts. "We didn't have the money to run a media blitz. The other side had these corporations pouring in big bucks to kill off land-use planning.

"We had one weapon. Tom McCall. There was no other way to explain it. Alone, Tom McCall told Oregonians what he believed in. McCall alone changed its course."

His declaration of his own imminent death, linked as it now was to preservation of the state's land-use laws, drew the national press once more to him. Before election day, the Associated Press and United Press International wrote stories on Oregon's land-use fight. This was followed up by putting McCall on both the NBC evening news and the "Today" show. Terry Drinkwater, the CBS reporter to whom McCall first gave his "visit, but don't stay" quote, also produced two separate stories on McCall.

In late October, McCall used his failing strength for a side trip into California where voters would decide the fate of a statewide bottle bill then on the ballot. He arrived at a San Francisco news conference to promote the measure looking worse than ever. He needed a cane to walk. His clothes hardly fit him. His shirt collar, once snug around his thick neck, now hung gaping. Still, he was becoming famous again, and reporters from all over California jammed the news conference to hear his charge. "For the things I believe in," he said, "I'm going down fighting."

For the first time in years, Tom McCall felt useful again, and he tried to make up for lost time. At an appearance at an outdoor school camp in rural Clackamas County, McCall criticized the "wailing in high places" and Oregon's "so-called leaders' groveling apology" for his legacy. "To scapegoat the McCall administration, which hasn't even been in office for eight years, is the refuge of weak, frightened men."

When a reporter asked him if that was a veiled attack on Governor Vic Atiyeh, McCall snapped, "Don't consider it a veiled attack. It wasn't a *veiled* attack."

"I want to die in the saddle," he told an interviewer a few days before election day. "I want to keep working on the causes that have meant so much to my life." Clearly growing weaker as the days passed, McCall said he was determined to carry no regrets to his death. "Everybody is

McCall, in November 1982, pondering the fate of Oregon, and the remainder of his life. (Courtesy of the Eugene *Register-Guard*; OrHi 90788)

allowed a death-bed wish, for Christ's sake," he said. "There's no use going, when you go to your last bedding down, thinking, by God, why hadn't I fought harder closer to the end? Why didn't I use the last of my power?"

His mailbox filled with letters of hope and cheer. To one old friend, who had applauded his final fight, McCall wrote that the battle "stimulated this ancient frame to live it up again because the challenges that set my jaw remain, in general substance if not in exact form. So you bolstered my resolve to stick around, workable, for awhile, to smite a few more bastards."

THE EFFORT TO PASS BALLOT MEASURE 6 emerged as one of Oregon's most expensive initiative campaigns of 1982, and in state history. In all, advocates of repealing land-use planning spent $206,760, more than one-fourth of which came from timber companies. Opponents of Measure 6 only mustered $126,524 to fight land-use planning's repeal.

On election day, 2 November, a solid majority—565,065 voters, or fifty-five percent—said they wanted to preserve land-use planning. Of all the initiative efforts to repeal land-use planning, the 1982 vote had come the closest to passing. The repeal measure passed in twenty-three of Oregon's thirty-six counties, and only the overwhelming majorities in the urban counties had defeated the measure. Tom McCall had made an unmistakable difference in the results.

On election night, McCall, resting at home, told a reporter his faith in Oregon was restored. "It was just great to see," he said, "that the response is still there to leadership that goes out for a cause."

With the joy of this last victory, he found solace, and, finally, he could rest.

24

No Final Victory

YOU'RE TERMINAL from the minute you arrive," Tom McCall said, in late 1982. "You've been going to go ever since you got here. Still it is unacceptable when the calendar hints that the prospect has lost its open-endedness. Despair strikes you and what was vaguely inevitable is barely down the road anymore."

McCall's campaign had taken a greater toll on his health than he had imagined. He continued to write and deliver his television commentaries, joking to colleagues at KATU-TV of his declining physical appearance. "I don't want to look too awful or I'll have to go back on radio," he said. Eventually he could no longer make the trip to the station, and KATU-TV sent a camera crew to his house where the gaunt McCall taped his commentaries while sitting at his dining room table.

He entered Good Samaritan hospital in late November for eight days, and when released took strong pain medication to ease the agony of the cancer that had burrowed into his bones. On 14 December, Audrey became concerned that McCall's medication was not correct and checked him back into Good Samaritan for observation.

He never left the hospital. The next morning, McCall awoke, unaware of where he was, and tried to get out of the raised hospital bed. His bad knee failed and he crashed to the floor. The accident created a hematoma in his back that required surgery. He showed signs of improvement Christmas Day, and opened a few of the hundreds of presents sent him by well-wishers around the state.

Two days later, McCall contracted pneumonia, and he turned his mind to death. To visitors he talked incessantly of the defeat of Ballot Measure 6 and the need to be vigilant against future threats to his legacy. Privately, he worried about his son, Sam, once again living in his parents' house. He expressed deep guilt about leaving Audrey alone to deal with their son's problems.

Other than McCall's family, Ron Schmidt spent the most time at McCall's bedside. Schmidt had been, in many ways, closer to McCall than his own sons had been. Together they discussed plans for McCall's funeral, and Schmidt kidded McCall about the old days, when despite Schmidt's best efforts to coordinate news events, McCall would rush to reporters and scoop his own office.

Despite the pain McCall laughed at the memory, and the irony, as they planned McCall's last event. "Now all we need," Schmidt said as he chuckled, "is for you to die on a Saturday, so your obituary will appear on the front page of all the Sunday newspapers."

McCall laughed again at the thought. "Well," he replied, "you know I've always tried to cooperate with your needs."

After the 28 December news of McCall's pneumonia, press reports on his condition stopped due to McCall's final request for privacy. Soon after the start of 1983, Tad McCall arrived at the hospital from his home on the east coast and was shocked by his father's deterioration. On Friday, 7 January, McCall appeared suddenly peaceful. "He said that he had enough of the pain," Tad McCall said. "I guess I didn't know it at the time. He was saying good-bye."

Audrey, Tad and Sam stayed awhile longer that night, then left for home. Later, a hospital official called Ron Schmidt to tell him McCall had entered what doctors called the "terminal phase." Schmidt reached the hospital after midnight to find McCall sleeping. He took McCall's hand and talked and reminisced. When a nurse entered to attend to McCall, Schmidt asked her, "Can he hear me?"

"Just keep talking," the nurse replied.

Schmidt kept talking until three in the morning when, exhausted and hoarse, he could no longer contain his emotions. Distraught, he went

McCall in the State Capitol's rotunda. (Courtesy of the Eugene *Register-Guard*)

home to wait. McCall, alone, never awoke. By ten minutes before eight that morning, 8 January 1983, he was dead.

The news of Tom McCall's death flashed across the state. By noon, reporters had solemnly gathered outside the McCall home, where Governor Vic Atiyeh had come to pay his respects to Audrey. After awhile, Audrey emerged and greeted reporters. "I had him for forty-three years," she said. "It wasn't enough."

The reporters quietly turned and left to file their stories. Outside, the sky was white, the day was quiet. It was a Saturday. The obituary would make it into the Sunday papers after all.

MCCALL'S DEATH came at the darkest moment for Oregon. The state had failed economically as he had failed physically, as if the decline of the man and the state were in synch. During the month in which he died, January 1983, Oregon posted the worst unemployment figures of the recession, 12.5 percent. The next month, the number of jobless in Oregon dropped slightly and kept improving until the recovery had run its course. That recovery would be as bitter as the recession itself: within three years the Oregon timber industry was producing as much lumber as it had before the crash, but with nearly thirty thousand fewer workers.

Oregon had already become a vastly different place, a state suddenly self-conscious of its past glories and fame. That fame had come from environmental protection—namely, the protection of Tom McCall's widespread arms stretched across the Oregon border—and carried an important lesson.

What saved Oregon's economy—what brought people back to the state—was not the contrition practiced by politicians but the invaluable character of its land and rivers and air. People came to Oregon because of the place—a place of surviving beauty that one man had cherished like no one before. The Bottle Bill had become the precursor to the national push toward recycling. Energy conservation had become a standard nationally. But in the months and years that followed, Oregon would continue to carry its reputation as an environmental leader, often in reputation only.

The recession had given those who opposed McCall and his dream a fierce new stature. The safeguards—the Land Conservation and Development Commission (LCDC) and the Department of Environmental Quality (DEQ)—were still in place, but these agencies were not always the watchdogs they once were. Land-use planning survived, and the economic recovery tested the program's ability to control growth for the first time.

Meanwhile, at the time of Tom McCall's death, the Willamette River, once running clean, grew polluted again. The list of pollutants that concerned scientists, including dioxins produced by pulp mills, had grown well beyond those first regulated in McCall's time, and the environmental regulations had not kept pace. Even the American Can plant, built in 1967 and touted as having the most modern controls, was now itself long out of date. When the DEQ celebrated its twentieth birthday, state officials claimed the Willamette was the nation's longest river still meeting local and federal pollution standards, but they admitted that oxygen levels often slipped below those necessary to sustain life.

McCall had inspired an environmental movement that had grown beyond what he thought was proper. Environmentalists had expanded their fights, using the courts to halt timber harvests. The legacy in McCall's absence was not balance, but polarization and division. His determination that jobs did not have to be traded to protect the environment seemed too often forgotten.

Oregon's future was as murky as the fog-shrouded night of McCall's funeral in the Oregon State Capitol. His body lay in state in the building's rotunda, and an estimated six thousand people came to pay their respects. The night of the service, 12 January 1983, the state came to a halt, out of respect for McCall and because of the dense mist that filled the Willamette Valley. Television stations across Oregon interrupted their programming to broadcast the funeral. At McCall's request, the services were held in the Oregon House of Representatives chambers with no reserved seating. At his funeral, as he had all his life, McCall wanted no one's status to reign. He wanted the public—as it came to him, one person at a time—as his congregation.

Governor Victor Atiyeh had won a second term in November 1982, and, as frustrated as he had been that McCall's fame had overshadowed his own, Atiyeh nonetheless had delivered touching words at McCall's funeral. He noted that McCall had once wondered aloud what it took to become a hero. "Wonder no more, Tom," Atiyeh said in his eulogy. "You have shown us what constitutes a genuine hero."

Later, pallbearers carried McCall's casket of Ponderosa pine to a hearse outside. He was to be buried the next day in Redmond, not far from the graves of Hal and Dorothy Lawson McCall. But due to the weather, the state police escorts did not know whether to put the casket in a plane for the trip or drive it across the mountains. While decisions were being made, the hearse idled at the Capitol's front door, its lights glowing in the fog.

As McCall's hearse waited at the curb outside, Atiyeh, followed by a few friends and aides, walked back to the governor's office after the funeral. As they reached the breezeway outside the office that opened to the rotunda, Atiyeh peered out through the tall front windows and spotted the crowd around the waiting hearse.

"Haven't they gone yet?" Atiyeh asked.

There was a long silence.

"No," someone standing nearby finally replied. "Tom doesn't want to leave."

Notes

Abbreviations used in the Notes

CJ	*Capital Journal* (Salem)
CKD	*Copper King's Daughter*, by Dorothy Lawson McCall
DLM	Dorothy Lawson McCall
DLMP	Dorothy Lawson McCall Papers
FOIA	Freedom of Information Act records
KATU	KATU-TV Tape Library
NYT	New York *Times*
OHS	Oregon Historical Society
OJ	*Oregon Journal* (Portland)
OR	The *Oregonian* (Portland)
OS	*Oregon Statesman* (Salem)
OSA	Oregon State Archives
PA	Presidential archives
RG	*Register-Guard* (Eugene)
RUR	*Ranch Under the Rimrock*, by Dorothy Lawson McCall
SJ	*Statesman-Journal* (Salem)
TM	Tom McCall
TM:M	*Tom McCall: Maverick*, by Tom McCall with Steve Neal
TM:Tapes	Oral history produced for *Tom McCall: Maverick*
TM:OHS	Tom McCall Papers, Oregon Historical Society
TM:OSA	McCall Administration Papers, Oregon State Archives
WSJ	*Wall Street Journal*

WP   Washington *Post*
WW   *Willamette Week*
UOSC   University of Oregon Special Collections

Prologue

1   the sign: this often-told myth is repeated by O'Donnell, *Oregon Blue Book*, 1991-1992, p. 400.
     "In their own time": Clark, *Eden Seekers*, p. 5.

2   Eden: Northwest history is replete with references to the Oregon country as "Eden." In particular, see Clark, *Eden Seekers*.

4   "Where the future works": *Newsweek*, 1/7/74, p. 49.

5   "Come visit us again and again": RG, 2/14/71, p. 10B.

7   Atiyeh wanted to blow up the sign: KATU.
     "Governor McCall will now be": KATU.
     "I want the terms of this understood": and remainder of McCall quotes: KATU.

Chapter 1

Key Sources

Thomas Lawson: Lawson, *Frenzied Finance*; Weinberg, *Muckrakers*; Holbrook, *Age of the Moguls*; *National Cyclopedia of American Biography*, Vol. 26, pp. 23-24. Dorothy Lawson McCall's memoirs were helpful, as was a valuable forty-part series on Lawson's life appearing in the Boston *American* in December 1923.

Sam McCall: Evans, *Samuel W. McCall*; Hennessy, *Four Decades of Massachusetts Politics*; Massachusetts Historical Society *Proceedings*, December 1923 and May 1924; Howe, *Later Years of the Saturday Club*.

13   the thousand-acre dominion he called Dreamwold: for description of the estate, CKD, pp. 53-75.
     a tower of kings: *Historic Preservation*, Sept.-Oct. 1993.

14   The chimes signaled Tom McCall's birth: no newspaper record could be found recording McCall's birth. The chiming of the Dreamwold tower bells for the birth of Lawson's grandchildren was a tradition: NYT, 10/12/13; author's interview with Jean McCall Babson.

Lawson ordered that his horses be shot: Samuel Walker McCall II, oral history, TM:OHS 35.

the Lawsons lived amid slums: Boston *American*, 12/1/24; interviews with Jean McCall Babson.

he watched as one sister died: interviews with Jean McCall Babson.

15   "I have been shoveling gold": CKD, pp. 1-7.

first fortune: Weinberg, *Muckrakers*, p. 261; Filler, *Muckrakers*, p. 172; Holbrook, *Age of the Moguls*, p. 169; Boston *American*, 12/1/24.

"most powerful weapon": NYT, 2/9/25, quoted in Weinberg, *Muckrakers*, p. 261.

Grand Rivers: Filler, *Muckrakers*, p. 172-173, 175; Boston *American*, 12/11/24.

16   gems in his pocket: Boston *Globe*, 2/9/25.

Lawson built one with seven: CKD, p. 72.

"smacked too much": Filler, *Muckrakers*, p. 176.

the New York Yacht Club refused him: Filler, *Muckrakers*, p. 177.

$30,000 to have a hybrid carnation: Filler, *Muckrakers*, p. 176.

He threw away tens of thousands of dollars: CKD, p. 84; Filler, *Muckrakers*, p. 177; Terkel, *American Dreams*, p. 331.

"responsible for more hell": Lawson, *Frenzied Finance*, p. 1.

17   outsmarted them: Holbrook, *Age of the Moguls*, p. 170.

Amalgamated Copper Co.: Lawson, *Frenzied Finance*, generally; Filler, *Muckrakers*, p. 177; Malone, *Battle for Butte*, p. 137-40; Sonnichsen, *Colonel Greene*, p. 139; Holbrook, *Age of the Moguls*, p. 170-73.

18   "Go your limit": Holbrook, *Age of the Moguls*, p. 172.

$5 million fee: Boston *American*, 12/19/24.

"The System": Filler, *Muckrakers*, p. 179.

"The people had dreamed": Filler, *Muckrakers*, p. 171.

"[T]here was a strange streak": Reiger, *Era of the Muckrakers*, as quoted in Weinberg, *Muckrakers*, p. 263.

"Lawson Panic": Sonnichsen, *Colonel Greene*, p. 139.

19   reclaim his stature: Weinberg, *Muckrakers*, p. 262; Filler, *Muckrakers*, p. 180.

inspired the Securities and Exchange Commission: Boston *American*, 12/19/24.

Lawson went wild with grief: interview with Sandy McCall; CKD, p. 7; Boston *American*, 12/5/24.

20   "Old Roman": Evans, *Samuel W. McCall*, p. 38, 44; Howe, *Later Years of the Saturday Club*, p. 343.

21   "an intellectual thoroughbred": Evans, *Samuel W. McCall*, p. 35; Howe, *Later Years of the Saturday Club*, p. 340.
"Sam McCall's voice": Boston *Globe*, 11/5/23.
"the backbone of an angleworm": Boston *Transcript*, 11/5/23.

22   by record margins: McCall once received the largest majority ever given a Massachusetts congressional candidate. Evans, *Samuel W. McCall*, p. 28.
thirty-one ballots: Boston *Globe*, 1/14/13; Hennessy, *Four Decades of Massachusetts Politics*, p. 186-87.
"To exaggerate the depths": Mayo, in Massachusetts Historical Society *Proceedings*, May 1924, p. 510.
"became obsessive": Storey, in Massachusetts Historical Society *Proceedings*, December 1923, p. 187.
the path of the McCall ancestry: Evans, *Samuel W. McCall*, p. 10.
Too many laws: Mayo, in Massachusetts Historical Society *Proceedings*, May 1924, p. 504; Evans, *Samuel W. McCall*, p. 4-5, 43.

23   corrupt practices act: Evans, *Samuel W. McCall*, p. 22-24, 26-27; Howe, *Later Years of the Saturday Club*, p. 337-38; Hennessy, *Four Decades of Massachusetts Politics*, p. 16.
winning election to Congress: Maisel, *Political Parties in the United States*, p. 351; Abrams, *Conservatism in a Progressive Era*, p. 35; Howe, *Later Years of the Saturday Club*, p. 338.
"severe and clean cut": Slayden, *Washington Wife*, p. 195.
"his characteristic independence": Howe, *Later Years of the Saturday Club*, p. 338.
McCall ran for governor: Evans, *Samuel W. McCall*, p. 45; McCoy, *Calvin Coolidge*, p. 66; Hennessy, *Four Decades of Massachusetts Politics*, pp. 218, 211.

24   compromise candidate for president: Hennessy, *Four Decades of Massachusetts Politics*, p. 244; Boston *Globe*, 11/5/23; newspaper clips, DLMP; Boston *Transcript*, 11/5/23; OR, 12/19/71, p. NW7.
illness and age: McCoy, *Calvin Coolidge*, p. 76.
vigorous campaign: Boston *Globe*, 8/8/18.

25   "repugnant to my inclination": Boston *Globe*, 8/20/18.
Dorothy Lawson, for one: CKD, generally; interview with Jean McCall Babson.

26   "The Lawsons had more charm": interview with Jean McCall
          Babson.
      She had known Henry McCall: undated clipping, "Harvard Man
          wins Lawson girl as bride," DLMP; Boston *Globe*, 7/26/09.
      he loved the game so much: interview with Jean McCall Babson.
      "sensational": Harvard *Crimson*, 6/18/08.
      began courting Dorothy: CKD, p. 113-117; RUR, pp. 2-4; interview
          with Jean McCall Babson.

27   pretended to try to drown herself: interview with Jean McCall
          Babson
      to perform an abortion: interview with Jean McCall Babson. DLM
          makes no mention of the abortion in her memoirs, although she
          talked of it publicly later.

28   "I know a fellow": DLMP.
      the state already worried about its growth: for early Oregon history;
          generally, see Dodds, *The American Northwest*; Carey, *General
          History of Oregon*; Merk, *The Oregon Question*; O'Donnell in
          Oregon Blue Book, 1991-92; Clark, *Eden Seekers*.
      "Oregon welcomes the man": *Oregon Almanac*, p. 5.

29   "City bred people": *Oregon Almanac*, p. 319.
      well-attended brothels: MacColl, *Shaping of a City*, pp. 401-410.
      "The rain came": RUR, p. 8.

30   Hal's health: Samuel Walker McCall to Hal McCall, 3/31/11,
          DLMP; CKD, p. 138-39; RUR, pp. 9, 15-21.

32   "Without forage": Clark, *Eden Seekers*, p. 38.
      Westernwold: Redmond *Spokesman*, 12/14/11 and 8/22/55; CKD, p.
          150.

33   "The family used to say": interview with Jean McCall Babson.

Chapter 2

34   painful arrival: interview with Jean McCall Babson.
      stays in Oregon: no precise record could be found to determine
          exactly when or how long the McCall children lived at Dream-
          wold, but a combined total of four years is a minimum, based on
          various records. The longest stay lasted more than two years,
          from the spring of 1919 to October 1921. CKD, pp. 176, 180;
          Central Oregonian, 10/6/21, p. 5; enrollment records, Derby
          Academy, Hingham, Massachusetts, and Crook County School
          District, Prineville. For DLM's effort to obscure how long she

kept her children at Dreamwold: OR, 11/19/54.

"They had the run": interview with Alma Litchfield.

35   "sweeping terraces": CKD, p. vi.

vowed she would never go back: interviews with Jean McCall
   Babson, Dorothy "Bebs" McCall Chamberlain.

Derby Academy: Clarke to Merrill, 9/22/69, TM:OHS Box 35.

"I found myself": CKD, p. 179.

36   "Granddaddy was king": interview with Thomas Lawson II.

"Everyone more or less": interview with Thomas Lawson II.

"magic spell": CKD, p. vi.

threatening divorce: interview with Jean McCall Babson.

he sank the Guggenheims: Green, *Gold Hustlers*, pp. 110-20;
   Filler, *Muckrakers*, p. 187.

37   "If the ship": Boston *Globe*, 9/6/54.

$200,000 a year operating costs: NYT, 10/7/22.

fiery populist speeches: Boston *Globe*, 8/23/18.

"No one could influence": OR, 12/19/71, p. 7.

Lawson did sap the Republican vote: Hennessy, *Four Decades of
   Massachusetts Politics*, p. 263.

Lawson's limousine overturned: Boston *Globe*, 10/24/18; NYT,
   10/24/18; Boston *American*, 12/5/24.

38   fitful midnight wanderings: interview Jean McCall Babson.

Massachusetts convicted Lawson: NYT, 3/26/20, 4/22/20.

The McCalls fled: the date of the McCalls' return to Oregon is
   uncertain. DLM was vague about the period of their stay at
   Dreamwold. The best evidence of timing is a report of the
   family's return in the *Central Oregonian*, 10/6/21, p. 5, which
   reported, "Henry McCall returned to Prineville the first of the
   week from Boston, Mass., where he, with his family, has been
   spending the summer. Mrs. McCall and family are in Portland at
   the present." If accurate, the news item fairly marks Tom's final
   return from Dreamwold and is consistent with other evidence:
   Clarke to Merrill, 9/22/69, TM:OHS Box 35; CKD, p. 180-181;
   interviews with Dorothy "Bebs" McCall Chamberlain, Alma
   Litchfield.

debts of $180,000: NYT, 12/13/23.

39   gave Lawson $550: Holbrook, *Age of the Moguls*, p. 174.

At his death: NYT, 4/9/23, 10/13/22, 10/14/22, 11/22/23; Boston
   Globe, 2/9/25, p. 1.

DLM . . . could not return: NYT, 2/11/23.

"It was such a change": interview with Dorothy "Bebs" McCall
Chamberlain.

Tom cared little about money: interviews with Jean McCall Babson, Sandy McCall.

McCall traced his own love: among many sources, Willis Tapes.

40   "My father was a hell of a good guy": Willis Tapes.

"no place for a dairy": interview with Charles McCormack.

line of credit: Crook County Recordings, 2/20/22 and 10/6/22.

could not afford decent feed: interview with Andrew Schmidt.

routinely shut off the ranch's electricity: Shattuck to Hal McCall,
1/12/25, DLMP; interview with Jean McCall Babson.

"The gold coins were gifts": interview with Maude Butler Knorr.

lawsuits: Crook County Courthouse, Buick, Case No. 4011; equipment, Case Nos. 3303, 3495, 3780; workers unpaid, Case Nos. 3153, 3439, 3445; state of Oregon, Case Nos. 3448, 3718. Nine of ten recorded judgments against Hal were by defaults.

41   "He finally gave up": Beck Tapes.

"because of the hat": interview with Jean McCall Babson.

"My husband was ashamed": Terkel, *American Dreams*, p. 332.

"I'm sorry you are holding": Shattuck to Hal McCall, 1/12/25, and
Shattuck to DLM, 1/22/25, DLMP.

"When she started a fight": interview with Maude Butler Knorr.

42   "I used to see dad go roaring": Beck Tapes.

with a shotgun: interview with Jean McCall Babson.

Her suicide threats: interview with Jean McCall Babson.

"We whistled through [the books]": KATU.

43   "She taught us what it meant": interview with Jean McCall Babson.

"that energy and the ability": interview with Maude Butler Knorr.

"He was a curious child": interview with Dorothy "Bebs" McCall
Chamberlain.

"My granddaddy was the governor of Massachusetts!": interview
with Dorothy "Bebs" McCall Chamberlain.

"It was reckless play": interview with Maude Butler Knorr.

"To my mother, life was this stage": interview with Jean McCall
Babson.

44   "She seemed to be punishing": interview with Dorothy "Bebs"
McCall Chamberlain.

weighed down with Harry's resentment: interviews with Sandy

McCall, Dorothy "Bebs" McCall Chamberlain.
"The World": DLMP; RUR, pp. 139-47.

45   Tom worked at expanding: interview with Richard Devers.
"Each of the children": interview with Maude Butler Knorr.
"He was the picture of innocence" and other quotes and descrip-
tions of TM at school: interview with Maude Butler Knorr.

46   "an uncoordinated, clumsy": TM:M, p. 2.
"I couldn't go into a room": TM:M, p. 2.
"drab nobody": McCall to Andrew Schmidt, 7/14/82, given to
author by Schmidt.
"He always could figure ways": Redmond Spokesman, 1/12/83,
p. 3.
"I was much better writing about [sports]": TM:Tapes 2.

47   hocked the pearl-handled revolvers: Terkel, American Dreams, p.
332.
delays forced him: interview with Jean McCall Babson; TM's
academic transcript, University of Oregon Registrar's Office.
moonshine: interview with Susan Knowland.
Harry's determination to punish: interview with Lagrande
Houghton.
"At Harry's direction": interview with Lagrande Houghton.
"a gregarious soul": TM:M, p. 3.

48   "Chas, ol' pal": interview with Charles Heltzel, Muriel Heltzel.
a drunken McCall: interview with Robert Lucas, Frank Nash.
an even C average: TM transcript, University of Oregon, Registrar's
Office; TM:M, p. 3.

49   To graduate from the journalism school: Turnbull, Journalists in
the Making, p. 56.
"He had the smarts": interview with Malcolm Bauer.
"He wasn't the least bit worried": interview with Richard Devers.

50   thesis earned him only a C: TM transcript, University of Oregon
Registrar's Office.
Inter-Fraternity Council: Oregon Daily Emerald, 10/11/35, p. 1.
impromptu write-in campaign: interview with Grant Eade; Oregon
Daily Emerald, 5/7/35, p. 1, 5/14/35, p. 1; TM:M, p. 4-5.
"We weren't protesting": interview with Robert Lucas.

51   "I intend to be President": interview with Frank Nash.
"That 'forgotten man' campaign": interview with Robert Lucas.

Chapter 3

Key Sources
TM's naval service: TM's letters to Audrey and DLM, September 1944 to
    August 1945, located in TM:OHS and DLMP.

53   "Louis would pound": interview with Dick Westwood.
      "Louis was never happy": interview with Bill Anderson.
      "movie scoop": TM:M, p. 6.
54   "Girls to Tom": interview with William Brown.
      "He was a witty": RG, 11/24/74.
      "He was amazing": interview with E. J. "Mike" Sullivan.
55   "He could hardly see": RG, 11/24/74.
      "He was not a lady's man": interview with Art Crossler.
      "I had a little gambling": TM:Tapes 2.
      "What he meant": interview with E. J. "Mike" Sullivan.
      "He was lousy ": interview with William Brown.
      "fell in love with the slot machines": TM:Tapes 2.
      "Every week he got his paycheck": interview with Ruth Brown.
      "I can remember going to the Elks": interview with E. J. "Mike"
          Sullivan.
      "He was playing the slots too much": interview with William
          Brown.
56   McCall often paid his debts: interview with Bill Anderson, William
          Brown.
      "On some occasions, the air in our tiny": TM:M, p. 8.
      hoped his reporter would grow out: interview with Audrey McCall.
      "Everybody read that column": interview with Dick Westwood.
      "His column was especially popular": interview with Ruth Brown.
57   "Unsung as a multiplier": Idahoian, 10/5/40, p. 6.
      "A spot of rhyme": Idahoian, 11/7/40, p. 6.
      "horizontal Hades": Idahoian, 10/14/40, p. 6.
      [A] couple of the west's: Idahoian, 10/14/40, p. 6.
58   "Knights of the Underwood": Idahoian, 3/13/42, p. 6.
      "this darling blond girl": TM:M, p. 6.
      "a very hungry reporter": interview with Audrey McCall.
      "I hadn't had anything to eat": TM:Tapes 2.
      "this hungry, hard-writing": TM speech, 9/17/74, author's files.
      Audrey Owen had grown up: interview with Audrey McCall.

59   "Tom, you made an ass of yourself": interview with Darrel Buttice.
      "I can't remember how many times": interview with Audrey
          McCall.
      "He didn't see any of [the money]": interview with William
          Brown.

60   "Every down-on-his-luck guy": interview with Ruth Brown.
      "This love of the land": interview with E. J. "Mike" Sullivan.
      "Those farmers were not too receptive": interview with E. J.
          "Mike" Sullivan.

61   "Tom could speak so well": interview with E. J. "Mike" Sullivan
      "I'm interested": interview with E. J. "Mike" Sullivan
      "It was always understood": interview with Audrey McCall.
      "[I]n 1940, Mayor Bill Anderson": TM:M, pp. 7-8.
      "The word was out": interview with E. J. "Mike" Sullivan.
      turned down the city leaders' offer: *Idahoian*, 9/20/74; RG,
          11/24/74; TM:M, p. 8.

62   running that year for the first time: city of Moscow records.
      "Why would I want him to run": interview with Bill Anderson.
      "I do remember": interview with Bill Anderson.
      His tenure in Moscow ended: *Idahoian*, 9/24/74; RG, 11/24/74;
          TM:M, p. 10-11.
      "tiff with Boaz": interview with Art Crossler.
      "Louis just canned me": interview with Bill Anderson.
      "Marineau just felt it was time": interview with Audrey McCall.

63   skulked out of town: TM:M, p. 10-11.
      $1,200 in debts: TM:M, p. 6.
      "He just grew up": interview with Ruth Brown.
      "hostage to my creditors": TM:M, p. 10-11.
      McCall had been told by the military: interview with Audrey
          McCall.

64   "I saw this tall, Lincolnesque": interview with Hollis Goodrich.
      "He had a good command": interview with J. Richard Nokes.
      "A lot of us were good": interview with Hollis Goodrich.
      "By-lines were like winning": interview with Audrey McCall.
      "He [was] an emotional": interview with J. Richard Nokes.
      "He took great pride": interview with Hollis Goodrich.
      "I'll kill that son of a bitch": interview with J. Richard Nokes.

65   "He loved to play poker": interview with Don McLeod.
      offered McCall a job: TM:M, pp. 12-13.

"He was such a wreck": interview with Arden Pangborn.

McCall adopted his middle name: Arden Pangborn; TM:M, p. 41.

66   "I think you'd be great": interview with E. J. "Mike" Sullivan.

"You don't understand": interview with Arden Pangborn.

67   "Heavens": interview with Audrey McCall.

"I had a great job": TM:M, p. 13.

"elderly idiot": TM to Audrey McCall, 11/9/44, TM:OHS Box 1.

McCall spent a frustrating four months: TM naval service files, National Personnel Records Center, Military Personal Records, service number 884 12 62; TM to Audrey McCall, 1/22/45, TM:OHS 1.

"make a name": TM to Audrey McCall, probably 2/20/45, TM:OHS 1.

68   "Lucky Lou": National Personnel Records Center, Military Personal Records, service number 884 12 62; *Jane's Fighting Ships of World War II*; TM:OHS Box 1; NYT, 7/25/45, p. 6.

"always bumping the noggin" and TM's life on the *St. Louis*: TM to Audrey McCall, 3/12/45, 3/28/45, 3/30/45, TM:OHS Box 1.

69   record 26,265 rounds: NYT, 7/25/45, p. 6; U.S.S. *St. Louis* history, TM:OHS Box 1.

"Plane after plane": TM to DLM, 7/28/45, DLMP.

"I don't think I care much": DLMP.

"[T]he ancient knees": TM to Audrey McCall, 5/3/45, DLMP.

"in a manner": TM to DLM, 7/28/45, DLMP.

"[I]t becomes impersonal": TM to DLM, 7/28/45, DLMP.

70   "Six months ago": TM to Audrey McCall, 8/4/45, TM:OHS Box 1.

"The experience will make me": TM to Audrey McCall, 8/1/45, TM:OHS Box 1.

Chapter 4

71   the navy rejected his application: TM naval service files, National Personnel Records Center, Military Personal Records, service number 884 12 62.

72   "It's full of the things": TM:OHS Box 32.

Hal had operated Westernwold with a profit: RUR, p. 166.

Hal told Dorothy he had pains: interview with Jean McCall Babson.

$735 to his name: Henry McCall, Sr., estate, Crook County Probate No. 1180; Redmond *Spokesman* 1/30/47; Beck Tapes.

73   "He wanted to be on [the symphony] board": interview with
       George Birnie.
       "A lot of us didn't have strong ambitions": interview with Robert
       Elliott.
       "The thought of Granddaddy McCall": interview with Clay Myers.
       "The group gave him the kind of exposure": interview with Robert
       Elliott.

74   McCall earned $7,200 . . . offer him only $6,000: TM:M, p. 19.
       "ability, aggressiveness": OR, 6/11/49, p. 8.
       "Clearly McCall": OS, 6/20/49.
       "Western carpetbaggers": Hendrickson, *Joe Lane of Oregon*, p. vii.
       "Oregon was in that stage of corruption": Steffens, *Upbuilders*, p.
       307.
       "There was never a time": OJ, 7/15/10, as quoted in MacColl,
       Shaping of a City, p. 188.
       Votes of a single legislator: Steffens, *Upbuilders*, pp. 306-14, and
       Autobiography, pp. 548-51; MacColl, *Shaping of a City*, pp.
       204-10, 288-98; Bone, *Oregon Cattleman/Governor/Congress-
       man*, pp. 40-42; Puter, *Looters of the Public Domain*, generally.

75   "Forty years of corruption": *McClure's*, as quoted in Bone, *Oregon
       Cattleman/Governor/Congressman*, p. 42.
       initiative and referendum: Steffens, *Upbuilders*, pp. 285-326;
       MacColl, *Shaping of a City*, pp 207-09; *Oregon Blue Book*,
       1989-90, p. 442; Lindstrom, *W. S. U'Ren and the Fight for
       Government Reform*, generally; LaPalombara, *The Initiative and
       Referendum in Oregon*, generally; Eaton, *The Oregon System*,
       generally.
       progressive reforms did not shake: Burton, *Democrats of Oregon*,
       pp. 6-7; Dodds, *The American Northwest*, pp. 273-74.
       links to the local Klu Klux Klan: MacColl, *Growth of a City*, pp.
       162-72; Burton, *Democrats of Oregon*, pp. 87-88.
       Martin, a retired major general: CJ, 7/14/36 and 4/29/38, as cited in
       Burton, *Democrats of Oregon*, p. 70.

76   McKay was a patriot: Sobel and Raimo, *Biographical Directory of
       Governors*, pp. 1284-85; Turnbull, *Governors of Oregon*, pp.
       88-90, 93-95.

77   "Did you hire": OJ, 1/27/52, p. 12.
       "He was a tremendously feisty guy": TM:Tapes 3.
       "I'll be damned if you'll impugn": TM:M, p. 24.

78   "This is the speech": TM:Tapes 4.
       "He never really understood me": TM:Tapes 4.
       "[Politicians] had been very bland": TM:Tapes 4.
       "I think we've got a way": TM:M, p. 28.
79   "You don't need legislation": interview with Robert Elliott.
80   craft a bill: *Oregon Laws* 1951, Chapter 425.
       "It was really a preamble": TM:M, p. 22.
       "Boys, if you think": TM:M, p. 23.
       "The bill came off the table": TM:M, p. 23.
81   McKay was at first uncomfortable: interview with Claire Argow.
       two prison guards decided to discipline: OJ, 8/20/51, p. 1; OR,
           8/17/51; 8/21/51, p. 1; RG, 8/19/51; 8/21/51, p. 1.
       "Warden Alexander is right": CJ, 8/21/51, p. 4.
82   reforms would die: interview with Claire Argow.
       to settle the strike: OS, 8/22/51, p. 1; OR, 8/22/51, p. 1.
       "They had eight murderers": TM:Tapes 10.
       "A great, coarse shout": TM:Tapes 10.
       made them look weak: TM:Tapes 10.
83   "a strong sense of public relations": interview with Robert Elliott.
       "lieutenant governor": TM:Tapes 5.
       "This is getting out of hand": interview with Travis Cross.
84   "We could hardly make ends meet": interview with Audrey McCall.
       "If the call to public duty": OR, 12/13/51, p. 15.

Chapter 5

85   "desirous eyes fixed": TM:Tapes 4.
       providing little reason: Clark, Public Opinion Study, December
           1953, Bardsley Papers, OHS.
87   Hells Canyon: TM:OHS Box 2.
       McKay had supported federal development: Mahar, *Douglas
           McKay*, p. 198.
       "You can tear up": Smith, *Tiger in the Senate*, p. 299.
88   fight over control of the utilities: interview with Monroe Sweet-
           land.
89   "Wasn't it refreshing": TM:M, p. 33.
90   "When you see a purse": *Oregon Democrat*, June 1953, as quoted
           in Burton, *Democrats of Oregon*, p. 127.
       single biggest political issue: Burton, *Democrats of Oregon*, p. 129.

Angell was a survivor: OR, 4/1/68, p. 28; Angell Papers, UOSC Box 2; *Biographical Directory of U.S. Congress*, p. 541.

91   a dam Homer Angell did not want: Angell congressional newsletters, generally, Angell Papers, UOSC Box 1.

92   Ike remained popular: Clark, Public Opinion Study, December 1953, Bardsley Papers, OHS.

These three men sought: TM:OHS Box 1, 2; TM:M, pp. 33-34.

"There was an Eisenhower wing": TM:M, p. 33-34.

93   "a man who has watched": *Commerce*, Portland Chamber of Commerce, 4/24/53.

local game show: KPTV program schedule, 11/15/53, TM:OHS/author's files.

$5,000 in bank loans: McCall for Congress, Statements of Contributions and Expenditures, National Archives, U.S. House of Representatives, Record Group 283, File No. 9E2A.

"Some influential Republicans": OR, 2/7/54, p. 1.

94   McCall talked about Hells Canyon: TM:Tapes 5.

He proposed that the federal government: TM:OHS Box 1; TM:M, p. 36.

"a cop out": TM:M, p. 36.

"Youth vs. Age": OR, 2/7/54, p. 1.

the Portland press: OJ, undated, TM:OHS Box 1; OR, 10/7/54.

95   "I have decided to stand": Angell Congressional newsletter, 1/13/54, Angell Papers, UOSC Box 1.

"I have always followed the practice": Angell Congressional newsletter, 5/25/48 and 5/21/52, Angell Papers, UOSC Box 2.

most Multnomah County voters agreed: Angell Papers, UOSC; Clark, Public Opinion Study, December 1953, Bardsley Papers, OHS.

questionnaire: Angell congressional newsletter, 3/26/54, Angell Papers, UOSC Box 1.

"surprised to learn": OJ, 5/7/54.

96   He collected 40,026 votes: Oregon Elections Division, 1954 primary election abstracts; OR, 5/23/54, p. 1.

the national press viewed McCall's victory: WP, 5/23/54; TM:OHS Box 1.

with $288 in cash and with the initial $5,000 loan outstanding: McCall for Congress, Statements of Contributions and Expenditures, National Archives, U.S. House of Representatives, Record Group 283, File No. 9E2A.

"Power, Payrolls and Prosperity for Portland": TM:OHS Box 1.

businessmen upped their loans to $11,000: McCall for Congress, Statements of Contributions and Expenditures, National Archives, U.S. House of Representatives, Record Group 283, File No. 9E2A.

97 the Democratic Party had been in shambles: Burton, *Democrats of Oregon*, pp. 88, 103-33; interview with Monroe Sweetland.

"We've got the best ideas": interview with Monroe Sweetland.

98 "We knew in 1952": interview with Monroe Sweetland.

"She always had this facade": interview with Jean Young.

Newbry won statewide by 68,322 votes: Oregon Elections Division, 1952 general election abstracts.

99 "We thought Edith would run well": interview with Monroe Sweetland.

"For Tom to win": interview with Monroe Sweetland.

100 "There wasn't a union": interview with Ken Rinke.

"we contacted every Townsend Club": interview with Ken Rinke.

"he did not take to criticism": interview with Ken Rinke.

"You get straight answers from Edith Green": interview with Ken Rinke.

"We planned to set out to show": interview with Ken Rinke.

"I challenge my opponent": interview with Ken Rinke.

"The beauty of that": interview with Ken Rinke.

102 chairman of the local Easter Seals: undated clippings, TM:OHS Box 1.

"There was a picture of the boys and the dog": TM:Tapes 6.

Lawson or Tom?: TM:M, p. 41.

"We may not have changed": interview with Ken Rinke.

"It was just a bunch": TM:Tapes 6.

103 "Tom had been brought up": interview with Audrey McCall.

"They shrewdly exploited our joint appearances": TM:M, p. 40.

104 "a spokesman for the influences": OJ, 10/2/54, p. 2.

"McKee, McKay and McCall": TM:M, p. 39; Mahar, *Douglas McKay*, p. 283.

"Morse was the hardest hater": TM:Tapes 7.

"I was shrouded by these affiliations": TM:M, p. 40.

record amount . . . $27,366: McCall for Congress, Statements of Contributions and Expenditures, National Archives, U.S. House of Representatives, Record Group 283, File No. 9E2A.

told a few friends: interview with Travis Cross.

a poll published by the *Oregonian*: OR, 10/24/54, p. 1.

105   "the raunchiest speech": TM:M, p. 41

"I wouldn't touch one word": TM:Tapes 6.

"I'm going to ask you": TM:M, p. 42.

he had thought his campaign was lost: TM:M, p. 41.

106   "Among the many things" and remainder of the speech: TM:OHS
       Box 1.

107   "I did go to the gutter": TM:M, 42.

108   joint appearance: OJ, 10/14/54, p. 3.

"I'm going to rule": interview with Ken Rinke.

"You wouldn't believe that he said that": interview with Ken Rinke.

Green's supporters stomped and howled: interview with Audrey
       McCall; OR, 10/29/54, p. 5; TM:M, p. 40.

"just did violence to my psyche": TM:Tapes 6.

109   Newspapers carried accounts: OR, 10/31/54.

Tom and Audrey grinning and embracing: OR, 11/3/54.

At midnight: OR, 11/3/54, p. 1.

Out of the 198,344 votes cast: Oregon Elections Division, 1954
       general election abstracts.

Democratic flood: Burton, *Democrats of Oregon*, p. 132.

111   McCall agreed to meet Green: interview with Audrey McCall; OR,
       11/4/54; TM:M, p. 43.

"They made me do it": interview with Ken Rinke.

112   "If there is anything": interview with Ken Rinke.

Chapter 6

115    $2,500: McCall for Congress, Statements of Contributions and
       Expenditures, National Archives, U.S. House of Representatives,
       Record Group 283, File No. 9E2A.

No one wanted him without a sponsor: TM:M, pp. 44-45.

116   three small newspapers: The Albany *Democrat-Herald*, Corvallis
       Gazette-Times and the Hillsboro *Argus* carried "The Second
       Look" until June 1957; TM:OHS Box 1.

"It was as presidential": interview with Hollis Goodrich.

"just hacking and whacking": TM:Tapes 11.

"His heart was not in it": interview with Ed Snyder.

"Many of us": interview with Ivan Smith.

117   "People were turned off": interview with Dick Altoff.
       extolling the sponsor's chocolates: interview with Ivan Smith.
       "The urge would come": interview with Dick Altoff.
       "I only wish": interview with Ed Snyder.
118   "I'm no Quisling!": interview with Ivan Smith.
       "Television was like a pulpit": interview with Dick Altoff.
       "a very imaginative fellow": TM:Tapes 8.
       "Dargan gave McCall a long leash": interview with Ken Yandle.
119   "Viewpoint": OR, 10/13/57.
       "He punched up": interview with Ken Yandle.
       "People would call": interview with Richard Ross.
       chronic disorganization: interviews with Richard Ross, Dick
           Altoff, Ken Yandle, Ivan Smith, Jack Capell.
121   a lengthy report: Report of the Legislative Interim Committee on
           Indian Affairs: A Reintroduction to the Indians of Oregon,
           October 1958. For more detail on the threat to the Klamath
           forest: Neuberger in Neal, *They Never Go Back to Pocatello*, pp.
           309-17.
122   "Boom or bust": TM:M, p. 52.
       "priceless scenic values": Report of the Legislative Interim Com-
           mittee on Indian Affairs, p. 68.
       Richard Neuberger: Neal, *They Never Go Back to Pocatello*, pp.
           xix-xxxiv.
123   "The federal government": TM:Tapes 7.
124   McCall thought the film: TM:M, p. 55.
       "The age of Sputnik": TM:M, p. 55.
125   "Oregon will never have a better senator": TM:M, p. 55.
       "I'm in politics": OR, 10/13/57.
       "I'm convinced you could get elected": interview with Marko
           Haggard.
       Mark O. Hatfield: Hatfield, *Not Quite So Simple*, pp. 6-26; Eells
           and Nyberg, *Lonely Walk*, pp. 19-25; Sobel and Raimo, *Bio-
           graphical Directory of Governors*, p. 1288; interviews with
           Mark Hatfield, Travis Cross.
127   Incumbent Governor Robert Holmes background: Turnbull, *Gover-
           nors of Oregon*, pp. 102-04.
       one of the more scurrilous attacks: Smith, *Tiger in the Senate*, pp.
           370-78; Eells and Nyberg, *Lonely Walk*, p. 37; interviews with
           Mark Hatfield, Travis Cross, Warne Nunn.

Aware that the incident: Smith, *Tiger in the Senate*, p. 371; interview with Travis Cross.

"Those who conspire": Smith, *Tiger in the Senate*, p. 375.

128   Their differences: interview with Audrey McCall.

"They were as different": interview with James Welch.

duties of secretary of state: interviews with Travis Cross, Ken Johnson.

During their meeting: TM:M, p. 57; interview with Travis Cross.

McCall said later: interviews with Audrey McCall, Dick Althoff.

Hatfield, in recollecting the meeting: interview with Mark Hatfield.

"Hatfield never seriously": interview with Travis Cross.

129   McCall even told Dargan: interviews with Audrey McCall, Dick Altoff.

McCall expected Hatfield: interview with Dick Altoff.

"You could just see him collapse": interview with Dick Althoff.

"He couldn't understand why": interview with Dick Althoff.

130   "I took complete responsibility": interview with Audrey McCall.

"If I had just one-tenth": *This Week*, 1/5/83, p. 3.

"We never had an abundance of money": interview with Audrey McCall.

131   "a kid at heart": interview with Thomas McCall, Jr.

"Tom, I want you to take care of this," interview with Samuel W. McCall III.

C.B. McCall: *This Week*, 1/5/83, p. 3.

"These were the best years for the family": interview with Audrey McCall.

car accident: OR, 4/10/60; medical report, Dr. Jack E. Battalia, TM:OHS Box 35; interview with Audrey McCall.

"I looked in my rear-view mirror": OR, 4/10/60.

Chapter 7

134   "spill water": McArthur, *Oregon Geographic Names*, p. 909.

135   Portland started the first careful study: Gleeson, *Return of a River*, p. 14.

"intolerable": Council on Environmental Quality 1973 Report, p. 48; Gleeson, *Return of a River*, p. 13.

136   mills were . . . major culprits: Gleeson and Merryfield, "Industrial

and Domestic Wastes of the Willamette Valley," Oregon State
University, May 1936, as cited in Gleeson, *Return of a River*, p.
17.

"sludge banks forming": Charlton Food and Sanitary Laboratory,
Preliminary Report, 10/5/34, as quoted in MacColl, *Growth of a
City*, p. 544.

137   "The fish would live longer": OR, 9/22/37, as quoted in MacColl,
Growth of a City, p. 545.

1937 legislature proposed a bill: Council on Environmental Quality
1973 Report, p. 50; MacColl, *Growth of a City*, p. 545-46.

138   He vetoed it on sight: Sources about the measure (Senate Bill 414,
1937 session) disagree about its fate. See 1935 Oregon Senate
calendar, final edition, p. 52.

voters approved a $6 million bond: Gleeson, *Return of a River*, p.
16; MacColl, *Growth of a City*, p. 546.

E. coli: OR, 9/3/38, p. 12. The original newspaper story reported the
finding of "B. Coli."

no oxygen at all: Gleeson, *Return of a River*, p. 22.

140   biggest source of pollution: Washington State Pollution Commission and Oregon State Sanitary Authority, *Report of Investigation in the Lower Columbia River*, 1943, p. 10.

In September 1950, low water levels: Gleeson, *Return of a River*, p.
26; OR, 9/21/50., p. 11.

surprised that so many fish survived: OR, 9/21/50, p. 11.

"The only real tool": interview with B.A. "Barney" McPhillips.

141   "I had sort of been hinting": TM:M, p. 59.

"get on the back": TM:M, p. 59.

142   McCall . . . was reluctant: Willis Tapes.

"We were beginning to develop the symptoms": Willis Tapes.

"portrayed as culprits": interview with Dick Altoff.

$18,000 . . . an enormous budget: TM:M, p. 60.

threatened to sue: interview with Dick Altoff.

143   "America is wild and clean" and other quotations from the documentary: KATU.

147   "When Tom blew the whistle": interview with Ken Yandle.

"a shocker": OJ, 11/21/62, p. 8.

the legislature responded with a bill: Senate Bill 259, Enrolled
Chapter 171, 1963 Laws.

Chapter 8

Key Sources
Glenn Jackson: Many people familiar with Jackson spoke only on the basis
   of confidentiality. For Jackson's early career: Glenn Jackson Papers, OHS,
   Mss. 2626. For his financial background and wealth: Oregon Government
   Ethics Commission records, OSA E17 80A-28 Box 1; probate file number
   133388, Multnomah County. For his career generally: WW, 4/14/75;
   Portland Board of Realtors, "Portland's First Citizen for 1971"; Pacific
   Power & Light, "The Pacific Power Story"; *Northwest Magazine*, OR,
   3/20/77; *Oregon Business*, January 1986; and obituaries, SJ, and OR,
   6/21/80. On the Commonwealth deal: General Accounting Office report
   B-118653 and its related correspondence.

149   "My 'inside inside' sources": OJ, 5/20/63, p. 2.
150   "line will form on the right": KGW-TV script archives, 12/13/63 and
            12/20/63.
         "Despite the temptation": OR, 12/28/63, p. 5.
         "We saw this as a means to my end": TM:Tapes 4.
         "Damn it": TM:M, p. 62.
         Oregon Junior Chamber of Commerce state convention: interview
            with Ron Schmidt; OS, 2/9/64.
151   Edward Westerdahl: interview with Edward Westerdahl.
         Ron Schmidt: interview with Ron Schmidt; OR, 11/9/92, p. B1.
         "OK, I'm running": interview with Ron Schmidt; also, TM:M, p. 62.
            McCall and Schmidt disagree about who got stuck with the bill;
            Schmidt's version is more believable.
         his portrait from the ceremony: OR, 2/25/64, p. 1.
         "I am running as an extension": OS, 2/27/64, p. 18.
         "Oh Fateful Day!": KGW-TV script archives, 2/26/64.
152   "We were not the choice": interview with Ron Schmidt.
153   "You give this to Tom McCall": interview with Ron Schmidt; also,
            TM:M, p. 63.
         McCall obliterated Mosee: Oregon Election Division, 1964 primary
            voting abstracts.
         In 1964, out of 932,461 registered voters: Oregon Election Divi-
            sion, 1964 general voting abstracts.
154   "[McCall] should be happy": CJ, 3/23/64, p. 4.
         "His loss in 1954": interview with Ed Westerdahl.

"He never looked at a poll": interview with Ron Schmidt.

"My whole weakness as a politician": TM:Tapes 9.

"big dog, little dog": TM:Tapes 11.

155   "This attack was a big nothing": OS, 10/18/64, p. 20; OR, 10/17/64,
p. 7; interview with Floyd McKay.

"Tom was making even dull Alf Corbett look good": interview
with Ed Westerdahl.

"Tom isn't doing very well": interviews with Ed Westerdahl, Ron
Schmidt. Westerdahl declined to identify Tom Dargan in the
anecdote, but Schmidt did.

"He generally knew that the strain": TM:Tapes 9.

Corbett was trying to link: OS, 10/29/64, p. 2.

156   "Affidavit of Conscience": TM:OHS Box 2.

"You rotten son of a bitch!": TM:Tapes 9.

He put McCall in a local hospital: OR, 10/23/64

"He was fine": interview with Raymond Engelcke.

"I had campaigned so hard": TM:M, p. 64.

"A lot of the reporters knew where Tom was": interview with Ed
Westerdahl.

157   collecting 432,150 votes: Oregon Elections Division, 1964 general
election abstracts.

"I am tremendously stirred by it": OR, 1/5/64.

His duties put him in charge: TM:OSA 70A-95 Box X3.

"He was terribly disorganized": interview with Wanda Merrill.

158   Robert Straub: interviews with Robert Straub, Ken Johnson; Sobel
and Raimo, *Biographical Directory of Governors*, p. 1289.

"Hatfield would go after Tom": interview with Floyd McKay.

"Mark was just cutting up Tom": interview with Ken Johnson.

they repeatedly outvoted Hatfield: OS, 1/4/66, p. 5.

159   the Sanitary Authority had seen only humble results: Gleeson,
Return of a River, generally; OJ, 2/28/66, p. 1.

160   "jammed with dreary records": OJ, 2/28/66, p. 1.

"he never showed all that much interest": interview with B.A.
"Barney" McPhillips

less than $2,000 a year: 1965 Legislative Interim Committee on
Public Health, OSA L6 68A-32 Box 3; OJ, 3/1/66, p. 3.

"Hatfield was a grabber of payrolls at any cost": TM:M, p. 65.

161   "grossly derelict": CJ, 8/13/65, p. 1.

"Oregon is at a crossroads": CJ, 10/8/65, p. 1.

"McCall said a 'line must be drawn'": OR, 10/9/65, p. 8.

"McCall is fighting": Bend *Bulletin*, 6/28/65.

launching an investigation into the local John Birch Society:
TM:OSA 70A-95 Box 1; OS, 1/20/66, p. 9.

162   "Our people were as much anti-Tom": interview with F.F. "Monte"
Montgomery.

"Rinke will put me in": TM memo, 12/31/65, OSA 70A-95 Box 3.

163   "I oppose such manipulating": Quotes and details of the meeting
were recorded by McCall in the memorandum to himself intended to protect him later, 12/31/65, OSA 70A-95 Box 3. In the
three-page, typewritten memo, McCall often refers to himself in
the third person, a common habit of his. Authorship of the
memo is clear, however, from later first-person references,
hand-written notes and the broadcast-style typewriter he often
used. Smith, later a U.S. congressman from Oregon's Second
District, repeatedly declined to be interviewed for this book.
F.F. "Monte" Montgomery confirmed in an interview with the
author that he was aware Smith had offered McCall the deal.

164   "The General": WW, 4/14/75, p. 1.

business interests spanned the state: Oregon Government Ethics
Commission, Glenn Jackson Statement of Economic Interest,
4/14/75, OSA E17 80A-28 Box 1.

Jackson was worth $20 million: Estate of Glenn Jackson, Mult-
nomah County, Probate No. 133388

165   Jackson was born in Albany: background on Jackson generally
comes from Glenn Jackson Papers, OHS; WW, 4/14/75; Portland
Board of Realtors, "Portland's First Citizen for 1971"; Pacific
Power & Light, "The Pacific Power Story"; OR, 3/20/77, *Northwest Magazine*; *Oregon Business*, January 1986, pp. 24-25; SJ,
6/21/80, p. 2D; OR, 6/21/80, p. A8.

"I've always been a little squirt": Pacific Power & Light, "The
Pacific Power Story," p. 33.

White City: Glenn Jackson Papers, OHS; OR, 5/21/66, p. 36; Medford *Mail-Tribune*, 1/5/64, p. B1.

behind the back of COPCO's president: Interviews with confidential
sources.

"Jackson was a doer": interview with Travis Cross.

166   "Doesn't he have a conflict of interest?": interview with Travis
        Cross.
        The ceremony celebrating the freeway's completion: OR, 10/23/66,
        p. 31.
167   Commonwealth also gave Jackson: General Accounting Office,
        Report B-118653, contains the investigation into Jackson and
        details of his relationship to Commonwealth that did not be-
        come public when the sale of White City was announced; OR,
        3/11/64, p. 1 and 1/6/65; Medford *Mail-Tribune*, 3/10/64, p. 1;
        Green to Weitzel, 4/7/66, GAO B-118653.
168   Jackson admired Schmidt: interview with Ron Schmidt.
        "loose cannon": interview with Ron Schmidt.
        McCall was so thrilled: interview with Ron Schmidt.
169   hanging effigies of Jackson: CJ, 7/25/65, p. 1.
        hanging Straub in effigy: OS, 5/9/66, p. 1.
170   the highway would run over two BLM parcels: TM:OSA 70A-95 Box
        38.
171   "For State Park Purposes": Patent application by Oregon Park and
        Recreation Division, Oregon State Highway Department,
        5/14/62, Bureau of Land Management records, Land Patent No.
        1237615.
        "Supporting that highway ran contrary": interview with Ron
        Schmidt.
        "Tom's heart was in the right place": interview with Robert Straub.
        McCall visited Pacific City: OS, 7/19/66, p. 1.
        "I had expected McCall to oppose": interview with Robert Straub.
172   editorial writers blasted Straub: for example, Medford *Mail-
        Tribune*, 6/2/66.
173   "Progress to me is measured": McCall for Governor, radio ad copy,
        TM:OHS Box 2.
        "the 'Tom and Bob' show": TM:Tapes 9.
174   The waters were still polluted: RG, 9/20/66, p. 1.
        "two men with the same mind": interview with Ken Johnson.
        "It totally diffused the issue": interview with Robert Straub.
        "It was just the two of us": interview with Ed Westerdahl.
175   "We were ready to air the debate": interview with Forest Amsden.
176   "I still remember the note": interview with Bill Anderson.

Chapter 9

179   In 1967, one third of Oregon: *Oregon Blue Book*, 1967-68, pp. 125-
        49; 1959-60, p. 278.
180   "A pleasant, homogeneous self-contained state": Schlesinger,
        Robert Kennedy and His Times, pp. 903-04.
        "in the proudest hour": 1967 Oregon Legislative Assembly, House
        Journal, 1/9/67, p. 254.
181   "Health, economic strength, recreation": 1967 Oregon Legislative
        Assembly, House Journal, 1/9/67, p. 254.
182   Hatfield's staff had stripped: OR, 11/12/86, p. B1; interview with
        Ron Schmidt.
        "No governor before Tom ever cared much what we did": inter-
        view with B. A. "Barney" McPhillips.
        cited the authority for its failure: U.S. Department of the Interior,
        Federal Water Pollution Control Administration, Water Quality
        Control and Management, Willamette River Basin, 1967; OR,
        2/27/67, p. 1.
        "Oregon has propounded—and enforces to the hilt": OR, 3/15/67;
        TM testimony, 3/14/67, TM:OHS Box 3.
183   Harold Wendel: OJ, 4/18/67, p. 1; TM:M, p. 79.
        "[Wendel] would have dropped dead anyway": TM:M, p. 79.
        "[Wendel's] departure leaves a void": OJ, 4/18/67, p. 1; press
        statement, 4/18/67, TM:OHS Box 3.
184   Democratic governor Oswald West: Sobel and Raimo, *Biographi-
        cal Directory of Governors*, pp. 1273-74; Turnbull, *Governors
        of Oregon*, pp. 63-65.
        "He found himself": MacColl, *Shaping of a City*, pp. 396-97.
        West rode horseback: Friedman, *Tracking Down Oregon*, pp. 256-
        58.
186   "I came up with a bright idea": OJ, 8/8/49; Oswald West Papers,
        OHS.
        West's sixty-six word bill: *General Laws of Oregon* 1913, Chapter
        47.
        "The legislature and the public": OJ, 8/8/49, Oswald West Papers,
        OHS.
        112 miles of dry sands: OR, 5/7/67, p. 20.
187   "private beach": Nokes to Rohde, 8/15/66, TM:OSA 70A-95 Box 6.

188   the amended bill lacked enough votes: 1967 House Highway
           Committee minutes, 4/6/67 and 4/18/67, OSA.
        "Beach goers joined the battle": OS, 5/3/67
        Bazzett tried again unsuccessfully: 1967 House Highway Commit-
           tee minutes, 5/2/67, OSA.
        "We cannot afford": Bazzett Papers, OHS Box 1; OR and OS, 5/5/67,
           p. 1.
        "When Tom did that, holy cow": interview with F. F. "Monte"
           Montgomery.

189   "Do you really want this bill?": interview with F. F. "Monte"
           Montgomery.
        to the attention of the Oregon press: OJ, 5/5/67, p. 14; TM:OSA 70A-
           95 Box 6; Bazzett Papers, OHS; interview with Forest Amsden.
        40,000 responses: Cannon to Sollen, 11/6/73, TM:OSA/author's
           files.
        "Every politician rode off wildly": TM:M, p. 82.
        Republicans' bill actually surrendered: OR, 5/11/67, p. 1.
        Smith and his allies: Bazzett Papers, OHS; 1967 House Highway
           Committee minutes, 5/12/67, OSA; OR, 5/13/67.

190   "The politicians and the lawyers": OR, 5/14/67, p. 1.
        sixteen-foot elevation line: TM:OSA 70A-95 Box 6; TM:M, p 82.
        "This is where the state's ownership now ends": interview with
           Don Jepsen.
        "He wasn't talking to anyone in particular": OR, 5/14/67, p. 1;
           interview with Don Jepsen.

191   the correct elevation was 13.7 feet: OR, 5/14/67, p. 32.
        Redden and Johnson rewrote the Beach Bill: Interviews with James
           Redden, Lee Johnson, F. F. "Monte" Montgomery; 1967 House
           Highway Committee minutes, 5/19/67, OSA.

192   "No local selfish interest": TM:M, pp. 82-83.

194   "Glenn explained it to me": interview with James Redden.
        approved construction of the Inn at Spanish Head: OR, 11/18/67,
           p. 1.
        highway project, in fact, would sit just above: Cannon to TM,
           7/26/67, TM:OSA 70A-95 Box 38.
        planned to build similar beachfront highways: interview with Floyd
           McKay.

195   Cannon could hardly be heard through the jeers: OJ, 8/4/67, p. 5.

"Oregon's noisiest minority": *Oregon Voter*, 8/19/67, p. 4; NYT, 9/3/67, p. 29.

"In the main": TM to Allen, 7/13/67, TM:OSA 70A-95 Box 38.

"Tom was the environmentalists' golden boy": interview with Ron Schmidt.

"We were getting creamed": interview with Ed Westerdahl.

full retreat as McCall's only route: Cannon to Westerdahl, 8/14/67, TM:OSA 70A-95 Box 38.

196   "Mr. Secretary": interview with Robert Straub. Straub's visit: OJ, 8/15/67.

"Quite frankly, it is my opinion": Udall to TM, 8/24/67, TM:OSA 70A-95 Box 38; OR, 8/27/67, p. 28.

"This closes the Nestucca Spit issue": press statement, 8/27/67, TM:OSA 70A-95 Box 38.

"If I ever catch": OJ, 8/26/67, p. 1.

"We in Oregon are not beauty wreckers": TM to Udall, 8/28/67, TM:OSA 70A-95 Box 38.

Jackson's engineers drew up a new plan: OR, 9/21/67, p. 42.

the highway would no longer line the beach: maps, TM:OSA 70A-95 Box 38.

197   "You said there would be no highway" and remainder of the scene in Hilton: interview with Robert Straub; *Reader's Digest* 9/83; OR, 9/22/67, p. 14.

"We had to remind Glenn Jackson": interview with Ed Westerdahl.

198   "There will be a pinch of stink, that's true": RG, 5/7/67, p. 1; 5/8/67, p. 1; and 5/9/67, p. 1.

199   "As soon as I became chairman": interview with John Mosser.

During a hearing in Eugene: OJ, 8/29/67, p. 1; interview with John Mosser.

"Why do you need to know": interview with John Mosser.

"Mosser's vote for approval": TM:M, p. 181.

200   On the same day, the authority: OR, 9/7/67, p. 26.

Chapter 10

Key Sources

Prison riot: Investigations by the Oregon State Police and two secret inquiries conducted by the McCall Administration, TM:OSA 70A-95 Box 28; and a Marion County grand jury report. A first-hand account of the riot came from McCall's assistant, Doris Penwell, who took shorthand notes on the scene. I found her original notes in TM:OSA, and Penwell graciously transcribed them for me. They are cited as Penwell notes below.

201   "Understanding why McCall was as loved": interview with Darrel
             Buttice.
         weekly open house: OR, 1/12/69, p. F1.
         "It was like someone opened the windows": interview with Harold
             Hughes.
202   "That's the trouble with politicians": TM:Tapes 7.
         "Nobody was a stranger to him": interview with Doris Penwell.
         "He loved people and people loved him": interview with Ron
             Schmidt.
         "In all my years as a broadcaster": Hess and Broder, *The Republican Establishment*, p. 390.
203   "Tom snuck out to my desk": interview with Wanda Merrill.
         "He just cringed and sank into his seat": interview with Ron
             Schmidt.
         "When the last group came in": interview with Darrel Buttice.
206   "You're in the legislature, aren't you?": interview with Jason Boe.
207   "Tom immediately ordered and demanded": KATU.
208   "I get scolded that I would live longer": CJ, 1/14/70, p. 14.
         "I wear my heart on my sleeve": TM to Rockefeller, 4/9/76,
             PA:Ford.
         When Democratic legislators delivered floor speeches: interview
             with James Redden.
         "This is Tom McCall": interview with Ron Schmidt.
         "He truly disliked deceit": interview with Henny Willis.
209   "People were naturally curious": TM:M, p. 149.
         "He was always a walking press conference": interview with
             Harold Hughes.
         "When he showed up": interview with Don Jepsen.
         "Silence, to a radio man": OR, 10/2/67, p. 24.
         "We just had the most interesting meeting": interview with Ron
             Schmidt.
         "The fastest way to get information": KATU.
         "He couldn't keep his mouth shut": interview with Lee Johnson.
         "I'll just open my mouth": Willis Tapes.
210   "A reflex action": draft article by Floyd McKay, author's files.

"because he had written enough news": interview with Russell Sadler.

"He was a master": interview with Don Jepsen.

"In politics you have to take": NYT, 11/26/67.

"The press is wont to talk": TM speech, 1/27/67, TM:OHS Box 3.

"You could tell he'd been running": interview with Harold Hughes.

211   He could be calculating: TM to Hinman, 3/4/68, TM:OHS/author's files.

He maintained a private correspondence with editors: *Oregon Times*, June 1972, p. 22. For example, Allen to TM, TM:OSA 70A-95 Box 38.

"The press always knew": TM:Tapes 16.

"It is done with sincerity": CJ, 1/14/70, p. 14.

"I'm an incurable old pro as a newsman": CJ, 1/14/70, p. 14.

"Harold, what are you doing?": interview with Harold Hughes; the story: OR, 4/16/67.

"They were brethren": interview with Ed Westerdahl.

213   Morse was one of only two senators: Karnow, *Vietnam*, pp. 374-76.

"I'm neither a hawk nor a dove": OR, 1/5/66, p. 4.

"I have supported your policy": TM to Johnson, 11/8/66, PA:LBJ.

"Tom was a red-hot patriot": interview with Ed Westerdahl.

"Tom had staked out his position": interview with Ron Schmidt.

"Oregon is back on the track on Vietnam": OR, 3/21/67, p. 14.

214   "honest manpower against the tide": OS, 4/17/67, p. 1.

"contempt for the apologists": OR, 7/14/67.

"A governor owes his support": memo, TM to Executive Office Staff, PA:LBJ.

215   Political survey results: OR, 4/1/67, p. 1.

"Oh, I could beat him": OR, 3/25/67, p. 8.

50,000 men . . . income tax surcharge: Johnson, *Vantage Point*, pp. 173, 263.

more than half of Americans polled: OR, 8/13/67.

McCall joined twenty-one other observers: NYT, 8/24/67, p. 1; Johnson, *Vantage Point*, p. 264.

Frustrated by the restrictions: WP, 9/1/67, p. A8; NYT, 9/2/67, p. 6; 9/3/67, p. 2; 9/4/67, p. 2

216   "I don't think the people know": NYT, 9/2/67, p. 6.

dispatch for the Associated Press: OR, 9/8/67, p. 1.

"sterile exercise": OR, 9/3/67, p. 1.

"seemed to have a dogged faith": TM:M, p. 87.

McCall joined the chorus: NYT, 9/3/67, p. 2; 9/4/67, p. 2.

"Though not flagrantly fraudulent": Karnow, *Vietnam*, p. 451

217   "If we had as much composure": NYT, 9/5/67, p. 1; OR, 9/5/67, p. 4.

McCall expressed doubts: interview with Eugene Patterson.

McCall shrugged off any doubts: PA:LBJ.

"Lyndon Johnson had . . . a Saigon regime": Karnow, *Vietnam*, p. 452.

McCall had eagerly asked Johnson: TM to Johnson, 10/23/67, PA:LBJ.

218   McCall recruited a core: OR, 4/12/67, p. 11; 4/20/67; NYT, 4/13/67, p. 20; TM:OHS Box 3; Hess and Broder, *The Republican Establishment*, p. 240.

"lying dead in the water": Witcover, *Resurrection of Richard Nixon*, p. 206.

whose mean-spirited politics McCall detested: interview with Ron Schmidt.

"A silence such as when a child": quoted in OS, 12/7/67, p. 4.

219   Montgomery had felt jilted: interview with F. F. "Monte" Montgomery.

McCall considered the biggest tragedy of his career: interview with Ron Schmidt.

rough ways of handling prisoners: Board of Control memos, TM:OSA 70A-95; OJ, 8/17/67, p. 4.

220   Randall, though, was not forthright: interview with Ed Westerdahl; Gladden memo, 7/9/68, TM:OSA 70A-95 Box 28.

"throwing him to the wolves": Gladden memo, 7/9/68, TM:OSA 70A-95 Box 28.

Montgomery wrote McCall a scathing letter: Montgomery to TM, 3/7/68, TM:OSA 70A 95 Box 28.

"I must further warn you": TM to Montgomery, 3/8/68, TM:OSA 70A-95 Box 28.

221   headlines McCall thought would defuse: OS, 3/9/68, p. 5; OJ, 3/9/68, p. 1

McCall flew off on the morning of 9 March: Westerdahl to Myers, 3/8/68, TM:OHS Box 21.

the Rockefeller apartment: NYT, 3/11/68, p. 1; TM:M, pp. 97-98.

The Oregon State Penitentiary had exploded: For history of the prison riot, Howard memos, undated and 4/1/68; undated

chronology "Oregon State Penitentiary Riot"; Cogan to Westerdahl, 4/4/68; Westerdahl memo, 4/6/68; Randall memo, 7/9/68;
Penwell notes; Carkin & Sherman, Fire and Riot Damage Evaluation, March 1968; all TM:OSA 70A-95 Box 28. Also, TM:M, pp.
98-101; Gaddis in Lucia, *This Land Around Us*, pp. 872-83; OR,
OJ, OS, 3/8/68 through 3/11/68; *Time*, 3/22/68, p. 22; interviews
with Ed Westerdahl, Ron Schmidt, Doris Penwell, Clay Myers.

222   "My prison is burning": OR, 1/12/69, p. F1; interview with Ron
Schmidt.

224   "The Oregon State Penitentiary": OR, 3/11/68.
"Why did they destroy?": interview with Ron Schmidt.
$1.6 million in damage: Howard memos, 4/1/68; Carkin & Sher-
man, Fire and Riot Damage Evaluation, March 1968; TM:OSA
70A-95 Box 28.
"hatchet job": OR, 4/25/68, p 1, 29-32.

225   he forced his prison chief to resign: Howard memos, undated and
4/1/68; Cogan to Westerdahl, 4/4/68; Westerdahl memo, 4/6/68;
TM:OSA 70A-95 Box 28.
"That was a major failure in his life": interview with Ron Schmidt.
"Imprudent comments to the press": Cogan to Westerdahl, 4/4/68,
TM:OSA 70A-95 Box 28.

226   "Quote from the street of Redmond": TM:OHS/author's files.

Chapter 11

227   "She was at once proud": interview with Audrey McCall.
Dorothy strutted about town: DLMP.

228   "The head Rosarians were just being awful": interview with Jean
McCall Babson.
"We can't say anything to defend ourselves": interview with Jean
McCall Babson.
"She knew how to get to them": interview with Borden Beck.
demands took heavy tolls: interview with Jean McCall Babson.
"She was jealous of his fame": interview with Audrey McCall.

229   "She would call—talk and talk and talk": interview with F. F.
"Monte" Montgomery.
"If I had a call at three o'clock": interview with Ron Schmidt.
"This is Dorothy Lawson McCall": interview with Robert Straub;
KATU.

231   "She could get anyone on the phone": interview with Jean McCall
          Babson.
        "I'm the governor's mother": interviews with Doris Penwell and
          Ron Schmidt.
        "Call your mother": interviews with Doris Penwell and Ron
          Schmidt.
        "I had a nice talk with your mother. Lyndon.": Johnson to TM,
          3/31/67, PA:LBJ.
        "Will have you impeached" and other telegrams: TM:OHS/author's
          files.
232   dark cloud hanging over the McCall family: interview with Jean
          McCall Babson.
        would be for the rest of his life: Samuel Walker McCall III died in
          April 1990 of a drug overdose.
        "My parents called me the sunshine boy": interview with Samuel
          Walker McCall III.
233   "Sometimes I was doubled up and screaming": interview with
          Samuel Walker McCall III.
        medically addicted: interview with Samuel Walker McCall III.
        "our favorite son": OS, 7/28/68, p. 1.
        "He went out the door": *Oregon Magazine*, March 1978, p. 35.
234   "I never liked to admit it": interview with Samuel W. McCall III.
        memorized the *Physicians Desk Reference*: interview with Samuel
          W. McCall III.
        "The whole thing snowballed": CJ, 7/1/70, p. 3.
        "I became very manipulative": RG, 4/17/90, p. 1.
        "I passed out": CJ, 7/1/70, p. 3.
        "We couldn't trust him at all": confidential source.
        "Audrey believed the world was ganging up on her son": interview
          with Ed Westerdahl.
235   "Damn the doctors!": interview with Charles and Muriel Heltzel.
        "He would look like hell": interview with Jason Boe.
        "Tom was a tremendously emotional person": confidential source.
        "Tom never wanted to believe": confidential source.
236   "It was a tragedy": interview with Harold Hughes.
        "It was a very private thing": interview with Henny Willis.
        recognized Sam's potential for violence: interview with Ron
          Schmidt.
237   "I don't want to hear": interview with Samuel Walker McCall III.

"We would say, 'We have a problem'": interview with Ron Schmidt.

"It wasn't big dough": OJ, 3/9/78.

How much they raised is unclear: interview with Ron Schmidt and Ed Westerdahl.

the cash gifts remained secret: news of the payments became public in 1978; OJ, 3/9/78.

"I don't think Audrey could stand": confidential source.

238   she insisted Sam be sent: interviews with Ron Schmidt and confidential sources.

"All they do": CJ, 7/1/70, p. 3.

"conned": CJ, 7/1/70, p. 3.

"They never would leave": confidential source.

239   "The publicity did not help anyone": confidential source.

"His moods changed for the better": interview with Ed Westerdahl.

"He had so much on his mind": interview with Doris Penwell.

Chapter 12

242   "the overriding issue": 1967 Oregon Legislative Assembly, House Journal, 1/9/67, p. 254.

243   statewide land-use planning: Logan, *Oregon Land Use Story*, p. 6; Babcock, *Zoning Game*, pp. 3-6; Plotkin, *Keep Out*, pp. 97-98.

"ticky tacky treadmill": Little, *New Oregon Trail*, pp. 7-8.

244   "twenty miserable miles": TM:M, p. 65.

local health officials in Lincoln County: Health Division, 1973 Lincoln County Report, TM:OSA 74A-98 Box 14.

"sagebrush saboteurs": Little, *New Oregon Trail*, p. 10.

Clackamas County . . . lost one-third of its farmland: DeGrove, *Land Growth and Politics*, p. 236.

"Oregonians have reason to fear": Little, *New Oregon Trail*, p. 13.

245   the provisions had little effect: Leonard, *Managing Oregon's Growth*, p. 6.

land-use programs in other states: Bosselman and Callies, *Quiet Revolution*, pp. 5-7.

246   "[W]e don't have a 'no growth' policy": Little, *New Oregon Trail*, p. 35.

"Tom never put much reliance": interview with Eldon Hout.

"commensurate with the character": Senate Bill 10 (1969) OSA
    RGL6 69-I2 Box 1.

247   campaigned mildly for the tax: OR, 5/4/69, p. NW10, and 5/17/69,
        p. 17.
    "McCall sales tax": for example, OR, 2/4/69, p. 1.
    "I knew in my bones": press conference, 6/4/69, TM:OHS Box 7.

248   "I have heard from my board of directors": RG, 11/29/74.
    "was very distasteful": TM:M, p. 166.
    "The steady scatteration": TM message to Oregon Senate, 2/7/69;
        author's files.

249   "I didn't revel in the knowledge": TM speech, 11/14/72, TM:OHS
        Box 20.

250   "We have a high standard of prohibition": OR, 3/6/69, p. 33.
    At least $11 million of industrial investments: TM:OHS Box 7.
    "Oregon has not been a lap dog": OR, 3/6/69, p. 33.

251   "He's telling them to bring": OR, 3/6/69, p. 33.
    "When you live in Oregon": TM speech, 9/23/69, TM:OHS Box 7.
    "So massive is our degradation": TM:OHS Box 7; OS, 11/1/69.

Chapter 13

Key Sources

All quotations from Richard Chambers' wife, Kay Chambers; his daughter,
    Victoria Chambers Berger; and his brother, Douglas Chambers, come
    from interviews for this book.

254   "It's nobody's business what I did": interview with Victoria Cham-
        bers Berger.

256   "Paul, you've got to get down here": interview with Paul Hanne-
        man; Corvallis *Gazette-Times*, 5/2/74, p. 10.

257   returnable bottle was a way of life: Savage and Richmond, *Ore-
        gon's Bottle Bill*, pp. 3-8.

258   breweries nationwide shrank: Savage and Richmond, *Oregon's
        Bottle Bill*, pp. 3-8.
    173 million bottles and 263 million cans: Gudger and Bailes, as
        cited in Savage and Richmond, *Oregon's Bottle Bill*, p. 25.
    Vermont . . . bottle bill: Savage and Richmond, *Oregon's Bottle
        Bill*, pp. 2-3.

Keep America Beautiful: Savage and Richmond, *Oregon's Bottle Bill*, pp. 2-3.

260   "I was desperate for support": interview with Paul Hanneman.

The bill impressed Cannon, who persuaded McCall: Reports that McCall opposed the Bottle Bill are inaccurate; House State and Federal Affairs Committee, minutes, 3/3/69, OSA L6 1969.

a parade of enthusiastic backers: House State and Federal Affairs Committee, minutes, 3/3/69 and 3/28/69, OSA L6 1969.

lobbyists . . . attacked the bill: House State and Federal Affairs Committee, minutes, 3/28/69, OSA L6 1969.

261   Martin, who secured promises: interviews with with Paul Hanneman, Roger Martin.

262   "There aren't many bills that escape": interview with Paul Hanneman.

Martin, despite his promise: OR, 4/12/69, p. 11.

McCall delivered a final blow to the bill: interviews with Paul Hanneman, Don Jepsen.

"blow the cover": interview with Don Jepsen.

"He was convinced the time wasn't right": interview with Paul Hanneman.

Chapter 14

Key Sources

Operation Red Hat: PA:Nixon, FOIA:DOD and FOIA:HEW. A helpful history is "Movement of Toxic Chemical Munitions," by Col. Harry L. Foradori for the Industrial College of the Armed Forces, Report No. M75-020, released in FOIA:HEW.

264   make environmental issues the theme: OJ, 3/9/70, p. 7.

Harris poll: Louis Harris And Associates, Inc., *The Public's View of Environmental Problems in Oregon*, March 1970.

ecology movement: Carroll, *It Seemed like Nothing Happened*, pp. 124-26; Barone, *Our Country*, pp. 477-78; Barney, *Unfinished Agenda*, pp. 81-84, 114-22; Davies, *Politics of Pollution*, pp. 7-57, 114-18, 130-38; Manchester, *Glory and the Dream*, pp. 1436-38; Hodgson, *America in Our Time*, pp. 401-04.

265   "The environment has just been": Commoner, *The Closing Circle*, p. 1.

"The great question of the seventies is": NYT, 1/23/70, p. 22.

266   "inform [McCall]": Dent to Cole, 10/17/69, PA:Nixon File ST37.

McCall again was with tall company: OR, 11/14/69, p. 25.

nerve agents included: Foradori, "Movement of Toxic Chemical
        Munitions," FOIA:HEW; Hersh, *Chemical and Biological War-
        fare*, p. xi; Beal to TM, 12/1/69; Oregon State Board of Health
        memo, 1/15/70, TM:OSA 72A-53 Box 17; OS, 1/2/70, p. 5;

6,400 sheep: Seagrave, *Yellow Rain*, p. 260.

267   thirteen thousand tons: Foradori, "Movement of Toxic Chemical
        Munitions," FOIA:HEW.

a leaky bomb: Foradori, "Movement of Toxic Chemical Muni-
        tions," FOIA:HEW; *Newsweek*, 12/8/69, p. 43; WSJ, 7/18/69, p. 1
        and 3/4/70, p. 18; Seagrave, *Yellow Rain*, p. 266.

a Pentagon official called Schmidt: TM:OSA 72A-53 Box 17; inter-
        view with Ron Schmidt.

268   "I'm going to listen to the Pentagon": interview with Ron Schmidt.

"Transportation of this material": Beal to TM, 12/1/69, TM:OSA
        72A-53 Box 17.

"It was as if they knew": interview with Ron Schmidt.

McCall took detailed notes: Beal to TM, 12/1/69; notes and memo,
        "Information for Governor McCall," 12/3/69, TM:OSA 72A-53
        Box 17; OS, 1/30/70, p. 2.

"Flawless": TM:OSA 72A-53 Box 17.

"You can't go along with this": interview with Ron Schmidt.

269   His fight with Schmidt had disturbed him deeply: interviews with
        Ron Schmidt, Audrey McCall.

"Are you mad at me?": interview with Ron Schmidt.

270   McCall thought, then why not destroy it?: For example, TM to
        Nixon, 12/5/69, PA:Nixon ST37.

McCall did his own math: TM:OSA 72A-53 Box 17.

"Put together a plan": interview with Ron Schmidt.

"He wanted to say no": interview with Ron Schmidt.

271   "To say that the citizens of Okinawa": TM to Nixon, 12/5/69,
        PA:Nixon ST37; TM:OSA 70A-95 Box 116; OS, 12/6/69, p. 1.

McCall was not alone in his opposition: OS, 12/4/69, p. 1; OR,
        12/11/69, p. 46.

"I can't recall an issue": Los Angeles *Times*, 1/19/70, p. 3.

272   the number grew to 23,000: CJ, 1/6/70, p. 1.

"We need poison gas here in Oregon": TM:OHS.

"I conclude (reluctantly)": Oliver to TM, 12/12/69, TM:OSA 70A-95 Box 112.

"[T]he President renounced": Laird to TM, 1/8/70, TM:OSA 70A-95 Box 112.

"By the Army's own definition": press release, 1/13/70, TM:OSA 70A-95 Box 112.

273   had reached 62,000: Foradori, "Movement of Toxic Chemical Munitions," FOIA:HEW.

Resor refused: Resor to Laird, 2/27/70, FOIA/DOD.

"was more implacable than ever": TM to Nixon, 3/4/70, PA:Nixon ST37; TM:OSA 72A-53 Box 17.

"I believe Tom McCall has done": TM to Nixon, 3/4/70, PA:Nixon ST37; TM:OSA 72A-53 Box 17.

"Can the Republican governor": WSJ, 3/4/70, p. 1.

"We were naive": interview with Ron Schmidt.

274   "Governor McCall has reluctantly": Hughes to Erlichman, 4/11/70, PA:Nixon ST37.

army sent him a classified copy: OR, 4/7/70, p. 1.

"Our previous information": OR, 4/11/70, p. 1.

"It was hollow talk": OR, 4/11/70, p. 1.

Earth Day: NYT, 4/23/70, p. 1, 23; OR, 4/23/70, p. 1, 22.

275   "In Oregon we use the phrase" and remainder of Earth Day speech: TM:OHS Box 9.

277   "What is going on in Albany": RG, 11/24/74, p. 13A.

Steinfeld disagreed: Steinfeld to TM, 5/1/70, FOIA/HEW; TM:OSA 72A-53 Box 17; OR, 5/7/70, p. 1.

278   "I have remonstrated until I am hoarse": TM to Agnew, 5/2/70, TM:OSA 72A-53 Box 17.

The lawsuit provided: OR, 4/22/70, p. 1; OS, 5/22/70, p. 1.

"die-in": OR, 5/18/70, p. 1.

a resolution to block the army's funding: OS, 5/22/70, p. 20.

279   he discovered hostile voters: Prochnau and Larsen, A Certain Democrat, p. 291.

Jackson told Nixon he was changing: OR, 4/23/70, p. 1.

280   "It was a near-perfect political approach": Prochnau and Larsen, A Certain Democrat, p. 291.

"I was the only one": OJ, 5/23/70, p. 1; Ognibene, Scoop, pp. 221-22; Prochnau and Larsen, A Certain Democrat, p. 292.

The president completely ignored the one person: interview with
Ron Schmidt.

"Tom wasn't mad": interview with Ron Schmidt.

"McCall deserved better": Prochnau and Larsen, *A Certain Democrat*, p. 292.

"tedious six-month battle toward reason": press statement, 5/23/70,
TM:OSA 72A-53 Box 17.

Chapter 15

282 The Oregonian had published a poll: OR, 4/12/70.

"Our surveys showed substantial numbers": interview with Ken
Johnson.

283 University of Oregon: Metzler, *Confrontation*, generally.

"Without the right of dissent": RG, 11/24/74, p. 13A

"fed up to their eardrums and eyeballs": Manchester, *Glory and the Dream*, p. 1347.

284 "that this kind of depraved mischief be stopped": RG, 1/16/83.

"We are in danger of becoming a society": RG, 11/24/74, p. 13A.

"He was a hot head": interview with Ed Westerdahl.

invasion of Cambodia: Shawcross, *Sideshow*, generally; Carroll, *It Seemed Like Nothing Happened*, pp. 11-12; Karnow, *Vietnam*, pp. 606-10.

"eradicate": Karnow, *Vietnam*, p. 611.

At PSU, protesters called a strike: Metropolitan Human Relations
Commission, *Campus Disorders at Portland State University*;
OJ, 5/6/70, p. 1; 5/7/70, p. 1; 5/8/70, p. 6; 5/9/70, p. 1; 11/6/70,
p. 5; OR, 5/7/70, pp. 2, 8; 5/8/70, p. 1; 5/9/70, p. 1, 10.

285 to endorse the president's policy: TM to Nixon, 9/29/69 and
11/12/69, PA:Nixon ST37.

"The president is on notice": TM to Agnew, 5/2/70, TM:OSA 72A-53
Box 17.

"one percent of the students": RG, 5/12/70, p. 1.

"You wouldn't want me to say": RG, 5/12/70, p. 1.

286 one-hundred-man police riot squad: OJ, 5/12/70, p. 1; 11/6/70, p. 5;
RG, 5/12/70, p. 3; Metropolitan Human Relations Commission,
Campus Disorders at Portland State University.

"It has not been a Victorian lawn party": TM:OHS Box 9.

287   "Not long after Kent State": TM:M, pp. 132-33.
        FBI had opened a routine security file: TM:M, pp. 132-33; OJ,
            5/25/70, p. 7; 9/23/70, p. 4; OR, 9/5/70, p. 4; SAC memorandum,
            6/9/70, FOIA:FBI.
        "[R]adical 'New Left'": Portland SAC to Hoover, 6/18/70, FOIA:FBI.
        "Although at this early date": Portland SAC to Hoover, 6/18/70,
            FOIA:FBI.
        he wired the Portland office: 7/1/70, FOIA:FBI.
        "all current information": Portland SAC to Hoover, 7/27/70,
            FOIA:FBI.
288   "pro-Bureau": 11/21/66, FOIA:TM.
        "a great admirer of the Director": 2/20/67, FOIA:TM.
        "We couldn't run the risk": interview with Ed Westerdahl.
        "intelligence sources": Portland SAC to Hoover, 6/18/70, FOIA:FBI.
        seventy thousand protestors: OJ, 6/4/70, p. 8.
        "People were just burned out": interview with Peter Fornara.
        "We had heard that the Legion expected": interview with Peter
            Fornara.
289   "There was a feeling of surprise": interview with Sidney Lezak.
        "more important than the intelligence": interview with Lee
            Johnson.
        "Pretty soon there was a legitimacy": interview with Ron Schmidt.
        "We exploited it": interview with Robert Wollheim.
        FBI also claimed that convoys: FOIA:FBI.
290   "The Nixon Administration kept warning": interview with Ron
            Schmidt.
        "They're going to play this": interview with Ron Schmidt.
        "Tom was well aware": interview with Ron Schmidt.
        Jamboree's following was in shambles: interviews with Glen Swift,
            Michael McCusker; OJ, 9/5/70, p. 4
        alternative event: interview with Glen Swift; OJ, 7/23/70, p. 4;
            Willamette Bridge, 7/24/70, p. 2; OR, 8/2/70, p. 27; 8/5/70, p. 7.
        "a peaceful coming together": files of Glen Swift.
291   "They identified the right way": interview with Ed Westerdahl.
292   "Westerdahl, are you crazy?": interview with Ron Schmidt.
        "Ron, you're the political man": KATU.
        "Whether it works or not": KATU.
293   "I've made my decision": KATU.
        Eugene Doherty: interview with Eugene Doherty.

"What do you know about rock festivals": interview with Eugene Doherty.

294   Westerdahl made his orders: interview with Ed Westerdahl.
"[McCall] should get the chair for this": OR, 8/7/70, p. 1.
"We're not going to put up with it": TM:M, p. 134.
"You're telling these people": OJ, 8/28/70, p. 9
"Government officials would be naive": OS, 8/6/70.

295   "A number of the people": interview with Ed Westerdahl.
Jackson shook down his business friends: interview with Ed Westerdahl.
thought of naked, drug using: Interview with Ken Johnson.
Johnson recognized the brilliance: interview with Ken Johnson.
"[L]et us use dope": NYT, 8/31/70.
"You didn't have to be a genius": interview with Peter Fornara.

296   make the National Guard's numbers: interview with Ed Westerdahl.
A rumor control center: OJ, 8/27/70.
"Citizens Urged": FOIA:FBI.
"Until we treat [protestors] as common criminals": OJ, 8/27/70.
rose petals: KATU; interview with Ron Schmidt.
Multnomah County gave the sheriff: OR, 8/28/70, p. 1.
city and county emptied their jails: OJ, 8/24/70, p. 3.
fifty thousand to ten thousand: OR, 9/5/70, p. 4.
"Outsiders are filtering into the city": Portland FBI to Hoover 8/25/70 FOIA: Vortex.

297   "[I]ntelligence sources" and rest of TM's speech: OR, 8/26/70, p. 18.
298   a small, little noticed story appeared: OJ, 8/25/70.
299   McCall guessed: OJ, 8/21/70.
when the festival officially opened: OR, 8/26/70, p. 33; 8/29/70, p. 16; 8/30/70, pp. 1, 38; 9/2/70, p. 15; OJ, 8/28/70, p. 8.
Sky River: OJ, 8/31/70, p. 4.
300   "Any movement": Portland SAC to Hoover: 8/30/70 FOIA:FBI.
thirty-five thousand to eight thousand: 8/30/70 memo, FOIA:FBI.
no more than a thousand people: OR, 8/31/70, p. 1; OJ, 8/31/70, p. 2.
"Go back, you police just make trouble": OJ, 9/1/70, p. 2.
301   a single broken window: OR, 9/3/70, p. 34.
"The Legion convention": interview with Sidney Lezak.
302   "weekenders": Portland FBI to Hoover 8/30/70 FOIA:FBI.
"We knew going in ninety-eight percent of the kids": interview with Ed Westerdahl.

303   "Hell of a job": interview with Eugene Doherty.
304   "And the turning point": interview with Ken Johnson.
       "If [Vortex] hadn't happened": interview with Robert Straub.
       "They smoked marijuana widely": OS, 9/4/70, p. 1.
       "If I had to do it": OJ, 9/12/70, p. 1.
       "If the press had really wanted to do McCall in": interview with
           Lee Johnson.
       "McCall showed courage and ingenuity": OR, 9/4/70, p. 39.
       a lousy debate performance: OJ, 10/16/70, p. 4; 10/19/70, p. 2; CJ,
           10/19/70, p. 7.
       "Straub is going to lose the election": OR, 10/22/70, p. 19.
305   "I'm his mother": OR, 10/29/70, p. 21.
       "That's enough promotion": OR, 10/29/70, p. 21.
       "Goddamn it, Mother": interview with Harry Bodine.
       "Well, you've got nothing to lose": OR, 10/29/70, p. 21; interview
           with Harry Bodine.
       eleven GOP governors: Witcover, *White Knight*, p. 403.
306   "like a man with a knife in his shawl": RG, 12/20/70, p. 10; Wit-
           cover, *White Knight*, p. 407.
       "The press would set me up": TM:M, p. 157.
       "Tom, I'm mad as hell at you": TM:M, p. 157.
       "There's only one way to campaign": as quoted in TM:Tapes 16.
307   "Tom, the vice president asked me personally": KATU.
       "to reaffirm our political friendships" and rest of Agnew speech:
           Peterson, *Agnew*, p. 141.
       "When you read the speech": KATU.
       "smoldering eyes would burn": TM:M, p. 158.
       "Nothing is more unreasonable": Peterson, *Agnew*, p. 141.
308   "Is that son of a bitch": KATU.
       "There was the most unbelievable": RG, 12/16/70, p. 1.
       "Listen Tom, now is the time to be cool": KATU.
       "David, thanks for helping me": KATU.
309   "fine, right and proper": Witcover, *White Knight*, p. 406.
       "Tom, I can't believe you said this!": TM:M, p. 158; TM:Tapes 16.
       "The wind roared in my ears": TM:M, p. 157.
       "Tom's impression as a wishy-washy leader": interview with Ken
           Johnson.

Chapter 16

314   "Come visit us again and again": RG, 2/14/71, p. 10B.
       "impugning western hospitality": TM:Tapes 17.
       "The personal freedom to live": RG, 2/14/71, p. 10B.
       "How refreshing it is": RG, 2/14/71, p. 10B.
       "We here are currently under siege": RG, 2/14/71, p. 10B.
       "You are the first person": RG, 2/14/71, p. 10B.
315   "Oregon: Keep Out": Los Angeles *Times*, 9/4/71, p. 1.
       "I think you yourself": TM to Longstreet, 4/13/71, TM:OSA 72A-89
           Box 19.
       "An office holder would have to be: TM speech, 4/13/71, TM:OHS
           Box 14.
       "I think I might be able to anticipate": TM speech, 10/13/71,
           TM:OHS Box 17.
316   "He thought SOLV was a bunch of crap": interview with Victoria
           Chambers Berger.
       SOLV had collected nearly three-fourths: *Oregon Times*, 3/29/71, p.
           6; OJ, 3/30/71, p. 2; TM:OSA 72A-53 Box 14.
317   "I want to make it very clear": CJ, 1/10/70, p. 3, and 1/17/70, p. 1.
       "The environmental crisis towers over us": TM:OHS Box 13.
318   similar container deposit laws: Savage and Richmond, *Oregon's
           Bottle Bill*, p. 11.
319   Plaid Pantry stores: OR, 4/16/70.
       "I hope that [Oregonians] bury me in litter": CJ, 4/1/70.
       "the companies were highly suspicious of Rich": interview with
           Kay Chambers.
       "My father was not a paranoid man": interview with Victoria
           Chambers Berger.
       "By the time the 1971 legislature opened": interview with Jason
           Boe.
320   Initiative 256: *Washington Monthly*, February 1971; Savage and
           Richmond, *Oregon's Bottle Bill*, p. 11.
       companies lined up their defenses in Salem: 1971 Senate Consumer
           Affairs Committee minutes, OSA; OR, 3/24/71, p. 7; 3/23/71, p. 7.
       "They did the most awful job": interview with Betty Roberts.
321   "Is this bottle covered": interview with Betty Roberts.
       Roberts quickly rounded up: interview with Betty Roberts; OJ,
           5/22/71, p. 4.

"If you can kill this bill": interviews with Betty Roberts, Ted Hallock; KATU.

322   "to turn us away from": CJ, 7/2/71, p. 1

"I am in no way qualified": Corvallis *Gazette-Times*, 5/2/74, p. 10.

"I accomplished what I set out to do": interview with Victoria Chambers Berger.

"ecology session": RG, 6/13/71, p. 4A.

323   "The 'captains of industry'": interview with James Faulstich.

"Oregon suffered from": interview with James Faulstich.

"We've got to have a little balance": WSJ, 11/3/71, p. 1.

324   "the woodsy witch doctors of a revived nature cult": NYT, 11/28/71, Section 3, p. 13.

"overkill": OJ, 5/13/71, p. 5.

"Add it all up": OJ, 5/13/70.

"hysteria" and "environmental McCarthyism": NYT, 12/26/71, p. 36.

325   "You have to understand L.B.": interview with Arnold Cogan.

L.B. Day never knew: interview with Frank Day.

"He had a talent for persuading people": interview with Frank Day.

"L.B. was a bully": confidential source.

"'Vicious' does not begin": interview with Robert Oliver.

326   EPA: OR, 10/1/72, p. F1.

"Sometimes it seems as if I'm shouting": OR, 10/1/72, p. F1.

"If the Corps of Engineers is environmentally concerned": TM speech, 2/8/73, TM:OHS Box 22.

"a pick, a shovel and a mule": TM speech, 2/8/73, TM:OHS Box 22.

"There was always a feeling": interview with B.A. "Barney" McPhillips.

327   "We are going to continue to be militant": CJ, 1/27/72, sec. 4, p. 33.

"Recognizing the ecological ills": *National Geographic*, June 1972, p. 834.

328   "showing little concern": TM:OHS Box 20.

dumping 145,000 gallons of waste. . . . 400,000 gallons of waste: TM:OHS Box 20.

329   Why the hell did it take you so long?: CJ, 7/26/72, p. 1; TM:OHS Box 20.

Day in turn had DEQ's attorneys draft: TM:OHS Box 20.

the DEQ did not file: OS, 7/27/72, p. 22; KATU.

"Hitler!": TM:M, p. 182.

330   "Why should one company": CJ, 7/27/72, p. 1.

331   "No one denied": TM:M, p. 294.
332   clearcutting: OR, 7/16/71, p. 25.
       opposed expanding wilderness designations: for example, OR,
           7/28/70, p. 12.
333   "the wave of the future": OS, 10/4/70, p. 2.
       "When swinging through the energy forest": OS, 4/6/78, p. 4C.
       A geologist's report raising concerns: WSJ, 1/26/72.

Chapter 17

335   "I'm going to veto that son of a bitch": interview with Robert
           Oliver.
338   "He had a very good public relations sense": interview with Jules
           Witcover.
       "He was his own man": interview with Jules Witcover.
       "For beginners": TM:M, p. 159.
339   "squeezed unduly": OJ, 7/13/71, p. 1.
       "Apparently Gov. McCall is not aware": OS, 7/12/71, p. 1.
       "The president is a guest in California": OJ, 7/13/71, p. 1.
       "When I said 'Hi, Ron!'": TM:M, p. 160.
340   "Which is something he overlooked": TM:Tapes 16.
       "the necessity of saying something": TM:Tapes 16.
       "People forget": NYT, 7/13/71.
       McCall said he intended to challenge: OS, 7/13/71, p. 1.
341   Hatfield quietly organized: TM:M, p. 106; OR, 8/1/68, p. 10.
       "Things have changed": Schmidt to TM, 6/24/68 TM:OSA 70A-95
           Box 61.
342   "I would feel safer": OS, 7/29/68 section 2, p. 13.
       "yellow, chicken kind of resolution": OS, 7/29/68 section 2, p. 13.
       "seething inside of me for the last four years": OS, 7/29/68, p. 1.
       "told friends that he was glad": OS, 7/29/68, p. 1.
       so he could have an aisle seat: interview with Howell Appling.
343   "Hatfield threw himself at Nixon": TM:M, p. 106.
       "Whenever you saw them together": confidential source.
344   "I am tired of your public tantrums": OS, 3/7/69, p. 4.
       "garrulous ex-broadcaster": OS, 3/7/69, p. 4.
       "I thought initially it was as cruel": TM to Smith, undated, TM:OHS
           and author's files.
345   "The criticism of [Hatfield]": OJ, 7/3/71, p. 2.

"I wish 95 percent of the people": WP, 9/26/71, p. 2.

McCall had confided that the Senate: Schmidt to TM, 3/12/74, author's files.

"Tom was a very unpredictable person": interview with Mark Hatfield.

346   "Come into the race": WW, 6/29/81, p.1; interview with Mark Hatfield.

"[Tom] knew I would": WW, 6/29/81, p. 1.

347   "All in all": TM:OHS Box 18.

"eyes popped wide": TM:M, p. 153.

"It's an unclear right": RG, 2/27/72, p. 1.

"That just shocked the shit": interview with Clarence Zaitz.

348   "He said what he thought": interview with Clarence Zaitz.

two announcements: TM:OHS Box 21.

he delivered the latter: RG, 3/7/72, p. 1.

"could turn me into a lame duck": TM to Welch and Frazier, 8/10/72, given to the author by James Welch.

"When McCall was asked": RG, 5/25/72, p. 1 and 6/11/72, p. 15A.

349   biopsy: TM:M, p. 230.

350   his office kept the trip's true reason: press statement, 9/8/72, TM:OHS Box 20.

did not allow himself to rest": TM:M, p. 231.

Chapter 18

Key Sources
Senate Bill 100's passage: The best history is Little, *New Oregon Trail*.

351   "You didn't!": TM:OSA 74A-98 Box 26.

"Oregon's leadership in fighting pollution": Detroit *News*, 2/27/73; TM:OSA 74A-98 Box 26.

352   The deadline had come and gone: Logan, *Oregon Land Use Story*, pp. 4-5; Leonard, *Managing Oregon's Growth*, pp. 6-7.

fifteen thousand more acres: *Oregon Times*, December 1972, p. 14.

"I'd like to hold on to my land": *Oregon Times*, December 1972, p. 13.

353   "The system hasn't failed": House Committee on Interior and Insular Affairs, Hearings, Serial No. 93-50, p. 27.

"Scratch a farmer": Little, *New Oregon Trail*, p. 26.

"raw-boned and somewhat cerebral": Little, *New Oregon Trail*, p. 9.

"Visualize the alternative": Little, *New Oregon Trail*, p. 9.

"Oregon had this environmental wave building up": interview with Hector Macpherson.

354   He soon found kindred spirits: interview with Hector Macpherson; DeGrove, *Land Growth and Politics*, pp. 239-40; Leonard, *Managing Oregon's Growth*, p. 8.

McCall and Macpherson's new land use bill: Logan, *Oregon Land Use Story*, p. 16.

"I knew nothing would get done": Leonard, *Managing Oregon's Growth*, p. 135.

355   "Project Foresight": Halprin, *The Willamette Valley*, generally; Logan, *Oregon Land Use Story*, pp. 6-9.

"[McCall] threw a great deal": interview with Hector Macpherson.

"We need growth" and the speech generally: OR, 11/21/72, p. 12; RG, 11/20/72, p. 1; CJ, 11/20/72, p. 1.

356   "There is a shameless threat to our environment": *Journals and Calendars of the Senate and the House*, House Journal, 1/8/73, p. J-313.

357   "[Tom] had the same distaste": interview with Ted Hallock.

"from unconvinced to hostile": Little, *New Oregon Trail*, p. 17.

sewer lines from subdivisions went nowhere: TM:OSA 74A-98 Box 14.

The study identified thirty-eight: TM:OSA 74A-98 Box 14.

358   "My first thought was that King Tom": RG, 1/18/73, p. 5A.

"There is a valid public interest": House Committee on Interior and Insular Affairs, Hearings, Serial No. 93-50, p. 3.

359   "There are no tomorrows": OR, 2/8/73, p. 13.

"Whenever Tom was around": interview with Henny Willis.

"just get me $500,000": interview with Ted Hallock.

360   "The first meeting consisted of L.B. haranguing": interview with Fred Van Natta.

Day beat down opposition: Little, *New Oregon Trail*, pp. 18-20.

"We're talking about planning": Logan, *Oregon Land Use Story*, p. 16.

361   "I told them not to change that bill": interview with Ted Hallock.

Unaltered, SB 100 sailed: DeGrove, *Land Growth and Politics*, pp. 243-44.

"Senate Bill 100 is tremendously hedged": Little, *New Oregon Trail*, pp. 36-37.

"We have just really got to pay attention": Little, *New Oregon Trail*, p. 36.

363   "Tax reform was the one issue": interview with Doris Penwell.

364   "get along like two long separated brothers": OJ, 4/7/73.

"They screwed Tom": interview with Jason Boe.

365   "Some opponents treat tax reform": TM speech 4/24/73, author's files; TM:M, p. 172.

"The school finance program offered": TM speeches, author's files.

367   "You son of a bitch": TM:M, pp. 171-72.

Last minute polls: Bardsley Papers, TM:OHS, Box 7; OR, 5/1/73, p. 28.

"The people have rejected me": interview with Jason Boe.

"He was personally wounded": interview with Elizabeth Myers.

"I'm resigning": interview with Ron Schmidt.

368   "Feeling of hopelessness": OJ, 5/3/73.

"Once he started getting the calls from people": interview with Ron Schmidt.

"Goddamn it, it was for the people": WW, 1/20/75, p. 1.

"McCall disappeared": WW, 1/20/75, p. 1.

Chapter 19

369   "Tom aged visibly that night": interview with Jason Boe.

"You defeated my plan": interview with Forest Amsden.

370   "the bastard at a family reunion": RG, 3/18/74, p. 8D.

371   He privately suspected Nixon: interview with Ron Schmidt.

"simply clear the air": OR, 5/10/73, p. 16.

"As far as changing parties is concerned": TM:Tapes I

372   "As a maverick soul": TM:M, p. 249.

the United States imported only ten percent: Johnson, *Modern Times*, p. 665.

A dramatic change occurred in 1971: Carroll, *It Seemed Like Nothing Happened,* pp. 119-23; Sherrill, *Oil Follies*, pp. 164-207.

373   shortages in Oregon: OS, 5/19/73, p. 1 and 9/24/73, p. 1.

"It's like losing": OR, 6/3/73, p. F1; *Time,* 11/18/73, p. 108.

375   "The fact remains that we face": TM statement, 5/31/73, TM:OSA 74A-98 Box 4.

"[McCall] overstated his case": OR, 6/3/73, p. F3.

"raise the hackles": RG, 6/1/73, p. 1.

"I think we can look first": OR, 6/3/73, p. F6.

376   "I've been in the rumpus room": OR, 7/25/73, p. 1 and 8/1/73, p. 1.

a nitroglycerin bomb: OR, 8/13/73, p. 1, 8/17/73, p. 1, 8/21/73, p. 1

377   one martini: TM:OHS Box 35.

"The prostate is hardly": TM:M, p. 235.

"distasteful to have the Governor's glands": TM:M, p. 235.

"One Ball" McCall: interviews with Darrel Buttice, Ron Schmidt.

"I just want you to remember": TM speech, 11/14/74, TM:OHS
    Box 25.

378   "Jobs are at stake": TM statement, 8/22/73, TM:OSA 74A-98 Box 4.

executive order: Executive Order 73-5; TM statement, 9/23/73,
    TM:OSA 74A-98 Box 4.

"People wouldn't believe there was a crisis": TM speech, 11/20/73,
    TM:OSA 74A-98 Box 4.

379   "risk of catastrophe": TM:OSA 74A-98 Box 4.

"wasteful practices": TM:OSA 74A-98 Box 4.

"But as a hard fact of life": TM:OSA 74A-98 Box 4.

"That danger to a governor": Executive Order 73-7; TM statement,
    9/23/73, TM:OSA 74A-98 Box 4.

the Oregon *Statesman* named on its front page: OS, 9/25/73, p. 1
    and 9/29/73, p. 7.

McCall anxiously sought a business to take to court: KATU.

"[W]hen the motel owner went to the hospital": TM:M, p. 223.

"loom like abandoned hulks": *Time,* 11/12/73, p. 108.

380   Oregon's 1,300 public schools close: OR, 10/13/73, p. 1.

"Somebody claimed the order was issued,": TM:OHS Box 25.

employ 800 people: OR, 1/28/71, p. 19.

he changed his mind: OS, 10/23/73, p. 9.

381   "We cannot invite industry": TM to Conkling, 10/17/73, author's
    files.

oil companies: Sherrill, *Oil Follies*, pp. 174-76.

382   "The Governor has a Cold": NYT, 11/9/73, p. 26 and 11/12/73,
    p. 12.

"The public is—or can be—convinced": TM speech, 11/20/73,
    TM:OSA 74A-98 Box 4.

that month polls had shown: Lukas, *Nightmare,* p. 339

enemies list: Lukas, *Nightmare,* p. 13.

383   "People have the right to know": Lukas, *Nightmare,* p. 455.

"I won't be a party": OR, 11/19/73, p. 1; also, NYT, 11/19/73, p. 22; WP, 11/19/73, p. 1.

"more credible": OJ, 11/19/73, p. 1.

"If I have added to your burden: Lukas, *Nightmare,* p. 455; WP, 11/21/73, p. 1.

"Are we going to be blindsided": Lukas, *Nightmare,* p. 456.

384   "All of us are going home feeling better": Lukas, *Nightmare,* p. 456.

History has shown that Nixon had known: Lukas, *Nightmare,* p. 456.

"[Nixon's] insensitivity to what a bombshell is": NYT, 11/25/73, p. 35.

"third force": *Newsweek,* 12/3/73, p. 21.

Chapter 20

385   "Energy crisis, drugs, pollution": *Newsweek,* 1/7/74, p. 49.

"All of [his work] finally reached": *Newsday,* 2/4/74.

386   "Oregon Story": TM speech, 3/17/72, TM:OHS Box 18.

"People are yearning to hear": TM to Kerr, 11/26/73, TM:OSA 75A-12 Box 29; RG, 11/27/73, p. 1.

calling for Nixon's resignation: CJ, 1/31/74, p. 1.

Agnew resigned: Lukas, *Nightmare,* pp. 402, 412.

"I'm mapping out the creation": Miami *Herald,* 6/2/74.

387   "Governor go back to the mainland": KATU.

"It's no political bandwagon I'm building": *Newsday,* 2/4/74.

"The Oregon story is a hopeful force": RG, 12/13/73, p. 1.

"I thought everybody would laugh": OR, 12/20/73, p. 24.

"How d'ya shut this thing off": author's files.

"Oregon's Gov. Tom McCall is a throwback": as quoted in Miami *Herald,* 6/2/74.

"McCall can hardly be described": Boston *Globe,* 5/7/74.

388   "There's no point in being coy about it": *Newsday,* 2/4/74.

"It may be that": RG, 5/23/74, p. 1

thirty-five other states: Los Angeles *Times* 8/26/73, p. 1.

"It has challenged the people": Honolulu *Star-Bulletin,* 12/5/73.

Oregon's gasoline and oil quotas: OS, 12/31/73, p. 1 and 1/3/74, p. 5.

389   "Was it true, as many Oregonians claimed": Sherrill, *Oil Follies*,
        p. 210.
        McCall privately suspected: TM speech, 1/3/74, author's files.
        independent stations: OS, 2/8/74, p. 8.
        "I sat there watching it": interview with Don Jarvi.
        McCall threatened mandatory rationing: Los Angeles *Times*
        1/10/74, p. 25.
390   "That the state of Oregon": *New Yorker,* 2/25/74.
391   he had given Packwood his word: TM:M, p. 249.
        "Can you believe he's a United States senator?": interview with
        Ken Johnson.
        "All of them thought": interview with Ken Johnson.
        Packwood had invited him: interviews with Ron Schmidt, Bob
        Packwood, TM:M, p. 252; OR, 3/12/74, p. 14.
392   "It was at least one martini": interview with Ron Schmidt.
        "He had it all figured out": interview with Bob Packwood.
393   "This made a mess of the evening": TM:M, p. 252.
        "I can't believe what I just saw": interview with Bob Packwood.
        "highly reliable Republican source": OR, 3/8/74, p. 1.
        Timber companies were now angry at Packwood: Davis to TM and
        Schmidt, 4/7/72, TM:OSA 74A-2 Box 8.
        "make the shootout at the OK Corral": RG, 3/8/74, p. 1.
394   he began spreading word: OR, 2/7/93, p. D1.
        Packwood's threat: interviews with Ron Schmidt, Leonard Fors-
        gren, confidential sources. A contemporary memo in Schmidt's
        handwriting puts "Financial help for Sam" as the number one
        concern about Packwood's line of attack, and a Schmidt memo
        to TM lays out other factors. Schmidt to TM, 3/12/74, author's
        files.
395   Packwood, or someone working on Packwood's behalf: interview
        with Ron Schmidt.
        "Even the suggestion of the smear": interview with Ron Schmidt.
        "My electoral successes tempted me": TM statement, 3/14/74,
        TM:OHS/author's files.
        "Tom had told me": interview with Jean McCall Babson.
396   "It was sort of a pathetic thing": interview with Robert Oliver.
        "Nobody is being asked to stop the world": *Vital Speeches,* 9/1/74.
        "Regeneration, damn it": author's files.

397   "As governor, he's done what we say": Von Hoffman, quoted in
            RG, 5/23/74, p. 1.
       newspaper and network news: for example, *Time,* CBS-TV, NBC-TV;
            RG, 11/27/73, p. 1.
       "60 Minutes": OR, 6/8/74; CJ, 8/9/74.
398   "the CBS management decision": TM:M, p. 265.
       "What is Tom McCall doing out there?": OR, 5/26/74.
       "It is an open question in fact": OR, 6/6/74,
       "Oregonians, beset by field burning smoke": OR, 9/9/74.
       speaking fees: "Honorarium and fees for Gov. Tom McCall,"
            1/7/75, TM:OHS/author's files.
399    $10,000: Duckworth to TM, 6/1/74, TM:OHS Box 24.
       "The title of my address": Congressional Record, 7/15/74, pp.
            E4718-20; TM:OHS Box 24.
402   the fall salmon count: RG, 10/29/89.
       twenty-pound salmon: *National Geographic,* June 1972, p. 818.
403   ninety-five percent of bottles and cans purchased: Gudger and
            Bailes, *Economic Impact of Bottle Bill,* p. 67; Savage and
            Richmond, *Oregon's Bottle Bill,* pp. 24-25.
       2.26 million people: *Oregon Blue Book* 1975-76, p. 144; and 1967-
            68, p. 140.
404   "How do you know?": TM speech, 4/29/74, TM:OHS 23.
       "He tried, oh Lord": RG, 1/10/75, p. 1; TM:OHS Box 34.
       "What's it like to be governor?": CJ, 4/19/71, p. 18.
405   "I will feel both relief and sadness": CJ, 4/19/71, p. 18.

Chapter 21

409   "I hate to find myself": TM:OHS Box 25.
       "I will never be content": author's files.
410   awards: NYT, 10/31/75; OR, 1/21/75, p. 1.
       teaching position with a $30,000: NYT, 1/15/75.
       $50,000 grant: OR, 1/17/75, p. 1; TM:OHS Box 30.
       $25,000 of the energy grant: TM:OHS Box 30; interview with Gene
            Maudlin.
411   "I thought the teaching": WW, 5/16/77, p. 1.
       "The winding down process": author's files.
       $37,000 . . . $13,000 for radio: TM:OHS/author's files.
       free of cancer: Hodges to TM, 10/13/77, TM:OHS/author's files.

"The whole point is": *Oregon Magazine*, March 1978, p. 30.

412   both Ford and Carter recognized: OJ, 10/26/76, p. 2.

McCall preferred Carter: interview with Ron Schmidt; TM to
    Schmidt 3/27/76, TM:OHS/author's files.

"writing his own ticket": interview with Ron Schmidt.

413   Alcoa produced a campaign: Don Waggoner Papers, OHS.

"Oregon has almost become": OS, 10/19/75, p. 5.

"which seem to be either deceptive": Packwood to Bernstein,
    7/22/76; Herzog to Packwood, 9/17/76; Don Waggoner Papers,
    OHS.

Hatfield had struggled: CJ, 6/30/76, p. 1.

414   "The pluses are absolutely so numerous": Detroit *News,* 10/6/76.

Oregonians "are incredulous": RG, 10/17/76, p. 6; CJ, 11/2/76, p.
    2A; NYT, 11/4/76, p. 22.

Land Conservation and Development Commission: Leonard,
    Managing Oregon's Growth, generally.

415   "Over my dead body": OR, 1/8/76, p. E1.

"Why so slow?": *1,000 Friends of Oregon Newsletter*, 10/76, as
    quoted in Leonard, *Managing Oregon's Growth*, p. 56.

416   "If there's anything that characterizes Oregon": RG, 9/16/76.

"Some people would subdivide the village graveyard": RG, 8/31/76,
    p. 7A.

"I've seen all that crap": RG, 9/16/76.

417   gave McCall a whopping lead: CJ, 11/3/75, p. 19.

"I must say I haven't decided": CJ, 4/19/77, p. 4.

IRS pressed McCall: Ormseth memo, 8/8/77 TM:OHS Box 27; TM to
    Schmidt 3/27/76, TM:OHS/author's files.

418   "Our CPA is": TM to Schmidt 3/27/76, TM:OHS Box 25.

"a political satrap": TM:OHS Box 25.

He was arrested: Rhoten to Samuel W. McCall III, 8/24/76 and
    9/24/76, TM:OHS Box 35; Marion County Circuit Court Case No.
    96681, Sloper order 9/22/76.

"a poor dear creature": TM to Walker 9/11/76 TM:OHS Box 33.

"our frightening battle": TM to Walker 9/11/76 TM:OHS Box 33.

charged Sam with a felony: OS, 7/12/77, p. 5A; Spokane *Daily
    Chronicle,* 7/11/77, p. 1.

asked the judge for mercy: Spokane *Daily Chronicle,* 7/11/77, p. 1.

"There's been a lot": OS, 7/12/77, p. 5A.

419   "I can sympathize": Washington State Superior Court, Spokane

County, Case No. 24527, 7/11/77; TM:OHS Box 35.

probation violation: Oregon Corrections Division Violation
    Reports, 10/10/77 and 10/12/77, TM:OHS Box 35.

"The governorship had always been": interview with Ed
    Westerdahl.

"Tom would just die": confidential source.

McCall was earning $52,000: Philadelphia *Inquirer*, 1/11/76; NYT,
    3/10/78, p. 16.

agreed to settle for $12,300: RG, 2/15/78, p. 2A; Ormseth to TM
    10/17/77, TM:OHS Box 27.

420   "He wanted to recapture": interview with Ron Schmidt.

"You'll get your heart broken": interview with Ron Schmidt.

"If all the people": Howell Appling, quoted by Travis Cross,
    interview with Cross.

421   "Can you see a politician": *Oregon Magazine*, March 1978, p. 36.

'You're dead a long time.': *Oregon Magazine*, March 1978, p. 36.

"When I announced I was going to run": NYT, 3/10/78, p. 16.

"Just having conventional party hacks": *Oregon Magazine*, March
    1978, p. 31.

422   Martin and Atiyeh thought their candidacies: interviews with Roger
    Martin, Jack Faust, John Mason.

"The legend always grows bigger": TM speech 2/15/78, author's
    files.

"He really wasn't geared": interview with Victor Atiyeh.

"McCall was shitty in raising money": interview with Ted Hallock.

424   McCall, as if in a confessional: OJ, 3/9/78. For evidence of the
    Republican Liaison Committee, TM:OHS Box 6 and TM:OSA 70A-
    95 Box 61.

"You could tell all of this stuff": interview with Doug Yocom.

"Tarnished image for McCall?": CJ, 3/18/78, p. 6D.

"reinspire the the team": KATU.

425   staff and supporters wondering: interviews with Phil Keisling,
    Marko Haggard, Ted Hallock.

"I just think he was fuzzy": interview with Ted Hallock.

"[W]hy should I rent the hall": CJ, 3/6/78.

"Too arrogant to debate?": CJ, 3/8/78.

"Let McCall stand up": OS, 3/11/78.

"I felt completely out of character": OR, 3/11/78, p. 8.

"It was obvious": interview with Roger Martin.

426   "Tom looked tragic," interview with Ted Hallock.

"Here was a hero": interview with Ted Hallock.

"We knew that if he got mad": interview with Roger Martin.

427   "Unlike Tom McCall, I don't think": RG, 4/29/78, p. 1.

"It was a very clever conspiracy": Hass Tape.

"I said to myself, 'That's not Tom McCall'": interview with Henny
    Willis.

"It was sad": interview with Henny Willis.

"wearing two hats": RG, 5/5/78, p. 2A.

428   More than 200,000 people: *Daily Astorian*, 3/6/78.

"jungle of neon": OS, 4/6/78, p. 4C.

"over a cocktail at the Elks Club": OS, 4/6/78, p. 4C.

429   "[Mine] is a pragmatic environmentalism": CJ, 5/14/78, p. 4.

"thinking as keenly about the environment": OS, 4/11/78.

"willful, childish, temper-tantrum": OJ, 5/14/78.

"Never let go of one limb": OS, 4/6/78, p. 4C.

"brown out, black out, cold houses and cold food": OR, 4/18/78.

"Damn it": OR, 4/18/78.

"Candidate Tom McCall appears": CJ, 5/14/78, p. 4.

430   fourteen-percentage-point lead over Victor Atiyeh: RG, 5/14/78,
    p. 3A.

"We thought we were where we should be": interview with Phil
    Keisling.

$390,000: Oregon Elections Division. Summary of Contributions
    and Expenditures, 1978 Primary, pp. 7-11.

"Six months out you were supposed": interview with Ted Hallock.

431   angrily berating his young campaign staff: confidential sources.

"I may have run once too often": NYT, 5/25/78.

"I'm not going to bicker with you": interview with Victor Atiyeh;
    KATU; CJ, 5/24/78, p. 1.

Atiyeh collected: Oregon Elections Division, 1978 primary ab-
    stracts.

432   refused to endorse him: interview with Victor Atiyeh; OR, 5/25/78,
    p. B1.

McCall first lent his name: TM:OHS Box 28.

$10,000 fee: Oregon Elections Division, Summary of Contributions
    and Expenditures, 1978 General, p. 77; OS, 11/3/78, p. 1A.

"I wasn't bought": ww, 10/13/80, p. 1.

433   "Governor Blunderbuss and Senator Milquetoast": os, 10/27/78, p.
          12A.

McCall had his first chance: interview with Ron Schmidt.

"Bob Straub could never": interview with Paul Hanson.

434   "Tom McCall was emancipated": RG, 11/8/78.

Chapter 22

Key Sources

Oregon's recession: Of the hundreds of newspaper articles written about the
    era, most helpful were: Foster Church in OR, 1/25/81-1/28/81 and
    12/2/81; assorted writers in OS, 2/28/82; and ww, 5/26/80; 6/2/80; 6/9/80
    and 6/16/80.

435   Kinzua: OR, 9/8/29 section 4, p. 6; 10/29/69, p. 10; 1/27/78, p. E5;
          3/12/78, p. 1; OJ, 1/27/78; 5/26/78.

8.2 billion board feet: U.S. Forest Service, Production, Prices,
          Employment and Trade, Second Quarter 1982, p. 6.

436   Champion International: OR, 5/10/79, p. D9; 6/9/79, p. E7.

437   ten percent: SJ, 2/28/82, p. 12J.

"We had an artificial economy": ww, 10/2/86, pp. 11, 12.

Federal Reserve Board: Greider, *Secrets of the Temple*, pp. 75-125.

"The alcoholic who goes on the wagon": Friedman, *Free to
          Choose*, p. 271.

438   44,000 lumber industry workers: OR, 4/18/80, p. 1.

"Companies are operating": ww, 5/26/80, p. 1.

Willamina: ww, 6/2/80; 6/9/80; 6/16/80; OR, 1/25/81, p. 1, C6, C7.

"It was like a vacation": ww, 6/10/80, p. 1.

"You don't even see them in the bars": ww, 6/10/80, p. 1.

439   Coos Bay: OR, 1/26/81, p. A9; 1/27/81, p. C7; 12/29/81, p. A14;
          12/29/81, p. A14; OJ, 3/11/81, p. 35; 10/14/81, p. 7; 10/21/81, p.
          19; 4/29/82, p. 1; WSJ, 4/21/82, p. 31.

Oregon's unemployment rate: OR, 3/13/81, p. 1; 11/6/81, p. B7;
          12/27/81, p. D7; 1/14/82, p. 1; WSJ, 4/21/82, p. 31.

Oregon's historic population: NYT, 12/20/81, p. 16.

440   "These suddenly jobless people": author's files.

"We raise [our children]": NYT, 3/6/82, p. 16.

"They tell their friends": OR, 12/27/81, p. D7.

"Oregon should be more pro-business": *Oregon Business*, June 1982, p. 25.

441   "I was thrown out trying to stretch": OS, 8/9/79.

"Damn fool!": RG, 7/19/81.

He quit the Republican party: OR, 5/16/80, p. B2.

He campaigned for bottle bills: OJ, 2/14/79.

442   "nitpicking over how to dress a corpse": *Rocky Mountain News*, 5/17/79.

"don't you try to foist the Luddite ways": TM speech, 11/28/79 TM:OHS Box 34; OR, /20/82, p. B3.

443   due to his drinking: OR, 2/24/79; interview with Jean McCall Babson.

the ranch went up for sale: OJ, 9/19/80, p. 7.

The family that bought the ranch: OR, 4/12/83, p. B1.

"I've never seen so much doubt and suspicion": WW, 1/7/80.

"I'm sort of shattered, but I'm still useful": Terkel, *American Dreams*, p. 337.

444   "cannot hold a candle to Jimmy Carter": RG, 2/9/81, p. 12A.

"Dirty Water Jim": unidentified clip dated, 4/23/81, DLMP.

"thumbed his nose": unidentified clip dated, 4/23/81, DLMP.

"You just don't have the attitude": unidentified clip dated, 4/23/81, DLMP.

"I don't ever expect": OJ, 4/30/81, p. 3; 5/1/81, p. 2; OR, 4/30/81, p. C1.

"They say take it easy": OJ, 5/1/81, p. 2.

446   "People throughout the country": *Oregon Business,* December 1981, p.47.

"My famous speech": *Oregon Business*, September 1981, p. 18.

447   "I've been called": RG, 10/18/81, p. 1B.

"Reagan bootlickers": RG, 10/19/81, p. 1B.

"We have an image problem": WSJ, 10/13/81, p. 35.

"This has happened in a state": NYT, 3/3/82, p. 16.

Atiyeh declared a state of disaster: WP, 1/17/82; OJ, 2/18/82, p. 1; NYT, 1/19/82, p. 18.

448   "I cry for it": RG, 10/18/81, p. 2B.

"Why did I have to wake up?": confidential sources.

McCall appeared in public on crutches: OJ, 11/21/81, p. 3.

"at times have been victims of abuse": Multnomah County Circuit Court Case No. 8112-68964.

Sam's violence toward his father: confidential sources.

450   loyally clipped out news stories: OR, 3/29/82, p. 1; clipped stories:
DLMP.

When they found her body: interview with Jean McCall Babson;
OJ, 4/12/82, p. 22.

the tumor in his back had grown: SJ, 4/16/82, p. 14A.

"The seemingly innocent McCallism": OJ, 4/30/82.

"It would be unfair to say": OJ, 4/30/82.

451   "Tom is misunderstood and maligned": OJ, 4/30/82.

"There's always in time of recession": OJ, 4/30/82.

statewide initiative: OR, 4/6/82, p. B1; OJ, 4/6/82, p. 4.

Chapter 23

452   one out of eight: Oregon Employment Division; *Oregon Business*,
July 1982, p. 21.

the rest of the nation: *Time,* 3/8/82, pp. 74-83.

"Oregon is as green": WP, 5/5/82.

453   "These local officials are playing": Leonard, *Managing Oregon's
Growth*, p. 135.

"If it hadn't been for us": NYT, 10/26/82, p. 18.

poll had recently placed: OR, 11/14/81, p. D1.

"we all have a little schlock": KATU.

454   Atiyeh said the state should blow up the sign: interview with Victor
Atiyeh; OR, 5/6/82, p. 1.

"speaker at the funeral of his own prose": KATU.

"Vic thinks he's trapped me": interview with Ron Schmidt.

455   "Wouldn't a little paint be more reasonable": KATU; OJ, 7/22/82, p.
10.

"There's been a lot of bad mouthing": KATU.

456   doctors guessed he had six months: SJ, 8/6/82, p. 1E; interview with
Ron Schmidt.

"like talking to the wind": OJ, 8/6/82, p. 1.

"I'm restless": OJ, 8/6/82, p. 1.

corporate Oregon: Oregon Elections Division, Summary of Contributions and Expenditures, 1982 General, pp. 331-33.

457   The report also issued a firm conclusion: OR, 9/16/82, p. 1.

A new generation of corporate power: Oregon Elections Division,

Summary of Contributions and Expenditures, 1982 General, pp. 328-29.

A whopping fifty-one percent of Oregonians: "Voter Opinion Toward Ballot Measure 6," September 1982, TH Research.

"Almost everyone who wanted to repeal": interview with Tim Hibbitts.

Only twenty-five percent of voters: "Voter Opinion Toward Ballot Measure 6," September 1982, TH Research.

"Having McCall as a spokesman": "Voter Opinion Toward Ballot Measure 6," September 1982, TH Research.

458   "We realized we had to get Tom Involved": interview with Eldon Hout.

"They want us to give up the gains we've made": OR, 9/28/82, p. B3.

"No matter how momentous the victory is": OR, 9/28/82, p. B3.

459   "I haven't much time left": OR, 10/9/82, p. 1.

460   "Now is the time to plan for growth": OR, 10/10/82, p. C2.

"Oregon owes Tom McCall something better": SJ, 10/13/82.

survey taken by the measure's opponents: "Voter Opinion Toward Ballot Measure 6," September 1982, TH Research.

Bardsley & Haslacher, showed a seventeen-point gap: OR, 10/19/82, p. 1.

The results, published 19 October: OR, 10/19/82, p. 1.

461   "We had done almost nothing": interview with Tim Hibbitts.

side trip into California: OR, 10/19/82, p. 1; San Francisco Chronicle, 10/19/82, p. 10; SJ, 10/19/82, p. 1.

"For the things I believe in": SJ, 10/19/82, p. 1.

"wailing in high places": SJ, 10/21/82, p. 1.

"Don't consider it a veiled attack": SJ, 10/21/82, p. 1.

"I want to die in the saddle": RG, 11/7/82, p. 1F.

"Everybody is allowed a death-bed wish": Hass Tape.

462   "stimulated this ancient frame": RG, 11/7/82, p. 4F.

one of Oregon's most expensive initiative campaigns: Oregon Elections Division, Summary of Contributions and Expenditures, 1982 General, pp. 328-33.

463   On election day: Oregon Blue Book 1983-84, p. 364.

"It was just great to see": OR, 11/4/82, p. C1.

Chapter 24

464   "You're terminal": KATU.
       "I don't want to look too awful": KATU.
       he crashed to the floor: SJ, 12/16/82, p. 1A; OR, 12/16/82, p. 1 and
              12/26/82, p. E9; interview with Audrey McCall, Samuel W.
              McCall III.
465   McCall contracted pneumonia: SJ, 12/18/82, p. 1; interview with
              Ron Schmidt.
       He expressed deep guilt: interview with Ron Schmidt.
       "Now all we need": interview with Ron Schmidt.
       "enough of the pain": interview with Thomas McCall, Jr.
       "terminal phase": SJ, 1/8/83, p. 1.
       "Can he hear me?": interview with Ron Schmidt.
467   ten minutes before eight: OR, 1/9/83, p. 1. Good Samaritan Hospital
              & Medical Center erroneously reported Audrey, Tad, Sam and
              Ron Schmidt were by McCall's side at he time of his death.
       "I had him": OR, 1/9/83, p. B1.
       30,000 fewer workers: Sources vary on actual job loss. For a range,
              see *Oregon Blue Book* 1993-94, p. 211.
469   "Wonder no more": OR, 1/13/83, p. 1.
       "Haven't they gone yet?" interview with Travis Cross. Cross said
              that he was the person who responded to Atiyeh.

Sources

COLLECTIONS

TM:OSA   McCall Administration Papers, Oregon State Archives

The state archives contain 338 boxes of records compiled during the McCall administration and his two years as secretary of state. Generally containing letters and official documents, the boxes are organized by year. Identification numbers of each year are 1965-69 (70A-95, 137 boxes); 1970 (72A-53, 27 boxes); 1971 (72A-89, 32 boxes); 1972 (74A-2, 43 boxes); 1973 (74A-98, 42 boxes) and 1974 (75A-53, 57 boxes).

TM:OHS   Tom McCall Papers, Oregon Historical Society

The Tom McCall Papers in the OHS archives (Mss. 625) include forty-one boxes of personal records. These records were extraordinarily revealing and are a testament to McCall's desire that his whole life be open for review. Copies of source material lacking specific box numbers in the footnotes are also in my files.

DLMP   Dorothy Lawson McCall Papers

Dorothy Lawson McCall left behind nine boxes of assorted letters, photographs and family records when she died in 1982. Her daughter, Jean McCall Babson, had the boxes in 1987 and allowed me access to them.

TM:M   *Tom McCall: Maverick*

McCall's memoir, published in 1977 and co-written by Steve Neal, runs 290 pages and is largely an off-the-cuff look back at his governorship. The book, while sometimes entertaining, was short on substance and perspective. However, the book contains important source material for his early life and personal reflections on his political career.

TM:Tapes   Tom McCall oral history

In July 1976 McCall filled thirty audio tapes with his recollections in preparation for his memoir, *Tom McCall: Maverick*. Conducted by his co-author, Steve Neal, the interviews when transcribed ran 303 pages. Much of the material went directly into *Maverick*. However, the unedited transcript is used when his comment proved more accurate and revealing.

RUR, CKD   *Ranch Under the Rimrock* and *Copper King's Daughter*

Dorothy Lawson McCall's two memoirs provided basic background for the family's origins and history in Massachusetts and the Oregon desert. *Ranch Under the Rimrock*, published in 1968, covers the construction of Westernwold and the McCalls' life there. *Copper King's Daughter*, published in 1972, looks at Dorothy's early years living in Lawson luxury. The books tend to gloss over Thomas Lawson's questionable business dealings and her initial opposition to raising her children in Oregon.

KATU   KATU-TV Tape Library

The station's tape library contains the finished work and raw interview footage for its 1982 documentary about McCall, "A Nice Place to Visit," produced by reporter Paul Hanson and photographer Bill Weaver. The interviews include long sessions with McCall and his associates, many of whom tell stories not available elsewhere. The library also contains a copy of "Pollution in Paradise," McCall's 1962 documentary on the state's environmental problems.

Assorted audio and video tapes

Many people who kept personal recordings of McCall made them available to me, including Chris Beck, who allowed me to use an interview his father, Borden Beck, had conducted with Tom about his early years; Mark Hass, Henny Willis and Doug Yocom. The footnotes cite the tapes by the owners' names (for example: Beck Tapes).

FOIA   Freedom of Information Act records

I filed more than a dozen requests that federal agencies release records relating to McCall and Oregon history under the disclosure law called the Freedom of Information Act. Most records had never been released before, and some were declassified subject to these requests.

To simplify the footnotes, records cited that were produced through these requests are noted by agency.

FOIA:FBI. An estimated 1,200 pages released by the Federal Bureau of Investigation that cover law enforcement activity before and during the American Legion Convention held in Portland during September 1970. The records, from FBI File Nos. 100-11705 and 100-459278, are a small portion of the 3,000 pages in FBI archives. The FBI claimed that, twenty years later, the remaining 1,800 pages were too sensitive to be released. Many of the 1,200 disclosed pages were heavily edited, but many passages were valuable nonetheless.

FOIA-TM. McCall's own FBI file, File No. 94-49461, thirty-eight pages in length, of which the FBI disclosed twenty-two pages. The file is largely laudatory and routine. A background check of McCall in 1969 found no "derogatory" information. Notably, the FBI withheld the file's first two pages. The nature of the exemption cited by the FBI suggests the agency either collected background information on McCall while he was a television reporter, or McCall himself provided the FBI with information, a common practice for journalists at the time and well within McCall's character. In November 1989, I filed suit in United States District Court to have the pages released. A federal judge later ruled in the FBI's favor and against disclosure.

FOIA:DOD. An estimated two hundred pages released by the Department of Defense. The records cover the army's and Pentagon's decisions and plans to launch Operation Red Hat, the proposed shipment of nerve gas into Oregon, during 1969 and 1970.

FOIA:HEW. An estimated three hundred pages released by the federal Department of Human Services. The pages relate to records kept by the former Department of Health, Education and Welfare in 1969 and 1970 that covered safety issues regarding the nerve gas shipments.

OHS   Oregon Historical Society

Other collections in OHS offered important information: the Edith Green Papers, Mss. 1424; Don Waggoner Papers, Mss. 1668, for background on the Bottle Bill; Sidney Bazzett Papers, Mss. 1826, for history of the Beach Bill fight; Glenn Jackson Papers, Mss. 2626, for his background; Oswald West Papers,

Mss. 589, for his background and history of beach protection legislation; and the Bardsley and Haslacher Papers, Mss. 1818, containing four decades of political polls and surveys.

OSA   Oregon State Archives

The state archives house legislative and state agency records, which provided background and detail on the Beach Bill, the Bottle Bill, land-use planning, early pollution controls and the financial disclosure statement of Glenn Jackson.

UOSC   University of Oregon Special Collections

These archives contain the Homer Angell Papers and Wayne Morse Papers. Both collections provided background on Hells Canyon and the 1954 Third District congressional campaign.

PA   Presidential archives.

Five presidential libraries and archives provided much useful information. The libraries include the Dwight D. Eisenhower Library in Abeline, Kansas; the Lyndon Baines Johnson Library in Austin, Texas; the Gerald R. Ford Library in Ann Arbor, Michigan; and the Jimmy Carter Library in Atlanta, Georgia. Richard M. Nixon's presidential papers are held by the National Archives and Records Administration. In each case, material cited can be found or referenced through the libraries' White House Central File Name File. Where possible, specific file numbers are noted. The notes cite each library by president (for example: PA:LBJ).

INTERVIEWS

Many people spoke with me for this book, some only for a few minutes, others for hours on end, totalling more than 250 interviews in all. The footnotes cite information and quotations from these interviews by noting the subject's name. In only a few cases did interview sources ask that their names not be used for attribution.

The book's interview subjects include: Ron Abell, Dick Althoff, Forest Amsden, Howell Appling, Vic Atiyeh, Jean McCall Babson, Malcolm Bauer, Charles Beggs, Victoria Chambers Berger, Ruth Brown, William Brown, Peggy Lucas, Robert Lucas, Claire Argow, Ed Armstrong, Borden Beck, Frankie Bell,

George Bell, George Birnie, Ron Blankenbaker, Harry Bodine, Jason Boe, Edward Branchfield, Darrel Buttice, Jack Capell, Dorothy "Bebs" McCall Chamberlain, George Chamberlain, Douglas Chambers, Kay Chambers, Arnold Cogan, William Crosbie, Travis Cross, Mark Cushing, Frank Day, Nan Dewey, Eugene Doherty, Kim Skerritt Duncan, Grant Eade, Robert Elliott, Raymond Engelcke, Daniel J. Evans, Jim Faulstich, Jack Faust, Peter Fornara, J.W. Forrester, Leonard Forsgren, Gerry Frank, Rosemary O'Donnell Freeman, Maradel Gale, Kim Gilbert, Richard Godfrey, Hollis Goodrich, Mary Goodrich Peden, William Goss, Alan Green, Tallant Greenough, William Guy, Marko Haggard, Ted Hallock, Paul Hanneman, Paul Hanson, Mark O. Hatfield, Charles Heltzel, Muriel Heltzel, Tim Hibbitts, Eldon Hout, Harold Hughes, Don Jarvi, Don Jepsen, Ken Johnson, Lee Johnson, Phil Keisling, Cathy Kiyomura, Maude Knorr, Amos Lawrence, Arnold Lawson, Thomas W. Lawson II, Sidney Lezak, Robert Logan, Herb Lundy, Audrey McCall, Samuel Walker McCall III, Sandy McCall, Thomas McCall, Jr., Steve McCarthy, Michael McCusker, Skeets McGrew, Jack McIsaac, Floyd McKay, Hector Macpherson, Roger Martin, Ed Martindale, John Mason, Gene Maudlin, F.F. "Monte" Montgomery, John Mosser, Clay Myers, Frank Nash, Steve Neal, J. Richard Nokes, Paul Nordstrom, Robert Notson, Warne Nunn, Robert Oliver, Bob Packwood, Arden X. Pangborn, Eugene Patterson, Norma Paulus, Ancil Payne, Doris Penwell, Gerry Pratt, James Redden Sr., Henry Richmond, Ken Rinke, Betty Roberts, Richard Ross, Russell Sadler, Andrew Schmidt, Ron Schmidt, A. Robert Smith, Ivan Smith, Ed Snyder, Kenneth Spies, Tim Storrs, Robert Straub, Monroe Sweetland, Glen Swift, E.J. "Mike" Sullivan, Wayne Thompson, Wallace Turner, Fred Van Natta, Don Waggoner, Jim Welch, Edward Westerdahl II, Wanda Merrill Wahus, Dick Westwood, Henny Willis, Robert Wise, Jules Witcover, Robert Wollheim, Wendell Wyatt, Ken Yandle, Doug Yocom, Jean Young, Anthony Yturri and Clarence Zaitz.

PUBLISHED

Abrams, Richard M. *Conservatives in a Progressive Era: Massachusetts Politics 1900-1912*. Cambridge, Massachusetts: Harvard University Press, 1964.

Babcock, Richard F. *The Zoning Game*. Madison, Wisconsin: University of Wisconsin Press, 1966.

Barney, Gerald O. *The Unfinished Agenda: The Citizen's Policy Guide to Environmental Issues*. New York: Crowell, 1977.

Barone, Michael. *Our Country: The Shaping of America from Roosevelt to Reagan*. New York: Free Press, 1990.

Biographical Directory of the United States Congress, 1774-1989. Bicentennial Edition, United States Senate Document 100-34. Washington, D.C.: United States Government Printing Office, 1989.

Bone, Arthur H. *Oregon Cattleman/Governor/Congressman: Memoirs and Times of Walter M. Pierce*. Portland, Oregon: Oregon Historical Society Press, 1981.

Bosselman, Fred and David Callies. *The Quiet Revolution in Land Use Control*. Washington, D.C.: Citizens Council on Environmental Quality, 1972.

Bureau of Governmental Research and Service. *Guide to Local Planning and Development*. Eugene, Oregon: University of Oregon, 1984.

Burton, Robert E. *Democrats of Oregon: The Pattern of Minority Politics, 1900-1956*. Eugene, Oregon: University of Oregon Press, 1970.

Carey, Charles H. *General History of Oregon*. Portland, Oregon: Binford and Mort, 1971.

Carroll, Peter N. *It Seemed Like Nothing Happened: The Tragedy and Promise of America in the 1970s*. New York: Holt, Rinehart and Winston, 1982.

Carson, Rachel. *Silent Spring*. Greenwich, Connecticut: Fawcett Publications, Inc., 1962.

Clark, Malcolm, Jr. *Eden Seekers: The Settlement of Oregon, 1818-1862*. Boston: Houghton Mifflin Co., 1981.

Commoner, Barry. *The Closing Circle: Nature, Man and Technology*. New York: Bantam Books, 1972.

Conservation Foundation, *The State of the Environment, 1982*. Washington, D.C.: Conservation Foundation, 1982.

Davies, J. Clarence and Barbara S. Davies. *The Politics of Pollution*. Indianapolis, Indiana: Pegasus, 1975.

DeGrove, John M. *Land, Growth and Politics*. Washington, D.C.: American Planners Association, Planners Press.

Dodds, Gordon B. *The American Northwest: A History of Oregon and Washington*. Arlington Heights, Illinois: Forum Press, Inc., 1986.

Eaton, Allen H. *The Oregon System: The Story of Direct Legislation in Oregon*. Chicago: A. C. McClurg and Co., 1912.

Eells, Robert, and Bartell Nyberg. *Lonely Walk: The Life of Senator Mark Hatfield*. Chappaqua, New York: Christian Herald Books, 1979.

Eisenhower, Dwight D. *Mandate for Change 1953-1956*. Garden City, New York: Doubleday and Company, Inc., 1963.

Evans, Lawrence B. *Samuel W. McCall, Governor of Massachusetts*. Boston:

Houghton Mifflin Co., 1916.

Filler, Lewis. *The Muckrakers: Crusaders for American Liberalism.* Chicago: Henry Regnery Co., Gateway Edition, 1968.

Friedman, Milton, and Rose Friedman. *Free to Choose.* New York: Harcourt Brace Jovanovich, 1980.

Friedman, Ralph. *Tracking Down Oregon.* Caldwell, Idaho: Caxton Press, 1978.

Fuess, Claude M. *Calvin Coolidge: The Man From Vermont.* Hamden, Connecticut: Archon Books, 1965.

Gleeson, George W. *The Return of a River: The Willamette River, Oregon.* Corvallis, Oregon: Oregon State University Water Resources Institute, 1972.

Green, Lewis. *The Gold Hustlers.* Anchorage, Alaska: Alaska Northwest Publishing Co., 1977.

Greider, William. *Secrets of the Temple: How the Federal Reserve Runs the Country.* New York: Touchstone, 1987.

Gudger, Charles M., and Jack C. Bailes. *The Economic Impact of Oregon's "Bottle Bill."* Corvallis, Oregon: Oregon State University Press, 1974.

Hatfield, Mark O. *Not Quite So Simple.* New York: Harper and Row, 1968.

Hendrickson, James E. *Joe Lane of Oregon: Machine Politics and the Sectional Crisis, 1849-1861.* New Haven, Connecticut: Yale University Press, 1967.

Hennessy, Michael E. *Four Decades of Massachusetts Politics, 1890-1935.* Freeport, New York: Books For Libraries Press, 1971.

Hersh, Seymour. *Chemical and Biological Warfare: America's Hidden Arsenal.* Indianapolis, Indiana: Bobbs-Merrill, 1968.

Hess, Stephen, and David Broder. *The Republican Establishment.* New York: Harper and Row, 1967.

Hodgson, Godfrey. *America in Our Time.* Garden City, New York: Doubleday and Co., Inc., 1976.

Holbrook, Stewart. *The Age of the Moguls.* Garden City, New York: Doubleday and Co., Inc., 1953.

Howe, M. A. DeWolfe, ed. *Later Years of the Saturday Club 1870-1920.* Freeport, New York: Books For Libraries Press, 1968.

Johnson, Lyndon. *The Vantage Point: Perspectives on the Presidency 1963-1969.* New York: Popular Press, 1971.

Johnson, Paul. *Modern Times: The World from the Twenties to the Eighties.* New York: Harper and Row, 1983.

Karnow, Stanley. *Vietnam: A History.* New York: Viking Press, 1983.

LaPalombara, Joseph G. *The Initiative and Referendum in Oregon: 1938-1948.* Corvallis, Oregon: Oregon State College Press, 1950.

Lawrence Halprin and Associates. *The Willamette Valley: Choices for the Future*. State of Oregon, Willamette Valley Environmental Protection and Development and Planning Council, 1972.

Lawson, Thomas W. *Frenzied Finance: The Crime of Amalgamated*. London: William Heinemann, 1906.

Leonard, H. Jeffrey. *Managing Oregon's Growth: The Politics of Development Planning*. Washington, D.C.: Conservation Foundation, 1983.

Lindstrom, David Elvin. *W. S. U'Ren and the Fight for Government Reform and the Single Tax: 1908-1912*. Unpublished master's thesis, Portland State University, 1972.

Lippman, Theo, Jr. *Spiro Agnew's America*. New York: W.W. Norton and Company, Inc., 1972

Little, Charles O. *The New Oregon Trail*. Washington, D.C.: Conservation Foundation, 1974.

Logan, Robert K., and others. *The Oregon Land Use Story*. Salem, Oregon: Oregon Local Government Relations Division, 1974.

Louis Harris and Associates, Inc. *The Public's View of Environmental Problems in the State of Oregon*. Report prepared for Pacific Northwest Bell Telephone Co., 1970.

Lucia, Ellis. *This Land Around Us: A Treasury of Pacific Northwest Writing*. Garden City, New York: Doubleday, 1969.

Lukas, J. Anthony. *Nightmare: The Underside of the Nixon Years*. New York: The Viking Press, 1976.

McArthur, Lewis A., and Lewis L. McArthur, ed. *Oregon Geographic Names*, Sixth Edition. Portland, Oregon: Oregon Historical Society Press, 1992.

McCall, Dorothy Lawson. *The Copper King's Daughter*. Portland, Oregon: Binford and Mort, 1972.

———. *Ranch Under the Rimrock*. Portland, Oregon: Binford and Mort, 1968.

McCall, Samuel W. *The Patriotism of the American Jew*. New York: Plymouth Press, 1924.

McCall, Tom, with Steve Neal. *Tom McCall: Maverick*. Portland, Oregon: Binford and Mort, 1977.

MacColl, E. Kimbark. *The Growth of a City: Power and Politics in Portland, Oregon 1915 to 1950*. Portland, Oregon: Georgian Press, 1979.

———. *The Shaping of a City: Business and Politics in Portland, Oregon 1885 to 1915*. Portland, Oregon: Georgian Press, 1976.

McCoy, Donald R. *Calvin Coolidge: The Quiet President*. New York: Macmillan, 1967.

Mahar, Franklyn Daniel. *Douglas McKay and the Issues of Power Develop-

ment in Oregon, 1953-1956. Unpublished doctoral dissertation, University of Oregon, 1968.

Maisel, L. Sandy. *Political Parties and Elections in the United States: An Encyclopedia.* New York: Garland Publishing, 1991.

Malone, Michael P. *The Battle for Butte: Mining and Politics on the Northern Frontier, 1864-1906.* Seattle: University of Washington Press, 1981.

Manchester, William. *The Glory and the Dream: A Narrative History of America 1932-1972.* Boston: Little, Brown and Company, 1973.

Massachusetts Historical Society. *Proceedings,* October 1923-June 1924, Vol. 57. Boston: Massachusetts Historical Society, 1924.

Merk, Frederick. *The Oregon Question: Essays in Anglo-American Diplomacy and Politics.* Cambridge, Massachusetts: Belknap Press of Harvard University Press, 1967.

Metropolitan Human Relations Commission. *Campus Disorders at Portland State University,* 1970.

Metzler, Ken. *Confrontation: The Destruction of a College President.* Los Angeles: Nash Publishing, 1973.

National Cyclopedia of American Biography, Vol. 26. New York: James T. White and Company, 1937.

Neal, Steve. *McNary of Oregon: A Political Biography.* Portland, Oregon: Western Imprints, 1985.

———, ed. *They Never Go Back to Pocatello: The Selected Essays of Richard Neuberger.* Portland, Oregon: Oregon Historical Society Press, 1988.

New York *Times. The White House Transcripts.* New York: Bantam Books, Inc.,1974.

Ognibene, Peter J. *Scoop: The Life and Politics of Henry M. Jackson.* New York: Stein and Day, 1975.

Oregon Advisory Committee on Environmental Science and Technology. *Environmental Quality in Oregon 1971.* Corvallis, Oregon: Oregon State University, 1971.

Oregon Legislative Assembly. *Report of the Legislative Interim Committee on Indian Affairs: A Reintroduction to the Indians of Oregon.* October 1958.

Peterson, Robert W. *Agnew: The Coining of a Household Word.* New York: Facts on File, 1972.

Plotkin, Sidney. *Keep Out: The Struggle for Land Use Control.* Berkeley, California: University of California Press, 1987.

Popper, Frank J. *The Politics of Land-Use Reform.* Madison, Wisconsin: University of Wisconsin Press, 1981.

Powers, Thomas. *Vietnam: The War at Home.* Boston: G.K. Hall and Co., 1984.

Prochnau, William W., and Richard W. Larsen. *A Certain Democrat: Senator Henry M. Jackson*. Englewood Cliffs, New Jersey: Prentice-Hall, Inc., 1972.

Puter, Stephen A. Douglas. *Looters of the Public Domain*. Portland, Oregon: Portland Printing House, 1908.

Rathlesberger, James, ed. *Nixon and the Environment: The Politics of Devastation*. New York: A Village Voice Book, Taurus Communications, Inc., 1972.

Reiger, Cornelius C. *The Era of the Muckrakers*. Chapel Hill, North Carolina: University of North Carolina Press, 1932.

Robbins, William G. *Land: Its Use and Abuse in Oregon, 1848-1910*. Corvallis, Oregon: Oregon State University, 1974.

Savage, John F., and Henry R. Richmond. *Oregon's Bottle Bill: "A Riproaring Success."* Portland, Oregon: Oregon Student Public Interest Research Group, 1974.

Schlesinger, Arthur M., Jr. *Robert Kennedy and His Times*. Boston: Houghton Mifflin, 1978.

Seagrave, Sterling. *Yellow Rain*. New York: M. Evans, 1981.

Shawcross, William. *Sideshow: Kissinger, Nixon and the Destruction of Cambodia*. New York: Simon and Schuster, 1979.

Sherrill, Robert. *The Oil Follies of 1970-1980*. Garden City, New York: Anchor Press/Doubleday, 1983.

Slayden, Ellen Maury. *Washington Wife: Journal of Ellen Maury Slayden from 1897-1919*. New York: Harper and Row, 1963.

Smith, A. Robert. *The Tiger in the Senate: The Biography of Wayne Morse*. Garden City, New York: Doubleday and Co., Inc., 1962.

Sobel, Robert, and John Raimo, eds. *Biographical Directory of Governors of the United States 1798-1978*, Vol. 3. Westport, Connecticut: Meckler Books, 1978.

Sonnichsen, C. L. *Colonel Greene and the Copper Skyrocket*. Tuscon, Arizona: University of Arizona Press, 1974.

Steffens, Lincoln. *The Autobiography of Lincoln Steffens*. New York: Harcourt, Brace and Company, 1931.

————. *Upbuilders*. Seattle, Washington: University of Washington Press, 1968.

Terkel, Studs. *American Dreams, Lost and Found*. New York: Pantheon Books, 1980.

Thompson, Cecil T. *The Origin of Direct Legislation in Oregon: How Oregon Secured the Initiative and Referendum*. Unpublished master's thesis, University of Oregon, 1925.

Turnbull, George S. *Governors of Oregon.* Portland, Oregon. Binford and Mort, 1959.

———. *History of Oregon Newspapers.* Portland, Oregon: Binford and Mort, 1939.

———. *Journalists in the Making.* Eugene, Oregon: University of Oregon School of Journalism, 1965.

Udall, Stewart. *The Quiet Crisis.* New York: Avon Books, 1963.

Washington State Pollution Commission and Oregon State Sanitary Authority. *Report of Investigation in the Lower Columbia River.* 1943.

Weinberg, Arthur, and Lila Weinberg, eds. *The Muckrakers.* New York: Capricorn Books, 1961.

White, William Allen. *A Puritan in Babylon: The Story of Calvin Coolidge.* New York: The Macmillian Co., 1938.

Witcover, Jules. *The Resurrection of Richard Nixon.* New York: Putnam, 1970.

———. *White Knight: The Rise of Spiro Agnew.* New York: Random House, 1972.

Acknowledgments

T HIS BOOK IS THE PRODUCT OF SEVEN YEARS OF WORK, years during which I wondered if I would ever finish, but years during which I was bolstered by true believers who helped me keep faith that this book would someday be published. Whatever strengths this book might have come from these people, and I wish to thank them here.

Shannon Buono, my wife and best friend, has extended her endless patience and love, and that has meant everything. My family—my parents Conrad and Megan, and my brother, Kent—also encouraged me throughout and taught me to never give up.

Mark Zusman and Richard Meeker, respectively the editor and publisher of *Willamette Week*, Portland's alternative newspaper, early on gave me invaluable support, both personal and financial. Phil Keisling was the first person to encourage me to take up this project, even when the odds against it were formidable. E. Kimbark MacColl, an august historian in his own right, became the book's greatest champion. Bruce Taylor Hamilton, as director of the Oregon Historical Society Press, most of all shared the vision for this book, keenly recognizing not only the need to tell McCall's story, but also understanding how it should be told.

Hall Templeton gave me a generous grant to support the writing of the book, and I am sorry he did not live to see the completed work. Other support came from Paul Hanson, Lars Larson, Tom Landye and Ron Buel, and I am grateful to them.

I am blessed with friends whose contributions were many and whose support never waned: Paul Brown, Linda Campillo, Greg Kerber, Joe Hart, Steve Kadel, Carol Cruzan Morton, Jim Redden and Jan Wilkerson. Lee Barrett really delivered when I needed his help. And I wish to give special and heartfelt thanks to Katherine Dunn in particular; she is a hero for writers if there ever was one.

I BEGAN THINKING ABOUT WRITING THIS BOOK in 1986 and started work in earnest the following year. In that time, there have been many dead ends that may well have led to failure. But without exaggeration, there would have been no book at all without the help of Audrey McCall and Ron Schmidt. Audrey talked with me for hours about her forty-three years with Tom McCall, opened doors to other people, allowed access to her personal materials and, most of all, provided thoughtful insight and memories.

It is difficult even now to think that Ron Schmidt did not live to see this published book, although he did read versions of the draft before he died in November 1992. He was the keeper of the McCall myth, but his candor and honesty was unrivaled in helping me understand McCall's humanity.

I am also thankful to Jean McCall Babson, McCall's youngest sister, who died in July 1987. As she battled cancer, Jean spent hours with me describing their childhood at Westernwold and the influence of their mother, Dorothy Lawson McCall. She also made Dorothy's papers available to me. Most importantly, from those valuable hours talking with Jean I learned what it meant to be a McCall and a Lawson.

Brian Booth, of the law firm of Tonkon, Torp, Galen, Marmaduke & Booth, is foremost a lover of books, and his counsel was valuable, insightful and wise. Stuart Brown, Diane Bridge, and Jim Loy, of the same firm, donated their time in a legal effort to wrest records from the Federal Bureau of Investigation, and I appreciate their effort.

Bennett Hall provided much-needed advice and ideas on the book's early drafts. And Carla Perry of Northwest Writers, Inc., skillfully oversaw that group's participation in this book, and I thank her for her time and attention.

AT THE OREGON HISTORICAL SOCIETY, Chet Orloff, the society's director, took on the formidable challenge of making this book a reality; I
want to thank him and the society's staff for their work.

Sharon Elaine Thompson did an outstanding job of editing this man-
uscript. Her talent as an editor, her own instincts as a writer, and her
care with my often unruly prose has made a tremendous difference.

TOM MCCALL LEFT BEHIND an exhaustive public record that made understanding his life easier, even if the volume of material made the re-
searching itself a greater chore. Kathy Dimond helped immensely in
the indexing of hundreds of cartons of previously unopened McCall
records in the Oregon State Archives. Many people at libraries and research centers also helped my work: James Clark, Tim Backer and
Michael McQuade at the Oregon State Archives; and Peggy Haines and
Kris White at the Oregon Historical Society. Erica Goodwin is the
skilled OHS volunteer who took on the daunting task of organizing the
original sixty-four boxes of material McCall donated as his private papers. She did a grand job of it, and her work made my life much easier
and made the papers accessible to everyone.

Kathleen Laidlaw, president of the Scituate Historical Society, in Scituate, Massachusetts, is the curator of Lawson lore. The society's office
is located within sight of the Lawson tower on the former Dreamwold
estate, and she spent hours walking me through the society's collections. I also appreciate the assistance of Bro. Frank Drury of the University of Portland Library; Mark Fischer at the Nixon Project of the
National Archives in Washington, D.C.; and Steve Yount at the Lyndon
Baines Johnson Library in Austin, Texas. And for her hospitality during
my research in Boston, I wish to thank Pat Linn.

I also wish to acknowledge those people who opened their personal
records to me. Steve Neal, political editor of the Chicago *Sun-Times*, allowed me to quote from the oral history he collected for McCall in 1976.
KATU-TV in Portland opened its archives and its general manager at the
time, Tom Dargan, graciously granted me permission to quote from the
file video tapes. Others who opened their files to me include Mark Hass,
Floyd McKay, Henny Willis, Chris Beck, Charles Gould, Glen Swift
and James Welch.

AT THE END OF THIS VOLUME the Oregon Historical Society acknowledges the people whose financial donations helped make the society's publication of this book possible. Some of these people are mentioned in the book itself while others were interview subjects who had earlier provided information about McCall.

Readers should know that none of the donors had or exercised control over any portion of the writing or editing of this book.

Index

The production of *Fire at Eden's Gate* was supported by
major contributions from:

The Conservation Fund
The Samuel S. Johnson Foundation

&

The Thomas Vaughan Fund for Publication
in Oregon Country History

Additional generous financial support was provided by:

Cecil D. Andrus, Anonymous, R. William Babson,
Ted & Marie Baker, The Borden F. Beck, Jr. Family,
Frankie & George Bell, Edward & Edith Branchfield,
Mrs. W. Lyons Brown, James & Jane Bryson, Blanche Cannon,
Don Clark, Elaine & Arnold Cogan, Charles T. Duncan,
Jim & Gretchen Faulstich, Evelyn Scott Ferris, J. W. (Bud) Forrester,
Mike & Pam Forrester, Gerry Frank, Otto & MarAbel Frohnmayer,
Dan & Genevieve Goldy, John D. Gray, Bruce Taylor Hamilton,
Charles & Muriel Heltzel, Edward B. Kaye, Mrs. Leonard Kirby,
Mrs. Louis Lang, Eric D. Lemelson, Sidney I. Lezak,
Robert K. & June D. Logan, Ned Look, Ron Lovell, Dan Lufkin,
Bill Lunch, Audrey O. McCall, Tad McCall & Kitty Taimi,
Wm. A. McClenaghan, E. Kimbark MacColl, Jr.,
E. Kimbark MacColl, Sr., Hector Macpherson, Irvin Mann,
Kate Mills, John D. Mosser, Elizabeth & Clay Myers,
Frank E. Nash, Wade Newbegin, Jr., Patrick F. Noonan,
Mr. & Mrs. Robert H. Noyes, Jr., Dale Parnell, Nick & Merna Peet,
Doris Penwell, Public Affairs Counsel, David & Patricia Pugh,
Jim & Joan Redden, Nathaniel P. Reed, The *Register-Guard*,
Lisa & Russell Sadler, Mr. & Mrs. Ron Schmidt,
Donald & Julie Sterling, L. L. (Stub) Stewart,
Robert W. & Patricia S. Straub, Sedley N. Stuart,
Monroe M. Sweetland, The Herbert A. Templeton Foundation,
Wilhelmine K. Waller, *Willamette Week*, Joella Werlin,
Robert B. Wilson, Mary T. Winch, Tom & Marguerite Wright,
The Wyss Foundation, Anthony Yturri

Colophon

Fire at Eden's Gate was set in Times Roman by
Irish Setter of Portland.

The printing and binding of this volume was by
Edwards Brothers of Ann Arbor, Michigan.

The book design was by Bruce Taylor Hamilton,
who supervised the editing and production of this project.

The "Tom McCall's Oregon" map was produced by Christine Rains.

The volume editor was Sharon Elaine Thompson.

Julie Kawabata indexed the text.